The Finance of Climate Change
A Guide for Governments, Corporations and Investors

Edited by Kenny Tang
with special assistance from Andrew Dlugolecki

Risk*books*

Published by Risk Books, a Division of Incisive Financial Publishing Ltd

Haymarket House
28–29 Haymarket
London SW1Y 4RX
Tel: +44 (0)20 7484 9700
Fax: +44 (0)20 7484 9800
E-mail: books@riskwaters.com
Sites: www.riskbooks.com
        www.incisivemedia.com

Every effort has been made to secure the permission of individual copyright
holders for inclusion.

ISBN 1 904339 62 X

British Library Cataloguing in Publication Data
A catalogue record for this book is available from the British Library

Managing Editor: Laurie Donaldson
Development Editor: Tamsine Green
Copy Editor: Andrew John
Head of Design: Simon Bogle

Typeset by Mizpah Publishing Services Private Limited, Chennai, India

Printed and bound in Spain by Espacegrafic, Pamplona, Navarra

The Finance of Climate Change

Contents

List of Contributors   ix

Foreword   xxv
Alderman Michael Savory

Foreword   xxvii
Jonathon Porritt

Foreword   xxix
Gao Guangsheng

Introduction   xxxi
Kenny Tang
Oxbridge Capital

SECTION 1: FRAMEWORK AND FINANCE POLICY ISSUES

1   A Changing Climate for the Finance and Insurance Sector   3
    Kenny Tang; Andrew Dlugolecki
    Oxbridge Capital; University of East Anglia

2   Climate Change and Capital   15
    James Cameron, James Allen
    Climate Change Capital

3   The "Finance-Policy" Gap: Policy Conditions for Attracting   25
    Long-Term Investment
    Kirsty Hamilton
    International Policy Consultant

4   REEEPing the Benefits: The Case for Renewable Energy   39
    Marianne Moscoso-Osterkorn, Mike Allen
    REEEP

SECTION 2: FINANCING AND CARBON FUNDS

5   Commodifying Carbon   51
    Martijn Wilder, Monique Willis, Katherine Lake
    Baker McKenzie

6   Securing Investment for Climate-Friendly Projects: 65
    Uses and Limitations of Carbon Trading
    Karen McClellan
    CIP

7   Unlocking Additionality in CDM Projects   77
    Gerhard Mulder
    ABN AMRO Bank

8   Procuring Carbon: The Dutch JI/CDM Approach   89
    Through ERUPT/CERUPT
    Stefan Leclaire, Daniël van der Weerd
    SenterNovem

9   Financing Photovoltaic Projects – Plus ça change,   103
    plus c'est la même chose?
    Stefan Schmitz
    Field Fisher Waterhouse

SECTION 3: TRADING PERSPECTIVES

10 Carbon Facilities as a Means of Sourcing   117
    Emission-Reduction Credits
    Pedro Moura Costa; Bruce Usher; Allan Walker
    EcoSecurities; Standard Bank

11 Purchasing Pools in Corporate Carbon Compliance: 129
    Survey of the Strategic Advantages
    Dirk Forrister; Paul Vickers
    Natsource Europe (London); Natsource Asset Management

12 Choices Facing Firms in a CO$_2$ Cap-and-Trade Emissions   145
    Trading Scheme
    Charles Donovan; Mustafa Hussain
    Enviros Consulting; Frontier Economics

13 Banking the Valuation of the Commons   155
    Claire Byers
    Fortis Bank

14 Weather Derivatives and Carbon Emissions Trading   165
    Stephen Jewson; Stuart Jones
    RMS; Centrica

15 Verifying Value: The Anchor for the Carbon Emissions Markets 177
    James Anderson
    BSI

SECTION 4: INVESTOR PERSPECTIVES

16 Corporate Carbon Disclosure – The Work of the CDP   189
    Paul Dickinson
    Carbon Disclosure Project

17 Investor Collaboration on Climate Change: 197
    The Work of the IIGCC
    Rory Sullivan; Nick Robins; David Russell; Helen Barnes
    Insight Investment; Henderson Global Investors;
    Universities Superannuation Scheme; IIGCC

18 Climate Change, Investment Risk and Fiduciary   211
    Responsibility
    Matthew Kiernan
    Innovest Strategic Value Advisors

SECTION 5: SECTOR DEVELOPMENTS

19 Climate Change and the Automotive Industry – Impact   227
    on Companies' Value
    Philipp Mettler
    SAM Research AG

20 Climate Change Policies and Energy Intensive Industry   245
    David Pocklington, Richard Leese
    British Cement Association

21 Best Practice in Strategies for Managing Carbon   259
    Abyd Karmali
    ICF Consulting

22 Aviation and Climate Change: Can Emissions   271
    Trading Deliver a Solution?
    Andrew Sentance, Andy Kershaw
    British Airways

23 Insuring Climate Change: Implications for the   281
    Insurance Industry
    George Walker; Charles Crosthwaite Eyre; Alan Punter
    Aon Re Australia; IRMG, Aon Ltd; Aon Capital Services Ltd

24 Protecting Your Carbon Asset: Risk and Insurance in   293
    the Greenhouse Gas Markets
    Christopher Walker, Brian Thomas
    Swiss Re

SECTION 6: GLOBAL DEVELOPMENTS

25 **CDM Financing and its Practice – An Asian Perspective**   305
    Kyoko Tochikawa, Mari Yoshitaka, Junji Hatano
    Mitsubishi Securities

26 **CDM and Renewable Energy in China**   319
    Lu Xuedu; Li Junfeng; Song Yanqin; Liu Yingchun
    Tsinghua University; Chinese Renewable Energy
    Industries Association; Energy Research Institute of
    National Development and Reform Commission;
    Building Capacity for CDM in China

27 **Making Climate-Change Investments in**   337
    Emerging-Market Countries
    Mark Goldsmith, Ben McKeown
    Actis Capital LLP

28 **The Clean Development Mechanism in Sub-Saharan**   353
    Africa: Left Out but not Left Behind
    William Greene
    africapractice

29 **The Spectre of Liability: Part 1 – Attribution**   367
    Myles Allen
    Oxford University

30 **The Spectre of Liability: Part 2 – Implications**   381
    Myles Allen
    Oxford University

    Index   401

List of Contributors

James Allen is an analyst in the policy and markets analysis team for Climate Change Capital. Prior to joining Climate Change Capital, he worked with the Westminster Energy Policy Forum (hosted by the Adam Smith Institute) as a freelance consultant, researching energy and climate change policy. James graduated from Imperial College, London, in September 2004 with an MSc in environmental technology (Distinction). For his masters' thesis, James investigated the scientific and economic uncertainties associated with climate change mitigation, and analysed the implications of uncertainty and risk on UK, EU and US climate change policy. James has an MA in natural sciences from Clare College, Cambridge.

Mike Allen is Finance Advisor for REEEP, working on the development of REEEP's programmes to support finance and funding for renewables. With a background in engineering, Mike has spent over 25 years involved in the geothermal industry undertaking project developments in Asia, Africa, Latin America and the Mediterranean. In 1995 he was appointed as Executive Director of E+Co, a US based not-for-profit organisation established with the support of the Rockefeller Foundation. E+Co provides business development services and seed capital for the promotion of renewable energy in emerging economies. Since 2002 he has also worked as an independent consultant for the IFC, Sustainable Project Management.

Myles Allen is a lecturer in the department of physics, University of Oxford, where he leads the climate dynamics group and is principal investigator of the climateprediction.net project. After graduating in physics and philosophy from Oxford, he worked for two years in Nairobi, Kenya, including a stint at the energy unit of the United Nations Environment Programme. He returned to Oxford to undertake a doctorate in atmospheric, oceanic and planetary physics, researching internal climate variability. He then moved to the Rutherford Appleton Laboratory to work on satellite missions for monitoring global change, and then to the Massachusetts Institute of Technology on a NOAA Global Change Fellowship to work with Professor Richard Lindzen on the problem of quantifying uncertainty in climate analysis and prediction. Myles contributed to the *Third Assessment Report* of the Intergovernmental Panel on Climate Change, and is a review editor for the chapter on predictions of global climate change for the *IPCC Fourth Assessment*. He is married with two children.

James Anderson is Head of Sustainability and Global Verification Services for the British Standards Institution (BSI), based in London. His remit spans corporate development to the environment, climate change, and sustainable development. Previously, he founded BSI Japan as managing director in 1999 and later became vice president of BSI Asia region, based in Hong Kong. In 2001 James launched BSI's global climate change services. James is a chartered environmental engineer with a master of science degree in environmental management and risk, a corporate member of the Chartered Institution of Water and Environmental Management and an independent writer to the UNEP. He advises the European Commission, and the UK, Korean, Japanese and Canadian governments on climate change.

Helen Barnes joined the UK Social Investment Forum (UKSIF) in 1999. Helen was Collaborative Engagement Officer from April 2003 to March 2005, providing support to two major collaborative investor initiatives on the pharmaceutical sector and climate change – the Pharmaceutical Shareowners Group and the Institutional Investors Group on Climate Change respectively. Her previous roles at UKSIF include acting as UKSIF's Parliamentary Officer and a secondment to the European Sustainable and Responsible Investment Forum. Helen developed her interest in socially responsible and sustainable investment during roles with Prudential, the UK Environment Agency and a small firm of Independent Financial Advisers. She gained an honours degree in geography from the University of Newcastle upon Tyne in 1996.

Claire Byers is Manager of Environmental Global Markets at Fortis Bank in The Netherlands, where she is responsible for the development of carbon products and services within Fortis Bank. She started her career as a production geologist working in the offshore sector for Shell. After three years she decided on a change in direction and went to work for Ecofys, providing energy and environmental consulting services mainly to the European Commission. Following that she worked for Nuon structuring and trading environmental products. She holds masters degrees in natural science and environmental technology from Cambridge University and Imperial College, University of London.

James Cameron is a founder of Climate Change Capital, head of Climate Change Policy Advisory and Chairman of the Advisory Board. He is counsel to Baker & McKenzie and was the founder and, until recently, the head of their climate change practice. He was a founder director of CIEL and FIELD, he negotiated the UNFCCC and Kyoto Protocol as an adviser to the Alliance of Small Island States and wrote the first law review article on climate change and State Responsibility in 1990. James has held academic positions at Cambridge, London, Bruges and Sydney and is currently affiliated with the

Yale Center for Environmental Law and Policy. As a barrister he has appeared in several of the leading cases in environmental law, including the case concerning the arrest of General Pinochet. He is the Chairman of the Carbon Disclosure Project and of Cameron May, the international law publishers. He is also a member of the governing board and treasurer of REEEP.

Pedro Moura Costa is the Founding Managing Director of EcoSecurities, a company that specialises in emerging environmental markets. Pedro has worked for over 15 years in the field of carbon trading, including the development and implementation of two of the first carbon offset projects in the world. In 1999, Pedro co-ordinated the development of the carbon trading component of a U$50 million forestry investment fund in Australia. In 2002, he coordinated the creation of the NovaGerar landfill gas to energy project in Brazil, which has already sold €8 million in carbon credits to the World Bank. Since 2003, he has also been the Facility Manager of the Denmark Carbon Facility. Pedro has a PhD from the University of London and has published more than 20 articles and books on the subject of environmental science and carbon trading.

Paul Dickinson is Coordinator of the Carbon Disclosure Project, which is a public interest organisation providing the world's largest registry of Greenhouse Gas Emissions. Paul is a member of the Environmental Research Group of the UK Faculty and Institute of Actuaries and the UK Department of Trade and Industry Innovation and Growth Team for the Environmental Goods and Services sector. He is Founder of EyeNetwork, the largest video-conference booking service in Europe, a board director of Social Venture Network Europe and a founder of Rufus Leonard Corporate Communications. He has an MSc in responsibility and business practice from the University of Bath and is the author of five books including *Beautiful Corporations* (2000, Financial Times Prentice Hall).

Andrew Dlugolecki is a visiting research fellow at the climatic research unit, University of East Anglia, a director of the Tyndall Centre for Climate Change Research, and the Carbon Disclosure Project, and an advisor to UNEP Finance Initiative. He also consults privately. Andrew worked for 27 years in Aviva, retiring from the position of Director of General Insurance Development in December 2000. He served as the chief author and, later, reviewer for the Intergovernmental Panel on Climate Change in its Second, Third and Fourth Assessment Reports, carried out similar duties for official UK and EU reviews of climate change, and chaired two studies of climate change by the Chartered Insurance Institute. Andrew obtained BSc (Hons) in pure mathematics at Edinburgh, an MA in operational research at Lancaster, a PhD in technological economics at Stirling, and is a fellow of the Chartered Insurance Institute and Royal Meteorological Society.

Charles Donovan is a commercial manager with the Enviros Group, a multidisciplinary environmental consultancy with offices in North America, Europe and Africa. Charles began his work on climate change with the US Environmental Protection Agency and subsequently worked for the Enron Corporation in its London and Houston offices, where he was responsible for project financing and investment risk analysis for electric power asset developments. His experience includes financial structuring for a range of renewable energy and advanced power generation technologies. Charles holds a bachelor degree from the University of Washington and graduated with honours from The Owen Graduate School of Business at Vanderbilt University. His MBA work included a concentration in corporate finance and international management studies at the Escuela Superior de Administración de Empresa in Barcelona.

Charles Crosthwaite Eyre is an associate director of IRMG, the risk consulting and risk financing division of Aon Ltd, the global provider of insurance broking and risk management services. He joined Aon in 2000, as the practice leader for climate change solutions, advising companies in energy and power generation, manufacturing, renewable energy and forestry on the identification, management and mitigation of emerging climate change policy risks. He has undertaken assignments in the public and private sector, evaluating risks from a national, corporate and project perspective. He is a regular speaker at climate change conferences, a member of the UK Emissions Trading Group, the UK Renewable Power Association, the Association of Energy Producers and the Finance and Investment Working Group of the Renewable Advisory Board.

Dirk Forrister is Managing Director of asset management and advisory services at Natsource Europe in London. He advises European financial, energy, industrial and government clients on environmental markets. Prior to joining Natsource, he was Chairman of the White House Climate Change Task Force under President Clinton. Dirk holds degrees from David Lipscomb (BA in political science) and Rutgers University School of Law (JD).

Mark Goldsmith is an investment principal at Actis Capital LLP – a leading private equity investor in emerging markets. Mark received an honours degree in manufacturing engineering from Nottingham University and a masters degree in environmental pollution control from the University of Leeds. Mark worked for five years for Shell International on various research and technical service projects. On leaving Shell, Mark joined the environmental, safety and risk section of Arthur D. Little and managed several environmental assignments for blue chip clients. In June 2002 Mark joined Actis, formerly CDC Capital Partners, where he has concentrated on further developing the health & safety, environmental and social management systems, he has specific responsibilities for environmental areas and leads the Actis approach on climate change issues.

William Greene is a climate change consultant for africapractice, a communications consultancy that works with governments and corporations in Africa, where he is also currently the editor of a new report on the Clean Development Mechanism in Africa. He was educated at Bristol (MSc) and the Institute of Development Studies, Sussex (MPhil), where he wrote his thesis on stakeholder relations around a large-scale mining project in Madagascar. He has written academically on climate change finance and was a representative of the United States Environmental Protection Agency at legislative hearings for the US Climate Change Bill. His recent research interests include carbon finance for sustainable community development and climate change adaptation in Africa. William's published work includes: "Aid fragmentation and proliferation: Can donors improve the delivery of climate change finance?" *IDS Bulletin*; "Black sand, green forest: Mining and sustainable development in South East Madagascar" published MPhil Thesis.

Kirsty Hamilton currently works as a consultant on international energy and climate policy issues, including a retainer with the UK Business Council for Sustainable Energy, representing the main UK utilities. She has been based in London since the end of 2001. This follows 12 years of involvement in the climate policy arena as an observer at the UNFCCC negotiations, latterly leading Greenpeace International's work on the corporate sector and the international policy process. Kirsty is currently an associate fellow at Chatham House (Royal Institute of International Affairs), and on the advisory board of UNEP Finance Initiative's Climate Change Working Group. Kirsty's published work includes the business module in *The Kyoto-Marrakech System: A Strategic Analysis* (IC consultants, 2003).

Junji Hatano is currently the Chairman of the clean energy finance committee for Mitsubishi Securities Co, Ltd. Prior to this he was Director and Deputy President for Tokyo-Mitsubishi Securities. Junji has been with Mitsubishi Bank since 1966, where he has held the positions of: Chief Manager, Securities Division; President and CEO, Mitsubishi Bank of California; General Manager, Investment Banking Division; and Director & General Manager, Investment Banking Division. He has a BA in psychology, a BA in economics from the University of Tokyo, and an MBA from Stanford University.

Mustafa Hussain is a consultant at Frontier Economics, a micro-economic consultancy that provides regulatory and policy support to governments, and extensive advisory support to high profile private sector clients. He has worked on energy markets across Europe and advised multi-lateral agencies in a number of developing markets. In the UK, Mustafa has worked on all the key policy instruments making up UK climate change policy. Prior to Frontier, Mustafa worked at Enron Europe in its origination and government affairs teams, and for Citigroup. He is a regular speaker at training seminars and has been a guest lecturer on the City University masters programme in economic regulation. He holds postgraduate qualifications in economics from the London School of Economics and the Université Catholique de Louvain.

Stephen Jewson runs the weather derivatives business at Risk Management Solutions in London, supplying weather data and software to the weather derivatives industry. Prior to working at RMS he was an academic researcher studying climate variability, and worked at the universities of Oxford, Bologna, Monash and Reading. He has a doctorate in climate science from Oxford University and degrees in mathematics from Cambridge University. Stephen has published a large number of scientific articles spanning fundamental climate research, applied meteorology and weather derivatives. He is the lead author of *Weather Derivative Valuation* (Cambridge University Press).

Stuart Jones is currently Head of Emissions Trading at Accord Energy Limited, a wholly owned subsidiary of UK Utility Centrica plc. Based at the Centrica headquarters in Windsor, he is responsible for all proprietary and compliance trading, deal structuring and business development. Previously, Stuart was a weather derivatives trader for Accord Energy Limited, trading proprietary and portfolio management books.

Li Junfeng is the General Secretary of the Chinese Renewable Industrial Association and also works at the Energy Research Institute of National Development and Reform Commission as a senior research fellow and chair of the academic committee. He is heavily involved in the REEEP programme in China and project development for GEF and World Bank, UNDP and other programmes for renewable energy development in China. In recent years, he has also been involved in Climate Change issues, particularly in technology transfer, CDM and carbon trading. He is the lead author for the development of Chinese Renewable Energy Law. His main publications include "Issues and options of greenhouse gas emission and control in China", "Renewable technology assessment in China", "Renewable energy planning and development strategy" and "Potential analysis of carbon trade in China". He graduated from Shandong Mining Institute in 1982.

Abyd Karmali is Director of European Climate Strategy Services with ICF Consulting's London office, and a Senior Vice President. Abyd has provided strategic support on issues relating to the commercial impacts of carbon constraints to many European, US, and Japanese companies in the Global Fortune 500. He has previously served in ICF Consulting's offices in Washington DC and in Toronto. From 1996–97 Abyd was Climate Change Officer at the United Nations Environment Programme's industry office in Paris, and he participated in the negotiations leading to the Kyoto Protocol. Abyd is also on the board of trustees for the Focus Humanitarian Assistance Europe Foundation. He holds an MS in technology and policy from the Massachusetts Institute of Technology.

Andy Kershaw is Climate Change Programme Manager at British Airways. He has worked in the field of aviation environmental policy since 1998 and currently serves on climate policy committees of the UK Emissions Trading Group and the Association of European Airlines. Andy has contributed to research into aircraft noise effects, noise abatement flight procedures and safety risk assessment for aircraft operations.

Matthew Kiernan is Founder and Chief Executive of Innovest Strategic Value Advisors, Inc, a specialist investment research advisory firm based in New York, London, Paris, Melbourne, Toronto and San Francisco. Matthew had previously co-founded a strategy consulting company that he later sold to KPMG Peat Marwick, where he served as a senior partner. From 1991–2, he was Director of the Business Council for Sustainable Development, which served as the principal business and industry advisor to the Secretary General of the UN Earth Summit in Rio de Janeiro. He has lectured on environmental finance in senior executive programmes at the Wharton School, Columbia Business School, and Oxford University. Matthew holds advanced degrees in political science and environmental studies, as well as a PhD in strategic environmental management from the University of London. His recent publications have appeared in a number of leading business journals, and his book, *The 11 Commandments of 21st Century Management*, has been translated into six languages.

Katherine Lake is a lawyer in the global climate change practice at Baker & McKenzie in Melbourne, Australia, where she works on the development of climate change law and policy at local and international levels. Prior to joining Baker & McKenzie, Katherine worked as an associate to a Judge of the Federal Court of Australia. She has a BSc with a major in environmental science, and a bachelor of laws (Hons) from the University of Melbourne. Her research interests include climate change, water law (she has published articles on the recent water law reforms in Australia) and biodiversity. She chairs the Law Institute of Victoria Young Lawyers' Environmental Law Reform Committee.

Stefan Leclaire is a project officer within the Carboncredits.nl team, where his main activities include identifying and evaluating greenhouse gas reduction projects in central and eastern Europe. He is also responsible for additionality and baseline studies within the Carboncredits team. Prior to joining the Carboncredits team, Stefan worked as project officer in the field of energy and environment at EG-Liaison, the department of SenterNovem dealing with the framework programme for research and development of the European Union. His tasks there comprised project consultation, training activities and participation in EU-projects. Prior to this, Stefan worked as a consultant with Tebodin, consultants and engineers in energy and environmental technology. Stefan holds master degrees in process engineering, environmental technology and european studies from the University of Aachen in Germany.

Richard Leese is currently the Manager of legislative and regulatory programmes for the British Cement Association, where he has specific responsibility for climate change issues as well as a broad remit of environmental and government issues. Richard has a first degree in environmental science and a masters in conservation biology. He is currently working toward a PhD on the implementation of integrated pollution prevention and control legislation in the chemical industry by part-time research study. Richard spent ten years in the chemical industry working for an SME fine chemical manufacturing company as Group Regulatory Affairs Manager. Richard's representations for the chemical and cement industries include international panels on climate change, best available techniques, IPPC and life cycle analysis.

Richard Lord (QC) is a barrister specialising in commercial litigation, practising at Brick Court Chambers in London. He has a particular interest in the legal implications of climate change. He was educated at Stowe School and Sidney Sussex College, Cambridge and was called to the bar in 1981, becoming a Queen's Counsel in 2002. His legal publications include textbooks on controlled drugs and the arbitration act, as well as papers on climate change and the law.

Karen McClellan is currently Director of Investment for Climate Investment Partnership, an international partnership of government and private investors seeking to invest in carbon emission mitigating projects. She was previously Senior Banker, Energy Efficiency, at the European Bank for Reconstruction and Development. Karen is a frequent speaker at conferences and events related to carbon finance. Her recent publications include "JI and CDM projects – Finance in practice" in *A Guide to Emissions Trading: Risk Management and Business Implications* (Risk Books, 2004) and she is a contributor to *The Global Climate and Economic Development*, to be published by the University of Minnesota in 2005. Karen holds a BA in economics from Yale University and an MBA from Stanford Graduate School of Business, where she co-authored and taught a case study on private equity investment in emerging markets for several years.

Ben McKeown is an investment principal at Actis Capital LLP – a leading private equity investor in emerging markets. Ben graduated as a mining engineer from Imperial College, London and completed an MBA at IESE, Barcelona. Prior to joining the minerals, oil & gas team in Actis, Ben worked in the upstream oil & gas industry in technical and commercial roles for BP and Total. He has also worked in a corporate development role for a large diversified Spanish industrial group, which amongst other activities was one of the largest private wind-farm and co-generation developers in Spain. Ben was on the board and investment committee of African Lion Ltd, a US$33m early stage-mining fund and, along with Mark Goldsmith, has been instrumental in developing Actis' awareness of the investment opportunities in the renewable energy sector in emerging markets.

Philipp Mettler is the Equity Analyst for Consumer Discretionary at Sustainable Asset Management Research. After attending the University of Applied Sciences (HWV) in Zurich, Philipp spent a number of years in the investment research departments of Swiss Volksbank and UBS. There he was in charge of the analysis of equity markets in Europe and in the Asia Pacific region, respectively. He also co-managed the global mutual fund UBS Portfolio Invest. In 1998 he joined Forbo International in the corporate treasury department where he was responsible for liquidity management. From 1999 to 2005 he worked as a senior portfolio manager for European equities at Swiss Life, managing several mutual funds. Philipp holds diplomas as a Chartered Financial Analyst, and as a Certified EFFAS Financial Analyst, as well as an executive masters in corporate finance.

Marianne Moscoso-Osterkorn has been the International Director of the Renewable Energy and Energy Efficiency Partnership (REEEP), since 2004. She obtained her PhD in business administration at the University of Economics in Vienna, and received an MA in industrial psychology from the University of Michigan. She started her career in the banking sector as a project manager for organisational projects at several Austrian banks. From 1981–2004, Marianne was employed by Verbund, the largest Austrian utility company. During this time, she held various management positions. For more than 10 years she was the International Relations Manager of the group and was responsible for international lobbying and market development; she followed closely the liberalisation process of the European energy market. During these years Marianne was strongly involved in the development of the European green certificate market and was for several years President of RECS International, a European green certificate organisation.

Gerhard Mulder is Vice President, Sustainable Development, with ABN AMRO Bank in the Netherlands, where he coordinates the development and introduction of new environmental financial products, including emissions trading and the market for CDM and JI under the Kyoto Protocol. Prior to joining ABN AMRO, Gerhard was employed by SenterNovem, an agency of the Netherlands Ministry of Economic Affairs. There he identified and evaluated greenhouse gas reduction projects and acted as focal point on technical and political aspects of baselines and additionality. Before that, Gerhard lived in the US for 10 years where he worked as an emissions broker for Natsource in New York and consultant on energy and environment for ICF Consulting in Washington, DC. Gerhard has a masters degree in international affairs from Columbia University and a master of political science from the University of Amsterdam.

David Pocklington is Director, Industry Affairs, for the British Cement Association. David is a professional engineer with experience in the metals, engineering, transport, and construction industries. After graduating in metallurgy at the University of Sheffield, he undertook research into the thermodynamics of slag/metal reactions, and became Research Fellow, heading a group working on the chemistry of steelmaking. He also holds a research degree in environmental law from De Montfort University. Following a period in the metals industry, David joined London Underground and later the Society of Motor Manufacturers & Traders. David publishes widely, he is author of the book, *The Law of Waste Management* and his column in *Environmental Law and Management* reviews current environmental issues from an industrial perspective.

Alan Punter is CEO of Aon Capital Services Limited, the UK-based unit responsible for raising capital for insurance operations and arranging securitisations of insurance risk, primarily for natural catastrophes. Alan has had a number of risk financing roles in 20 years with global insurance brokers, following 10 years of college lecturing in statistics. He holds degrees in mathematics, statistics and an MBA in finance and is a visiting lecturer at Cass Business School, City University, in London. He has published many papers in the trade press and academic journals, including the

Journal of Insurance Research & Practice and *The Geneva Papers*, and is the author of *Risk Financing and Management* (Institute of Finance Services). He was awarded the inaugural Lumina Award for outstanding research in reinsurance in 2001.

Nick Robins is Head of SRI Funds at Henderson Global Investors in London. He also leads Henderson's work on climate change, and is leader of the public policy workstream of the Institutional Investors Group on Climate Change. Prior to Henderson, Nick spent seven years with the International Institute for Environment and Development (IIED), where he worked as Director of the sustainable markets group. Prior to IIED, Nick was a special advisor to the EC's Environment Directorate working on the preparations and follow-up to the 1992 Earth Summit, and contributed chapters on strategy and innovation to the Business Council for Sustainable Development's landmark report, *Changing Course*. He has a BA in history (first class) from Cambridge University, and an MSc in international relations (distinction) from the London School of Economics.

David Russell is an advisor on responsible investment for the Universities Superannuation Scheme, the UK's third largest pension fund with assets of about £20 billion. A specialist in environmental issues, David is also a steering committee member of the Institutional Investors Group on Climate Change. He was previously environmental manager for a UK DIY retail multiple, dealing with the broad spectrum of business sustainability issues. He was also a lecturer at the University of Wales, Aberystwyth, specialising in environmental management systems and auditing, and providing consultancy services to companies. David has a masters in environmental impact assessment and a degree in zoology.

Stefan Schmitz works in London as head of the wind energy practice at city law firm Field Fisher Waterhouse. He is also head of the wind energy practice group of the European Legal Alliance. Stefan is admitted as a solicitor in England and Wales, and as a Rechtsanwalt in Germany. Stefan studied law in Germany and England, and holds a doctorate from Christian-Albrechts-University at Kiel and a masters degree from Cambridge University (Magdalene College). After working in Germany, Stefan joined the project finance practice at US law firm Orrick Herrington & Sutcliffe, in London, where he specialised in renewable projects. Stefan speaks regularly at conferences and seminars on topics relating to the financing of renewable energy projects. He is currently involved in a number of wind and PV projects.

Andrew Sentance joined BA as Chief Economist in January 1998. Since 2002 he has also been responsible for BA environmental and corporate responsibility policies. He was one of the five senior managers appointed by Rod Eddington in 2001 to prepare the company's "Future size and shape" turnaround plan and is also a trustee of the two main BA pension funds. Andrew is a former director of economic affairs at the Confederation of British Industry and a director of the London Business School Centre for Economic Forecasting. He also holds visiting professorships at Royal Holloway (University of London) and Cranfield University.

Rory Sullivan is Director, Investor Responsibility, for Insight Investment, where he leads the company's engagement activities on climate change. Rory has 15 years of experience in environmental management and public policy, and has worked on these issues for the public and private sector in Australia, South East Asia, Africa and Europe. His experience includes advising organisations on greenhouse, energy and environmental management issues, and advising Environment Australia and the OECD on the development and implementation of pollutant release and transfer registers. He is the author or editor of numerous articles, book chapters and papers on greenhouse and environmental policy issues. Rory holds a first class honours degree in electrical engineering (University College Cork), masters degrees in environmental science (University of Manchester) and environmental law (University of Sydney), and has a PhD in law (Queen Mary, University of London).

Kenny Tang is founder and CEO of Oxbridge Capital. With postgraduate degrees from the universities of Oxford and Cambridge, he has worked in corporate finance with the Union Bank of Switzerland and has strategy consultancy experience with KPMG Consultants and Stern Stewart. He is European Partner at Enhancement Partners LP, is the Founder President and CEO of SUSTAIN, and is part of the Asian Strategic Leadership Institute. Kenny earned his doctorate at The Judge Institute of Management Studies, Cambridge University's business school, and is a member of the board of governors of Middlesex University. He is a Chartered Financial Analyst and holds the Investment Management Certificate. Kenny is the lead author of *Taking Research to Market: How to Build and Invest in Successful University Spinouts* (Euromoney Books, 2004). He has written for the *Wall Street Journal Europe* and *Asian Wall Street Journal* and was a member of the Global Judging Panel of the *Wall Street Journal*'s Global Technology Innovations Awards, 2004.

Brian Thomas is a content manager and member of management at Swiss Re America Holding, where he focuses on sustainability issues. He has worked for many years as a writer on financial and other topics at various capital markets firms. He has a BA in philosophy from Brown University.

Kyoko Tochikawa is a CDM/JI consultant for Mitsubishi Securities' clean energy finance committee. Her role includes project management, developing project design documents and developing successful methodology applications. Recently relocated to Hong Kong, she continues her work mainly in Asia for energy- and forestation-related projects. She has a BEng (Hons), majoring in environmental engineering and process control, from the Faculty of Engineering of Sydney University in Australia. Her published work includes an article entitled "The spirit of the CDM", published in *Carbon Finance*, August 2004.

Bruce Usher is CEO of EcoSecurities, and structured the Austrian Small-Scale Facility and the 2C Carbon Access Facility. Prior to EcoSecurities, Bruce was co-founder and CEO of TreasuryConnect LLC. For the previous six years, Bruce was responsible for managing sales, trading and administration as COO of The Williams Capital Group. Prior to that he spent four years as a vice president and trader of structured derivative securities at Lehman Brothers in both New York and Tokyo. Prior to this Bruce worked for several years trading derivatives at the Chuo Trust & Banking Company in Tokyo. Bruce received an MBA with distinction from Harvard Business School and is an adjunct professor of finance at Columbia Business School, where he teaches a course on finance & sustainability.

Paul Vickers is Managing Director at Natsource-Tullett (Alberta) Co, where he is a portfolio manager for the Greenhouse Gas Credit Aggregation Pool (GG-CAP), a joint purchasing initiative of several companies globally valued at over €72,000,000. Prior to joining Natsource, he designed and implemented emissions market strategies for Transalta, as well as a range of businesses for Shell Canada. Paul holds an MEng and a BEng in chemical engineering from McGill University in Montreal, Quebec.

Allan Walker joined Standard Bank, London, in 2002 as Head of Power and Infrastructure within project finance, where he is also responsible for the bank's carbon credits activities and its cooperation agreement with EcoSecurities. Allan has over 22 years of experience in commercial and investment banking. Prior to Standard Bank he was a director in the global energy and project finance group for Credit Suisse First Boston in London. Prior to this he ran the energy group at CSFB Garantia in Sao Paulo, Brazil. Allan has closed numerous M&A, privatisation, project and structured finance transactions in countries as diverse as Saudi Arabia, Peru and South Korea. Allan has an MA in economic geography (Cambridge) and received his financial training on a one-year residential course with JP Morgan in New York. He has also worked for Samuel Montagu (HSBC) and ING Barings. Allan speaks Portuguese and Spanish.

Christopher Walker is the Managing Director of Swiss Re's Environmental/Greenhouse Gas Risk Solutions, the unit charged with developing commercial applications to Swiss Re sustainability commitments and in particular business and investment risks and opportunities in the emerging greenhouse gas emissions reduction area. Christopher has worked in various capacities at Swiss Re for nine years. An attorney, he has a BA in government and JD from St. John's University.

George Walker, who is partially retired, works for Aon Re Australia as Senior Risk Analyst, following nine years as their Head of Strategic Development. He was a pioneer in the development of catastrophe insurance loss modelling in Australia. This followed five years in senior government research management as Assistant Chief of the CSIRO division of building construction and engineering. Before this, George was Associate Professor of civil engineering at James Cook University of North Queensland, where he was an academic for 21 years. He obtained his PhD in earthquake engineering at the University of Auckland in 1966. At James Cook University he specialised in the design of housing to resist tropical cyclones, leading the investigation of the damage to Darwin by Cyclone Tracy in 1975. George was also a peer reviewer of the insurance input into the financial sections of IPCC 2nd and 3rd reports.

Martijn Wilder heads Baker & McKenzie's global climate change group advising governments, multi-laterals (such as the World Bank), carbon funds and corporations on all matters of climate change law and policy. In particular he is regarded as a leader in advising on carbon deals, emissions trading and the CDM. Martijn has published widely and has honours degrees in both law and economics, and an LLM from the University of Cambridge where he studied as a Cambridge Commonwealth Scholar.

Monique Willis is an associate in the global climate change practice group at Baker & McKenzie. She advises corporations and governments on many aspects of the emerging national and international climate change regulations. Her clients include the World Bank, Rabobank, the Japan Carbon Fund, The United Nations Environment Program and BP. Monique specialises in advising on carbon finance and CDM projects and is co-author of the UNEP Guidebook *Legal Issues and the CDM*. Monique holds a bachelor of arts and a bachelor of laws (Hons) from the Australian National University, and is Assistant Secretary on the Management Committee of the International Law Association (Australian branch).

Daniël van der Weerd is Programme Manager of carboncredits.nl. This programme executes the ERUPT and CERUPT tenders that the Dutch government is using for acquiring carbon credits from JI and CDM projects. Prior to this, Daniël worked as a legal counsel for SenterNovem. In this capacity he provided legal advice regarding ERPAs and public procurement law. After being appointed to legal counsel for the carboncredits.nl programme he became more involved in negotiating all aspects of carbon contracts. As part of this he also participated in the IETA initiative to negotiate a standard contract for carbon procurement. In addition, he assisted the Dutch Ministry of Economic Affairs in negotiating their framework contracts with the World Bank/PCF and the EBRD. Daniël holds a masters degree in Dutch law with a specialisation in international law from the University of Utrecht.

Lu Xuedu is Deputy Director General for the Office of Global Environmental Affairs with the Ministry of Science and Technology of China. He has been involved in climate change negotiation as a member of the Chinese delegation since 1996. He was elected as the alternate member of the CDM Executive Board in 2001, as member of the board in 2004, and as vice chairman of the board in 2005. In June 2004, he was elected as chairman for the Host Country Committee of the World Bank Carbon Finance Business. He is now also acting as the focal point for China for the Asian-Pacific Network for Global Change Research, and focal point for China for the Carbon Sequestration Leadership Forum. He has published two books, *CDM in China* and *Climate Change Study: Progress and Perspective*, as well as many CDM and climate change academic papers.

Song Yanqin is Deputy Director of the Centre for Renewable Energy Development, Energy Research Institute, National Development and the Reform Commission, as well as the project coordinator for the Building Capacity for CDM in China. His main task is to manage international cooperation projects in the renewable energy commercialisation and CDM capacity building area. His research interests include renewable energy policy and development planning at the national level. Previously, he was working in the human resource management office of the Beinei Group as the Deputy Director. His major publications include "Renewable energy development plan and strategy for China", "Introduction of CDM and its implementation in China" and "CDM and solar energy development in China".

Liu Yingchun graduated from Dalian University of Foreign Languages, majored in science and English and acquired a national translator qualification. She works at the Project Management Office of Building Capacity for the CDM in China as assistant to the project coordinator. Her main task is to assist in organising CDM training workshops, policy study workshops, and to conduct on-the-spot research of pilot CDM projects and facilitate the dissemination of CDM knowledge and information. Her research interests include the practical experiences of CDM projects and potential carbon trading markets. At present, she is making preparations for the CDM Country Guide together with many other CDM experts from the Institute for Global Environment Strategies.

Mari Yoshitaka is a project manager and senior analyst for Mitsubishi Securities' clean energy finance committee, a working unit that specialises in CDM and JI, with experience in projects in Asia, Eastern Europe and Latin America. She has both a financial and environmental background, her previous positions include fixed income business management at Nikko City (previously Nikko Salomon Smith Barney) in Tokyo. She has a BA in law (international and civil law) from Meiji University, Tokyo and an MSc from the School of Natural Resource and Environment, University of Michigan.

Foreword

On behalf of the Corporation of London, I am delighted to write a foreword for this book.

The City of London's financial district is a dynamic group of financial institutions operating in all environments. Global climate change has emerged as a challenge faced by every nation in the world. I therefore warmly welcome the role of the City in producing innovative financial solutions that meet these challenges – whether in the financing, insuring or investing side of climate change.

The City of London is already an important international centre in the area of climate change. As we expand climate change services overseas into key global financial centres, we feel it is imperative that London has a platform to establish and leverage our current pre-eminent position in the field of climate change. Therefore I am delighted that this book originated in London and reflects the contributions of major City-based organisations – both UK and foreign institutions.

I welcome *The Finance of Climate Change* as a significant breakthrough to bring climate change into the global arena and I am delighted that London – the climate change capital of the world – has taken the lead to do this. All governments, corporations and investors should read it!

Alderman Michael Savory
The Rt. Hon. the Lord Mayor of London

Foreword

If you were sitting down now to write "the history of the climate change debate between 1985 and 2015", it would go something like this: in the beginning, there were the radical scientists, raising hypotheses and risking the scorn of their mainstream colleagues; with the establishment of the Intergovernmental Panel on Climate Change the radical became the mainstream, gradually generating a scientific consensus that embraced all but a handful of genuine dissenters and a dwindling army of ideological naysayers; that consensus brought in a first wave of rich world governments through the Kyoto Protocol, which in turn unleashed the creativity of the "market-makers" and the financiers. For most ordinary citizens, as capital markets aligned with governments, that was the point at which climate change become a reality, finally setting to one side the confusion and disempowerment caused by endless scientific disputes; it wasn't long after that moment that the laggard governments in the rich world grumbled their way on board, as did the heavy-hitters of the poor world such as China, India and Brazil – the rest, as they say, is history.

That potted history of climate change puts the catalytic role of capital markets pretty much at the mid-point of the thirty year cycle. For many people, those markets constitute the new "realpolitic", the place where realities are first manifested. When the UK Sustainable Development Commission was recently compiling a group of "tipping point moments" (after which, progress towards a more sustainable world is unstoppable), high on our list was the moment at which the world's first self-made carbon billionaire hits the headlines. We're not there yet, but this book demonstrates why it might not be too long before that moment is reached.

Not before time. Although I welcome the enormous dynamism and ingenuity that the contributors to this book bring to bear on the challenge of climate change, there's still a worrying feeling that the full import of what the scientists now tell us hasn't as yet worked its way into most of today's "mainstream mindsets".

To achieve the 60% cut in CO_2 emissions by 2050 that the UK and other European Governments now believe to be necessary demands a *pace* of change and a *depth* of engagement that remain elusive. We are still allowing ourselves the luxury of imagining that climate systems will change gradually and predictably over the next two or three decades, enabling our financial and political systems to adapt in an equally gradual and measured way. That assumption now looks increasingly unwise as the scientists surface more and more radical discontinuities from the historical climate record.

That's the scary bit. The reassuring bit lies in the sense of our financial systems and institutions building up in-house capacity, exploring new market mechanisms, creating new products and new intellectual capital. In other words, there is much to celebrate, even as the white-knuckle ride involved in adapting to climate change begins to accelerate.

Jonathon Porritt
Chairman of the UK Sustainable Development Commission and Director of Forum for the Future

Foreword

I am delighted to write this foreword for the first ever book on "the finance of climate change" to celebrate the coming into force of the Kyoto Protocol in 2005.

The global climate change has emerged as a challenge faced by every nation in the world, since more and more research and observation has shown that climate change has affected human life, society and economy.

China, with its fragile ecological environment, is vulnerable to the negative impact of climate change. According to the preliminary studies by Chinese scientists, climate change will continue to exert profound influence on the ecological environment as well as the social-economic system in China, and such influences are mainly negative.

The future population expansion and the urbanisation expansion in China will unavoidably boost energy demand, resulting in more greenhouse gases emissions. As a developing country susceptible to impacts of climate change, the Chinese government has attached great importance to this issue and adopted active response measures. The Chinese government earnestly implemented its responsibilities under the United Nations Framework Convention on Climate Change.

In order to take advantage of opportunities offered by the Clean Development Mechanism defined in the Kyoto Protocol, we will work closely with developed countries, especially in the area of finance. We thoroughly welcome this book as a major move to bring climate change into the mainstream consciousness and the boardrooms of financial institutions and corporations in developing countries.

Climate change has brought about a great challenge to China and the world as a whole. It is imperative for the international community to make full preparation for this challenge. This book is a major breakthrough to bring climate change onto the centre stage of the financial sector.

I commend this book to China and to all developing countries!

Gao Guangsheng
Director General
Office of National Coordination Committee on Climate Change Policy
National Development and Reform Commission of China

Introduction

Kenny Tang

Oxbridge Capital

"Climate change is an issue of justice as much as of economic development. It is a problem caused by the industrialised countries, whose effects will disproportionately fall on developing countries."

Gordon Brown, UK Chancellor of the Exchequer, 15 March 2005

WHY PRODUCE THIS BOOK?

When one sees pictures of the effects of human-induced climate change, such as the melting ice cap in the Arctics, one is tempted to think that it is years away and, in any case, it is also thousands of miles away! But, when the UK recorded its highest ever temperature of 37.9°C (100.2°F) in London on 10 August 2003 (with statistics attributing an extra 2,142 deaths of mostly elderly folk over 10 days in August 2003[1]), we begin to realise it is happening right now and right in our own backyard.

It is a wake-up call! It is time for us to act, even in our own limited way, not only to prepare for the effects that are upon us, but also to preserve the environment for today and the future. As the father of two young children, I'd like to pass on this earth to them in a far better shape than when we came in. Instead, the earth that we pass to them is considerably worse off, and the earth that they themselves pass to their own children will not be in much better shape either!

We wanted to mark 2005 as the year the Kyoto Protocol finally became law (eight years after the Protocol was adopted in 1997 and 15 years after the UN adopted the United Nations Framework

Convention of Climate Change). The UK government also raised the profile of climate change as an international issue highlighting it as a key objective during the UK's presidency of the Group of Eight (G8) nations in 2005.

The creation of the world's first trading exchange in "hot air" will mean the generation of carbon credits in the developing countries, which is crucial in determining whether sustainable clean-energy projects in such countries can be successfully financed. But these developing countries are probably the last to know about these credits. As Gordon Brown said, the effects of climate change fall disproportionately on developing countries, yet they do not have the resources or the expertise to deal with the effects of climate change. Our hope is to raise the issue of climate change and its threats among the key influencers in government, business and the financial community in both developed and developing countries, to urge all to take serious and immediate action while there is still time. We need a comprehensive global response.

The role of finance

Our objective for this book is to showcase and promote international excellence, expertise and leadership in the field of climate change. As the Kyoto Protocol envisages a global system of caps in carbon emissions and the setting up of a trading system in carbon credits from 2008, a whole new area is evolving. This is essentially a book on the evolving area of the finance of climate change and carbon emissions, involving the mechanics of project finance, setting up of carbon facilities, development of weather derivatives, creation of carbon equity funds, development of insurance products, analysis of investors' perspective on risk exposures to climate change, development of investment strategies that utilise climate risk analysis, and so on.

PURPOSE AND STRUCTURE

To achieve these goals, this book will provide a clear and comprehensive guide to the financing, insuring and investing aspects of climate change. It aims to present a collection of chapters including real-world examples and cases supplemented by detailed industry notes that explore the dynamic world of climate change, investing, financing and international policymaking.

The Kyoto Protocol took at least 15 years – from initial conception in 1990 through adoption in 1997 to formal ratification in 2005. The formal coming into law of the Kyoto Protocol on 16 February 2005 and the start of the EU Emissions Trading Scheme (EU ETS) on 1 January 2005 shows that international, regional and national policymakers have come to understand that market-based solutions will play a key role in providing a framework for effective international action to deal with the issue of climate change.

Successful politically driven market-based solutions require two key imperatives to function effectively: the development of a robust policy framework (including the protection of property rights, the enforceability of legal ownership provisions and requirement for transparency and disclosure), and the engagement of the financial services industry, intermediaries and service providers both in its evolution and its ongoing development.

Governments need to create robust policy frameworks that will provide the clarity and long-term stability vital to investors, project developers, corporations and financiers. The finance sector has a key role to play in creating the right conditions for market-based solutions to flourish. We discuss both imperatives throughout this book, while recognising that practical issues still remain.

Purpose

Momentum in recognising the climate threat and taking immediate and long-term action to curb carbon emissions is gathering pace in major parts of the globe. The purpose of this book is to drive the climate-change issue, its opportunities and threats and its full financial impact into mainstream consciousness within the financial services community, onto the board agendas of company directors, senior executives, pension fund trustees and institutional investors, and onto the policymaking frameworks of national, regional and international policymakers. Climate change must become a board issue, rather than a climate or scientific issue!

Specifically, they need to realise that carbon is gradually being recognised by both the financial community and the wider financial environment as a factor that needs to be incorporated into all calculations of equity value, credit risk, corporate risk management, capital spending and project viability. In other words, carbon is a determinant of corporate and financial value.

The primary task is to improve the ability of investors, host governments, policymakers, leading global corporations and project developers to realise potential benefits from the development of viable and robust climate-change policies, and in particular the finance and financing of key carbon mitigation/adaptation projects and new renewable-energy technologies while enabling intermediaries (such as investment and commercial banks, insurance players, providers of risk management services, project consultants and project verifiers) to provide relevant and appropriate services and products to assist in such major endeavours.

Specifically this book has five goals.

❑ First, it seeks to plug the knowledge gap that exists between governments and policymakers in the developed countries and those in the developing countries in this key area of the finance and financing of climate-change programmes and initiatives.

❑ Second, it tries to inform, educate and manage expectations of investors, governments, project developers, corporations and financiers into the emerging and evolving area of the finance and risks of climate change, and to enable these parties to operate more effectively in the carbon-constrained economy of the future, based on a better understanding of each other's requirements and risk appetites.

❑ Third, the book aims to facilitate greater interaction and develop closer involvement between, on the one hand, major corporations (who are potential purchasers of carbon credits) and financiers in the developed countries and, on the other hand, potential project developers and intermediaries engaged in the development of climate change and renewable-energy projects in the developing countries through the dissemination of best practices, case studies and lessons learned.

❑ Fourth, the book seeks to increase awareness among governments and policymakers in the developing countries that creating, developing and financing potential climate-change projects is a dynamic and intensive endeavour. The book will emphasise that realising success is based on a multitude of factors, including successful collaboration with developers and financiers, and that national governments have a critical role to play through the development of effective policies in education, investment and so on.

❏ Fifth, the book aims to become the essential guide for anyone involved in the financing of climate change and renewable-energy projects by helping to uncover potential problems and showing what to look out for. As a result investors, project developers, policymakers, financiers and consultants can better plan to avoid common mistakes, manage risks more effectively and make smarter choices that lead them to implement projects more effectively, thereby maximising returns.

Structure

To date, the discussions about climate change have been dominated by policy issues and scientific debates, but much less attention has been paid to the financing and financial aspects, such as: the role of carbon as a determinant of financial and corporate value, unlocking the obstacles to securing renewable-energy projects, developing climate-related insurance products, analysing investors' perspectives on risk exposures to climate change, and developing investment strategies that utilise climate risk analysis.

This book aims to fill the gap with a challenging perspective. It poses the question: *what are the financing, insuring and investing effects of climate change, with their implications for governments, corporations and investors?*

This question is particularly pertinent for all businesses and industries facing the threat of climate change (there is increasing evidence that the potential financial consequences of climate change extend well beyond the obvious, energy-intensive industry sectors) as well as for their financiers, lenders, insurers, advisers and regulators, not to mention governments, policymakers and service providers. Is climate change and carbon a determinant of corporate and financial value within your industry, and, if so, where, how, when and in what way will it impact your business and industry?

Section 1 addresses the finance and policy issues, especially "finance–policy" gaps and the policy conditions for attracting investment.

Section 2 addresses a number of critical issues arising from the financing of Clean Development Mechanism/Joint Implementation projects to help with the successful financing and implementation of these projects.

Section 3 addresses the role of emissions trading and carbon funds to secure carbon credits, including the role of weather derivatives.

Section 4 addresses investor perspectives from two coalition groups of investors representing nearly US$22 trillion of assets under management and poses the intriguing question of whether climate change has now "arrived" as a *bona fide* mainstream investment issue.

Section 5 looks at developments in a number of key sectors such as aviation, auto, insurance and energy-intensive industry such as cement, including a survey of best practices.

Section 6 looks at developments around the world, including contributions on China, Japan, Southeast Asia and Africa.

The book concludes by assessing the real social cost of carbon and raises the spectre of liability in discussing a scenario of what could happen if international agreements such as the Kyoto Protocol were to collapse overnight.

ACKNOWLEDGEMENTS

My thanks to Laurie Donaldson, managing editor at Risk Books, for his support and encouragement to push for a first-ever book on the subject of the finance of climate change. Tamsine Green provided invaluable editorial and other support, and was a delight to work with. Antony Spence provided invaluable marketing support.

Thanks must also go to Tony Blair, Gordon Brown, Dato Abdullah Badawi, Lord Mayor of London Alderman Michael Savory, Gao Guangsheng, and Jonathon Porritt for contributing their respective quotes and forewords to this book. I owe a great debt to Andrew Dlugolecki for his unstinting work and challenging comments, and the team of external informal reviewers, including Kirsty Hamilton, Steve Jewson, Mike Allen, Karen McClellan, Mark Goldsmith and Michael Pao. There are fewer factual errors and erroneous insights thanks to your unstinting efforts.

A venture like this could not proceed without financial support from a number of key parties – in particular, we should like to mention Actis, Aon, British Airways, British Cement Association, BSI and Field Fisher Waterhouse for their generous support and assistance.

Thanks also to everyone connected with Oxbridge Capital, especially Sir Paul Judge (chairman), Gordon Young, Nigel Rich, Peter Pearson, Sir Geoffrey Pattie and Yap Hon Seeng for their continuing support. I would also like to thank Michael Pao, Lim Yew Seng and Anthony Teo of Enhancement Partners, Tan Sri Francis Yeoh of YTL, and Dato Michael Yeoh of ASLI and SUSTAIN. Quintin Vello was very helpful in Malaysia.

On a personal note, special thanks to my wife, Lorraine, for her cheerfulness and wifely support, as well as a keen interest in this project; my son Joseph, whose knowledge and interest in cars is astounding; and cute little Hannah, whose smile just melts Daddy's heart! I now have the book and the courage to tell my in-laws, Brian and Christine, why they should switch off unused lights in their house!

Finally our grateful thanks must go to all the chapter contributors – the real stars of the book – including James Cameron, Matthew Kiernan and others who have been involved in climate-change initiatives since the early 1990s. It is their devotion to furthering the cause of climate change and disseminating best practice that has brought them together to share their vision, thoughts, experiences and practices. With the editors' constant promptings to publish the book in time for the G8 Summit in July 2005, the authors delivered what they promised. Thanks for your time, energy, dedication and commitment in completing your excellent contributions![2]

---

[1] Office of National Statistics "Summer Mortality - Deaths up in August Heat wave" – see http://www.statistics.gov.uk/cci/nugget.asp?id=480. On each of the 10 days from Monday, 4 August 2003, to Wednesday, 13 August 2003, the numbers of deaths in England and Wales was above the average for those days over the past five years. There were 15,261 deaths over the period in 2003, 16 per cent (2,142 deaths) above the average for the past five years. The impact was greatest in the southern half of England, particularly in London, where deaths for all ages were 42 per cent (616 deaths) above the average. Deaths in the 75-and-over age group were 59 per cent (522 deaths) above the average. London experienced a maximum temperature of 37.9°C (100.2°F) on 10 August 2003.

[2] Responsibility for the contents of, and arguments advanced within, each individual chapter rests with its author(s). I have sought to ensure consistency of style and clarity of expression while avoiding overlap, which is unavoidable in many cases.

Section 1

Framework and Finance Policy Issues

A Changing Climate for the Finance and Insurance Sector

Kenny Tang; Andrew Dlugolecki

Oxbridge Capital; University of East Anglia

The Kyoto Protocol, conceived in 1990, and adopted in 1997, finally became law on 16 February 2005. We hope this marks a turning point in the public consciousness about climate change and a sea change in attitude where previously businesses and individuals were adopting a "wait-and-see" attitude!

In full flow, climate change will impact corporate performance, institutional investments, major energy projects and renewable technologies, insurance contracts and corporate lending. Clearly, financial services, intermediaries and providers are faced with a range of real threats – but these are also opportunities. How will financing, insuring and investing change in the light of these developments? How should governments, corporations and investors react in the face of such challenges? How can policymakers harness the financial sector to provide the necessary financing and risk mitigation to develop sustainable market-based mechanisms?

There are still widely differing views on the impact of climate change and the specific steps these financial services providers could be taking now and in the future. With the pace of action accelerating after the ratification of the Kyoto Protocol, financial services companies need to investigate the issues for themselves and develop strategic responses. As a consequence, best practice in meeting the challenge and threat of climate change is expected to evolve rapidly as companies strive to gain an edge in these new markets.

HUMAN-INDUCED CLIMATE CHANGE IS UPON US

International scientists and technical researchers have compiled reports that present compelling evidence that human-induced climate change is upon us. Its consequences now are already significant and its long-term consequences could be devastating.

However, several factors make it difficult to be sure the degree to which climate change is actually affecting us already. Because of the rapid changes in the socioeconomic system and the high natural variability of the climate, trends in economic losses have to be treated with caution, and are subject to estimation since there is no rigorous system for recording them. Insurance losses, too, are not comprehensive indicators, since the statistics are recent, the extent of insurance varies widely and the vulnerability of insured property and the behaviour of property owners has also tended to aggravate losses over time.

What is known is that property losses result from extreme weather conditions: freeze losses come from cold waves, flood losses from heavy rain and storm surges, subsidence from drought and heat, and storm losses from high winds. Therefore, the weather itself provides an objective measure of loss potential, which can be quantified. The UK data series on weather is the longest in the world (back to 1665 for temperature), and so we can examine it to see if the weather is already changing, and is therefore a factor in losses. Using temperature provides a short cut; rainfall is correlated with temperature systematically through the year, and also great storms historically have occurred in milder winters.

Figure 1 shows that, from the 1970s, monthly temperatures in the UK have been hitting the top decile (the level seen 10% of the time in the past) more often. For the last 15 years the rate has been 30%, almost three times the long-term rate. At the same time, the proportion of cool months has fallen, and in fact none have been seen for the last 10 years.

Changes of this nature have already affected the UK insurance industry through:

❑ more storm claims (as happened in 1987 and 1990, with near misses for mainland UK in 1993 and 1999);
❑ more flood claims (as happened in 1998, 2000 and 2002);

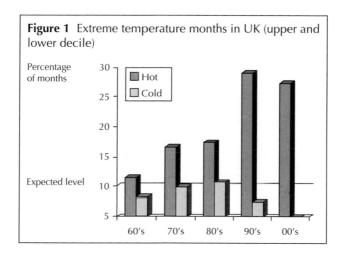

Figure 1 Extreme temperature months in UK (upper and lower decile)

❑ more subsidence claims (as happened in 1990–1 and 1997–8); and
❑ fewer freeze claims (1987 was the last significant event).

On mainland Europe, the insurance systems vary widely, so it is not possible to use claims statistics as evidence. In a very short period the overall economic damage from extreme weather has escalated dramatically – annual losses have doubled to US$11 billion in 20 years. Clearly this cannot be due to societal change over such a short time span, and the impacts are of just the type expected from predictions of climate change.

MOMENTUM FOR ACTION

Since the last Intergovernmental Panel on Climate Change (IPCC) report in 2001, much new evidence has arrived showing that the risk of climate change is considerably worse (see Hadley Centre, 2005). The actual sensitivity of the climate system has been underestimated. New factors such as acidification of the ocean have been identified. Faster melting and almost inevitable disappearance of polar icecaps is predicted,[1] and massive dieback of tropical forests that store CO_2. A Pentagon study comments that in the extreme "disruption and conflict will be endemic features of life – many countries' needs will exceed their carrying capacity".[2]

The EU goal to avoid dangerous climate change is a rise in temperature of less than 2°C and an atmospheric concentration of greenhouse gases (GHGs) of under 550 CO_2e.[3] These now look incompatible because of the new research. The appropriate target level for GHGs is now 450 CO_2e. To achieve this requires 60% cuts by 2050, according to the International Climate Change Task Force. Already we are over 400 CO_2e and rising fast. The business-as-usual view from the International Energy Agency (IEA) is that emissions will *rise by 63% by 2030*. Emissions could double by 2050, with the growth coming mainly from Asia. The best that can be done by 2030, according to the IEA, is to improve efficiency (particularly vehicles), reducing the growth in emissions to 44%, at the penalty of more expensive energy. No radical technology shift is expected in this timeframe. An alternative view from WBCSD promotes a scenario of strong development in developing countries, with emissions climbing to about 850 CO_2e, far above the safe level. The argument again is that there is too much inertia due to old capital plant and that nations will continue to prefer to rely on conventional resources such as coal.

While the "danger level" of 2°C may not be reached till 2050 on the mid-range IPCC projections, it will become unavoidable if energy demand continues on a business-as-usual trajectory from now until 2025, because of the inertia in the climate and socioeconomic systems. Early action is therefore essential from the precautionary point of view, and also provides greater certainty to business for long-term investment and technological change.

Within the financial and investment community, the momentum of climate-change initiatives is exploding (see Panel 1) with government investments in carbon funds, investor initiatives through coalitions of investors and the start of the EU Emissions Trading Scheme (EU ETS) culminating in the coming into force of the Kyoto Protocol on 16 February, 2005.

After 15 years of gestation, the activation of the Kyoto Protocol shows that international, regional and national policymakers have come to understand that market-based solutions will play a key role in providing a framework for effective international action. Successful market-based solutions require two key imperatives to function effectively: the development of a robust policy framework, and the engagement of the financial services industry, intermediaries and service providers both in its evolution and its ongoing development. Governments need to create robust policy frameworks that

PANEL 1 MOMENTUM OF CLIMATE CHANGE INITIATIVES IS EXPLODING

Powerful external forces are converging to make climate change and carbon-related issues relevant to financial services companies.
  These include:
❑ formal coming into law of the Kyoto Protocol on 16 February, 2005; and
❑ strengthening scientific consensus on the impacts of climate change.

Investors
❑ Carbon Disclosure Project, a coalition of institutional investors (with collectively over US$20 trillion in assets under management) pressing major companies to disclose investment-relevant information concerning their GHG strategies and emissions;
❑ Institutional Investors Group on Climate Change (IIGCC), with nearly US$2 trillion in assets, promoting research on asset valuation and property portfolio management, and conducting public policy discussions; and
❑ Investors Network on Climate Change (INCR) formulating rules of engagement for pension funds to influence corporate behaviour and strategy.

Carbon funds
❑ Success of the Dutch ERUPT programme, in which the Dutch government paid out nearly US$40 million to five successful project bids for 4 million tonnes of CO_2 allowances; and
❑ Experiences of the World Bank's Prototype Carbon Fund, which is expanding to match market interest, and which has led to the emergence of a series of similar "spin-off" funds from European governments.

Emissions trading market
❑ EU ETS started trading with effect from 1 January, 2005;
❑ The steady growth of the emissions trading market, where more than 70 transactions have now been reported involving some 95 million tonnes CO_2e; and
❑ Success of Australia's green energy certificates trading scheme.

Corporate governance
❑ Increasing focus on climate change as a corporate governance and accounting issue for pension fund trustees and fiduciaries;
❑ Growing willingness of respected mainstream financial institutions to initiate debate over implications of climate change for the finance and insurance business; and
❑ Formation of the Climate Group to promote best practice on climate-change issues among corporates and sub-national jurisdictions.

(Source: UNEPFI, Innovest and authors)

will provide the clarity and long-term stability vital to both project developers and financiers. At the same time they need to ensure that investment markets have access to the kind of information that will enable them to deal with climate change efficiently.

IMPACT ON THE FINANCE SECTOR

Recent reports have detailed the relevance of climate change for the financial services industry (see Figure 2). It will increase dramatically as climate change and its opportunities and threats get onto the board agendas of company directors, senior executives, pension fund trustees and institutional investors.

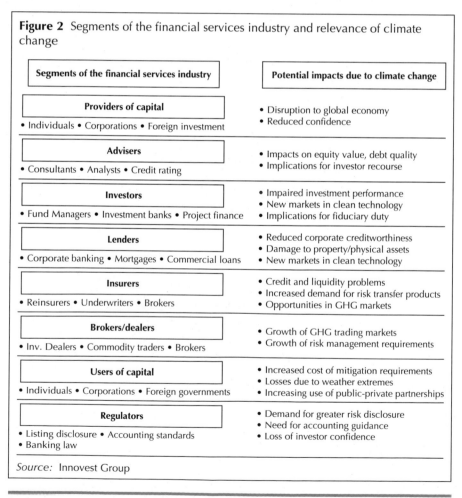

Figure 2 Segments of the financial services industry and relevance of climate change

Segments of the financial services industry	Potential impacts due to climate change
Providers of capital • Individuals • Corporations • Foreign investment	• Disruption to global economy • Reduced confidence
Advisers • Consultants • Analysts • Credit rating	• Impacts on equity value, debt quality • Implications for investor recourse
Investors • Fund Managers • Investment banks • Project finance	• Impaired investment performance • New markets in clean technology • Implications for fiduciary duty
Lenders • Corporate banking • Mortgages • Commercial loans	• Reduced corporate creditworthiness • Damage to property/physical assets • New markets in clean technology
Insurers • Reinsurers • Underwriters • Brokers	• Credit and liquidity problems • Increased demand for risk transfer products • Opportunities in GHG markets
Brokers/dealers • Inv. Dealers • Commodity traders • Brokers	• Growth of GHG trading markets • Growth of risk management requirements
Users of capital • Individuals • Corporations • Foreign governments	• Increased cost of mitigation requirements • Losses due to weather extremes • Increasing use of public-private partnerships
Regulators • Listing disclosure • Accounting standards • Banking law	• Demand for greater risk disclosure • Need for accounting guidance • Loss of investor confidence

Source: Innovest Group

Climate change will affect the finance sector from lending to investing, and from advising to financing. While not as pronounced as the insurance sector with its direct impact on property and physical assets, nevertheless the impact on financial institutions could be far-reaching. While there is growing experience among banks in financing renewable-energy projects to address the impact of climate change, there are several key issues that need to be addressed within the Kyoto framework: an obvious lack of innovative financing instruments, the risks associated with significant potential regulatory and policy change that could dilute the duration and value of carbon credits, and the initial costs of preparing project proposals that are considered too high for smaller projects and too cumbersome.

Lending institutions need to include climate change systematically in their risk assessment procedures. While banks are generally highly skilled in credit evaluation and risk management, the key step is in developing some form of carbon risk management and benchmarking tools for lending. Banks need to develop tools to quantify the risk management implications associated with their lending decisions. Coupled with industry and sector benchmarking tools, such quantitative risk management and credit evaluation tools will help ensure that carbon and climate change risks are factored into lending decisions. Furthermore, employee education and awareness building are essential to ensure the effective implementation of bank policies and the development of best practice for lending. On a wider front, commercial banks as leading pillars of society should consider the potential for involvement in projects concerned with clean energy and energy efficiency, and in awareness programmes to finance climate-friendly consumption by end-users, whether businesses or individuals. A prime example is the European Bank for Reconstruction and Development (EBRD), which incorporates a review of clients' energy efficiency into the due-diligence process for industrial lending, in order to encourage the cost-effective adoption of best available energy technology.

The financial services community has an incredible opportunity (not to mention an obligation to its clients and shareholders) to provide products and solutions to meet the increasing and diverse challenges of climate change. It needs to spread the message through investor and corporate education and awareness programmes that carbon is a determinant of corporate and financial value (see UNEP

Finance Initiative, 2002). It needs to overcome the barriers to action and instead take the lead by developing and structuring innovative solutions and risk mitigation techniques that assist corporates and individuals in adopting sound and sustainable climate-change practices. Such solutions will help transform today's corporate-responsibility statements and commitments on climate change into tomorrow's concrete actions with specific business activities and change processes – in doing so, it will help move climate change to centre stage of the financial services sector, and into the strategic mindset and onto the board agendas of company directors, senior executives, pension fund trustees and institutional investors.

Crucially the key role of institutional investors is being recognised. With over US$30 trillion of assets under management, these investors wield significant influence over future economic management and industrial activity, and therefore the scale and pattern of the future of global GHG emissions. With their focus on the long-term profitability of their investee companies, institutions can play a key role in influencing and shaping the climate-change debate as well as its ramifications. First, they can do so as owners in influencing corporate management and encouraging greater corporate disclosure through direct engagement and through voting their proxies. Such pressure from investors, because of pension funds expanding their fiduciary duties, is on the rise in line with the general trend towards shareholder activism. Voting with their feet is increasingly not an option!

Secondly, investors are increasingly incorporating the potential of climate-change and GHG policies to add or destroy value in investment holdings and impact equity prices, corporate earnings and relative sector risk. The ability to reflect the climate-change risk factor in equity/sector valuation and in asset-allocation decisions is an increasingly sought-after skill. As such, investors, through pricing and valuation of corporations, are making financial choices among firms and sectors that are effective in combating and mitigating the effects of climate change. Increasingly, a third role is in joining together as coalitions of investors in influencing public policy, in eliciting responses from top corporates and in stimulating debate and action among pension fund trustees. Having identified what should be done, it needs to be remembered that there are considerable barriers to action, particularly in asset management, because of the multiple parties involved in decision making and the focus on short-term performance.

In summary, carbon is gradually being recognised by both the financial community and the wider financial environment as a factor that needs to be incorporated into all calculations of equity value, credit risk, corporate risk management, project development, capital spending and project viability, but much more needs to be done.

IMPACT ON THE INSURANCE SECTOR

Climate change will affect the insurance sector from property insurance to pensions, and from underwriting to investment. Here we focus on property risk, because the effects are already happening and the sums at issue are large. The global insured cost of major weather-related incidents reached €32 billion in 2004,[4] with the total economic cost of weather-related damage in the region of €160 billion.[5] Climate change will create new extremes of sea level, heat waves, drought, flood and almost certainly storminess. In the coming decades, therefore, human activity will become more vulnerable to extreme events, and this will create greater demands for insurance.

To manage increases or uncertainty in risk, there are four traditional insurance strategies: limiting the cover, controlling the damage, reinsurance and price. However, conventional insurance is inadequate to meet the needs of the victims. Currently, about 80% of the global economic damage from natural events is not insured, but has to be borne by the victims, or alleviated with *ad hoc* disaster relief. A determined effort is needed to improve the overall efficiency of the system so that clients receive adequate cover on acceptable terms, but the insurer is not faced with a higher risk of ruin.

The sector has to increase its capitalisation, either directly through raising additional money or through innovative methods of "borrowing" capital from the wider finance sector in times of need. One way in which the latter might be achieved is by government institutions taking the risk off insurers' balance sheets. This has the advantage that the potential cost of the risk does not need to be quantified accurately, as the state will be the insurer of last resort. Using the commercial capital markets in the form of catastrophe bonds has been investigated, but the continuity of supply is uncertain, and the transaction costs are rather high.

Insurance (that is to say, risk transfer) is not the only way to manage financial risk. Controlling the underlying physical risk may be more effective, or self-insurance may be adequate. The sophisticated nature of the industry with its specialised functions (broking, underwriting, risk assessment, claims handling, reinsurance) helps to provide a rich variety of solutions for risk management. Quite often the service provided by the industry does not include "insurance" where there is a more effective way of managing the risk. The largest business corporations, covering about half the world's economic output, are now more highly capitalised than insurance companies, so they can withstand the financial shock of disasters themselves, and have become expert in managing their own risks, which go far beyond traditional insurable events.

In the mass markets (retail and SME), a basic question is how to apportion the costs of the insurance scheme. On the basis of social solidarity, all those who require insurance would receive it in return for a uniform premium (the *social* model), but this contravenes the need for economic efficiency; in other words, those exposed to a higher risk should contribute proportionately more (the *risk-related price* model). The social model can encourage unsustainable behaviour (such as flood plain development) and so alternative ways of risk control, such as strict regulatory standards for planning and design, would be necessary. The social model also runs the risk of creating large subsidies or very high premiums unless the insurance is compulsory, because low-risk people will not join the pool. On the other hand, the risk-related price system may result in at-risk people being unable to afford the premium. One way to resolve this might be to discriminate between existing risk exposure and future exposures, created *after* climate change has been recognised. In the former case a "social" model might apply, with a "risk-related price" model for all others. Proposals for natural-hazard insurance schemes in Belgium, Germany, Italy, Hungary and the Netherlands have all failed to make progress because of the practical and political problems. Hopefully in developing countries "micro-insurance" could underpin microfinance against climate change and help to support sustainable development.

For insurance schemes to be effective, two key stakeholders are the construction industry and the public sector. Repeatedly, post-loss analysis shows that a significant factor in catastrophe losses is that construction practices have been deficient. In addition, the construction industry often resists initiatives for more resilient design on the basis of the increased cost, and on major projects the possibility of extreme weather has been ignored with unfortunate results. Climate change will compound these issues, because of the tendency for more extreme conditions to occur. It is in insurers' interests to ensure that standards are raised, and then implemented. In fact in the US they have even contributed to the training costs of public building inspectors.

The public sector also has an enormous role to play: funding research into basic knowledge about the hazards, framing the regulations for the built environment, and setting the parameters for the insurance markets themselves. In both cases, the insurance industry can influence the decisions that are reached, and the Association of British Insurers has even gone to the extent of producing an "election manifesto" on flood insurance in 2005.

As with any change, there will be new business opportunities, as well as risks for those firms that do not recognise the need to adapt. Business clients will need to protect themselves against the risk of more variable weather because this can affect profitability greatly, even without damaging their assets physically. Traditionally, this has not been seen as an insurable contingency, but already the energy sector has been developing tools such as weather derivatives to deal with it, and insurers should try to incorporate this risk into their standard basket of insurable hazards.

Government policies to mitigate climate change and to adapt to its effects will generate a range of specific projects and processes to realise those strategies, for example clean energy technology, new or altered infrastructure. These will require careful underwriting and close cooperation with the developers during the design stages to ensure that risks remain insurable.

The international political process has been slow to grapple with global warming, and insurers themselves have not devoted much resource to lobbying, despite forming the UNEP Insurance Initiative in 1995. Under the auspices of the United Nations Environment Programme Finance Initiative (UNEPFI), some insurers recently called for a higher priority to be given to long-range emissions targets through the adoption of an approach such as "contraction and convergence", to limit the extent of climate damage (see

UNEPFI, 2002), and have supported a number of UNEPFI papers on key policies such as renewable energy.

CONCLUSIONS

Human-induced climate change is upon us. With political and investor momentum on climate change now snowballing after the formal ratification and coming into law of the Kyoto Protocol, it is clear that market-based solutions will play a key role in the framework for effective international action. Successful market-based solutions require two key imperatives to function effectively: the development of a robust policy framework, and the engagement of the financial services industry, both in its evolution and ongoing development.

The impact on the financial services industry is expected to increase significantly once climate change gets onto the board agendas of company directors, senior executives, pension fund trustees and institutional investors. The onus is on financial services companies to shape their strategic response. Banks, institutional investors and insurers have key roles to play. As a consequence, best practice in meeting the challenge and threat of climate change is expected to evolve rapidly, and will be a major determinant in the growth and standing of financial centres.

1   The Western Antarctic Ice Sheet is accelerating like "a cork out of a bottle" with a potential for 5m sea-level rise (Hadley Centre, 2005).
2   Schwartz and Randall, US Defense Department, Washington, DC, 2003.
3   Parts per million by volume of carbon dioxide equivalent (ppmv).
4   Munich Re, Catastrophe Statistics, 2004.
5   Estimated from €80 billion of major events, then doubled to allow for smaller incidents.

REFERENCES

Hadley Centre, 2005, *Conference on Dangerous Climate Change*, Summary Report, February.

UNEP Finance Initiative, 2002, "Climate change and the financial services industry", (Module 2), July.

2

Climate Change and Capital

James Cameron, James Allen

Climate Change Capital

The scientific case for climate change is overwhelming. Global average surface temperatures are rising and, if "business-as-usual" is our future, projected to unleash catastrophic damages upon the global environment (and thereby the global economy) in the course of this century. Efforts to mitigate climate change are under way, with the Kyoto Protocol now in force and expected to expand and intensify with future international agreements and domestic action.

In the private sector the most notable consequences of climate change have been felt in the insurance industry. Costs from weather-related damages have been rising by 10% year on year. Jeremy Leggett in *The Carbon War* cites the US$2 trillion of uninsured assets at the coastal margin of Florida – therefore exposed to sea-level rise and increased cyclonic activity – whilst the industry as a whole keeps less than half a billion dollars a year in reserve to cover all catastrophic losses everywhere in the world in any one year (see Leggett, 1999). As far back as 1990 the insurance industry had already determined that sea-level rise was an uninsurable risk, so certain was its arrival. Just imagine the implications for business assets at the coastal margin around the world, whether in cities, agricultural land or in expensive residential property. Adaptation is necessary, but adaptation without strenuous efforts at mitigation is also reckless. The solution is clear: we need to reflect the costs of emitting carbon in the price of carbon.

THE PRICE OF CARBON

A huge shift in relative value, from economic activities that are carbon-intensive to those that are not, will follow the creation, maintenance and enforcement of a price for carbon, provided the price is significant. The price will be significant if the ambition to reduce greenhouse-gas emissions by 60% from 1990 levels is matched by legal commitment. Central to this new paradigm is the creation of a new commodity, greenhouse-gas emissions (referred to here as carbon emissions) reductions, which may be traded between parties to realise climate-change mitigation at least cost. With the creation of any new market there are risks and opportunities for business to negotiate. Yet in this instance it is the policy-driven nature of the "Kyoto markets" (including markets in clean and renewable energies) that underlines the complex political, regulatory, environmental and financial risks that the business community, whether informed or not, must face.

For the time being the debate about business and climate change revolves around the price of carbon. Over the course of the last year or so the decision-making machinery of corporations throughout Europe has been grappling with this issue, thanks to the arrival of the EU Emissions Trading Scheme (EU ETS) in 2005. You may find yourself with a chief executive officer of a large energy-using company discussing the way accounting rules will treat allowances granted by the European Commission and allocated by the Member States. Businesses are now trying to understand how much asset and liability they have. Models are being developed to show what the price of carbon does to the options available to a large power company. When does the price argue for a switch from coal to gas? When and where are installing combined-cycle gas turbines economic? When, perhaps with other incentives, is substantial investment in renewables sensible?

MARKET DRIVERS AND POLITICAL DYNAMICS

Thus it is through organisations that best understand the market drivers – that is, the political dynamics that underpin the Kyoto markets – on that the rewards will flow. An understanding of the policy framework that underpins the Kyoto markets will be a key asset of successful new companies. It is this intellectual capital, combined with the innovative and entrepreneurial spirit that markets instinctively foster, that will be the distinguishing characteristic of leading companies in a carbon-constrained world. In essence, even if climate change is a real and terrible threat, it offers the potential for forward-thinking businesses to exploit and profit from a completely new market.

If setting a price for carbon is essential, so are a whole range of policies that deal indirectly with climate change. Climate policy is, in particular, having a growing influence on energy policy. A recent UK White Paper attaches environmental priorities to long-term energy policy and also considers the benefits of security of supply in reducing Britain's dependence upon imported oil and gas (see DTI, 2003). Policy measures are being adopted around the world to encourage more efficient combustion engines and fuels lower in CO_2 and other pollutants (notably improving air quality in large cities); energy efficiency in domestic and commercial buildings; reduced congestion on roads and an increased use of public transport; and, of course, the development of renewable sources of energy.

ALTERNATIVE SOLUTIONS

So what of the alternatives? Where will the solutions come from? Until recently it was a conventional wisdom among the fossil-fuels lobby and its governmental allies that low-carbon technologies are either too expensive or too unreliable to provide the answer to our need for increasing energy supplies concomitant with decreasing carbon emissions. The reality is rather different. Virtually all technologies show reduced costs with time and exploitation (known as "declining learning curves"), and renewables are no exception to this rule. In some instances they are already cheaper than conventional energy sources, and if anything it is the costs associated with replacing long-term capital stocks, such as national electricity distribution systems, that provide the greatest obstacle to their continued development.

However, there are encouraging precedents. Our favourite is, ironically, the development of the oil economy. Jeremy Rifkin tells us that the first gas/petrol station was put up in Detroit in 1911 (see Rifkin, 2002). Just five years later the US had more than 3 million cars and, by 1925, there were 23 million. In a similar vein, Winston Churchill's decision to fuel the British Royal Navy on oil rather than coal, despite unproven supplies of oil worldwide compared with tremendous reserves of coal on Britain's own doorstep, was brave and visionary. The Anglo Persian Oil Company, later British Petroleum/BP, was the direct beneficiary of the Royal Navy order and is now one of the most profitable companies in the world.

Besides, we know that the world is not going to stop using fossil fuels for some time yet. Huge coal and gas reserves will be needed to power growing economies until alternatives to fossil fuels can meet massive demand with confidence (when they have moved sufficiently along their declining learning curves). Carbon capture and sequestration, often combined with enhanced oil recovery, may enable a cheap and abundant resource to be exploited for decades to come, without jeopardising the future of our environment. And energy crops or biomass can be used in co-firing with fossil fuels to generate power, while biofuels (in the form of bioethanol or biodiesel) can be used to supplement and even completely replace the need for oil to fuel our vehicles.

Again, the past gives us clues for how we should plan our future. Sometimes regulatory intervention, and other times fiscal or other market instruments, can open up new opportunities for individuals and for business. Just as the early oil pioneers were greeted with scepticism when they suggested we should drill for oil (in fact, many were labelled as "crazy"),[1] so the proponents of renewable energy are often treated with scorn or derision. But we are much further down the road than that. Several EU countries already power 25% of their economies from renewable sources. While there is always a risk in moving away from structures and technologies with which we are comfortable and familiar, the winners in economic history are those who spot a new paradigm and confront it at the right time and with the right people.

EXPLOITING POLICY-DRIVEN MARKETS

A successful strategy for a financial firm seeking to profit from a significant price for carbon would be to align with the entrepreneurs, governments and non-governmental organisations that are developing, proposing and demanding new ways of producing and using energy. They will work with the established energy and power producers who are seeking to manage climate risk, and with entrepreneurs and innovators seeking capital to develop low-carbon technologies and solutions. Because, after all, it is a purpose of the policy-driven Kyoto markets to establish the conditions under which entrepreneurial innovators can be matched efficiently with entrepreneurial capital to supply solutions to the fundamental policy goal, namely reducing carbon emissions. It is important here to recognise the benefits of aligning interests between the policy-maker and the profit-making investor. Only then will sufficient capital flow to irrigate new markets and deliver emissions reductions at the required scale – IEA estimates 1 billion tonnes of CO_2 per year, every year until 2050.[2]

So how should companies go about exploiting the opportunities these new markets create? Recent research by the likes of the Carbon Trust, the Carbon Disclosure Project and the Institutional Investor Network on Climate Risk identifies an increasing awareness from institutional investors of the opportunities created by climate-change mitigation. The gap between large institutional investor awareness and investment in solution providers is still considerable, but there are encouraging signs in the UK. The enthusiastic reception to the recent listing of D1 Oils Ltd (see Panel 1) on the UK Alternative Investment Market (AIM) neatly exemplifies the market and policy drivers that are starting to grab investor attention.[3]

ASSET MANAGEMENT

Climate-change mitigation also offers opportunities for assets to be managed in new ways that are both productive and profitable. Several specialist funds have emerged that offer investment potential in (among others) fuel-cell technologies (Chrysalix), sustainability investments such as water technologies (SAM), and clean fuels and distributed energy systems (N[th] Power). The Clean Tech venture network is a for-profit business designed to develop an asset management response to climate change and a host of other environmental issues. Their website, www.cleantech.com, identifies a number of other specialist investors. Clearly there are opportunities for mezzanine finance as well as several other variations of debt, equity and hedge fund structures.

For many energy-intensive industries the start of the EU ETS in 2005 means they must quickly come to terms with the implications

PANEL 1 CASE STUDY: D1 OILS

D1 was established to address the growing global market demand for biodiesel, a blend of diesel and methyl esters derived from plant or animal sources (vegetable oil is a common source). Based in the UK, D1 has developed and is commercialising a modular biodiesel refinery technology, with each module able to produce 8,000 tonnes per annum. D1's approach combines innovative oil sourcing and crop production, unique refining technology and a phased roll-out plan in target markets.

They aim to be a large-scale producer of feedstock (from Jatopha plantations in West, East and South Africa, India and the Philippines), and have in excess of 6 million hectares under option. They raised £13 million when listing on admission to AIM (UK's Alternative Investment Market), thereby valuing the company at £34.4 million.

On the policy side, global biodiesel production and demand is being reshaped by international agreements such as the Kyoto Protocol and the European Biofuels Directive, creating demand for biodiesel estimated at 7 million tonnes by 2010, compared with production estimates of 3 million tonnes. Despite this clear opportunity for growth, nascent "solution providers" like D1 have had to struggle to raise capital to expand their operations because the policy-driven markets are unknown, and thereby too risky, for traditional sources of finance to invest in. New specialist firms, with the expertise to identify market winners and the capacity to avert policy risk (through understanding and influencing policy developments), will take the first steps in these markets and lead where others will eventually follow.

of restrictions on carbon emissions for their business. This emissions market will likely be volatile depending upon fuel prices and how "short" the market ends up. In addition, the demand and supply of electricity will fluctuate and the ability to transact smoothly in the marketplace will affect price. The timing of auctions and release of new entrant reserves will also affect liquidity. Markets notoriously tend not to trade at "fundamental value". In particular, the early stages of the EU ETS will likely be dominated by compliance-driven traders rather than profit maximisers. A well-informed company can therefore reduce its costs of complying with the legislation by timing its trades well. The EU ETS will be extended in Phase II to other greenhouse gases and more sectors of the economy. There is a possibility that aviation might be included, certainly the UK government is pushing for that outcome. In order

PANEL 2 CASE STUDY: VENTUS VCT

Ventus VCT plc is a new specialist venture capital trust established to invest in a portfolio of companies that will develop, construct and operate small onshore UK wind projects.[4] Ventus is an example of an investment vehicle being adapted to be relevant to clean power. When Chancellor Gordon Brown and the UK Treasury created the Venture Capital Trust (VCT) vehicle for private-sector investment, investing in renewable energy was not specified. However, fiscal policy that encourages venture capital investment will help grow these markets in climate solutions.

Ventus has so far raised over £13 million in the 2004/5 financial year and is seeking to raise upwards of £20 million. Investee companies will benefit from long-term power-purchase agreements (PPAs) provided by Geotrupes Energy Ltd for the sale of electricity, at an agreed price, pursuant to an existing framework PPA facility. The availability and use of this framework PPA facility will substantially mitigate a major risk of investing in the wind-energy sector, namely the uncertainty that would otherwise exist as to the future price of renewable energy.

For Ventus the key policy mechanism is the Renewables Obligation (RO), which requires all licenced electricity suppliers in the UK to secure a specified and increasing portion of their electricity from eligible renewable sources (such as wind power). Suppliers must either meet their targets (4.9% of total supply in 2004–5 and 10.4% in 2010–11) or pay a "buy-out price" in relation to any shortfalls.

The UK (and particularly Scotland) has one of the best wind resources in Europe, but it is far behind other Member States in taking advantage of this fact. Germany currently has onshore wind capacity in excess of 14,000 MW, while Spain and Denmark have onshore wind capacity of 6,000 and 3,000 MW respectively. In contrast, the UK currently has an installed capacity of under 1,000 MW. Recently, however, there is a significant development pipeline of projects at the planning stage; the RO is acting to provide a growing investment opportunity in UK onshore wind projects. Ventus therefore demonstrates the advantages on offer to businesses that can interpret the policy signals in new markets and form relationships with key market players to manage assets in a way that maximises their value to investors.

to manage carbon price risk companies will have to consider now how to release capital from their own balance sheets and in what circumstances they would seek 3rd party capital. The long lead times for most investments of scale in the power sector explains the importance of good analysis of the forward curve for carbon.

CARBON MODELLING, HEDGING AND LENDING

Models can predict carbon market fundamentals with some accuracy. But they are often most effective when used to help companies analyse the impact of various price scenarios on their business. Below roughly 100 million tonnes of carbon dioxide abatement required, we believe the coal–gas price differential will be the key driver of allowance prices in the EU. In general we expect volatility in price to increase with the start of Kyoto in 2008, together with higher carbon prices and a tighter allocation process. Detailed and accurate modelling of the emissions market can thus make the relative economics of companies affected by the price of carbon easier to predict.

Just as companies are familiar with dealing with exchange rates, interest rates and commodity prices, so they will need to start managing the carbon market in a similar way and start thinking about hedging their risks. Indeed, many companies are already buying forward in 2006–7 or have acquired the potential to use options. On the other hand, allowances are also an asset on the balance sheet. By leaving allowances on the books doing nothing, companies may be missing out on the opportunity to extract value from their allocation. For companies with active treasury groups, for example, allowances have a value that is not needed for a full year but can be lent out, into the marketplace, in order to create revenues.

Carbon credits can be lent and returned at a date negotiated by the lender and in the meantime "interest", or some form of premium, will be earned upon them. As time passes carbon will be traded all year and actively – it will not be an annual compliance-driven event. We expect volume and initially volatility. It would be an unwise business risk management decision to leave trading to the last minute. There are financial intermediaries and speculative traders already in the market and the market will benefit from the emergence of derivatives and structured products to smooth out compliance costs over time.

There is also the potential to make use of allowances as collateral. Although traditional financial institutions are still relatively uneducated about the value of allowances (and their value can move up and down), there is certainly the opportunity for reducing borrowing costs by using allowances in this way. So companies need to start factoring carbon prices into their investment decisions and they need to stay well informed in order to time their trades well.

CONCLUSIONS

The ultimate risk in the carbon market is to stay ignorant. Carbon is a new reality with attendant risks and opportunities. First and foremost companies must acquire knowledge and understanding of the value of reducing greenhouse gas and the means by which capital can be deployed in order to realise that value. Investing capital in emission reductions, carbon sequestration and related clean technologies brings returns in climate policy delivered as well as profits. The policymakers need to do more to keep momentum going and to achieve scale – it is all too small, too modest and too relative today – but investors can give government the confidence to be bolder when they know there is money to be made. The carbon price signal will release capital to parts of the economy. (Governments would not have been able to predict that discussions will be formed exclusively for the purposes of profiting by reducing emissions!) The carbon market ecosystem will attract a multitude of new and colourful species, which will be attractive to behold – the more so if you have put capital to work creating it.

1 Drillers whom Edwin L. Drake tried to enlist to his project to drill for oil in 1859.
2 Quoted from a 2005 presentation by Claude Mandil, IEA, at the Energy and Environment Ministerial Roundtable in London.
3 D1 Oils was a client of Climate Change Advisory, a wholly owned subsidiary of Climate Change Capital, throughout the course of this transaction.
4 Ventus VCT plc is managed by Climate Change Investments, a wholly owned subsidiary of Climate Change Capital.

REFERENCES

DTI, 2003, "Our energy future – creating a low carbon economy", White Paper, URL: http:// www.dti.uk/energy/whitepaper/ourenergyfuture.pdf.

Leggett, J., 1999, *The Carbon War: Dispatches from the End of the Oil Century* (London: Allen Lane, 1999).

Rifkin, J., 2002, *The Hydrogen Economy: The Creation of the Worldwide Energy Web and the Redistribution of Power on Earth* (New York: Tarcher/Putnam), pp. viii, 294.

3

The "Finance-Policy" Gap: Policy Conditions for Attracting Long-Term Investment

Kirsty Hamilton

International Policy Consultant

Substantial investment will be required in the near term to provide for rising global energy demand: the often-quoted International Energy Agency (IEA) estimate is that US$16 trillion will be needed between 2001 and 2030 (see IEA, 2003a) for energy supply and infrastructure, under "business-as-usual". How much of such investment is channelled towards the uptake of zero and lower carbon energy systems, infrastructure and technologies will play a critical role in determining the carbon intensity of economies in the coming decades, and the ability to tackle climate change.

Energy policy and market regulation will continue to perform a key role in setting the context for this investment. Getting finance-sector perspectives into the policy debate, in particular analysis of policy "impact" on risk and return, is arguably an important but missing element in increasing the effectiveness and precision of governments' intended actions in this area. Even within the European Union, there are still only a handful of countries where renewable energy markets have taken off, despite having nationally set renewable-energy goals, and an EU mandate.[1]

The scale of action required is significant: a 60% cut in CO_2 emissions is regarded as necessary by 2050, as acknowledged by UK Prime Minister, Tony Blair.[2] This implies a fundamental transformation of the energy sector in the medium term away from carbon-intensive fuels, with considerably greater effort to maximise

25

supply- and demand-side energy efficiency, and to accelerate the use of renewable energy, at scale.

CARBON MARKETS: NOT THE ANSWER, AT LEAST NOT YET!

Carbon emission trading markets alone are unlikely to drive the systematic growth of new sectors such as renewable energy, at least in the short term, while the value of carbon has yet to firm up and the market focus is on securing access to potential credits rather project implementation. The European Union Emissions Trading Scheme (EU ETS), for example, is designed to capture market "efficiency" by channelling investments into the lowest-cost carbon abatement options, not higher-cost but strategically important technologies and energy systems. The Clean Development Mechanism (CDM), under the Kyoto Protocol, is also bedding down at present, but is highly uneven in geography and scope thus far, and was never designed as a substitute for energy policy.

In its assessment of a lower-carbon, 30-year global energy scenario, the IEA estimates that US$724 billion will be needed for renewable-energy generation – around half of the total investment in new plant (see IEA, 2003b) and requiring "vigorous incentive strategies" in the OECD. In China alone, the government indicated that around €49 billion would be required to achieve the national 2010 renewable-energy target announced in June 2004.[3]

Concern over national energy security, related to volatile, escalating oil prices in 2004 and 2005, is also driving the international energy agenda. As well as a focus on increased oil production, high prices have shifted international attention onto reducing the energy intensity of economies, particularly those economically vulnerable to sustained high oil prices, and the ensuing transfer of wealth. The importance of energy efficiency and the development of alternative indigenous energy sources have now been recognised by the International Monetary Fund, and others in the mainstream political agenda.[4]

An approach that employs energy efficiency and conservation, distributed energy systems and renewable energy can reduce overall investment needs in the power system and its infrastructure.[5] In addition, the role of these in reducing the "cost" of fossil-fuel price volatility is now becoming explicit as new analytic tools are developed that are helping to reconfigure the traditional "least-cost" approach to assessing energy options.

Dr Shimon Awerbuch points out that financial investors commonly use "mean-variance" portfolio theory to create portfolios that deliver the best performance; and that such an approach should be used by policymakers in the economic evaluation of properly diversified generating mixes that minimise cost while delivering energy security and fossil price risk mitigation. Renewable energy may have a higher capital cost; however, within a portfolio of generation it can reduce the overall system risk associated with fuel price volatility, as production costs move independently from fossil fuel prices (see Awerbuch, 2004).[6]

"FINANCE – POLICY" GAP

Against this backdrop of rising political interest in sustainable energy, finance and investor expertise should play a central role in informing the policy conditions for attracting investment. While seeming a rather simple proposition, in practice a "finance–policy gap" does exist between the lexicon of policy and policy development, often focused on "least-cost" economic options, and that of bankability and access to capital. Bridging this is one means of reducing the perception of political/policy risk for financiers, increasing the precision and effectiveness of policies and reducing the cost of capital, including through the use of public funds to leverage private money.

The invitation to provide "finance sector" input on what constitutes "good policy" to an international ministerial-level conference on renewable energy in Bonn in 2004[7] was an opportunity to bring power-sector financiers from the City of London and Europe and financial innovators working in developing countries into the policy debate.[8] The conference itself was international in scope but without powers to mandate national policy change in participating countries, yet intended to forge greater consensus on how to scale up the use of renewable energy internationally, including the fundamentals of an effective enabling environment. Leading international and boutique banks, equity funds and insurers were involved, and the discussions raised matters for the finance sector itself to consider including issues in the area of risk management, awareness raising, capacity building, and new financial products.[9]

LOUD, LONG AND LEGAL

The take-home message for both developed and emerging markets was that policy frameworks need to be "loud, long and legal" in order to have a real impact on the bankability of projects.

❑ *Loud*: The signal to the market, through incentive structures or other means, needs to be "loud" and clearly designed to impact returns, and attract capital into the sector. Feed-in tariffs, and mandatory quota systems are two instruments specifically designed to give greater returns to renewables.

❑ *Long*: Rules and incentives need to be stable and sustained for a duration that reflects the financing horizons of the projects. For example, the UK's mandatory quota "renewables obligation" originally had a initial target ending in 2010, which was then rather rapidly extended to a new 2015 target, due in no small part to feedback that the original timeframe was too short to enable commercially attractive returns to be realised.

❑ *Legal*: a legally established regulatory framework based on binding targets or implementation mechanisms is needed to provide the basis for long-life capital-intensive investments. This helps creates confidence that regimes are not going to be subject to political mood swings, and allows for enforceability.

While this descriptive is rather general, it embodies core policy factors, applicable to most if not all markets, that could attract greater investment into renewable energy. This is more generally stated by one US financial consultant as, "policies must affect cashflow if businesses are expected to respond". Policy based upon political "aims" is in effect asking investors to speculate about political delivery and that speculation, in finance terms, will demand high or even venture capital level returns, making these technologies even less attractive (see Hamilton, 2004) – a factor not necessarily thoroughly understood by policymakers!

The assessment of policy issues in industrialised countries, mainly European markets, raised many contextual matters, a core message being policy stability: "pick a system and stick to it". Policy review, or the evolution of new policy, should not destroy the value of existing investments in renewable energy, as this sends a particularly damaging signal to investors at this stage in market development. The detrimental impact of stop-start policies, such as

LOUD, LONG AND LEGAL?

The different European mandatory incentive systems for renewable energy present different issues for financiers and investors, within the context of these "loud, long and legal" frameworks. At present, these fall into two principal categories: fixed tariff (or "feed-in") systems such as Germany and Spain, and the binding quota and trading system such as the Renewable Obligation Certificate (ROC) market in the UK.

The efficacy of the feed-in tariff system raised issues including: the fact it can encourage installations on low-quality resource sites (such as in poor wind-speed areas); does not overcome local planning complexities; and the fact that national and local "below-the-line" distortions such as taxation still exist. However, fixed tariffs provide strong price certainty for investors, reflected in the number of deals done, and have encouraged entrepreneurs and smaller-scale investors to enter the market. Germany and Spain, with the largest and highest growth wind markets in the world, both have systems using feed-in tariffs.

Issues around quota markets are illustrated by the UK's ROC market – a relatively new mechanism introduced in April 2002 – placing a binding obligation on electricity retailers to provide a percentage quota of renewable energy. Its relative sophistication means investors must take a forward view on future price (including, for example, income derived from recycling the "buyout fund"[11]) to arrive at the value of the ROC. These price uncertainties have tended to drive investment into the arena of parties that can both manage this risk and access the necessary level of capital, traditionally the bigger utilities. The ROC market is currently creating a strong incentive for mature and lower-cost technologies – typically onshore wind – leading to the conclusion that additional support mechanisms, or formulas, may be needed to boost returns and lower risks for other renewable-energy technologies, including potentially offshore wind.

EU renewables policy

The European Union "Renewables Directive", containing a *non-binding* 2010 EU-wide target, while politically important, was perceived as having little market relevance compared with the importance of the *national* policy or support regimes, to the financiers. The 2005 review of these EU support schemes,[12] and issues around greater harmonisation, could benefit from an assessment of the effectiveness of policy according to different parts of the finance and investment chain. If onshore wind is taken as a proxy, only a handful of EU countries are demonstrating strong growth in the sector – despite its very significant overall annual growth rate (see European Wind Energy Association, 2005) – indicating that national goals are not being translated through to investment-focused policy regimes and support mechanisms.

> Interestingly, no comparative analysis of the effectiveness of the different incentive and policy structures across Europe, specifically from a financing perspective, appears to have been undertaken, certainly with a view to informing policymakers.

the vagaries of the Production Tax Credit in the US, is also widely recognised.[10]

A summary of more detailed "good policy" and market characteristics, from an investor perspective, included:

❑ a solid basis for long-term contracts, or a legal regime, to secure revenue over a 10–15-year period;

❑ conditions that lead to big, liquid markets, if using tradable market incentives, with credible market players that can deliver the projects;

❑ ensuring oligopoly or monopoly control of access is not a barrier, and that network codes are consistent with a move to distributed and renewable generation;

❑ implementing a clear process for the planning and approval of new power plants and generation, including a preference for renewable-energy options: a framework setting out a more uniform process, involving local planning authorities, would reduce development risk such as that experienced by onshore wind projects in some countries;

❑ an expedited process for tackling "future" grid infrastructure and investment matters, including who pays, and issues related to balancing, security, distributed generation, to ensure these issues do not become a barrier to project investment and delivery;

❑ tackling existing subsidies, and other distortions in the market that favour conventional fuel sources, these are an issue for some markets in terms of creating an additional barrier to the perceived competitiveness of renewables; and

❑ a strong compliance regime, where relevant, including penalties for non-delivery.

FINANCE AND INSURANCE GAPS

On the finance side of the equation more generally, several gaps exist on what has been termed the renewable-energy financing "continuum" (see O'Brien and Usher, 2004), from the widely recognised "valley of death" faced by technology developers prior to commercialisation, to gaps between smaller, specialised commercial finance players dealing mainly with project developers and the major financial institutions seeking large-scale opportunities in the renewables sector. Small amounts of targeted public money can play a critical role in overcoming these gaps.[13]

A gap was also identified in the insurance and risk-transfer market for innovative approaches and new products for renewable-energy technologies, which, because of their small scale, have difficulties passing internal business hurdles.

While not arising as an immediate concern to the banks and equity investors, it is useful to note the importance of public investment in research and development. Taking the wind sector once more: the IEA finds that R&D accounts for about 40% of technology cost reductions (performance and design improvement), with commercial installation/market experience the other 60% (economies of scale) (see IEA R&D Wind Executive Committee, 2001). Therefore, public investment and policy need to target both of those areas to continue cost-reduction trends. The IEA notes that renewable-energy technologies received only 7.7% of energy R&D funding from 1987 to 2002 (see IEA, 2004).

EMERGING MARKETS

From a financing perspective, investment in emerging markets[14] is seen to face many of the same issues as industrialised nations in terms of the importance of stable, effective policy frameworks, but with the additional burden of significantly higher perceived risks and higher costs in securing capital.[15]

Indeed, reducing the cost of (and increasing access to) capital for renewable energy is a key issue in developing countries, where the supply of private finance is currently limited.[16] In many instances renewable energy must compete with subsidised conventional power, making investment in energy even less attractive when compared with alternative uses of capital in what are often rapidly expanding economies.

Rising carbon values in the OECD and reducing technology costs with the scale-up of OECD renewable-energy markets will contribute to renewable-energy development in emerging markets.

However it was generally accepted that the benefit of carbon credits alone, even if the value rises substantially, will be inadequate to make most renewable-energy investments profitable (with some exceptions such as methane capture from landfill gas projects under the CDM). Discussion remained inconclusive over whether or not it is possible to "export" the premium that consumers are willing to pay in the industrialised world for renewable energy to developing countries through, for example, the creation of an international market for renewable energy.

The financing issues for larger-scale, on-grid, renewable-energy investment and small-scale, off-grid, renewable-energy projects are distinct. The latter represents an important, very significant market in many developing countries with large land-mass and dispersed rural populations for which grid-based distribution is often uneconomic, or technically unsuited.[17] For small to medium supply companies working in this area, national energy market regulation is less important than lowering the cost of capital and front-end transaction costs associated with the smaller-scale projects while easing the credit criteria for borrowers. The availability of small amounts of grant money and "patient capital" is seen as strategically important for the development of the "small scale" sector, and a strong argument is put forward for a blend of grant and development finance funds where renewables-based projects are also cost-effective mechanisms for serving poverty alleviation, health and welfare benefits.

ENHANCED ROLE FOR REGIONAL AND INTERNATIONAL FINANCIAL INSTITUTIONS

A number of financial innovators are working in the energy-for-poverty-alleviation area, particularly looking at the opportunity to blend together the different expectations of returns of public and private funds to finance projects. They are also seeking to align policy objectives in the area of energy provision, sustainable agriculture, health and water supply for a more efficient, integrated approach at community level.[18]

The view was that modest amounts of grant funding to reduce transaction costs and foster the local equipment supply chain, and pooled and dedicated funds to diversify investment risk can both generate a leveraged return. Such approaches can foster the progressive engagement of private-sector finance in the market, and build confidence through successful and financially attractive project implementation.

Not surprisingly, therefore the importance of an enhanced role for regional and international financial institutions (including Export Credit Agencies) was a core part of the pre-Bonn and many other debates. In tackling the scarcity of viable, bankable opportunities in this area, these institutions can lower early development costs in markets, as well as playing a role in the development of legal, regulatory and governance frameworks that could lower risk. Additionally by underwriting or otherwise mitigating political and regulatory risk, they can significantly reduce project costs. An example would be the World Bank's US$202 million loan to two Turkish banks to supply credit to private investors in renewable energy.[19] Importantly, this would require explicit donor government support, and demand from client countries.

CREDIT ISSUES – BRIEF
Also important is the development of strong domestic credit markets for renewable energy in developing countries, and needing far greater recognition, in all markets, is the role of local government in creating demand, policy, and regulatory and planning functions, and offering various public–private collaborations that can lower costs.

The issue of the creditworthiness of local entrepreneurs, in terms of perceived credit risk by lenders, is regarded as particularly important in improving project and deal flow.[20]

PANEL 1: CHINA – ADOPTION OF RENEWABLE-ENERGY LAW
Perhaps one of the most significant policy developments since the Bonn discussions in 2004 has been the adoption of the Chinese Renewable Energy Law (28 February 2005). This establishes renewable energy as an important part of the energy mix in China and creates the legal framework for the introduction of a feed-in tariff-type mechanism, and an overall target for the sector, to be developed in the next months.[21] Some commentators have speculated that the centre of gravity of renewable-energy market development and investment could shift east, the devil being in the detail of the Law's implementing mechanisms, certainly something to watch.

FINANCIAL INSTITUTIONS AND ENERGY EFFICIENCY

In addition to approaches that accelerate growth of the renewable energy sector, energy efficiency and conservation should not be forgotten as offering very significant potential for immediate least-cost carbon savings and added economic efficiency. One effort to institutionalise energy efficiency is the European Bank of Reconstruction and Development's (EBRD's) industrial energy efficiency project, incorporating energy efficiency into its existing loan process, through a dedicated energy efficiency team. All EBRD projects are formally assessed for energy efficiency potential. With site visits and an energy-efficiency audit (EEA), high savings are recognised. Upfront costs are then incorporated into the investment programme.[22] If professional EEAs became widely recognised and instituted throughout the project finance and policy community, the gains could be substantial.

CONCLUSIONS

Alignment of political objectives on climate change and energy security with the reality of what needs to be done to mobilise finance in the necessary timeframe and at corresponding scale is essential. Such "clarity of purpose" will be essential to feed through into financeable business proposals that can deliver results in the next 5–15-year period, particularly as long-term infrastructure and power-capacity decisions could lock in very different emissions profiles.[23] The key requirement for policy designed to promote renewable energy investment is that it is "loud, long and legal", to positively affect project bankability, and to reflect a strong governmental commitment to delivery in this area.

Getting this message across, particularly in greater detail early in the national energy policy and consultation process, could make the difference between a policy framework that establishes an investment-friendly environment and markets that can work, and one that does not. The finance community would also understand better how to interpret policy risk.

International discussions – such as the G8 and the United Nations Framework Convention on Climate Change process – while far removed from the daily grind of energy project finance and implementation, can be seen as strategically important. This is particularly crucial if longer-term issues, including the development of effective international carbon markets (such as CDM), the emerging debate over the international renewable energy market, and technology transfer, are to reflect the thinking process of (and actively engage) the mainstream finance community.

Set within the wider context is the challenge of how the overall investment sector and financial regulation can create a consistent message on taking a long-term perspective on investor returns and carbon liability. Only when this is established will all these efforts help to systematically shift the balance of interest towards low-carbon options and renewable energy.

1   The "Renewables Directive": Directive 2001/77/EC of the European Parliament and Council, 27 September 2001, "on the promotion of electricity produced from renewable energy sources in the internal electricity market".

2   For example, in a speech en route to the World Summit on Sustainable Development, September 2002 in Mozambique, Mr Blair stated, "But we know from recent reports that to stop further damage from climate change, and to stabilise the global climate system, in fact we need a 60% reduction worldwide." The Royal Commission on Environmental Pollution in the UK had both recommended and demonstrated the feasibility of achieving a 60% cut in CO_2 emissions by 2050, in its report "Energy – a Changing Climate", June 2000.

3   Bonn International Conference on Renewable Energies, International Action Programme, page 43. See http://www.renewables2004.de/pdf/International_Action_Programme.pdf. Note that a Renewable Energy Law, was adopted in China in February 2005, establishing a framework for instituting a binding target.

4   For example: International Energy Agency: "Analysis of the Impact of High Oil Prices on the Global Economy", May 2004; Communiqué of the International Monetary and Financial Committee of the Board of Governors of the IMF, 2 October 2004 and 16 April 2005; World Bank Energy Sector Management Assistance Programme (ESMAP) report, "The impact of Higher Oil Prices on Low Income Countries and on the Poor", March 2005; *Financial Times* article "Energy Agency says high oil prices should boost hunt for alternatives", 12 March 2005.

5   Under the World Energy Investment Outlook, 2003, "Alternative Policy" scenario, emphasising renewable energy, overall investment in the power sector is reduced by US$2.7 trillion, compared with business-as-usual. Transmission investment is 40% lower and distribution 36% lower.

6   Dr Shimon Awerbuch is a Tyndall Centre Visiting Fellow, based at the Science and Technology Policy Research Unit, SPRU, University of Sussex, UK.

7   See http://www.renewables2004.de. This was the first time in a multilateral process of that nature, that the finance sector was formally recognised as a distinct category of "stakeholder" expertise, as distinct from "business" that, in the energy arena, has been traditionally represented by conventional energy interests.

8   The consultation roundtables took place in London and Basel, April 2004, and were held under the auspices of REEEP, Renewable Energy and Energy Efficiency Partnership, by the UK Business Council for Sustainable Energy, in collaboration with the Royal Institute of International Affairs, Chatham House; and the Sustainable Energy Finance Initiative, SEFI. A wider group of financiers working in developing countries were brought in through the REEEP financiers network. URL: http://www.reeep.org, http://www.sefi.unep.org.

9   For detailed work on the risk management side, see for example "Financial Risk Management Instruments for Renewable Energy Projects", 2004, at http://www.uneptie.org.

10 See, for example, the case study on ANZ Investment Bank's experience in the US, in "CEO Briefing on Renewable Energy", issued by UNEP Finance Initiative, June 2004, at http://www.unepfi.net.

11 Buyout payments by suppliers for any shortfall in holding the required level of Renewables Obligation Certificates (ROCs) go into a buyout fund, which is then recycled back to suppliers, proportional to the amount of ROCs they held at the deadline – this forms a potential additional income stream. See http://www.ofgem.gov.uk.

12 This is being undertaken by the European Commission, under the auspices of the EU Renewables Directive, 2001, and is due to report on 27 October 2005.

13 These issues were raised during the London roundtables, April 2004.

14 This includes both developing countries and economies in transition. There were mixed views at the time on whether central and eastern European countries are mature or emerging markets, from a finance perspective. A roundtable specifically on emerging markets took place in London.

15 At the London roundtable, the cost of political-risk insurance was regarded as a significant addition (3% per annum) to project cost.

16 IEA, 2003, p.65.

17 A commonly used statistic is that there are around 2 billion people without access to modern energy worldwide. The World Energy Investment Outlook, reference scenario, finds 1.4 billion without access to electricity in 2030.

18 See, for example, www.reeep.org.

19 See, http://lnweb18.worldbank.org/eca/eca.nsf/0/9B14296390CC7DA985256E62007E B958? OpenDocument – press release, 25 March 2004, "World Bank supports Renewable Energy in Turkey".

20 A renewable-energy-focused Finance Network has been set up among financiers in southern Africa with an aim to improve deal flow in the region – it involves private and public finance at different scales. See http://www.reeep.org.

21 For the legislation, and related news stories, see the Chinese Renewable Energy Industries Association website: www.creia.net.

22 See http://www.ebrd.com/country/sector/energyef/industry/leaflet.pdf.

23 This was the main conclusion from a G8-related business consultation on climate change and investment, organised by the UK Business Council on Sustainable Energy, to feed in to the G8-related Energy and Environment Ministerial Roundtable on 15–16 March 2005. A Co-Chair's Summary of the Ministerial Roundtable is available on the Website of the Department of the Environment, Food and Rural Affairs (http://www.defra.gov.uk), and contains the "loud, long and legal" policy message.

REFERENCES

Awerbuch, S., "Enhancing energy security & diversity", *REEEP News*, URL: http://www.awerbuch.com.

IEA, 2004, "Renewable energy – markets and policy trends in IEA countries", press release, 1 June.

IEA, 2003, "World energy investment outlook, 2003 insights", press release, 4 November.

IEA R&D Wind Executive Committee, 2001, "Long-term research and development needs for wind energy for the time frame 2000 to 2020", October.

Hamilton, K., 2004, interview with Tom Lord, then managing partner of the Distributed Energy Financial Group, US, in *Renewable Energy World*, September–October.

O'Brien, V. S. and E. Usher, 2004, background paper on mobilising finance for the International Conference for Renewable Energies, Bonn, URL: http://www.renewables2004.de/en/cd/default.asp.

4

REEEPing the Benefits:
The Case for Renewable Energy

Marianne Moscoso-Osterkorn, Mike Allen

REEEP

If climate change is to be avoided and if the impoverished are to get the energy services they need, the finance and business communities need to feel more confident in backing sustainable energy.[1]

THE MARKETPLACE

The promotion of renewable energy (RE) is much easier said than done. There are few governments, corporations or public bodies who would not agree that we need to make the mix of energy use more sustainable – using more renewable sources, promoting energy efficiency (EE) and using less oil and gas. However, our energy-intensive, high-carbon economies are so firmly established as political, economic and social structures that changing them is a multifaceted challenge. So action is often abandoned, postponed or watered down.

The investment models that support coal and oil are so well established and profitable that renewables with lower immediate returns are not considered bankable. As a consequence, many well-intentioned initiatives gather dust in government, multilateral and philanthropic institutions around the world. There are initiatives that are making a difference, but they tend to be low-key and behind the scenes.

The Renewable Energy and Energy Efficiency Partnership (REEEP) is one of these. Although REEEP rarely makes any head-lines, it is coming to be acknowledged as a global champion for a more sustainable, secure and reliable energy mix for both the

> ## PANEL 1 REEEP – A PARTNERSHIP OF PARTNERSHIPS
> REEEP, established by the UK government after the 2002 Johannesburg World Summit for Sustainable Development (WSSD), has its international secretariat in Vienna and is funded by the Austrian, Canadian, Dutch, Irish, Italian, Spanish, UK and US governments, and the European Commission. It is a partnership whose members are governments, businesses and NGOs committed to creating a regulatory environment and finance market that will accelerate the uptake of renewable energy and energy efficiency. Their representatives within REEEP are all committed energy practitioners, making REEEP a "partnership of partnerships" that has access to unrivalled expertise, local market knowledge and political leverage. The key is to share relevant global experiences that will build confidence in renewable energy and energy efficiency, and reduce the perceived risk of investing in it.

developed and the developing world. Much of what REEEP does is concerned with the unglamorous matter of helping to ensure that the regulations and systems that underpin the delivery of energy are supportive of the increase in the use of renewables and energy efficiency. Only if those systems are in place will the renewable sector be able to gain the support of politicians who will drive further change, and the confidence of the financial markets that will provide the money that makes change a reality.

Alongside other initiatives that are progressing the uptake of sustainable energy, including the Johannesburg Renewable Energy Coalition (JREC), the Global Village Energy Partnership (GVEP) and the Mediterranean Renewable Energy Programme (MEDREP), REEEP is one of the durable achievements of the 2002 Johannesburg World Summit for Sustainable Development (WSSD).

REGULATION
One of the key issues that REEEP is addressing is energy utility regulation. Electricity generation systems around the world have evolved into highly centralised grids for large-scale remote power generation using coal, oil, gas and nuclear power and long-distance transmission. Such systems have been very successful at delivering low-cost power, both in the developed world and increasingly in developing countries. The energy market reforms of the last 20 years have introduced to the power industry new and

more complex regulatory regimes that mix the private sector, governments and independent regulators.

Despite these changes in market structure, ownership, control and regulation, the emphasis on traditional technologies and systems has usually remained. Governments and regulators recognise that changes are needed to improve the energy mix. They may lack the time and the expertise to establish the regulatory foundations for such a change.

This is where REEEP has a vital role to play. Based on work carried out by the Centre for Management under Regulation at Warwick University in the UK, REEEP has established the Sustainable Energy Regulation Network (SERN) to do the behind-the-scenes work necessary to promote forms of regulation that support and encourage the use of energy efficiency and renewable energy. The structure is regional, with global links, and a wide range of stakeholders involved.

Much of this work is low-key and unglamorous: facilitating exchanges of experience and knowledge between regulators on the different policy and regulatory mechanisms; promoting better understanding of the economic benefits of renewable energy such as greater energy security, utilisation of indigenous resources and opportunities for income generation, particularly in rural areas. Good practice guides and training courses for regulators on all forms of renewables are prosaic, but they are essential for changing the energy environment to ensure greater energy security.

Various regulatory initiatives are now being developed through SERN. These include market obligations on energy companies to source some energy from renewable sources and targets to improve energy efficiency for their customers. Some governments and regulators are also beginning to examine the need for more fundamental changes to energy systems to promote localised and distributed power sources and demand management responses on an equal or preferential basis to traditional large-scale power generation and transmission.

REEEP has a number of projects under way that will facilitate a more conducive regulatory environment for renewable energy. The Renewable Energy International Law (REIL) project, for example, seeks to ensure that new and existing international treaties and agreements on everything from free trade to biodiversity take into account the emerging need for diversification into renewable energy, and do not unintentionally create barriers. Regulations make things clear, and raise the comfort levels of everyone involved.

Such assurance is particularly important for those financial institutions whose money will actually finance the introduction of renewable energy and energy efficiency. Bankers are conservative and cautious – which is why we trust our savings with them. However, that same attitude often inclines them against putting their financial weight behind new energy projects for which the technology and its application may appear immature and the economics untried. Renewable-energy and energy-efficiency investments do yield economic returns, but the perception of higher upfront capital costs and longer-term payback periods tends to deter investors.

Kirsty Hamilton (2004) summarises consultations with financiers that lead to a finance sector statement, which fed into the June 2004 Bonn policy process, and emphasises the critical importance of the strength and stability of government policy frameworks at this stage of market development. If investor confidence is to increase, and the bankability of projects to be improved, then policies must be "loud, long and legal" – "loud" meaning that the incentives are sufficiently strong to make a difference to business plans, "long" meaning of a sufficient time frame to be relevant to project lifetimes, and "legal" meaning legally binding, whether targets or mechanisms".

FINANCE

Historically the banking sector has been reluctant to consider renewables because the projects are often small and are seen as providing modest returns on investment. (It is often forgotten, however, that even traditional energy sources are not high-yield investments.) Furthermore, there is often limited capacity and awareness within existing financial institutions about the value of renewable energy and energy efficiency, and this issue needs to be addressed to free up funds for projects.

While the industry is still dominated by public-sector-backed programmes and developments, the opportunities are slowly being recognised by the broader finance industry, spurred on in part by the potential for trading in carbon credits under the Kyoto protocol and the trading system established within the European

Union. Given a relatively small energy service industry, the recognition that many renewable technologies can be more capital-intensive (but typically with lower operating costs) and that the current interest is to develop smaller, dispersed power distribution systems and/or to provide energy at a household level, it is little surprise that the orthodox finance markets have been slow to show significant interest in such opportunities. The result is a perception of increased risk.

Creating systems and networks that provide bankers with the necessary level of comfort to invest is a crucial REEEP role. Regulations and pricing that give preference to renewable-energy sources are an important part of this process. However, direct financial backing using government money is also essential to encourage investment. Public funds can be used to encourage a greater supply of financing to renewable energy and energy efficiency, either through guarantee mechanisms or by buying down the rate of return required by financiers. The role that the German and Japanese governments have played in the promotion of the wind and solar industries is a prime example of the role that the public sector can play in developing this market to build scale, increase exposure to newer technologies and attract more traditional investment.

REEEP partners in the Association of South East Asian Nations (ASEAN) identified finance as a particular need. In Asia as elsewhere, renewable energy and energy efficiency projects tend to be smaller-scale, modular and capital-intensive investments. Locally owned small and medium-sized enterprises (SMEs) in Asia could provide energy services to those most in need, but they often lack the business development skills and necessary financial resources.

There are a number of regional organisations involved in addressing the barriers to renewable energy, promoting such resources and providing development assistance. Few, however, have access to the level of financial support that is needed for project implementation. Asian bankers are as conservative in their attitude to renewables as their European and North American counterparts.

PATIENT CAPITAL
In response to the ASEAN needs, REEEP is promoting the creation of a Foundation for Sustainable Energy. This builds on a concept

suggested in 2000 and recommended by the Group of Eight (G8) Task Force on Renewables. It is envisaged that the finance to be offered through the facility would be "patient capital" – public- and private-sector investment sources melded together to provide finance that will yield a return but at lower rates than typically expected from the private capital market. This model is at the core of the European Commission's initiative to develop a Global Renewable Energy Fund of Funds. Envisaged as a not-for-profit entity, the Foundation will allow donor money to be attracted and utilised in a manner that will leverage public and private sector sources.

The key aims of the Foundation will be the provision to the private sector of business development skills, project preparation funding, seed capital and limited project finance. The available finance will be a combination of donor grant funds and investment sources that will provide borrowers and partners mutually acceptable terms and returns. An initial investment target over the first three years of operation of US$50 million is now under consideration. The proposal has been noted by the June 2004 ASEAN Energy Ministers' meeting and REEEP's efforts are recognised in the ASEAN Plan of Action for Energy to 2009. The facility is also seen as a vehicle through which a number of bilateral and multilateral donors, philanthropic organisations and corporations, regional institutions and the private sector can cooperate and build on the commitments made at the WSSD in Johannesburg to provide practical and appropriate support for the acceleration of renewable energy projects in Asia and the Pacific. The establishment of strong partnerships with existing organisations in the region will be of fundamental importance to maximise the impact of the Foundation.

The amount of money involved in the Foundation may seem small given the world's need to diversify its energy use from high-carbon sources to include renewables and energy efficiency. However, relatively small policy and financial initiatives of this sort have an impact way beyond their immediate size and scope. They are not limelight projects, but they put the structures and systems in place without which change will be impossible to implement, and they create the confidence and reduce the impression of risk that is essential for securing investment.

PANEL 2 EQUITY FUND FOR INDIA

With support from REEEP, India is to get its first private equity fund to back enterprises developing and servicing renewable energy projects. Although various Indian banks and financial institutions are providing debt financing to renewable-energy ventures, access to equity funds has been limited. Now two financial institutions, BTS Investment Advisors Private Limited and Rabo India Finance Pvt Ltd, have come together to create the Indian Renewable Energy Enterprise Development (IREFD) fund, a private equity fund that can invest in renewable-energy projects and earn superior returns on its investments.

The IREED fund will invest in projects in all renewable-energy generation sub-sectors, such as wind, small hydro, solar energy, municipal and industrial waste to energy, biomass and cogeneration, as well as in energy efficiency improvement projects. IREED will also invest in companies manufacturing renewable energy and energy efficiency equipment, thus diversifying its risk within the sector.

PANEL 3 ENERGY EFFICIENCY FINANCING

In June 2003, the APEC Energy Working Group (EWG) identified a project to strengthen the institutions for financing energy efficiency projects in APEC member economies. The project will create a locally managed financial intermediary with legal framework and standard project documents, which may be used for multiple EE projects in the Philippines. The project has been ongoing in Mexico and REEEP's support will contribute to the establishment of activities in the Philippines.

The project's objective is to secure financing for small-scale (smaller than US$5 million) clean-energy and efficiency projects via a financing intermediary. The role of the intermediary is to communicate with banks, borrowers and project developers while reducing costs by developing standard transaction documents and improving confidence for both borrowers and lenders by creating a process that is standard, transparent and more predictable. The financial intermediary will work closely with an energy service company (ESCO) and will target energy efficiency upgrades in schools, hospitals, water districts and industrial parks.

CARBON FINANCE – FRIEND OR FOE?

There is no question that the renewable energy and energy efficiency markets have received a significant boost through the efforts under way to address the global impact of climate change. There is also little doubt that the international debates about climate change and the Kyoto protocol in particular have attracted much limelight, shared in part by the RE and EE industries but perhaps diluted by the constant emphasis on CO_2 reduction, rather than the options that exist to provide the necessary solutions.

Ahead of the ratification of Kyoto, and since its formal inception, much effort has been directed at "carbon funds", led initially by the World Bank's Prototype Carbon Fund that drew a strong and positive response from the donor community. Today there are a significant number of similar funds, in both the public and private sectors, fuelled by the need to secure carbon offsets that will allow corporations and countries to meet their targets under Kyoto. The participants in these funds are seeking secured offsets that will become available through the various CDM/JI, projects that are now being submitted for approval. Though not all of these are renewables based (in fact only a small portion are) an emerging issue is that the investment needed to implement many of these projects may be no more readily available now that it was in the past. This will of course create a shortage of offsets to trade and, while this will no doubt provide some benefits for those who have an excess to trade, there could be a market shortage generating difficulties for those expecting that their obligations under Kyoto can be met through this mechanism.

The commitment of substantial funds into the carbon market effect is creating a perverse effect. The expectation has been that this market would provide a source of development capital, but it may in fact be more effective in fostering a trade in a relatively scarce commodity. While the risk of committing to the purchase of carbon credits for approved and established projects is limited, both in practice and in the eyes of the (carbon fund) investors, these funds are not available to finance the development phase of projects. There are some funds that will offer a partial prepayment against future credits, but this is typically only a small percentage of the overall capital cost of a project. The investment in the carbon funds is therefore an additional demand of a rather limited investment pool and, while superficially seen as supporting the accelerated development of RE and EE, it is not the panacea that many had expected. The upside is that this tension may in fact force a focus on sourcing development finance to ensure that the carbon offset market matures and can provide the credits that have been anticipated – only time will tell.

TAKING STOCK

We have to face the fact that, despite widespread efforts over the last ten to fifteen years and repeated assertions by many international agencies and conferences about the needs for the sustainable delivery of energy services, there has been limited practical implementation of RE and EE projects, particularly in developing economies. It has been easy to make announcements about aspirations, but such intentions are of little value if we do not make the effort to adjust established energy generation, transmission and financing systems to give RE and EE a necessary helping hand. The pressure of the "carbon market" may yet yield some medium-term solutions but its introduction needs monitoring and pragmatic evaluation.

If REEEP can put the "nuts and bolts" in place for an energy structure that will admit renewables and energy efficiency into the energy mix, the way will be open for politicians and financiers to deliver. REEEP's achievements in establishing the SERN, REIL and ASEAN Foundation for Sustainable Energy may not grab the headlines, but there has perhaps been too much of that in the history of encouraging renewables.

1   In this chapter, Marianne Moscoso-Osterkorn, international director of the Renewable Energy and Energy Efficiency Partnership (REEEP), outlines how regulatory and legal frameworks can help provide this confidence. Mike Allen, finance adviser to REEEP, addresses the efforts under way to introduce new sources of finance into the market and some unexpected influences of the carbon market.

REFERENCES

Hamilton, K., 2004, "Finance & Investment: a challenge of scale", *Renewable Energy World*, September/October.

Section 2

Financing and Carbon Funds

5

Commodifying Carbon

Martijn Wilder, Monique Willis, Katherine Lake

Baker McKenzie

The finance of climate-change projects is predicated on the idea that projects that reduce greenhouse-gas emissions create a recognisable benefit in terms of reducing global climate change. The international community, many national governments and a wide range of corporations and individuals, have recognised that emission reduction projects have a measurable advantage over other types of projects in terms of their contribution to climate change, through the creation of what is referred to in this chapter as the "carbon asset".

There are many types of carbon assets created under international and national legal regimes (for example, the Kyoto Protocol and the European Union Emissions Trading Scheme, or EU ETS) or through private contracts outside of legal frameworks (see Panel 1). What is common to most of these carbon assets is that they are based on a common unit of 1 tonne of carbon dioxide reduced or sequestered, or an allowance to emit 1 tonne of carbon dioxide (CO_2). "Emissions trading" or "carbon trading" is essentially the creation and sale of carbon assets.

The carbon asset is becoming a material consideration in the expected rate of return of projects and, ultimately, the financial worth of the companies that are involved in projects that create such assets (for example, renewable-energy companies or sustainable-plantation developers). In order for financiers to be able to properly invest in carbon projects, it is essential that they understand the nature of the asset that is being produced. This chapter discusses some of the key issues involved in creating, valuing and transacting carbon assets and illustrates through recent case studies some of the different carbon assets that are being produced.

WHAT IS A CARBON ASSET?
Nature of the asset
There are many types of carbon assets, including the following.

❑ *Contractually based rights*: rights that derive their existence from a contractual agreement, for example rights traded in a voluntary trading scheme or acquired to produce carbon neutral products.
❑ *Statutory-based rights*: derive their meaning from a statute or treaty and include those mentioned below.
❑ *Kyoto Protocol*: for example, the four types of carbon assets recognised under the Protocol are:

   ❑ CERs (Certified Emission Reductions), which are the emission reductions created through Clean Development Mechanism (CDM) projects;
   ❑ ERUs (Emission Reduction Units), which are the emission reductions produced from Joint Implementation (JI) projects; in essence they are not "new" assets but are converted from Assigned Amount Units (AAUs) into ERUs, in recognition of the other Annex I contribution to an emission reduction project in the first Annex I country; and
   ❑ AAUs, which are issued to Annex I parties at the outset of the Protocol that in effect is an allowance determining how much that country is entitled to emit (if the Annex I party exceeds its allocation of AAUs, it has to acquire other types of statutory assets recognised under the Protocol).
   ❑ RMUs (Removal Units), which are generated by forest sequestration projects. An RMU is produced for every tonne of carbon dioxide taken from the air and captured in the wood of forest plantations. RMUs will not be bankable for the second commitment period under the protocol.

❑ *National and Regional Carbon Assets*: carbon assets have also been created under various national and regional emissions trading regimes. For example:

   ❑ *EU Allowances*: These are carbon assets under the EU ETS, which are issued to liable installations under the scheme and represent an allowance to emit one tonne of CO_2.

❑ *US and Australian State Schemes*: Various states in the US and Australia have created emissions trading schemes recognising various types of carbon asset. For example, in New South Wales, Australia, an emissions trading scheme operates that recognises a carbon asset representing 1 tonne of CO_2 reduced below a baseline.

The value underlying every carbon asset is the reduction of greenhouse gas (GHG) emissions. The exact nature of the carbon asset will depend on the regulatory or contractual framework in which it is created. As there are numerous forms of carbon assets, derived from the various national and international statutory regimes, as well as privately in contracts, the most crucial element to transacting a carbon asset from a project is defining the exact nature of the asset and how it is transferred.

In any carbon contract, a definition of carbon asset being transacted should include:

❑ reference to the physical reduction in levels of GHG emissions in a clear unit of measurement (usually per tonne of CO_2 equivalent);
❑ reference to the clearly defined project creating the reductions;
❑ objective validation and assessment methodology; and
❑ the basis on which such reductions are measured (for example, against a predetermined baseline).

The Kyoto Protocol and the rules supporting it recognise a range of carbon assets and create a clear international framework for creating, registering and transacting those assets. As the Protocol is an international agreement, the carbon assets under that treaty are essentially sovereign rights. However, the Protocol allows countries party to that treaty to encourage the involvement of industry in reducing national emissions by specifically providing for the participation of public and private entities in the trading of the assets and, in the case of the CDM, in the creation of such assets. The tendency for many governments has been to devolve the rights and responsibility to undertake emissions trading to private industry, subject to a level of government supervision of the registry system and ultimate government responsibility for the compliance with Kyoto Protocol targets.

However, not all carbon assets require government endorsement. For example, two private companies could enter into a contract to transact carbon assets generated by a certain project. These assets may not be recognised in a legislative compliance scheme, but some companies and individuals have assigned a financial value to such "contractual carbon assets" because of the inherent environmental benefit they represent.

Broadly, carbon assets can be divided into contractual and statutory rights.

Contractually based carbon assets

As mentioned above, carbon assets can be created and transacted purely by way of contract with no government involvement. Contractual carbon assets are often used to offset emissions from certain activities (for example, to offset individual transport emissions or a company's emissions) and some companies, such as 500 ppm and Future Forests, have developed a business around the premium that consumers are willing to pay to purchase products and services that are "carbon-neutral". These companies purchase contractual carbon assets that have been verified to a certain standard and use these assets to offset the emissions involved in creating or providing products and services such as passenger flights

It is always possible for two parties to agree to transfer contractually based Emission Reductions (ERs) from a project or an activity for non-compliance purposes, as there are no statutory requirements that must be complied with. The financial value of such ERs will depend entirely on the premium that the purchaser of the carbon asset is willing to pay for the environmental benefit or the value they think the carbon asset may have in the future.

Set out below is a case study of a transaction involving contractual carbon assets.

Notwithstanding the "mere" contractual nature of such rights and their absence of regulatory recognition, it is still important that the contractual right be based on actual physical action to reduce, remove or abate GHGs. In such cases an agreed approach to verify (or audit) ERs, is usually provided in the contract terms. Accordingly it is common to refer to such tradable contractual rights as *verified emissions reductions* (VERs).

PANEL 1
Case Study: ST Microelectronics Investment in Australian Carbon Assets

Although this is a case study from outside the Kyoto Protocol context, it indicates that carbon assets can be a consideration in project finance for reasons other than compliance with a statutory framework.

ST Microelectronics, one of the world's largest semiconductor companies, has established an internal corporate target of achieving "carbon neutrality" in its operations by 2010. In addition to internal measures to reduce its emissions, the company has implemented a "carbon offsets programme", which will invest in regeneration projects around the world expected to sequester 3 million tonnes of CO_2 by 2010.

In 2004 ST Microelectronics invested AU\$172 million in carbon assets in Australian forests managed by the New South Wales government entity State Forests. In return for the investment, 10,000 hectares of cleared land will be revegetated, expecting to sequester around 5.4 million tonnes of CO_2. As Australia is not a party to the Kyoto Protocol, these plantations are not eligible to create Kyoto Protocol credits. In addition, although NSW has its own emissions trading scheme, by selling the credits to ST Microelectronics for compliance purposes, this means that the CO_2 sequestered cannot form the basis of a credit under the NSW schemes.

These investments are occurring on the basis of the value of the carbon asset for meeting the company's voluntary target. The company's view is that its carbon investments are not only environmentally responsible, but also good forward planning for potentially stringent targets in the future.

In addition, agreements to trade contractual carbon assets may also have an obligation on the parties to work together to transform these contractual carbon assets into credits recognised under a legal scheme (such as the Kyoto Protocol) when this becomes possible.

Statutory rights

Some carbon contracts are designed to transfer carbon assets recognised under an existing legal scheme. The definition of the carbon asset in such contracts refers to existing legislation or a treaty rather than a generic definition of the legal rights to a tonne of CO_2 abated or sequestered (which is the general way that contractual carbon assets are defined). There are a range of national and regional schemes that allow for the creation and transaction of carbon assets, including the EU ETS and US and Australian state-based emissions trading schemes.

The entry into force of the Kyoto Protocol has introduced long-sought regulatory certainty to the definition of the carbon asset in the international community. The three mechanisms introduced by the Marrakech Accords into the Kyoto Protocol produce different kinds of carbon assets, all of which carry the same value in the carbon accounting system. It is likely that these assets will trade for different prices, in recognition of the different sources and perhaps different qualities of the assets.

The Kyoto Protocol carbon assets are in effect sovereign rights agreed between parties to the Protocol. However, the Protocol specifically recognises the ability of private companies to create carbon assets and participate in Kyoto Protocol projects in return for the ability to receive, trade and use the sovereign Kyoto Protocol credits.

The carbon assets recognised in the Protocol are all equal to 1 tonne of CO_2 abated or sequestered. The carbon assets created and transacted through the Protocol's flexible mechanisms are discussed below.

(i) ERUs under JI

Article 6 provides for the industrialised Kyoto Protocol parties that have undertaken binding commitments to reduce their emissions (Annex I parties) to work together to develop projects to create ERUs.

An ERU can be created only by an agreement by one Annex I party to transform its AAUs into ERUs in recognition of the other Annex I party's contribution to an emission reduction project in the first party. AAUs are the credits issued to Annex I parties at the outset of the Kyoto Protocol, which equate to the number of tonnes of greenhouse gas they are "allowed" to emit during the Kyoto Protocol's commitment period, based on their agreed target.

At the end of the Kyoto Protocol's first commitment period (the end of 2012), each Annex I party must measure its emissions and then acquit enough Kyoto Protocol credits (including any AAUs it was initially issued or any credits purchased from projects or emissions trading) to meet its target. In transforming an AAU into an ERU for a JI project, an Annex I party must make a measured assessment that it will not require that AAU for compliance

---

PANEL 2
Case Study: New Zealand projects to reduce emissions programme
The New Zealand government has implemented a programme to encourage projects in New Zealand that can generate a "carbon asset" but, without the value from that carbon asset, would otherwise not be financially viable. It is providing such projects with the ability to secure project finance.

Essentially, the government has agreed to provide projects, on a competitive-tender basis, with Kyoto Protocol credits (either AAUs or ERUs) from New Zealand's assigned amount. Project owners can then sell these credits on the international market to achieve the rate of return required to secure project finance. Many successful project developers have already sold their allocation of credits to the Dutch government through the ERUPT procurement programme.

The actual transaction of the credits (to provide revenue from the projects) is between the successful tenderer and the Annex I purchaser of the carbon asset.

---

purposes. Overall, there is no "new" credit being created and the ERU is essentially sovereign-backed. For this reason, ERUs are considered more certain and potentially more valuable than CERs (which are "new" credits, as discussed below). However, AAUs will not be issued until 2008, so there has been limited progress in JI projects, other than some forward sales of AAUs or ERUs as and when they are created.

(ii) CERs under the CDM

Article 12 provides for Annex I parties to implement projects that reduce emissions in non-Annex I countries, in return for CERs and temporary CERs created from sequestration projects (tCERs).

CERs are created by projects in developing countries without targets under the Kyoto Protocol (non-Annex I parties). The logic behind the CDM is that an emission reduced in one part of the world has an equal environmental benefit to an emission reduced in any other part of the world. Therefore, it makes sense to allow emissions to be reduced in the most economically effective way, which could include developing countries, where costs of establishing a project may be less and where it is particularly important to facilitate sustainable development.

A CER is a carbon asset created by a CDM project through a certain verification process. CERs are rights that are additional to the initial Annex I party assigned amounts, so it is crucial to ensure that they have environmental integrity. To create a CER therefore requires a rigorous assessment procedure and proof that the CDM project that creates the CER is generating emission reductions that are "additional" to the emission reductions, which would have been achieved in the most feasible scenario if the CDM did not exist. Without these stringent safeguards, there is a concern that Annex I parties could meet their targets by purchasing CERs that represent emission reductions that would have occurred anyway, so no overall reduction in greenhouse gases is achieved and the fundamental goal of the Kyoto Protocol is thwarted.

However, because of these stringent verification processes (and the fact that the ultimate responsibility for issuing CERs lies with a United Nations body – the CDM Executive Board), there is some level of risk involved in CDM projects. Therefore, even though the CDM is operational and the EU ETS recognises CERs (so CERs are the first Kyoto Protocol credit able to be traded), CERs have not yet achieved a market value of the price for an EU Allowance.

(iii) Emissions trading

Article 17 provides for Annex I parties to acquire units from other Annex I parties. These units may be in the form of AAUs, RMUs, ERUs and the various types of CERs.

Emissions trading will constitute a "secondary" trading of the carbon asset. It does not require any actual involvement in the project that reduced the emissions, but, rather, will serve the purpose of ensuring that all Annex I parties can meet their targets at the least overall economic cost.

TRANSFERRING THE CARBON ASSET

After contracting to purchase the asset, it is essential to know how the asset is recorded and transferred to the party who has purchased it so that parties can be sure they are receiving what they have contracted to buy.

Under the Kyoto Protocol, the carbon assets are recorded in an electronic form and are traded within an international registry system. The registries will be in the form of standardised electronic databases with common data elements relevant to the issuance and trading of credits. The Kyoto Protocol registry system will consist of: (a) a national registry in each Annex I party; (b) a CDM Executive Board registry (operated by a registry administrator under the authority of the CDM Executive Board); and (c) an international transaction log, which will record and verify transactions of AAUs, ERUs and CERs.

Most national and regional legislative schemes recognising carbon assets also involve electronic registries through which the creation and transaction of carbon assets can be tracked. However, where a carbon asset transaction involves a "mere" contractual carbon asset, the seller and purchaser must agree on exactly how this asset is to be transferred. For example, a VER can be transferred by the submission of a report verifying the existence of the carbon asset (that is the reduction of a certain amount of greenhouse gas by a project activity) to the purchaser together with a transfer form specifying that the seller transfers all legal and beneficial title in the relevant carbon asset to the purchaser. It is important for contracts to carefully define exactly how and at what point the carbon asset is transferred from seller to buyer. If this is not done, a dispute may arise at a later date on the issue of whether the seller has fulfilled its delivery obligations and whether the buyer has the legal title required to sell-on or use the carbon assets.

LEGAL OWNERSHIP OF THE CARBON ASSET

All carbon assets (including Kyoto Protocol rights such as CERs or ERUs) are created by way of a verification process of monitoring the reduction abatement or sequestration of GHGs by certain types of activities or projects. In order for entities to be able to claim legal title to carbon assets they must also be able to claim legal title to the rights created from the abatement of GHGs by the activity or project. This is not always a straightforward issue.

The general approach of most governments has been to assume that the entity that owns or develops the project activity responsible for reducing GHGs is entitled to deal with any rights arising from the project (for example, CERs or ERUs). However, even if this assumption is correct, it is often difficult to tell who owns the project activity. For example, in a carbon sequestration project involving replanting cleared land, one entity may own the land, another may lease the land, a third may plant the trees, a fourth may harvest the trees and a fifth may wish to purchase the carbon sequestered in the trees. Even with regard to Kyoto Protocol credits, it should not be an automatic assumption that private developers are entitled to any carbon assets created from project activity.

Although the Kyoto Protocol is an international agreement providing rights and obligations for national party governments, the Marrakech Accords are silent on the ownership of credits and it could be argued that the reduction of GHGs is in effect the management of a natural resource. In many countries, natural resources (such as air and water) are seen to be the responsibility of the governments rather than private entities. Thus some governments may consider that ERUs and CERs are sovereign rights, which can be traded for profit only by the government. For example, initially the New Zealand government nationalised retention of all rights and obligations arising from certain sequestration activities, although the authors understand that the government has subsequently allowed permanent conservation project developers entitlement to the carbon asset and made arrangements with forestry plantation owners to recognise the financial value of the carbon sequestered by their plantations.

Although common law or statute law will eventually define rules for determining the ownership of carbon assets, in the meantime a major concern for purchasers when entering into contracts to purchase the ERs will be to ensure that the seller can establish legal title. A warranty to this effect should be included in any such contract, with appropriate remedies if the seller cannot ultimately deliver title that is free of encumbrances. When there are many parties that could claim title, each party's legal entitlement should be clearly set out in the contract.

THE CARBON ASSET AND PROJECT FINANCE

It is likely that under the Kyoto Protocol certain parties will have difficulty achieving emission reduction targets on a domestic level (that is by simply acquitting AAUs) and will need to look for project-based offsets (CERs and ERUs) and emissions trading for compliance purposes.

The discussions behind Article 12 of the Kyoto Protocol assumed there would be a high level of Annex I party involvement and technology transfer in CDM projects, with the Annex I providing underlying finance to the project or taking equity in the project. However, many of the early CDM projects have in fact been implemented independently by host country participants and the CERs sold directly to an Annex I CER purchaser with no further involvement of that purchaser in the project.

It is likely that with the new certainty brought to CERs, as a result of the Protocol entering into force, and as a greater understanding of the CDM develops, Annex I investment in the underlying project will increase. This is because not only will the investor receive the revenue from the project, but they will also be entitled to the CERs produced by the project and thus overall project returns are increased.

The Marrakech Accords provide no requirements as to how Annex I investment in a CDM project is to be structured and thus there is opportunity for investors to develop innovative and profitable project structures.

Below are some additional structures through which an Annex I investor may purchase the carbon asset.

The way forward: investment in the underlying project
Provision of debt finance in return for part payment in CERs
An investor can be involved as financier to the underlying project, providing a portion of project finance in the form of a loan. The loan will generally be secured against the assets of the project and will attract interest. Contracts can be entered into so that part of the repayment for the debt is made in CERs. In this case, the obligation to transfer CERs would be structured as consideration for a partial down payment on the loan received.

As the financier's interest in the project in this situation extends beyond a future interest in CERs, it may be more concerned to hedge various project and credit risks in the agreement and ensure that the project is likely to be successful. The legal arrangements for the transfer of CERs will be incorporated into the finance documentation as part of the repayment conditions.

Equity investment
An Annex I investor may become more involved in the project and purchase equity in the project. The return for the investor could be the transfer of the carbon asset arising from the project together

with a share in any revenues generated from the other products or services created by the project (for example, the sale of electricity).

Non-recourse project finance

This involves the funding of the construction of a new CDM project in circumstances where the debt financier's security consists wholly of real and personal property of the project and payments due under supply contracts (including CER supply agreements). Servicing and repayment of finance for the project is entirely based upon cashflows derived from the project. This means that, in the event of default, financiers can have recourse against only the assets of the project (for example, the assets of the special-purpose entity established to construct and operate the CDM project) and not against the project participants themselves.

Technology swap in return for CERs

This may occur where an investor provides or licenses technology to a project (that is, technology transfer as envisaged by Article 12), which is paid for by CERs from the project.

Bundling the asset with other commodities

Where CDM project developers may produce another commodity, such as coal, in addition to CERs, it is possible to structure take-off arrangements to bundle the product and the CERs created on the basis of emission reductions from the project. This will assist to off-set emissions from the purchase of the other commodity.

CONCLUSIONS

The key feature of emission reduction projects, which can make them a more attractive investment proposition, is their ability to create an additional "carbon asset" that has real value either to investors in the project for compliance purposes or as a source of additional revenue to the project.

The key issues for project financiers to consider when judging the attractiveness of a GHG mitigation project are:

❏ the exact nature of the carbon asset that the project can create (a contractual right or a statutory credit);

❑ the way in which the carbon asset can add value to a project (or ultimately add value to the company owning the project);

❑ the ownership and transfer of the carbon asset;

❑ the types of risk that can arise that are particular to the carbon asset (project financiers are already likely to be experienced in general project risks management, but carbon presents new and unique issues to consider); and

❑ the project structure that will derive the most value from the carbon asset while also presenting an acceptable level of risk.

6

Securing Investment for Climate-Friendly Projects: Uses and Limitations of Carbon Trading

Karen McClellan

CIP

Under the Kyoto Protocol, emission reduction credits are designed to help countries comply with carbon reduction targets, as well as to encourage sustainable development in emerging economies. As anticipated, carbon trading is becoming a global market. While the demand for carbon credits is high and the sale of such credits can add up to a double-digit increase in project IRRs and more secure financial structures, the opportunity to use credits to finance projects remains limited. This is due to both market and political risk. Investors must be aware of the practical difficulties in registering and operating projects under the CDM rules, and calculate the costs and benefits early on.

JI/CDM FLEXIBLE MECHANISMS AS INVESTMENT INCENTIVES

Concern about climate change has been on the rise for many years, but it is only now that governments and companies are assuming binding liabilities with respect to carbon emissions. With the Kyoto Protocol in force and governing more than 60% of the world's carbon dioxide equivalent (CO_2e) emissions, new "cap and trade" markets are emerging.[1] Most significant is the EU Emissions Trading Scheme (ETS), launched in 2005 and covering more than 25,000 installations in the 25 EU member states.

A cornerstone of the Kyoto Protocol is that it should stimulate foreign investment in "green" technologies in developing countries, thus encouraging alternatives to fossil-fuel-driven growth.[2] Two market mechanisms were developed for this purpose: Joint Implementation (JI) and the Clean Development Mechanism (CDM). Because CO_2 abatement costs among OECD countries can range from 5 to 30 times that of developing countries, these offset instruments also provide a low-cost source of "carbon credits" to carbon-constrained buyers. This chapter will examine how these instruments (predominantly CDM) are helping create the world's first global environmental market.

While carbon funds and investments have the flavour of the latest dotcom trend, the future of this new market is not yet clear. On one side, there has been an enormous increase in demand for emission offsets, as countries and companies seek to balance their new liabilities.[3] Most EU members, plus Canada and Japan have announced a carbon purchase scheme. Many intermediaries have emerged to help with this process. The World Bank manages a portfolio of "carbon funds" totalling US$1.4 billion, 80% of which commitments come from governments. New private-sector funds have emerged that will speculate on and seek arbitrage opportunities among the emerging carbon markets, drawing interest from large institutional players.[4]

The current supply of emission credits, however, is not sufficient to meet this demand. In the largest market for allowances, the EU ETS, prices have skyrocketed, increasing three-fold since January, and buyers have begun to look elsewhere. CDM and JI projects as alternative sources of emission reductions have not met expectations: as they must originate from commercially viable projects, these credits have been subject to all the difficulties of emerging-market infrastructure investment. In addition, they are being held back by the complex rules for project approval and registration created by the United Nations Framework Convention on Climate Change (UNFCCC).[5]

CDM EXPERIENCE TO DATE

A wide variety of CDM projects have been developed to date, and it is estimated that close to 55 million tonnes of CO_2e were sold from JI and CDM projects between April 2004 and March 2005, although most projects are still seeking formal registration.[6] The reduction in CO_2e comes from "clean energy" and other greenhouse-gas (GHG) mitigation projects, including renewable-energy generation; district and industrial heating; energy efficiency; distributed generation; chemical decomposition; waste management, such as landfill gas capture; sewage treatment and agricultural waste management; and forestry sequestration (with constraints). Each project must consistently and verifiably reduce greenhouse-gas emissions over a set period of time. Due to the higher global warming values of non-CO_2 gases, projects such as methane capture and HFC abatement stand to benefit substantially from the sale of CERs, and such projects have been among the first to submit methodologies to the CDM Executive Board.

The major sellers of carbon emissions have been project developers in Latin America (27%) and Asia (51%); the largest buyers are Japanese companies, together with the World Bank and the Dutch government. Most experts agree that China will eventually supply the lion's share of CERs.[7]

A major hurdle for CDM project developers has been getting the project and its methodology approved by the CDM Executive Board. At the end of Q1 2005, 21 methodologies had been approved by the EB, 10 were under revision and 32 were rejected. In addition, there were 30 waiting for assessment. To date, only five projects have received approval from the board, allowing them to sell CERs into the market as Kyoto-compliant instruments. A selection of the approved methodologies can be seen in Table 1.

This meagre portfolio of methodologies from which the world is to source its CDM demand will expand: at least 350 projects yielding 535 million tonnes of CO_2e have reached the level of project design document (PDD).[8] However, institutional bottlenecks and a lack of resources have stymied their development. While the ratification of the Protocol has led to much pressure on the board to move more quickly, it remains hampered by lack of resources as well as by ideological commitments to issues such as "additionality".

INVESTMENT CONSTRAINTS IN THE CDM MARKET

According to a recent World Bank study,[9] emission reductions from CDM projects in 2010 yielding 400 million tonnes of CO_2e would require an annual investment of about US$10 billion. This is small compared with total foreign direct investment flows to developing

Table 1 Approved baseline and monitoring methodologies

Type of project	Sector	Country
Landfill gas capture and flaring	Waste handling and disposal	Brazil
Grid-connected biomass power	Energy generation	Brazil
Industrial Fuel Switching from coal to natural gas	Manufacturing industries	Chile
GHG emission reductions from manure management systems	Agriculture/waste disposal and handling	Chile
Recovery and utilisation of gas from oil wells that would otherwise be flared	Fugitive emissions from fuels (solid, oil and gas)	Vietnam
Biomethanisation of municipal solid waste	Waste handling and disposal	India
Steam system efficiency improvements by replacing steam traps	Energy demand	China
Bagasse cogeneration with grid connection	Energy generation	Brazil
Geothermal power replacing electricity production of a fossil-fuel plant	Energy generation	Papua New Guinea
Natural gas-based cogeneration	Energy generation	Chile
Incineration of HFC 23 waste streams	Fugitive emissions from halocarbons and sulphur hexafluoride	South Korea

countries, which averaged US$140 billion per year during 1997–2002. However, the reality today is that many worthy and commercially attractive CDM projects, while able to sell emission reductions many times over, cannot find investment capital. This is because the carbon credit market today is a futures market, with little money available upfront, and limited opportunity to borrow against an emissions reduction purchase agreement, as a developer could against a solid power offtake agreement. The dearth of investment in CDM projects is attributable to sovereign risk, including risk related to the national CDM approval process, and project risk.

Sovereign risk
Sovereign risk reflects the current macroeconomic state of an emerging economy and the risk of default on government obligations. The threat of local currency devaluation, sudden interest-rate hikes, currency convertibility and even nationalisation of assets, is

of particular importance to CDM projects, as many are dependent on state-owned energy offtakers. As developing countries adopt policies and incentives that favour sustainable energy production, energy markets are liberalised (diversifying offtaker risk); local financial markets begin to back clean-energy projects and insurance products for foreign investors become more flexible,[10] sovereign risk can be mitigated.

Political risk for CDM projects is difficult to estimate and to hedge against. It is the possibility that the host-country-designated national authority (DNA) does not issue the letter of approval or that the country establishes barriers for the CER transactions.[11] Currently, this policy risk is being tracked by research companies such as Point Carbon based on the limited experience with the CDM approval process. Rating methodologies include assessment of the host countries' institutional conditions for CDM, the number and quality of projects that have been registered with the country's DNA, and the actual experience so far in approving projects.

Table 2 compares the current Point Carbon host-country ratings for the top five rated CDM countries, compared with the Sovereign rating by Standard & Poor's.

It is interesting to note that the correlation between approval for a CDM project and the macroeconomic strength of an emerging economy is not high. This reflects proactive government policies and the number and experience of CDM project developers in countries such as India and Chile.

Project risk

Many CDM projects are financed using a project finance structure, designed to mitigate risks to cashflows with which the project must

Table 2

Country	CDM host-country rating (Point Carbon)	Sovereign rating (S&P – foreign currency)
India	BBB	B
Chile	BB+	A–
Brazil	BB+	B+
China	B+	BBB
South Korea	B+	BBB+

service debt and repay investors. Key project risks include techno-logical performance, the lack of regulatory structure and natural resources data, construction and operating risk and the creditwor-thiness of offtakers. Mitigation for these risks can come in the form of local or international bank guarantees, performance insurance, documentation of natural resources such as wind, and manufac-turer's guarantees. Other tools include bundling projects to achieve portfolio diversification and upfront deposits to lenders. The expe-rience level and capitalisation of the development team is key, as is the state of development of the project, which typically needs to have all engineering studies, land acquisition and long-term con-tracts in place or near to completion prior to gaining finance.

While carbon finance is not a panacea, project developers are increasingly searching for ways to use CER sales to mitigate project finance risk. The following section will cover Emission Reduction Purchase Agreements (ERPAs) as a source of revenue, as well as a new tool in the containment of project risk.

STRUCTURING CERs IN PROJECT FINANCING

Developing a CDM project is not for the faint-hearted. Many pro-ject developers have spent months or years and significant sums of money on the various stages of project approval, which are as fol-lows:

❑ *project activity design* – submit project according to the desig-nated project design document (PDD);
❑ *proposal of a methodology* – secure approval of a new methodology (or use an already approved methodology) to govern the certifi-cation and verification of emissions;
❑ *validation of the CDM project activity* – receive independent evalu-ation of the project from a designated operational entity;
❑ *registration of the CDM project* – receive formal acceptance by the executive board that the project is eligible for verification, certifi-cation and issuance of CERs; and
❑ *certification/verification* – faciliate periodic independent review of monitored reductions in GHG that have occurred as a result of the project.

Given the complex development path, why is there so much inter-est in the JI and CDM investment incentives? To begin with, the carbon-emissions-derived cashflow that can accrue to a CDM project is a "free" source of revenue, which can have an impact on the financial structure of the project. Since this additional cashflow is not correlated to the core business of the project, it can help overcome financing hurdles, enabling the project developer to reach financial close.

The number of CERs that can be derived from a project is linked to its underlying technology – a wind farm is less profitable in terms of carbon revenues than a landfill gas recovery project. In addition, the same project will produce more credits in one country than another, as offsets are determined by a baseline, for example, underlying fuel mix that the clean energy is replacing. An estimate of the impact that carbon finance can have on expected rates of return from carbon (at US$4 per tonne CO_2e) is summarised in Table 3.

A recent World Bank report (see Haites, 2004) indicates that so far, of current and identified projects, the minimum size is about 100,000tCO_2e per year, while the average size 150,000tCO_2e per year. At current prices (US$5–$7 per tCO_2e), this means that an average project could receive more than US$1 million per year from the sale of carbon, although this could increase significantly as the market tightens.

Not only does the carbon-derived cash stream boost internal rates of return, but CERs can be used to buy down the project risk, secure debt, reduce leverage ratios, mitigate currency risk and improve returns to investors. An example of how carbon finance can be used to leverage project funding appears in Figure 1.

In this project the developer concludes an ERPA with a AAA-rated buyer in return for payment on delivery (ie, in the future) of US$400,000. The developer is now able to rely on a second source of project cashflow from its certified emission reductions, which

Table 3

Technology	Contribution to IRR
Hydro, wind, geothermal	0.5–2.5 + %
Crop/forest residues	3–7 + %
Municipal solid waste	5–15 + %

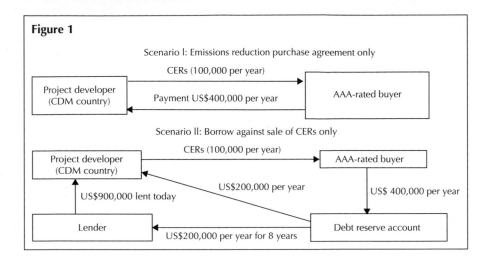

Figure 1

Scenario I: Emissions reduction purchase agreement only

will improve the project IRR; however, the developer still faces development costs to get the project under way and register it with the CDM board. In the second scenario however, if the developer is able to get a bank loan on the strength of its carbon offtake agreement with an AAA buyer, it can leverage the agreement into US$900,000 of upfront project capital.

This structure provides a reliable source of cash at a fixed purchase price, which is (1) denominated in hard currency, (2) backed by investment-grade purchasers (in this case, AAA-rated), (3) endorsed by the host country and (4) assignable to creditors, so revenues may be placed in escrow for debt repayment. As carbon prices increase, the potential of CERs to improve access to financing for clean-energy projects is thus an exciting development.

RISK MITIGATION: CARBON FINANCE IN ACTION

An example of how project risks can be mitigated is presented in the following run-of-river hydroelectric project in Ecuador.[12] Despite substantial hydro capacity, Ecuador had no previous private investment in hydropower. The project profile is as follows.

Country risk: Ecuador has a poor investment environment (S&P sovereign rating of CCC+), high interest rates (14–15% in US$ terms), low national savings rate (2.8%) and an uneven power offtaker history.

Project profile: A 30 MW run-of-river mini hydro plant capable of displacing 8 million gallons of diesel generation from highly polluting thermal plants.

Benefits:
- 250 direct jobs and 2,000 construction jobs in one of the most economically depressed regions of Ecuador;
- reliable supply of water to the city of Macas, saving US$3 million in municipal investment in water infrastructure;
- stabilisation of the national grid.

Financial gap: Despite strong fundamentals (high IRR of 15.5%, low investment cost of US$1.1 million per MW installed, a capacity factor above 85%, and secured power-purchase agreements with shareholders for 35% of its power sales) the project fell short of the main investor's requirements that more than 50% of sales are to be under firm PPA contracts and assigned to the repayment of debt service.

Emission reductions: Emission reductions result from the displacement of fossil-fuel generation in Ecuador.[13] Proceeds from the sale of carbon offsets increased the equity IRR from 15.6% to 16.3%.

Impact of carbon finance: The first 806 k tonnes of CO_2e was sold to the World Bank, in a purchase agreement that was structured so that emission proceeds accrue directly to a debt reserve account, eliminating Ecuadorian sovereign risk and reducing the cost of the loan.

Carbon finance was successfully used by the developer to achieve financing. The ability of the project to sell emission reductions directly to the World Bank, without prior registration with the CDM Executive Board (since the World Bank as buyer takes that risk), means that the project has obviated the most important policy impediment. Many buyers are not willing to take the registration risk, and prices will of course reflect the risk allocation between buyer and seller. Nevertheless, in the above project emission credits successfully offset credit, currency and sovereign risks, indicating the flexibility and relevance of carbon finance.

CONCLUSION AND TIPS FOR INVESTORS

Potential investors in and developers of CDM projects who are seeking financial benefits from the new environmental markets must be prepared to deal with both commercial and policy-related risks. Of these, the policy issues are the most difficult to control, but project risks are just as important to manage. The following tips may be useful.

❑ Calculate the cost and benefit of developing a CDM project before you begin, using experience to date as a guide.

❑ If you have a choice, invest in projects likely to receive host company approval and CDM registration. Seek out supportive CDM governments.

❑ Consider other stakeholders whose support could be solicited: national and international NGOs, the academic community and regional governments.

❑ Look at carbon finance as a whole picture in terms of structuring the deal, not just as a revenue stream; how can it secure debt and reduce risk as well?

❑ Pay attention to the structuring of the ERPA. For some projects, emission reductions are a major source of revenue and it will be critical that the lender understand the value of the ERUs. An ERPA can reduce the specific risks of the project, thereby increasing its bankability.

❑ Ensure that commercial and political project development is concurrent. While CDM project approval remains something of a lottery, if the timing can be correctly anticipated, financing will become more accessible. At this point the project must be ready with licenses, a management team, contracts and so on in order to raise funds as quickly as possible.

❑ remember that, ultimately, those closest to the development of a project development will control the sale of CERs.

❑ ERPAs will eventually be rateable, tradable commodities and should be drafted with this in mind.

As the market becomes more liquid, new financial structures will emerge, such as asset-backed, carbon-linked bonds and other secondary market instruments. Carbon finance is still in its infancy, however, and its impact on "plain vanilla" project financings in the coming months will be an important signal to policymakers as to whether the Kyoto market mechanisms can achieve their goals.

1   After Russia formally ratified the agreement on 18 November 2004, the Kyoto Protocol came into force on 16 February 2005. The countries that have ratified the Protocol account for 61.6% of the greenhouse gas emissions produced by the industrialised countries in 1990.

2   Both the Kyoto Protocol and the European Union's Emissions Trading Scheme make use of flexible mechanisms by which rich countries can buy emission reductions through climate-friendly projects in developing countries and count those reductions as part of the Protocol's established targets.

3   Estimates suggest that OECD countries' cumulative target reductions will be 5–5.5 billion tonnes of carbon dioxide based on their Kyoto obligations. If we assume that half are achieved from domestic measures within the OECD, this still leaves a "compliance gap" of around 2.5 billion tonnes.

4   In April 2005 a £135 million investment vehicle, Trading Emissions plc, was listed on the Alternative Investment Market in London, becoming the first special-purpose hedge fund to buy pollution credits.

5   See the UNFCCC website at http://unfccc.int/2860.php.

6   "JI and CDM Investments in 2004 and 2005 (mtCO$_2$e)", *CDM and JI Monitor*, Point Carbon, 19th April 2005. CDM and JI credits are sold forward prior to being registered as official Kyoto projects, with buyer, seller or both bearing the risk of registration.

7   Experts at the Massachusetts Institute of Technology recently predicted that China will supply 47% of total carbon traded, while India will offer just 11%.

8   A formal PDD has been submitted to the executive board (*Point Carbon*, April 2005).

9   Ibid.

10 These include reinsurance companies, development banks and export credit agencies.

11 It is estimated, for example, that too much delay in getting host country approval could jeopardise 10% of the total volume of 82 million CERs, which could be generated by Brazilian CDM projects submitted to date (*Point Carbon*, April 2005).

12 See Carbon Finance at the World Bank (http://www.carbonfinance.org) for a further discussion of this project.

13 This was estimated by multiplying expected annual generation of 223.5 GWh by an emission factor of 0.668 tCO$_2$e/MWh (calculated using the average of the operating and build margins, combination of oil, diesel, and hydro).

REFERENCES

Haites, E., 2004, "Estimating the market potential for the clean development mechanism: review of models and lessons learned", PCFPlus Report 19, Margaree Consultants for the World Bank, June.

"JI and CDM investments in 2004 and 2005 (mtCO$_2$e)", *CDM and JI Monitor*, Point Carbon, 19th April 2005.

7

Unlocking Additionality in CDM Projects

Gerhard Mulder

ABN AMRO Bank

Additionality has proved to be a contentious issue in the Clean Development Mechanism (CDM). As the Marrakech Accords did not provide a conclusive answer on additionality, the CDM Executive Board and its methodology panel finally settled on an "additionality tool" in October 2004. The tool reveals that "investment additionality" criteria, where project developers must prove that *income* from CDM was the decisive factor in carrying out the project, are not the sole criteria. Rather, the project developer must determine that its project scenario is not the "most attractive course of action", or in other words the baseline scenario. This allows for a comparison of different scenarios, if possible using economic or financial criteria.

INTRODUCTION

Since the Kyoto Protocol of 1997 the international community strived to operationalise the three flexible mechanisms, the Clean Development Mechanism (CDM), Joint Implementation (JI), and International Emissions Trading (IET). The CDM Executive Board was established under the 2001 Marrakech Accords to kick-start the CDM and lay down its ground rules.

The CDM intends to assist Annex I countries in meeting their reduction obligations under the Kyoto Protocol while assisting developing countries (non-Annex I) in their sustainable development. However, because non-Annex I countries do not have a reduction obligation under the Kyoto Protocol it is important that the CDM projects be "additional". After all, to procure 1 tonne of CO_2 equivalent through the CDM allows an Annex I country to emit one tonne CO_2 equivalent more.

The executive board has settled on a compromise text that was agreed to at its 16th meeting in October 2004.[1] This chapter will provide the context in which this compromise was derived and practical guidance on how the additionality tool should be interpreted.

BACKGROUND

The Marrakech Accords (MA) are the guiding document on baselines and additionality. It was approved by the Conference of Parties in 2001 in Marrakech and it aims to operationalise the Kyoto Protocol. Paragraph 44 of the CDM modalities and procedures defines baseline scenario:

> The baseline for a CDM project activity is the scenario that reasonably represents the anthropogenic emissions by sources of greenhouse gases that would occur in the absence of the proposed project activity.

In addition, Paragraph 43 states that:

> A [CDM] project activity is additional if anthropogenic emissions of GHG gases by sources are reduced below those that would have occurred in the absence of the registered CDM project activity.

The text of Paragraphs 43 and 44 is rather ambiguous and leaves room for interpretation. Some believed that additionality meant that the emissions of greenhouse gases had to be lower with the proposed CDM project activity than without the project. This was also referred to as "environmental additionality". The executive board rejected this interpretation and determined that an explicit project additionality test was required.

BASELINES AND ADDITIONALITY AND THE EXECUTIVE BOARD

The executive board meets six times per year, has a methodology panel that provides technical input, and is assisted in its work by the United Nations Framework Convention on Climate Change

(UNFCCC) secretariat in Bonn. The executive board approves baseline methodologies and additionality tools.

The executive board has consistently equated "project activity" with "baseline scenario" since the beginning of its work. In March 2003, the executive board stated that the baseline must explain "how, through the methodology, it is demonstrated that a project activity is additional *and therefore not the baseline scenario*" (italics added).

The ninth meeting of the CDM Executive Board (June 2003), provides clarification:

> a project activity using the methodology can demonstrate that it is additional ie, different from the baseline scenario. Project participants shall therefore describe how to develop the baseline scenario and how the baseline methodology addresses ... the determination of project additionality.

These clarifications suggest that project proponents can determine additionality by comparing different baseline scenarios and determine whether the project scenario is the most plausible option.

It must therefore be concluded that the executive board allows in its clarifications – that additionality can be established by equating a scenario that includes the project – with other plausible scenarios, and determines that the most likely course of action is the baseline. In this case, a project is additional if it is not the baseline scenario.[2] This shifts the focus away from a developer's individual motivations and instead compares the comparative disadvantages of the project with other plausible scenarios.

Not investment additionality

It is important to understand the difference between the two approaches. The executive board allows additionality be determined by comparing different baseline scenarios and determines whether or not the project scenario is the most plausible option, using economic and/or financial arguments or barriers to investment. Investment additionality instead focuses on the project developer by assessing whether returns on investment have improved such that CDM revenue makes the project viable from the investors' perspective.

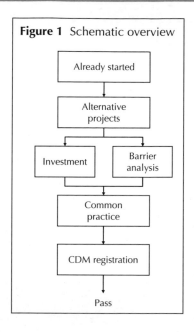

Figure 1 Schematic overview

The consolidated additionality tool

The first methodologies submitted in April 2003 were rejected in part because they insufficiently addressed additionality. The executive board opted for a bottom-up approach in which real projects were used to submit a new methodology.

In the ensuing 12 months many, often very similar, new methodologies were submitted. For example, many of the grid-connected electricity baseline methodologies were based on the same approach.[3] In response, the executive board instructed the methodology panel to develop a consolidated methodology for grid-connected electricity projects and landfill gas projects, and a consolidated tool for additionality. This new additionality tool is now widely accepted as the standard approach to additionality.

The consolidated additionality tool consists of several steps that each project must pass.

Step 1 Preliminary screening based on the starting date of the project activity

The Marrakech Accords allow for the registration of CDM projects if the project's starting date is after 1 January 2000. *Starting date* generally means the beginning of construction work. However, the project developer must "provide evidence that the incentive from the CDM was seriously considered in the decision to proceed with the project activity". This can be a challenge: the company must have evidence – such as minutes of board meetings, e-mails, financial analyses – that the CDM played a role in determining whether the project should go ahead. If such evidence is not available, it is assumed that the project would have gone ahead regardless of the CDM.

Step 2. Identification of alternatives to the project activity consistent with current laws and regulations
This step has two parts. First of all, it requires the project developer to develop different plausible alternatives, or scenarios, to the proposed project. However, in constructing the baseline, the additionality tool specifically mentions that the project itself "not undertaken as a CDM project" should be considered as one of the alternatives. Thus, if the project itself is the most likely alternative, the project is not additional. Another element to this step is that the alternatives, including the project itself, cannot be the result of a legal obligation. However, if non-compliance with this law is widespread, the project might even be additional if applicable laws exist.

In the next step, the project developer has the choice between an investment analysis (Step 3) and a barrier analysis (Step 4). This step goes to the core of the additionality question: determine what is the most likely scenario, or, rather, prove that your project is not the most likely scenario.

Step 3. Investment analysis
In this step, the project developer must determine whether "the proposed project activity is the economically or financially less attractive than other alternatives without the revenue from the sale of CERs" (Certified Emission Reduction credits). This is not investment additionality! Investment additionality would force the project developer to prove that the revenue from the sale of CERs made the difference between the project going ahead or not. Here, it must be determined that the project is less economically attractive than other alternatives.

Step 3 has several options. The first option applies to projects that have no other income or benefit that the income derived from the proposed project activity. Examples of this can be gas flaring projects with refineries or landfills, HFC-23 destruction projects and the like. In such cases, the project developer only needs to "document the costs associated with the CDM project activity and demonstrate that the activity produces no economic benefits other than CDM related income".

The second option requires the project developer to calculate a suitable financial indicator for the proposed CDM project activity and compare this with the same indicator of the other alternatives. Possible indicators can be IRR, NPV, cost–benefit ratio, or unit cost of service (for example, levelised cost of electricity production in US$/kWh or levelised cost of delivered heat in US$/GJ). In case the project developer calculates the IRR, it chooses either the project IRR or equity IRR.[4] Because the equity IRR represents the return to investors and is therefore a more reliable investment criterion, the equity IRR is considered more appropriate. In general, all relevant costs must be included, including for example the revenues such as subsidies and fiscal. Finally, the financial indicators of the different scenarios, including the project scenario, are compared with each other. If one of the other alternatives has the best indicator (say highest IRR), then the CDM project activity can not be considered as the most financially attractive.

Alternatively, the financial indicators can also be compared with a benchmark that represents a standard return in the market. For example, government bond rates, cost of financing and required return on capital, or a company's internal benchmark can be used (see example in Panel 1).

Step 4. Barrier analysis
Barrier analysis allows the project developer to take a non-quantitative approach to determining additionality. Such barriers must apply to the proposed project. However, they should *not* apply to at least one of the alternatives. After all, if these barriers applied to all other plausible scenarios, none of these projects would ever be realised and no baseline scenario could be established.

Possible barriers that prevent the CDM project from being implemented include investment barriers, technological barriers and barriers stemming from common practice. For example, an investment barrier can be that, even though a project is profitable

PANEL 1 CASE STUDY

The project is a 40 MW run-of-river hydro facility in Central America being built by a private developer. Historically, the installed capacity in this country was 70% hydro- and 30% fossil-fired; however, this mix has been reversed. The total installed capacity is approximately 1,500 MW, while currently there are negotiations to build a large gas-fired plant. This will further increase the contribution of fossil-fired plants.

Step 1. Preliminary screening based on the starting date of the project activity

The project started construction before the date of registration, in April 2004. Both the debt and equity investors considered the CDM as an integral part of their decision to move ahead with the project. Both the equity provider, who is also the project sponsor, and the debt provider, an international bank, will provide evidence upon request.

Step 2. Identification of alternatives to the project activity consistent with current laws and regulations

The project sponsor identified only two scenarios: either the project goes ahead or the current situation will continue. An examination of the legal and regulatory requirements of the country, including those sections of the law that pertain specifically to hydroelectric gener-ation, reveals that both scenarios apply with all relevant laws and regulations.

Step 3. Investment analysis

The option chosen is Option III – benchmark analysis – because plaus-ible investments defined in the previous step do not include invest-ment of similar nature. The most plausible benchmark for this case is to compare the project IRR with government bond rates in other Central American countries. A summary table of government bond rates is included in the additionality test. Finally, it is concluded that the bond rates remain higher than the project IRR, even including the CDM revenue. This analysis is complemented with a sensitivity analy-sis. In addition, the project sponsor lists several barriers, including access to financing for privately developed hydro plant, lack of skilled labour and uncertain hydrological conditions.

Step 4. Common-practice analysis

The national grid of this country was once dominated by hydro. However, the capacity additions over the last two decades were dom-inated by fossil-fired generation, in particular diesel. In fact, only one small hydro plant entered into service in the mid-nineties. A review of the National Allocation Plan reveals that, while there are some hydro facilities planned, it is not certain whether these will be implemented.

> *Step 5. Impact of CDM registration*
> Finally, the project sponsor lists the benefits and incentives brought by the CDM. These include the additional revenue derived from the investment; attracting new players who bring new technology and capacity to the country; reducing inflation/exchange rate risk; and that hydro is not subject to price risk for diesel and thus smoothes whole-sale electricity prices.
>
> *Conclusion*
> The additionality test is based on a comparison of only two scenarios: either the investor puts their money in the project, or they invest the money in a safe vehicle such as government bonds. It may be that the project developer felt it was difficult to construct plausible electricity supply scenarios for such a small grid. What makes this additionality test interesting is the emphasis on scenarios *to the project developer*. He or she also could have taken a more distant approach and compare costs of generation. While the additional "barrier analysis" is interesting, it was not necessary. In fact, adding more arguments can also backfire if claims need to be substantiated.

on paper, the project developer cannot obtain debt financing because banks are unwilling to lend to the type of technology. All evidence must be documented. For example, rejection letters that document that the project developer applied for financing in good faith with serious financial institutions are acceptable.

Step 5. Common-practice analysis
The common-practice analysis complements the previous two steps with an analysis of the extent to which the proposed project type (for example, wind energy) is already widely diffused in the sector and region. So, for example, if a project claims that it is additional, based on an investment barrier (such as having no access to financing), but the common-practice analysis shows that wind energy is already highly penetrated in the region, it must explain why this project is distinct from the other projects.

Step 6. Impact of CDM registration
Finally, the project developer must explain how the approval and registration of the project activity as a CDM activity contributed to the project approval. This can be explained in a quantitative and a

qualitative manner. While this section clearly focuses on the motivations of the project developer, it does not reintroduce investment additionality. Rather, it allows the project developer to build its case as to why it is committed to the project.

IMPLICATIONS FOR DEVELOPERS AND INVESTORS

So far, only a handful of projects have been registered with the CDM Executive Board. And, while many more are in the pipeline and even have been validated, we will not know until more projects are registered how the CDM Executive Board interprets and applies the tool.

Based on the approved methodologies and the additionality tool, a supply curve of CDM projects is emerging. At the current prices for credits from CDM projects (between €4 and €6 per tonne), the supply curve is dominated by low-capital-expense projects that generate many carbon credits, for example landfill gas projects, N20 and HFC-23 destruction projects, manure waste management projects, and in the future coalmine methane projects. While renewable energy in general should be able to demonstrate additionality under the current rules, it appears to be at a disadvantage at the current prices. This disadvantage is not the result of the additionality tool, but rather because these types of projects simply generate fewer carbon credits per unit of investment compared with some other technologies.

It is recommended that project developers have a dynamic approach to the additionality tool. If the additionality can be proven with investment criteria as described above, the project developer should not attempt to also define barriers but move to Step 5, the common-practice analysis. However, if the investment analysis shows that its proposed CDM project is indeed the economically most attractive course of action, but a common-practice analysis shows that the technology has not penetrated at all or in minor form, the project developer should consider why this is the case. This will lead to an examination of the barriers that the proposed technology is facing, arguments that can be used under Step 4, barrier analysis.

CONCLUSIONS

A project developer must build its additionality case bearing in mind that a foolproof additionality test does not exist. Instead, the goal is to screen out those projects that are blatantly business-as-usual. "The perfect is the enemy of the good" is often said in the CDM circles. This is true, and validators apply strict but reasonable standards to judge the additionality of projects. Nevertheless, the debate on additionality rages on. While it is certainly not perfect, the important thing at this moment is that we have something that works, that is the official standard of the UNFCCC and, that does not compromise the environmental integrity of the CDM.

10 tips for developers and investors

1. Do not underestimate the importance of additionality. Ask for expert advice if necessary.
2. Use examples of projects already registered with the CDM Executive Board or that have been submitted for registration.
3. Preferably, use the investment analysis, as it is more objective and thus easier to verify.
4. Develop a good relation with the validator. Ask for a pre-validation of the additionality test before you invest large sums to develop a complete project design document.
5. Keep a paper trail of all your discussions regarding additionality. Validators demand proof that the CDM played a role in deciding whether your project will go ahead.
6. If the technology of your project is already widespread in your region, determine how the circumstances have changed.
7. If your project is not registered before 31 December 2005, only assume reference from carbon credits after registration.
8. Have a dynamic approach to the additionality tool: it has various options to determine additionality.
9. Develop a good sense on what alternative scenarios exist for the proposed project. Only those scenarios that are plausible should be considered.
10. Do not believe those who say that "investment additionality" has been reintroduced. This additionality, while far from perfect, is a reasonable screening tool that will help to separate the wheat from the chaff.

1 See http://cdm.unfccc.int/EB/Meetings, Annex I.
2 A baseline scenario is generally defined as "the most likely course of action". The CDM Glossary of Terms states, "The baseline for a CDM project activity is the scenario that reasonably represents the anthropogenic emissions by sources of greenhouse gases (GHG) that would occur in the absence of the proposed project activity."
3 The standard methodology to determining the baseline carbon emissions factor is the *combined margin*. The combined-margin approach is the average of the generation-weighted average carbon emissions factor of all generation sources except must-run (*operating margin*) and the generation-weighted average carbon emissions factor of the most recent capacity addition (*build margin*).
4 Project IRRs calculate a return based on project cash outflows and cash inflows only, irrespective the source of financing. Equity IRRs calculate a return to equity investors and therefore also consider amount and costs of available debt financing.

8

Procuring Carbon: The Dutch JI/CDM Approach Through ERUPT/CERUPT

Stefan Leclaire, Daniël van der Weerd

SenterNovem

Since 2000 the Netherlands has been purchasing carbon credits through Emission Reduction Unit Procurement Tenders (ERUPTs) and Certified Emission Reduction Unit Procurement Tenders (CERUPTs). This chapter gives an overview of the Dutch approach regarding the Kyoto mechanisms. We start with the Dutch climate policy, in particular the Dutch activities in the framework of Joint Implementation (JI) and the Clean Development Mechanism (CDM). We describe how the ERUPT/CERUPT tenders have been set up and which procurement procedures have been applied, together with a focus on the financing of JI/CDM projects. Two case studies are presented in order to give some insights of concrete projects. We also stress the lessons learned from five-year tender experiences and the conclusions that can be drawn. Moreover, practical recommendations regarding the preparation of a JI/CDM-project are also provided.

BACKGROUND: DUTCH CLIMATE POLICY AND JI/CDM FRAMEWORK

The Kyoto Protocol adopted at the Third Conference of the Parties to the United Nations Framework Convention on Climate Change (UNFCCC) in December 1997 sets targets for the reduction of greenhouse gases (GHGs) in developed countries. Within the European Union's commitment to the realisation of the Kyoto Protocol, the Netherlands has to achieve a 6% reduction in GHG emission levels over the first commitment period (from 2008 to 2012) relative to the emission levels in the reference year 1990.

The Netherlands seeks to achieve half of its reduction target of 200 million tonnes CO_2e through domestically implemented measures. The remaining part is to be realised through the flexible Kyoto mechanisms such as JI and CDM. Within the Netherlands, the Ministry of Economic Affairs is responsible for the implementation of JI and the Ministry of Housing, Spatial Planning and the Environment for CDM. The Netherlands has allocated substantial amounts for purchasing JI and CDM credits. The initial overall budget was almost €1 billion.

Before the Kyoto Protocol had entered into force, the Netherlands was the first country in the world to decide to become an active player in the carbon market. The Netherlands started as early as 2000, while Kyoto only recently entered into force on 16 February 2005. The intention was to accelerate the establishment of a market by creating a demand for emission reduction certificates and to create possible standards for this market. Moreover, the pioneering risk was taken in order to realise the Kyoto targets at the lowest costs as the government was convinced that prices would rise in the build-up to the commitment period 2008 to 2012. However, the Netherlands would not buy just *any* credit: credits must be of good quality and be the result of a real reduction in the emission of greenhouse gases. Quality of credits will be assured by means of validation of projects and verification of reductions.

First experiences were gained with projects in the framework of Activities Implemented Jointly (AIJ), which served as a pilot phase for both industry and government. In 2000 the Ministry of Economic Affairs and the Ministry of Housing, Spatial Planning and the Environment have contracted SenterNovem, a governmental agency, to purchase carbon credits through public procurement procedures. As a consequence the Carboncredits.nl team was founded.

In order to maintain sufficient flexibility and also to spread risks, other possibilities for purchasing carbon credits besides Carboncredits.nl were established. The Netherlands now participates in the Prototype Carbon Fund of the World Bank and has signed agreements with several financial institutions. In 2003 the Ministry of Economic Affairs and the European Bank for Reconstruction and Development set up a Carbon Fund.[1] A similar fund has been set up with the International Finance Corporation and the International Bank for Reconstruction and

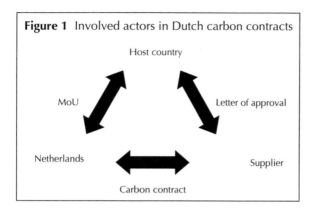

Figure 1 Involved actors in Dutch carbon contracts

Development. The Ministry of Housing, Spatial Planning and the Environment has signed agreements with the Rabobank, the International Finance Corporation, the International Bank for Reconstruction and Development and the Corporación Andina de Fomento.[2]

THE ERUPT/CERUPT TENDERS

The mandate of Carboncredits.nl consists of both JI and CDM measures. The procedure to purchase Emission Reduction Units (ERUs) is called ERUPT. Accordingly, the one for obtaining Certified Emission Reductions (CERs) in the framework of CDM is called CERUPT. Over the last five years Carboncredits.nl has carried out several procurement procedures through which it identified and contracted emissions reduction projects in Central and Eastern Europe and in developing countries. To date five ERUPT calls for tenders have been published. The fifth round is now in its second phase. The first four rounds have resulted in 18 contracted projects. Only one CERUPT call for tenders was launched. This happened in 2001 and resulted in 18 contracted projects, of which only five are remaining.

The underlying principle of the ERUPT/CERUPT tender procedure is to elaborate a stable relation between the three involved actors as shown in Figure 1. The Netherlands established contacts with various host countries by drawing up memoranda of understanding in order to create a mutual understanding on the realisation of the Kyoto targets. It is, however, up to the supplier to obtain a letter of approval from the host country, which eventually allows the transfer of emission reductions from the host country to the Netherlands.

Finally, the carbon contract between the Netherlands and the supplier sets out the conditions under which the payments are made. Another important principle is to equitably share the risks related to these carbon contracts. In recent years Carboncredits.nl played not only a role in realising carbon contracts but also in the field of capacity building in these host countries, as a consequence of contacts with host country governments when identifying potential JI projects in those countries.

As the target of ERUs to be purchased is within reach, the main focus of Carboncredits.nl will shift from identifying new projects towards contract management of ongoing projects in order to safe-guard the delivery of ERUs/CERs during the commitment period. This will mean that activities will be aimed at minimising risks of non-delivery of credits. To that end overall portfolio risk manage-ment is implemented and modalities of delivery such as under Track One or Two JI are being investigated.

PROCUREMENT PROCEDURES

The procurement procedures for ERUPT and CERUPT are set up and executed in accordance with the European directives on the procurement of goods and services,[3] even though neither of them seems to apply to carbon credits. The closest type of transaction to resemble contracts over the generation and transfer of a carbon credit would probably be the contract for the issue, sale, purchase or transfer of securities and other financial instruments. The European procurement rules aim to increase the transparency of the market and equality among suppliers.

The ERUPT/CERUPT tender procedure follows the rules of the European directive for restricted procedures and subsequently con-sists of two phases. During the Selection Phase Carboncredits.nl assesses the suitability of a supplier of emission reductions based on an *expression of interest* (EoI) made by the supplier. The EoI is evalu-ated on the following criteria:

❑ *exclusion criteria*: such as bankruptcy, proven professional mis-conduct, non-fulfilment of obligations relating to social security or taxes;

❑ *registration*: enrolment in a professional or trade register of the country of origin;
❑ *financial and economic standing*: total equity, solvency, stable positive development of turnover and profits; and
❑ *technical capacity*: ability of the supplier to realise the project.

Based on the results of this assessment selected suppliers receive an invitation to submit a full proposal in the contract-awarding phase. Submitted proposals are at first checked for their completeness. Complete projects are subsequently evaluated using the submitted written materials such as the project design document, the business plan, a validation report and a full environmental-impact assessment (if required by the host country). Additionally, on-site assessments take place.

Contracts are awarded to the economically most advantageous offers, so not solely based on price. Two contract-awarding criteria are taken into account for the contract-awarding phase, namely the certainty of delivery and the price per ERU or CER. In order to assess the certainty of delivery the following sub-criteria are applied:

❑ *project justification*: the project should conform to the market and the country;
❑ *investment plan*: solid financial closure should be reachable prior to the submission date;
❑ *implementation plan*: construction should be feasible to start within one year after submission and the commissioning of the project should be due in a reasonable period after that; and
❑ *exploitation plan*: the project should remain in operation until and including 2012.

When risks are identified in the above-mentioned categories this results in a deduction of points. The higher the risks are, the bigger the deduction in points will be. Projects that do not score at least 60 points on certainty of delivery will not be awarded a contract. All projects passing the 60-points threshold will be ranked on price. Contracts will be awarded, starting with the lowest-priced projects up to the budgeted amount for that round.

PORTFOLIO
The current ERUPT/CERUPT portfolio is one of the biggest for emission reduction certificates worldwide. It comprises to date

eighteen JI projects and five CDM projects spread over nine countries for JI and five for CDM. The contract value of the portfolio amounts to €60 million. Within ERUPT a total amount of 11.8 million tonnes CO_2e have been purchased with an average price of €5.30 per tonne CO_2e. The current CERUPT portfolio comprises 2.2 million tonnes CO_2e at an average price of €3.80 per tonne CO_2e.

Many different technologies came across in the tenders. They range from renewable technologies such as wind, hydro and biomass, to fuel switch, energy efficiency and finally landfill gas extraction. When renewables are used for producing energy, the baseline, or the existing situation in the energy sector, determines the reduction potential. In case of fuel switch or energy efficiency, the reduction greatly depends on the technology itself.

Table 1 gives an overview on the current ERUPT portfolio. It appears that almost all Central and Eastern European Countries are represented, with Romania in the fore regarding both the number of projects and amount of CO_2e. One can clearly observe differences between the various countries when it comes to the applied technology. For example, in Hungary three biomass projects were established.

As we saw earlier, the CERUPT portfolio has shrunk from originally eighteen projects to not more than five at this moment. With regard to the geographical spreading of the portfolio it appears that important emerging countries such as India, China and Brazil are represented as well as various technologies (see Table 2).

None of the five projects have been registered yet at the CDM Executive Board but it is expected that at least two projects are likely to obtain the registration within the coming months.

FINANCING OF JI/CDM PROJECTS
Financial aspects of the ERUPT/CERUPT-tenders
The overall idea of the flexible Kyoto mechanisms JI and CDM is to allow industrialised countries to partly achieve their GHG emission reductions targets abroad with an optimised cost–benefit ratio. For example, in the Netherlands it was estimated that for domestic measures investments of more than €30/tCO_2e would be necessary, whereas comparable measures in transition or developing countries would cost about €5 per tCO_2e.

Table 1 Overview JI-portfolio (ERUPT)

No	Country	Project type	Certificates (MtCO$_2$e)
1.	Bulgaria	Fuel switch	350
2.		Fuel switch	500
3.		Energy efficiency	490
4.		Energy efficiency	720
5.	Czech Republic	Biomass	520
6.	Estonia	Wind	990
7.	Germany	Mine gas	250
8.	Hungary	Biomass	710
9.		Biomass	410
10.		Biomass	320
11.	New Zealand	Wind	530
12.	Poland	Landfill gas	250
13.	Romania	Fuel switch	300
14.		Mine gas	550
15.		Hydro	2,600
16.		Energy efficiency	1,300
17.		Energy efficiency	500
18.	Slovakia	Landfill gas	550
			Total: 11,840

Table 2 Overview CDM-portfolio (CERUPT)

No	Country	Project type	Certificates (MtCO$_2$e)
1.	Brazil	Landfill gas	490
2.	China	Wind	580
3.	Costa Rica	Landfill gas	670
4.	India	Biomass	230
5.	Panama	Hydro	200
			Total: 2,170

The Kyoto Protocol requires that a JI/CDM project should generate a GHG emission reduction that is additional to any reduction that would otherwise occur. Among other ways, additionality can be demonstrated by carrying out an investment analysis to determine that the proposed project activity is not the most economically or financially attractive. As a consequence considerable costs have to be made in order to realise a JI/CDM-project.

Carboncredits.nl intends to support potential project developers in this respect. In order to compensate the costs made by the supplier

Carboncredits.nl grants a lump-sum fee of €37,500 for the preparation of a proposal under ERUPT/CERUPT. Prerequisites are that a complete proposal is submitted, comprising all necessary items, and that the project should score more than 30 points on the certainty-of-delivery criterion.

Once a project is contracted Carboncredits.nl provides an attractive financial scheme. Instalments counting up to 50% will be paid before the project is commissioned. The first 10% prepayment is made as the supplier completes the project development by finalising outstanding issues such as financial closure. Another 30% prepayments are made during construction and the last 10% prepayment after commissioning. In this respect Carboncredits.nl bears a high financial risk as half of the payments are granted before a project even starts to generate ERUs, the eventual "good" of the carbon contract.

PROJECT CO-FINANCING

In its purchasing activities ERUPT has seen not only technology suppliers enabling their customers and clients to be able to reduce their emissions, but also equipment suppliers that introduced the possibility of the carbon financing of a part of their new investment. This helped the customer to get the financial closure for the specific new investment.

The financing of the project strongly depends on the type of technology used. Table 3 illustrates that the revenues from the carbon credits can vary from 5% for hydro and wind installations up to 100% for methane recovery. For projects dealing with N_2O even a profit can be realised. Obviously revenues are higher when relatively economical technologies such as flaring of landfill gas are applied.

In order to reach financial closure, project developers need to find other sources of funding. Financing of non-economic viable projects often relies on subsidies from national programmes such as the State Environmental Fund of the Czech Republic (SEF) (see case studies below).

LESSONS LEARNED

The Netherlands has done pioneering work in the field of carbon projects. It was the first country to decide to implement the flexible mechanisms of the Kyoto Protocol and the Marrakech Accords, respectively, the CDM and JI. Prior to the elaboration of the

Table 3 Value of carbon credits of a JI-project (percentage of the total investment costs)

Project category	Revenues from ERUs/CERs (in % of total investment costs)
Hydro	5–20%
Wind	5–15%
Forestry	30–40%
Fuel switch	10–45%
Biomass	15–50%
Methane	up to 100%
N_2O	> 100%

PANEL 1
Case study: Biomass energy portfolio, Czech Republic
The project "Biomass energy portfolio" in the Czech Republic has been one of the first projects contracted by SenterNovem. In this project Bioheat International BV, a spin-off company of Biomass Technology Group BV from the Netherlands, implements a portfolio of nine biomass energy projects. They mainly consist of a replacement, renewal, extension or new construction of municipal heating systems, where biomass (wood and straw) boilers will replace old coal or gas-based boiler systems.

The first projects were implemented in 2001 and the last in 2004. The owners of the systems are mainly municipalities; two of them are private companies. In a few projects a co-generation system is installed for the production of heat and power. The thermal capacity of the installations ranges from 0.6 MWh to about 24 MWh. The total thermal capacity of the projects amounts to 130 MWh. With this project a minimum reduction of 520,000 tonnes CO_2e in the commitment period 2008 to 2012 can be achieved, of which 60% is realised by the burning of coal and 40% by the fermentation of the biomass.

The financial scheme mainly consists of three sources. The most essential part has been the State Environmental Fund (SEF) of the Czech Republic, which covers almost 75% of the initial investment. Half of it has been provided as a grant and the other half as a no-interest loan. The ERUPT contract covers 12% of the investment while the remaining part consists of own capital. Additional revenues can be realised by selling early credits in the period prior to 2008, as the projects have been in full operation from 2002 onwards. It is also very likely that due to a fairly conservative determination of the emissions reduction potential surplus credits can be generated.

PANEL 2
Case study: Landfill gas recovery in Konin, Poland
The Konin Landfill has been operating since 1986 and until today more than 1 million tonnes of waste has been disposed. The EU Waste Directives require the extraction of landfill gas but, as the Polish government will primarily focus on the construction of new landfills, financial sources for the closure and/or rehabilitation of existing landfills are scarcely available in Poland.

For contractor Arcadis Ekokonrem, the project meant an opportunity to expand its services in the Polish environmental market. The project proposes to build and operate installations for extraction of methane gas. The envisaged investments comprise a gas collection network, high-temperature gas flares, biogas monitoring and control equipment and gas engines with gas-cleaning equipment. It is planned to put the project in operation at the end of 2007. The emission reduction of methane is calculated by assuming that 80% of the produced emissions are captured and flared. The volume to be extracted is calculated at 600 to 900 Nm^3/hour, resulting in a total emission reduction of approximately 300,000 tCO_2e during the Kyoto commitment period.

The capturing and flaring of methane is relatively inexpensive compared with the revenues from the emission reduction credits that have been sold. The revenues of the ERUPT contract and the electricity generated from the collected biogas will even exceed the total investment. However, investments have to be done years before the first instalment by ERUPT will be paid.

tenders, memoranda of understanding (MoU) with various countries were signed in order to pave the way for lasting relations with the host countries. These MoU are also useful for establishing other business contacts in Eastern Europe. Also Carboncredits.nl has been active in capacity building in the respective countries on its missions to identify emission reduction projects.

When ERUPT/CERUPT started, neither a carbon market existed nor an actual price per tCO_2e was determined. Being an early player meant of course the ability to define standards regarding tender procedures and baselines. Buyers appraised the tender system as open, transparent and fair but considered it also as somehow inflexible and bureaucratic. In any case, taking the risk allowed the Netherlands to profit from lower carbon prices.

However, pioneers always face setbacks. Due to fact that no rules were established at the time the contracts were signed, the initial CDM portfolio especially has shrunken considerably. Once the CDM Executive Board established its rules for additionality of CDM projects it became clear that not all of the CERUPT projects would be eligible. Whether JI will experience similar developments remains a question and possibly a concern for the future.

Furthermore, it appeared that the time from contract to realisation of the project was often underestimated. Also, the costs for an eventual registration (CDM) were higher than expected. JI Track 1 could possibly attenuate this burden. In the first of the ERUPT/CERUPT tenders Dutch investors were well represented. Subsequently, over the years, project developers from the host countries themselves increasingly played a leading role.

CONCLUSIONS AND RECOMMENDATIONS

On the basis of five years' experience, Carboncredits.nl gained insight into various aspects of the JI/CDM procedure. Carboncredits.nl established clear guidelines (terms of reference) for the purchase of carbon credits from the buyer's point of view. A buyer is generally interested in carbon credits that provide a good balance between the offered price and the certainty of delivery. Moreover, Carboncredits.nl also supported several companies while successfully developing JI/CDM projects. Although every project is of course unique, some main conclusions can be drawn that can be useful for project developers in the future.

❏ *Buying conditions:* The conditions of the different buying institutions differ widely. It is therefore decisive which procedure fits the best with your ideas. A somehow strict but transparent tender procedure could be favourable over a less bureaucratic but less transparent fund. It is also important to assess whether a contribution for the proposal preparation is granted or not.

❏ *Risk spreading:* Every carbon contract aims at balancing the risks between contractor and supplier. The contract design differs from the various contracting organisations. While the contractor normally takes institutional risks – for instance, that the CDM Executive Board will not accept the guidelines used – the supplier must bear the more practical risks. For instance the board or supervisory committee may not accept the project as a JI/CDM project. Moreover, technical or financial risks should to be taken into account.

❏ *Timing of the project:* The timing of the project is essential. The feasibility study of the project should have been accomplished and a solid business plan should have been developed. The project shows progress in the development stage and a clear project design is available. Also, the financial scheme should be solid and near to closure. Otherwise the evaluating body may consider your project to be insufficiently ripe.

❏ *Project team:* The project team should be experienced in developing similar projects and preferably should have experience in the carbon business. Emission Reduction Units are a whole new commodity to most companies and therefore they should gain a thorough understanding of that kind of business. Furthermore, all partners should have a sufficient financial and economic standing, since selling your emission reductions means you'll have a contractual relation until 2013.

❏ *Local contacts:* Projects may be difficult to realise without sufficient local support. This applies for both technological partners and governmental organisations. Examples of the latter are the focal point of the host country or the authority that issues the letter of endorsement and letter of approval respectively. Contacts should be established at an early stage.

❏ *Type of technology:* Depending on the type of technology the revenues from ERUs can vary between 5% and 100% of the total investment costs. Furthermore, countries may differ in their specific economic needs and in preferred technologies.

❏ *Additionality:* In order to cope with the requirements regarding additionality, the project should not be a "business-as-usual" project. This means that you will have to be able to prove the additionality of your project. Basically, this can be done by either following investment/financial additionality or identifying barriers that prevent the development of your project.

❏ *Bureaucracy:* The JI/CDM procedures are characterised by an additional administrative burden besides the normal project administration. Extra costs are to be taken into account for validation, verification and the registration at the executive board (CDM only). JI will without a doubt have its own procedures. So far buyers of emission reductions and host countries have required validation of JI projects before projects are contracted.

1   The agreement between the Ministry of Economic Affairs and EBRD was signed in The Hague on 27 October 2003.
2   See the CDM homepage of the Ministry of Housing, Spatial Planning and the Environment, accessible at http://www.cdminfo.nl
3   Council Directive 92/50/EEC of 18 June 1992 relating to the coordination of procedures for the award of public-service contracts, PB 1992, L 209/1; and Council Directive 93/36/EEC of 14 June 1993 coordinating procedures for the award of public supply contracts, PB 1993, L 199/1. Both directives can be accessed at http://simap.eu.int

9

Financing Photovoltaic Projects – Plus ça change, plus c'est la même chose?

Stefan Schmitz

Field Fisher Waterhouse

Photovoltaic (PV) is often regarded as one of the most promising sources of renewable energy for the future. At a time when the reduction of carbon dioxide emissions is high on the agenda of governments and international organisations, developers are looking for technologies that are easy to put in place, cause little opposition from local residents and have as little volatility as possible. And all of this at a price that would make such projects economic.

Wind energy has certainly become the frontrunner on costs in recent years but this has run into problems on volatility and popular acceptance. Other sources, such as tidal power and geothermal energy, are usually more acceptable to the public and have lower levels of volatility, but the costs for such projects are still too high to make them commercially viable in the short term. Photovoltaic energy combines the positive elements of these other sources: it is more acceptable than wind turbines and less volatile. PV technology is set to become commercially viable, especially in countries where the price paid for PV-generated electricity is subsidised or otherwise incentivised, or where there is enough sunlight to allow the projects to generate sufficient electricity.

For PV projects, especially large projects, it is likely that similar financing structures to other renewable energy projects such as wind will be used, and there is ample experience in the financial world of how to structure finance for such projects. So, does that mean that the principles of project finance will be applied to PV projects and that merely small adjustments are needed, simply

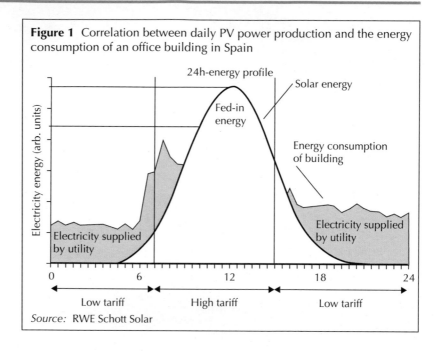

Figure 1 Correlation between daily PV power production and the energy consumption of an office building in Spain

Source: RWE Schott Solar

changing the description of the technology? The answer is that it is not that straightforward – and the fact that an entire chapter of this book is devoted to the details of PV project finance shows that there are several issues arising from financing PV projects which require special attention.

HOW DO PHOTOVOLTAIC PROJECTS WORK?

Photovoltaic systems transfer the energy in sunlight into electrons and thereby create an electric current whenever sunlight strikes their surface. Since PV depends on sunlight, the power curve of PV roughly parallels that of the sun as the source of light, and is basically the same every day in that it peaks when the sun is at its highest (Figure 1). It also means that there is no production at night and less during the months of winter, autumn and spring than there is in the summer.

Generally, PV projects can be divided into green-field and non-green-field (often also called rooftop) projects. They are also divided into on-grid and off-grid projects. Rooftop projects very often only supply the building on whose roof they have been

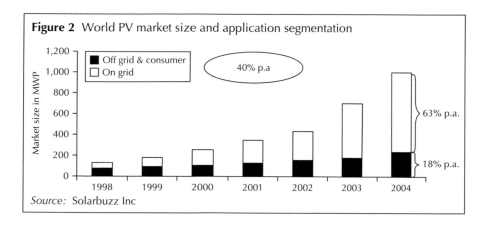

Figure 2 World PV market size and application segmentation

Source: Solarbuzz Inc

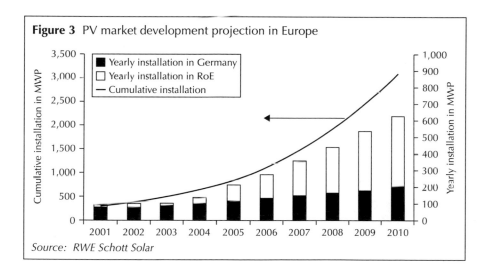

Figure 3 PV market development projection in Europe

Source: RWE Schott Solar

installed or of whose structure they form a part. Green-field projects are usually much larger and feed directly into the grid.

Currently, there are only a few projects large enough to be financed by project finance. Many projects are small-scale, notably the so-called "roof programmes", which have been set up by a number of countries. These programmes have been designed to encourage home owners or companies to install PV modules on their roofs to contribute to their energy consumption. It is only quite recently that larger PV projects have been established, most of them in Germany, the US, Japan and the Iberian peninsula.

MARKET DEVELOPMENT

The PV market has been undergoing rapid development in recent years. PV installations were 927 MW in 2004, representing a growth of 62% over 2003 installations (Figure 2). Once again, Germany showed the strongest growth rate with a staggering 152%, which is largely due to their favourable feed-in tariff regime. Japan – the other major host to PV projects – and Germany accounted for 69% of the world's PV installations in 2004. The consolidated world production of PV cells increased to 1,146 MW in 2004. It is estimated that the worldwide annual PV installation rate will reach 3.2 GW by 2010, a threefold increase over 2004 market installations. World PV annual turnover is set to grow from US$6.5 billion in 2004 to US$18.5 billion by 2010 (Figure 3).[1]

FINANCING PV PROJECTS – WHAT IS SPECIAL, WHAT TO LOOK FOR

While it is correct to say that the financing of PV products works along the lines of conventional project finance structures, there are a number of particular factors unique to PV projects that banks and sponsors will need to pay attention to.

PV Modules
Technology
The PV modules are the crucial element in any PV project. These modules have been used in commercial projects for more than a decade, so there are good data available about their performance and reliability. The efficiency rate of PV modules is currently around 13%, although this is expected to increase over the next few years.

There are basically two types of PV module: wafer-based crystalline silicon modules and thin-film modules. The latter has an advantage in that the film can be applied very easily, such as being rolled out on a structure; it is also cheaper to manufacture and to install. It does, though, have a disadvantage as far as financing is concerned, in that there is only limited data on its performance available.

Crystalline silicon technologies accounted for 92% of PV module production in 2002, and their share has been increasing at the expense of thin film during the last decade.

Photovoltaic modules are classified (or rated) by the power they produce under a specific set of standard test conditions. The most

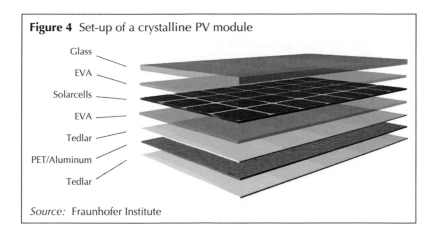

Figure 4 Set-up of a crystalline PV module

Glass

EVA

Solarcells

EVA

Tedlar

PET/Aluminum

Tedlar

Source: Fraunhofer Institute

common rating used in Europe is the peak rating. The peak rating of a PV system is the sum total of the PV modules' nameplate power under published standard test conditions (STC). The performance is then stated in watt peak (Wp). This approach is not too different from that, for example, applied to wind turbines, which are rated in MW to denote their peak performance.

PV modules can be certified, for example according to IEC61215. Lenders will usually expect modules to comply with this standard and in supply agreements with PV module manufacturers it is common that the manufacturer supplies the relevant certification for its modules.

PV modules are very reliable. Only 2.1% of the projects had a problem with modules and their cabling.[2]

Performance guaranty/degradation

One of the most positive aspects of PV technology is the reliability and low maintenance. With no moving parts, solar cells should be able to operate reliably for 25–30 years, with virtually no maintenance. In PV module supply contracts, the manufacturer usually guarantees that in the first 10 years of the PV module's operating life the performance of the PV modules, under STC, will be not lower than 90% of the specified minimum peak performance. These contracts typically accept that peak performance is subject to a general variance of +/−5%, which means that the acceptable minimum peak performance would be 95% of the peak performance under STC. In relation to the first 20 or 25 years of the PV module's operating life, the guarantee is usually for 80% of the minimum peak performance. The reason for this model is that it is generally believed that the performance of the PV modules would decrease over time. However, long-term studies have shown that after 10, or even 20, years there is no evidence of a general degradation and that the performance generally remains within the tolerance laid down by the manufacturer.

It would be impracticable to check every module to be installed in a project for its compliance with the specified peak performance. Therefore, purchase agreements usually contain a clause according to which the purchaser is entitled to have a certain percentage (usually fewer than 1%) of modules checked by its own engineers or an independent expert. It can also be agreed that the purchaser has the right to send its engineers to inspect the production facility and process.

Costs/supply bottleneck

A significant problem in the current PV market is the shortage of PV modules, which in turn is the result of a lack of silicon. The bottleneck in processed silicon is expected to continue for 2005 and probably well into 2006, which will make it difficult for PV modules to be obtained. Because of this lack of modules and the growing demand, the bargaining position of the suppliers is a very strong one. For the financing of PV projects, this means that it is essential to ensure a sufficient and timely supply of modules, accompanied by the appropriate guarantees. A project where the supply of the electricity-generating devices (and thus cashflow) is in doubt will have difficulties finding investors.

Four companies account for over 50% of solar cell production: Sharp, Kyocera, BP Solar and Shell Solar. Among the top four manufacturers, Sharp remains the largest and has shown the fastest growth over the last five years. Sanyo, the fifth largest, has shown the second highest rate of growth over the same period. Around 50% of the world's solar cells were manufactured in Japan in 2003. The United States accounted for 12%.[3]

Other issues

Because of the very nature of PV modules, precaution has to be taken in case individual modules break, get stolen or otherwise cease to function. This can become a significant problem after a number of years. Technically, it is quite easy to remove a broken module and replace it with another, as long as (and here lies a potentially major problem) spare PV modules that are compatible with the existing project set-up are available in sufficient numbers. As in other industries, the PV module technology develops very fast. This relates mostly to the efficiency of the PV modules but can also affect size, weight and other factors that may make a new PV module incompatible with older ones. Attempts to require the PV module manufacturer to keep a number of modules in reserve that could be used to replace broken ones have, unsurprisingly, met with little success. One possible alternative – namely that the purchaser acquires a certain number of extra PV modules as a reserve – can be dismissed because of the costs associated. These PV modules, bought at high cost, would not generate any revenue until they are put in place (which may of course never happen). It is also possible to build reserve structures, in addition to the main project, that would generate electricity and would, in effect, also function as a spare-part reserve. This approach would of course create additional costs but could ensure that the target size of a project could be maintained in the long term.

Costs/prices

Because of the supply bottleneck, prices for PV modules are high and, even if bought in large quantities, appear to currently range between €2.90/Wp and €3.50/Wp. Prices in the higher region of the scale would probably render the project unbankable as the projects cannot generate sufficient cashflow to meet the required debt servicing. As a consequence, projects can currently be developed only in areas with a lot of sunlight or with a sufficiently high feed-in tariff.

This scenario will change in the course of the next few years as prices of PV modules are expected to come down to €1.0/Wp by 2010 and €0.5/Wp by 2030,[4] so that projects will increasingly become viable in areas with less sunlight and/or a less attractive feed-in tariff. The total costs for 1 MW of PV power turn-key installed are currently around €4.5 million – a substantial amount when compared with other renewable projects, especially wind energy, where costs are closer to the €1 million/MW mark for onshore projects and where even offshore projects appear to cost, depending on the environment, between €1.5 million and €2 million.

The costs for PV electricity generation vary between €0.25 and €0.65/kWh, compared with the costs for wind energy of €0.04 and €0.12/kWh. It is expected that the PV generation costs will come down to 0.05 to €0.12/kWh by 2030 (see European Commission, 2005).

Energy yield study

Similar to other renewable energy projects, the financing banks or equity investors will require an energy yield report from one or more reputable experts. Due to the relatively short history of the PV market in the context of project finance, as well as the demanding nature of such reports and the work required, there are few institutions that can provide such reports. Since large PV projects have been done in only relatively few countries, there are many countries where no expert institutions have emerged and there has not yet been a strong movement towards international institutions, which has happened, for example, in the wind market.

As with other projects, the energy yield study will assess the likely electricity output of a project, based on the technology, location and other circumstances. For PV projects, the most important factor to be considered is sunlight and how the applied technology will perform with the sunlight available.

The two measures of sunlight most commonly used to evaluate PV system's performance are irradiance and insolation, of which irradiance is the more important factor. The higher the irradiance, the more sunlight hits the PV cells and the more electrons get an energy boost to flow through the PV system circuitry. The more electrons that flow, the higher the current (amperage) and the higher the current, the more electricity (kilowatts) are produced. Although irradiance varies from moment to moment during the day, the total energy received by the system from the sun in a given year remains relatively constant from year to year, usually varying only between 5 and 10% of the average.

Irradiance levels are affected by the angle of the sun, passing clouds, hazy weather, smog and other air pollution. All of these can affect the amount of sunlight available at any given moment. Hence, these are the factors that have to be looked at by the experts and applied to their calculations. Satellite data as well as data from local meteorological stations are typically used. As with wind-energy projects, the longer the duration of measurements, the less variation there is and more accurate predictions for energy yield can be made. While the variations can amount to about $+/-16\%$ after the first year, they can come down to less than 10% after three years and less than 5% after 10 years.[5] Total-year horizontal irradiation on the European subcontinent ranges from 700 kWh/sqm (Arctic Norway) to 1,800 kWh/sqm (Southern Spain and Sicily) (see "Putting PV on the Map", 2005).

Insurance, special risks

Comprehensive insurance cover is an integral factor in any project finance structure. For PV projects, as with any other energy projects, there are two cost factors that need to be covered by insurance: the costs of repairing the site if it has been damaged, and the costs of loss of electricity production.

One important factor, which usually does not play an important part in most other energy projects, is theft. It is quite easy for modules simply to be stolen, especially in green-field projects, which tend to be in remote places and not always sufficiently guarded. In the same category of unusual risk is damage caused by rodents, which appear to have a distinct appetite for the cables of PV projects.

Operations and maintenance (O&M)

Many of the O&M issues relating to PV projects are very similar to those arising on other projects. As with other project types, it needs to be considered whether availability should or could be guaranteed – for PV projects, the benchmark usually mentioned is 97%. It is easy to see how the technical availability of, for example, one wind turbine can be established: it has to be ready for generation on, say, 355 days per year. For PV projects, the issue is more complex. First, it has to be decided at which level availability relates. Should it relate to the entire project, to a panel of PV modules or just to each individual module? It would seem to be impossible to guarantee the availability of the entire project such that the failure of a single module would mean that the project is not available. The likelihood that, at any one time, one of the thousands of modules in large projects is not working is very high. Also, availability has to be defined very clearly. If, for example, there is dirt or snow on part of a PV module (so they do not perform fully), should this mean that the module or panel is available for generation? It has been suggested that, rather than having availability guarantees, the O&M contractor should guarantee only its engineers' reaction time. The problem with this approach is that the mere presence of an engineer on site does not guarantee that the project will become fully operational immediately. Needless to say, close attention should be paid to the obligations of the O&M contractor on site.

Additional sources of finance/hedging

Currently, for the reasons outlined above, PV projects are bankable only in countries where the electricity generated receives some form of incentive, for example a tariff that commands a substantial premium to the current market price for electricity. A number of countries have a feed-in tariff regime in place, which guarantees the offtake at a set price. However, many of these tariffs are still well below the generation cost so that projects that solely rely on these tariffs are unlikely to be bankable. Some countries offer additional sources of financial help, notably through direct subsidies or by granting tax breaks for investors (see European Commission, 2005, p 16). The EU Emission Allowance Trading Scheme (ETS), launched in 2005, does not benefit the actual producers of green energy and the international equivalent for developed countries, the Joint Implementation (JI) scheme, is not yet operational.

In order to add security to the cashflow of a PV project and, therefore, hopefully reduce the cost of the finance, the risk of insufficient sunlight can be hedged. At present, around 95% of weather derivatives are temperature-related and there is a natural correlation of temperature and sunshine (a more precise correlation of a particular site could be established as part of the technical expert's report). So, weather derivatives could be structured to hedge against the risk of "bad" months or years. As there is sufficient liquidity in the market, such hedges should be possible to put in place at a reasonable cost.

SUMMARY

For the financing community, PV projects should represent a safe investment. They offer a predictable cashflow, established technology and a business environment where many of the players are large companies that can back up the various guarantees with a substantial balance sheet. In view of the current costs of PV projects, large projects appear to be viable only in countries that have either a very high feed-in tariff or have many hours of unimpeded sunlight. With the current rate of growth of PV, the price for these projects will come down to a level at which projects are also economical in countries with less sunlight and no high feed-in tariff.

TIPS AND IMPLICATIONS FOR INVESTORS/PROJECT DEVELOPERS OF PV PROJECTS

❑ When taking security over PV projects, special attention has to be paid to how local law treats PV modules that are connected to frames and structures. Investors need to ensure that security can be taken over the entire structure, especially when the structure is connected to the ground, or, if security is to be taken over only the modules, that this is possible.

❑ Since large green-field projects are usually in remote locations, special attention must be paid to the issues of security at these sites. Guards or CCTV can add substantially to the O&M costs and electricity has to be available at the site.

❑ Very often, modules will not be repaired but replaced. Special attention has to be paid to the timeframe in which such a repair must be done and to what extent it is technically possible to replace a module, especially after a longer period of time during which the original (and compatible) type of module may have become unavailable.

❑ Because of the current shortage of PV modules and the fact that many modules are manufactured in Japan, special attention must be paid to long-term planning in order to ensure that the right number of modules will be available for installation when needed.

❑ The size of green-field projects makes it necessary to get the rights for substantial plots of land. Costs for leasing this property can be substantial.

1 Source: Solarbuzz Inc.
2 Source: Gute Noten vom Handel für die boomende Solarbranche, Erneuerbare Energien 4/2005, page 53.
3 For more information see http://www.solarbuzz.com.

4   These latter figures are based on the historic learning curve for PV modules, which show a 20% price reduction for every doubling of the accumulated sales.

5   Source: Meteocontrol.

REFERENCES

Suri, M., T. Huld and E. Dunlop, 2005, "Putting PV on the map: internet tods for solar resource assessment in Europe", *Renewable Energy World*, 2 (March/April).

Photovoltaic Technology Research Advisory Council, 2005, "A vision for photovoltaic technology", Directorate-General for Research – Sustainable Energy Systems, EUR 2/242.

Section 3

Trading Perspectives

10

Carbon Facilities as a Means of Sourcing Emission-Reduction Credits

Pedro Moura Costa, Bruce Usher; Allan Walker

EcoSecurities; Standard Bank

As the carbon market evolves, there is an increasing need for vehicles that provide simple solutions to the compliance needs of private- and public-sector parties in Annex I countries. One of the most comprehensive of these solutions is carbon facilities that play the role of procuring, selecting and acquiring carbon credits on behalf of their investors/participants. This chapter describes three facilities that target different niches of the market.

The first one is the EcoSecurities & Standard Bank Carbon Facility, an initiative to assist governments and industry to source Joint Implementation (JI) and Clean Development Mechanism (CDM) emission reductions for compliance with the Kyoto Protocol and other emission-reduction programmes (such as the EU Emissions Trading Scheme), currently focused on projects in Central and Eastern Europe. The first entity to take advantage of this facility and commit funds for the purchase of emission reductions is the Danish Ministry of the Environment. Our second facility is 2E Carbon Access, which focuses exclusively on the development of small-scale CDM projects, primarily in the renewable-energy sector. 2E Carbon Access is a joint venture with E+Co, the leading not-for-profit provider of services and capital to developing-country clean-energy enterprises. This facility is already developing a series of projects in Central America. The third is the Austrian Small-Scale Facility, which has the objective of acquiring credits from small-scale CDM projects structured by EcoSecurities and the 2E Carbon Access Facility. This chapter describes how carbon facilities work and provides three case studies of the facilities described above.

INTRODUCTION

Among all environmental challenges currently facing industry, the reduction of greenhouse gas (GHG) emissions is among the most topical. Given its direct link to global climate change, how countries and industries will reduce emissions of GHGs has become an issue of significant international relevance and public interest. It is widely acknowledged that the potential impact of climate change on the global economy could be enormous. Reinsurance companies estimate that it could be in the order of hundreds of billions of dollars per year in the form of natural disasters and disruptions to agricultural cycles. The extent of these impacts provides ample justification for the introduction of drastic measures for prevention and mitigation of climate change. The targets set out by the Kyoto Protocol of the Climate Convention are only a first step in this direction, but undoubtedly any measure to limit emissions will come with a cost.

Limitations on the emissions of GHGs could lead to reductions in the levels of industrial output and economic activity. In the absence of innovation, it has been estimated that the cost of compliance to meet the targets outlined by the Kyoto Protocol could reach tens of billions of euros per year in Europe alone. Moreover, traditional policy measures such as command-and-control systems and taxation mechanisms can be difficult and expensive to administer, can result in prohibitive costs for industry and do not provide any guarantee that targets will actually be met. Regulatory systems that cap overall emissions and allow for the trading of each participant's allocation of reductions (known as cap-and-trade systems), provide flexibility for individual companies to explore the full extent of their comparative advantages and are proven to be cheaper and more effective than other approaches. It is expected that an international trading system for GHGs could significantly reduce the cost of reaching global targets while at the same time rewarding innovation and entrepreneurship.

While the Kyoto Protocol allows the use of three flexibility mechanisms (see below) for assisting Annex I parties in reaching their GHG emission reduction targets at lower costs, the project cycles of these mechanisms are extremely complex and uncertain. Given the complexities of this market, and the highly specialised skills required for the identification and acquisition of credits and use of the Kyoto mechanisms, it is only logical that a series of market players are outsourcing credit-procurement activities to third parties specialised in this sector. In this context, carbon facilities that aggregate intelligence, expertise, skilled personnel and international exposure, are becoming popular as a means to effectively identify, structure and deliver project-based credits for investors.

This chapter describes three new facilities that were launched between mid-2004 and mid-2005, and how they are operating.

THE CLIMATE CONVENTION AND ITS FLEXIBILITY MECHANISMS

The underlying policy initiative steering international efforts to reduce GHG emissions is the United Nations Framework Convention on Climate Change. Launched in 1992 during the United Nations Conference on Environment and Development in Rio de Janeiro, the Climate Convention created the basis for current efforts related to controlling GHG emissions. Specifically, the Convention establishes the stabilisation of GHG concentrations in the atmosphere as its main objective.

In December 1997, the Kyoto Protocol was created to further define the rules and regulations for the implementation of the targets established in the Climate Convention. The most important aspect of the Kyoto Protocol is the adoption of binding commitments by 37 developed countries and economies in transition (collectively called the Annex I countries) to reduce their GHG emissions by an average of 5.2% below the year 1990 for the years 2008–12. The commitments are differentiated by countries, with some required to reduce up to 8% below their 1990 levels (for example, the EU as a whole), while others only have to limit the growth of their emissions to 1990 levels. At the same time, the Protocol establishes the use of three "flexibility mechanisms" for facilitating the achievement of these GHG emission reduction targets. These are:

❏ emissions Trading, allowing the international transfer of national allotments of emission rights between Annex I countries;

❑ joint Implementation (JI), the creation of emissions reduction credits undertaken through transnational investment between industrial countries and/or companies of the Annex I; and,

❑ the Clean Development Mechanism (CDM), which allows for the creation of Certified Emission Reduction (CER) credits from projects in developing countries and also promotes sustainable development in these countries.

While it is expected that these market mechanisms can lead to a reduction in the overall cost of compliance with the Kyoto Protocol's targets, the convoluted way in which they work creates barriers for the participation of many companies. For instance, Figure 1 shows the typical CDM project cycle, according to the latest rules. Each step of the way has its own rules and regulations, and on average a project takes a least one year from conception to registration, and CDM costs alone are in excess of €150,000.

The complexities of the CDM and JI project cycles suggest that the use of carbon facilities run by specialised entities is a safer and more efficient means by which to participate in the carbon markets.

Carbon facilities as a means to accessing emission reduction credits

It is clear that the complexities related to the CDM may prevent some parties from participating in this market. Carbon facilities, therefore, are a means to enable parties to participate in the carbon market without the need for investing in building their own internal capacity. The principal advantages of participating in a carbon facility are as follows.

❑ *Professional management*. One of the main advantages for participants is that carbon facilities provide the services of a management team with high technical and financial expertise in this field, removing from the carbon buyers the need to understand the dynamics of this fast-moving and convoluted market.

❑ *Portfolio diversification*. A primary advantage of carbon facilities is that they can pool resources from multiple buyers and acquire credits from a variety of different project types (such as technologies) in various countries, thus diversifying overall risk.

❑ *Flexibility*. Unlike carbon funds, carbon facilities are structured to meet the individual needs of buyers and project developers.

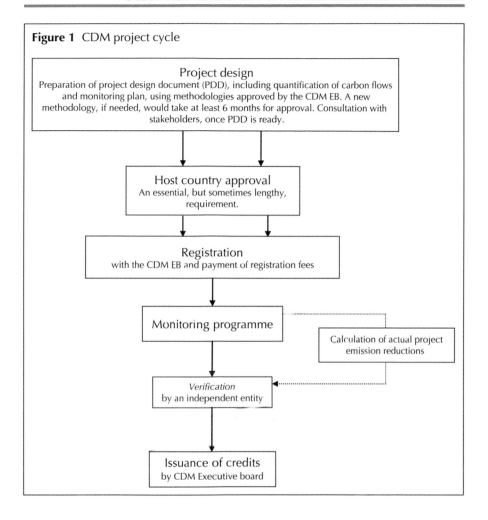

Figure 1 CDM project cycle

Project design
Preparation of project design document (PDD), including quantification of carbon flows and monitoring plan, using methodologies approved by the CDM EB. A new methodology, if needed, would take at least 6 months for approval. Consultation with stakeholders, once PDD is ready.

Host country approval
An essential, but sometimes lengthy, requirement.

Registration
with the CDM EB and payment of registration fees

Monitoring programme

Calculation of actual project emission reductions

Verification
by an independent entity

Issuance of credits
by CDM Executive board

Specifically, the low costs of establishing and managing a facility, when compared with the high fixed costs of a carbon fund, allow for much greater flexibility, and for the establishment of much smaller facilities (as small as €5 million in size).

❏ *Reduced administrative burden and transaction costs.* Facilities manage all of the administrative functions related to project structuring, document preparation, negotiations, registration and project development, and when they manage a large portfolio for various participants there are economies of scale in the preparation of the documentation and an overall reduction in transaction costs.

The overall combination of advantages suggests that the use of carbon facilities may be the most appropriate means for many parties to enter into this market. Panel 1 provides an example of a carbon facility established for sourcing JI credits from large scale projects.

Facilities as a means to promoting small-scale projects

One of the primary objectives of the CDM is also to promote sustainable development in developing countries. Towards this end, the CDM has created streamlined procedures for small-scale projects, which are generally considered to have proportionally greater sustainability benefits than larger projects. The rationale for streamlined procedures for small-scale projects is to provide project developers within an incentive to apply for certification of their emissions reductions, and therefore provide them with an opportunity to participate in the CDM. The definition of small-scale projects under the CDM is:

❑ renewable-energy project activities with a maximum output capacity equivalent of up to 15 MW;
❑ energy efficiency improvement project activities that reduce energy consumption by up to the equivalent of 15 GWh per year; or
❑ other project activities that both reduce emissions by sources and directly emit less than 15,000 tonnes of CO_2 equivalent per year.

Unfortunately, practical experience has shown that most of the volume of emissions reductions from projects participating in the CDM to date is from large-scale projects. This is despite the fact that the vast majority of renewable-energy projects in developing countries are, and will continue to be, small-scale.

The primary hurdle to CDM access is the significant time and cost required to complete the CDM process, combined with a significant risk that, despite the outlay of time and capital, the project will fail to receive CDM approval and/or will fail to find a buyer for its CERs. Specifically, the due-diligence process required to create CERs is too expensive in relation to the value of the emission reductions to be generated by many small-scale projects. As a result, most small-scale project developers have not attempted to access the CDM, and are therefore de facto excluded from the very mechanism that was established with a primary objective of supporting sustainable development.

PANEL 1 LARGE-SCALE PROJECT FACILITIES:
ECOSECURITIES & STANDARD BANK CARBON FACILITY

The EcoSecurities & Standard Bank Carbon Facility is an initiative created to assist governments and industry to source JI and CDM emission reductions for compliance with the Kyoto Protocol and other emission-reduction programmes (such as the EU Emissions Trading Scheme). The first entity to take advantage of the facility is the Danish Ministry of the Environment. This is part of a suite of initiatives currently being developed by the government of Denmark to meet its emission-reduction objectives. Other entities from the public and private sectors, however, may also be able to take advantage of this initiative.

The facility is initially sourcing JI and CDM credits from projects in the following regions and countries:

❏ *Balkan states* (Albania, Bosnia-Herzegovina, Croatia, Macedonia, Montenegro, Serbia, Slovenia);
❏ *Baltic states* (Estonia, Latvia, Lithuania);
❏ *Central Europe* (Bulgaria, Czech Republic, Hungary, Poland, Romania, Slovakia); and
❏ *Eastern Europe and Central Asia* (Armenia, Azerbaijan, Belarus, Georgia, Kazakhstan, Kyrgyzstan, Moldova, Russia, Tajikistan, Turkmenistan, Ukraine, Uzbekistan).

In the future, or on demand from participants, the facility may expand its area of project sourcing to include a wider range of developing countries. Furthermore, participants in a facility have the possibility to specify regions, countries or technologies they want to buy from, even if they are outside the regions and countries indicated above.

The facility will buy JI credits generated from 2008 onwards, from both Track 1 and Track 2 projects, but the facility will also consider early- and late-crediting AAU transactions under the International Emissions Trading Mechanism of the Kyoto Protocol. CDM credits from the countries allowed will also be sourced.

In an initial phase, the facility has already identified more than 100 candidate projects from a wide range of technologies and locations that can be further developed to meet the requirements of the participants. Initial feedback from participants has indicated that the services provided by the facility are such that it provides a full solution to those parties looking for carbon credits. It was also noted that this is a cost-effective and reliable way to source credits, in comparison with other internal or external options available to most parties.

Recognising this challenge, the CDM executive board in January of 2003 approved simplified procedures for small-scale projects. The simplified procedures eliminated the requirement to navigate the methodology panel, but the requirements for development of a project design document (PDD), validation, registration, monitoring and verification remain essentially the same as for large-scale projects. As a result, the small-scale procedures have not materially improved the ability for small-scale project developers to participate in the CDM. The hurdle is a shortage of both capital and expertise: small-scale project developers rarely have the financial resources or the in-house knowledge to navigate the simplified procedures of the CDM process.

A potential solution to this problem is to create carbon facilities exclusively designed for small-scale projects, providing a combination of CDM expertise and financing to cover the cost of completing the process. While the type of carbon facility for large-scale projects tends to provide advantages mainly to carbon buyers, carbon facilities for small-scale projects focus on providing an invaluable service for project developers that otherwise would not be able to enter into this market. Examples of small-scale carbon facilities can be found in Panels 2 and 3.

PANEL 2 SMALL-SCALE PROJECT FACILITIES: 2E CARBON ACCESS

E+Co, a leading investor in clean-energy projects in developing countries, analysed both the 2002 report of the Group of Eight (G8) Task Force, co-chaired by Sir Mark Moody Stuart, and the 2002 World Energy Assessment of the International Energy Agency (IEA). It concluded that, in order to meet the surging demand for energy in developing countries, a total of 12,000 off-grid energy service companies, and 500 on-grid projects will be developed over the next 10 years. Virtually all of the off-grid service companies and a substantial number of the on-grid projects will qualify as small-scale projects under the rules of the CDM, but most will be unable to access CDM financing.

2E Carbon Access is a joint venture of EcoSecurities and E+Co, the leading energy-investment company for entrepreneurs in the developing world (hence the name "2E"). 2E Carbon Access officially launched at COP 9 in Milan in December 2003.

In its first year of operations the 2E Carbon Access facility has contracted with nine project developers, located in Honduras, Guatemala and the Philippines. As of January 2005, the facility has three validated small-scale projects. The primary lesson learned from the first year is that it is possible, despite a great deal of early scepticism, to rapidly develop and guide a small-scale project through the CDM process.

The early success of the facility can be attributed to the following.

❑ The 2E Carbon Access facility covers all costs of CDM project development, including validation and registration. This removes the lack of financial resources as a hurdle for small-scale project developers to participate in the CDM.

❑ The facility leverages the expertise and relationships of its parent companies to assist small-scale developers in navigating the CDM process, including stakeholder consultations and applying for Host Country Approval.

❑ The 2E Carbon Access facility has only one objective: to complete the CDM process for small-scale project developers as quickly and efficiently as possible. This focus, combined with the fact that the facility is compensated purely on a success fee basis when CERs are sold, is a key factor in the facility's success.

❑ Finally, and perhaps most importantly, the 2E Carbon Access facility has made a clear decision to trade off profits for greater sustainable development. Even with the streamlined procedures of the CDM, it is not economically rational to focus on small-scale projects if profit maximisation is the primary objective. The 2E Carbon Access facility was established as a for-profit entity, but it is clear from early experience that even with a successful track record the many challenges of small-scale CDM projects will prevent significant financial returns for the facility.

PANEL 3 AUSTRIAN SMALL-SCALE CARBON FACILITY

In October 2004, EcoSecurities and Kommunalkredit Public Consulting (KPC), the Austrian specialist in public consulting, firmed an agreement to acquire Certified Emissions Reductions (CERs) from small-scale projects on behalf of the Republic of Austria. KPC is responsible for the management of the Austrian JI/CDM Programme (http://www.ji-cdm-austria.at) and acts on behalf of the Austrian Federal Ministry of Agriculture, Forestry, Environment and Water Management in this respect.

The Austrian CDM Small-Scale Project Facility is managed by EcoSecurities and has the objective to purchase CERs from small-scale projects in developing countries under the Clean Development Mechanism of the Kyoto Protocol. The projects may be based on production of renewable energy, energy efficiency, fuel switching, methane capture or reduction of industrial emissions. The facility started operating in November 2004, and will be acquiring 1.25 million tonnes of CERs generated between 2006 and 2012 inclusive. It is expected that this facility will contribute substantially towards Austria's international climate obligations under the Kyoto Protocol and the respective EU agreements in a cost-effective manner, while simultaneously fulfilling Austria's desire to support sustainable development in CDM countries.

KPC acts as a partner for public-sector clients in Austria and other countries around the world. KPC, a wholly owned subsidiary of Kommunalkredit Austria, the specialist bank for the public sector in Austria, works mainly for public and quasi-public institutions, such as the Federal and Provincial governments of Austria, local authorities, associations, sovereign states, international financial institutions operating under a public-sector mandate. Its clients benefit also from the bank's level of specialisation and its knowledge of the specific requirements associated with public services. In its main fields of activity – climate and energy, water management and the rehabilitation of contaminated sites, and international consulting – Kommunalkredit Public Consulting manages support and consultancy programmes in close cooperation with its clients.

CONCLUSIONS

It is increasingly clear that the facility model is one of the most efficient mechanisms for the acquisition of CDM projects on behalf of corporate and public-sector entities. Facilities work for both small- and large-scale projects because they provide the combined benefits of flexibility, portfolio diversification, risk mitigation and specialised professional services, reducing overall costs of credit creation and procurement for its participants.

For project developers and carbon credit buyers, when considering participating in a carbon facility it is recommended that you look for the following key characteristics.

❏ *Flexibility.* The CDM market is new and rapidly developing, requiring flexibility from both project developers and buyers to participate. The facility model allows for maximum flexibility while retaining all of the benefits of aggregation.

❑ *Diversification.* Successful carbon facilities are diversified geographically, by technology and by project type, in order to minimise the risk associated with the CDM and project development.

❑ *Volume.* Facilities succeed by dramatically lowering transaction costs, which means that successful facilities must be working on a minimum of five projects at any point in time to be successful.

❑ *Time.* The facility should be structured to work quickly and efficiently, thereby raising the prospect of a successful result, while minimising the risk of wasted time for all parties.

❑ *Experience.* The CDM remains a highly challenging process for creating value, and the results are binary, in that unsuccessful parties receive absolutely no credits or compensation. Therefore, it is essential that the managers of the facility have the practical experience necessary to successfully navigate the CDM and thereby improve the odds of success.

11

Purchasing Pools in Corporate Carbon Compliance: Survey of the Strategic Advantages

Dirk Forrister; Paul Vickers

Natsource Europe (London); Natsource Asset Management

The "buyers'-pool" concept could become a trendsetter, given its strategic advantages for companies in achieving compliance objectives using the Clean Development Mechanism (CDM) and Joint Implementation (JI).

Buyers' pools are not unique to carbon markets – in fact, the concept of joint activities is a proven winner, borrowed from more mature markets. Power companies have used coal-buying collaboratives to improve economies of scale and reduce risks. Oil companies often join forces to develop large oil projects so as to diversify risks across a number of companies.

Environmental commodity markets have also demonstrated the value of pooled purchasing initiatives. One of the earliest, the Greenhouse Emissions Gas Management Consortium in Canada, offered a number of valuable lessons, as has the World Bank's Prototype Carbon Fund (PCF). Building on those initiatives, the Greenhouse Gas Credit Aggregation Pool (GG CAP) is one buyers' pool that will use a number of proven risk management techniques from other markets to improve delivery potential for purchasers.

This chapter explores the strategic role of such a pool in achieving compliance objectives as part of a suite of activities. It explains the key elements of a carbon buyers' pool, comments on how risks are managed and provides case studies of corporations who are using a buyers' pool as part of their compliance regime. In closing, it reviews the emerging role of other carbon funds and purchasing initiatives appearing in the global carbon market.

A BUYERS' POOL IN THE CORPORATE COMPLIANCE STRATEGY

The basic financial premise of a buyers' pool is that purchasing Certified Emission Reductions (CERs) and Emission Reduction Units (ERUs) as part of a group effort enables companies to gain advantages of a large portfolio: better diversification, economies of scale to drive down fixed costs, and resources to retain an expert manager. Its greatest advantage is its improved risk management, compared with an individual corporate purchasing plan: rather than hedge risks across the CER flows from three projects that a company might purchase on its own, it can join a ten-company buyers' pool that purchases CER flows from thirty projects.

Each of these buyers is also engaged in a set of corporate activities to address greenhouse gas emissions. Most include:

❑ abatement of emissions at their own facilities – up to cost levels that do not exceed expected market price levels;
❑ a select number of long-term purchases of CER or ERU transactions tailored to corporate priorities;
❑ spot market purchases or forward transactions of EUAs;

some are also investing in various carbon funds (such as the World Bank's Community Development Carbon Fund).

WHAT IS A BUYERS' POOL?

In our model of a buyers' pool, each purchaser commits to purchase an overall volume as part of a group purchasing strategy. For example, 10 companies might commit to purchase 1 million tonnes (mt) each – for a total pool size of 10 million tonnes. In practice, commitments range from less than 1 mt to 5 mt.

In our model (see Figure 1), each pool member signs a parallel agreement that commits to their purchasing volume with a notional delivery schedule up to a specified price. The agreement appoints a portfolio manager, subject to a governance structure controlled by the buyers. The buyers' group sets an overall level of acceptable risk, which the portfolio manager must meet in its purchasing decisions. They also agree to a governance structure that ensures they can provide ongoing guidance to the portfolio manager to respond to changing market conditions.

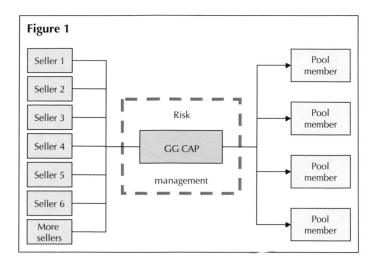

Figure 1

To assemble its 20–40 mt portfolio for the buyers, the portfolio manager will arrange 20–30 Emissions Reduction Purchase Agreements (ERPAs) for different project types. It will apply extensive risk management, using a proprietary delivery risk management model, to ensure that the portfolio can deliver a portfolio tailored to the level of risk sought by the buyers – in other words, for the equivalent of an investment-grade financial instrument. In so doing, the pool operates at a defined level of risk – but it is not a guaranteed "risk-free" purchasing strategy.

It is critical to understand that risk-free purchasing is elusive at this early stage of the carbon market. Brokers sometimes market offers on individual transactions that carry a high level of delivery assurance – such as one backed by an AAA-rated company that will agree to provide replacement credits if the CERs fail to arrive on schedule. Still, a residual risk usually exists – such as some mark-to-market price limit or financial upper limit. More importantly for many buyers, an AAA-rated company appropriately charges a higher price than the price performance of a purchasing pool.

More commonly, CDM credit offers involve "best efforts" to deliver CERs – with no guarantee, so no money is paid upfront. Often, the counterparty has no credit rating whatsoever, or it is rated as "speculative". In CDM, the jurisdiction is necessarily a developing country, where economic and regulatory risks exist given that the CDM is a new programme. The net effect of these risks, in market terms, has been to drive prices into a lower range than EUAs, which command higher prices since they bear lower risks. This should provide initial context for the underlying purpose of a greenhouse gas (GHG) buyers' pool.

HOW IS RISK MANAGEMENT CONDUCTED ON A BUYERS' POOL?

The portfolio manager's contract with the buyers' pool members stipulates that it must operate within defined risk management parameters in arranging ERPAs. In particular, it must screen, assess and score a large number of projects, using its delivery risk model. It must then assemble a portfolio of ERPAs that avoids the use of projects with highly correlated risks – in other words, it would not rely on too many similar projects in two countries with closely inter-linked economies, given the potential risk that a faltering economy in one country could cause the other country to decline as well.

With advice from numerous experts, both in buyer companies and research and financial institutions, on the common "root causes" of CDM and JI project failures, we clustered these risks into five "buckets" that could be addressed with specific contract or portfolio protections. The five risk categories, discussed more fully in Panel 1, include:

❑ *counterparty risk*: the risk that the project owner goes bankrupt or defaults;
❑ *performance risk – technology*: the risk that the technology involved fails for operational reasons;
❑ *performance risk – carbon*: the risk that emission reduction production variability could impact delivered volumes;
❑ *regulatory risk*: the risk that CDM- or JI-specific regulatory issues (executive board delays or host government difficulties) could impact delivery; and
❑ *country risk*: the risk that the host country has economic problems or impose restrictions that cause a project to fail to produce the credits.

The pool will utilise a delivery risk model to rate projects for aggregate risk – and it will rate portfolios of projects to understand their combined effects, in risk and delivery terms. Use of the above model will enable the portfolio manager to narrow its focus on a

PANEL 1 REVIEW OF THE GROWTH OF CARBON FUNDS

Many financial institutions, in particular national purchasing initiatives, have been emerging in a number of jurisdictions. In a 2003 study for the IEA/IETA/EPRI annual carbon review, they also demonstrate a trend of national purchasing to augment the ETS in many European member states. These funds also recognise, at some core level, the value of purchasing in bulk – improving the risk distribution across a variety of projects. However, few government purchasing strategies manage risk the same way private funds do. In a sense, the buyer pool provided a private-sector strategy for bulk purchasing on a par with these initiatives, but augmented with use of private sector risk management tools that are not yet required by governments.

This market context is important for other reasons: private purchasing vehicles such as buyer pools will compete with government funds for good projects at times, but at other times they will collaborate in syndications for combined purchases on large projects. We review the range of funds under development that will be increasingly engaged in the Kyoto-related markets in coming years.

Among financial institutions, the World Bank's Carbon Finance Group (WB CFG) became the market pioneer in the late 1990s, when it launched the Prototype Carbon Fund, a €138 million initiative aimed at purchasing a portfolio of early emissions reductions that it expected might meet Kyoto compliance requirements. However, given the market's early stage of development, investing governments and companies had no guarantee that purchases would comply with the Kyoto Protocol. Their purchases of "verified emissions reductions" (VERs) carried risks that they might not ultimately qualify as CDM or JI credits – but they recognised the importance of learning by doing with the World Bank's team.

More recently, the WB CFG has launched a series of other funds that place it as the dominant player in the current carbon fund market.

❏ the Community Development Carbon Fund, which closed in January at just over €60 million, is a fund of private and governmental purchasers focused on small, community-oriented carbon reduction projects.

❏ the Bio-Carbon Fund, which is closed at an estimated €25 million, will invest in forestry and agriculture-related carbon sequestration projects.

❏ the Netherlands Clean Development Facility, where €108 million is available for investment in projects that will produce 21–32 mt of CERs.

❏ the Italian Carbon Fund, which is targeted to raise €60 million from Italian government and industries and would invest in a range of CDM/JI projects (current level of investment is €12 million).

❑ the Spanish Carbon Fund, in which the government of Spain committed €200 million for CDM/JI projects.

Other national purchasing initiatives have also emerged:

The Netherlands has been the most active country in pioneering transactions in the carbon market. In addition to its World Bank fund, it sponsors a number of other purchasing initiatives aimed at meeting half of its Kyoto obligation or 40 mt over the decade.

❑ the Swedish International Climate Investment Programme, with €12 million available for purchasing of CDM/JI credits;
❑ the Baltic Sea Regional Energy Cooperation Testing Ground Facility (€10 million);
❑ the Danish government's purchasing facilities, which have €108 million budgeted over several years for purchasing of CDM/JI credits;
❑ the Finnish government purchasing programme, which has €10 million budgeted; and
❑ the Austrian government's purchasing programme, which has €287 million budgeted for CDM/JI purchases over the next several years.

Government-owned banks are also collaborating with private-sector investors on funds, such as the following.

❑ The European Investment Bank (EIB) is developing a European Carbon Fund with the World Bank, which was due to be launched in late 2005. It hopes to raise €100 million from European governments. Previously, the EIB committed €500 million in financing for Kyoto-friendly projects, but it did not plan to purchase carbon credits with the money, preferring to provide debt financing for climate-friendly projects.
❑ The European Bank for Reconstruction and Development is developing a carbon fund aimed at purchasing carbon reductions from its project portfolio; it hopes to raise €50–150 million.
❑ The KfW Carbon Fund, which is working to raise €50 million for CDM/JI purchases.
❑ The Japan Carbon Fund, launched in late 2004 as a joint effort of the Japanese Bank of International Cooperation and the Development Bank of Japan – and a number of private Japanese energy and industrial firms; it has more than US$100 million available for CDM/JI investments.
❑ France's deposit investment corporation, CDC Ixis, has joined forces with Fortis Bank on a €60 million carbon speculation fund, which it hopes other banks and private investors will join. It is targeted to grow to €100 million, for purchasing credits and reselling them in the European carbon market at a profit. Unlike the other funds, it operates with an investment philosophy of providing maximum financial returns rather than the compliance focus of most other funds.

short list of projects for negotiation and transaction. The manager can design the portfolio to deliver within the acceptable level of risk defined by the buyers.

The portfolio design and formation is, of course, only the foundation of a more elaborate risk management structure. The portfolio manager also tailors specific risk management features into the ERPAs with the buyer – using a variety of techniques to reduce, transfer or accept risks. These include use of credit limits, contract remedies and collateral, as well as insurance, financial guarantees, default recovery and reserve margins. Some of these techniques can be applied at the individual contract level, and others are applied across the portfolio as a whole.

In summary, the delivery risk model enables the portfolio manager to understand how to: (1) establish purchasing priorities to meet portfolio targets; (2) value reductions from different projects; (3) allocate risks in contracting; and (4) determine risk management techniques to mitigate them. Figure 2 illustrates how the model

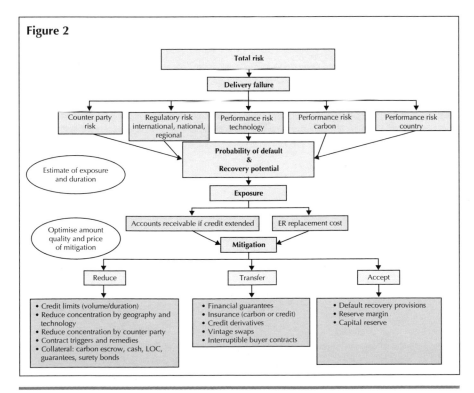

Figure 2

will assess project risk and implement risk management strategies to reduce, accept and transfer risk.

The model is just one example of how private-sector entities are now analysing risks – some market participants use less formal systems, some use no formal system at all. But virtually every buyer undertakes some form of systematic assessment of project risk, which it factors into price. Lending institutions specialise in assessing risk, and often consider their assessments of value and risk to be highly proprietary. Thus, there is wide scope for different valuations of risk and price for forward streams of compliance instruments created by projects.

WHY COMPANIES JOIN A BUYERS' POOL: TWO CASE STUDIES

Each of the companies that have joined had its own strategic reasons for joining – and, given the market sensitivities existing in this new market, their complete reasoning is often confidential. For purposes of this chapter, we thought it wise to focus generically on two companies – from Europe and Japan – to offer insights on how the strategy is viewed in each jurisdiction.

Chugoku Electric (Chugoku)

This was the first company to commit to the buyers' pool in late spring 2004. It announced that it would join at a 3.6 mt level. From its previous experience as a participant in the World Bank PCF, it understood the value of a group purchasing initiative and the benefits of a portfolio of CER/ERUs. Given the seriousness of its voluntary commitment to reduce emissions as part of the Kaidanran's agreement with the government of Japan, Chugoku had begun to carefully manage its own emissions with a series of efficiency improvements. But, given its load growth, it also needed to join additional purchasing programmes. It joined the World Bank's Community Development Carbon Fund (CDCF), and the BioCarbon Fund. The three initiatives would provide a balance of purchasing in nearly every realm of carbon asset – CDCF for small, community-oriented projects; BioCarbon for sinks projects; and buyers' pool for larger CDM/JI projects. Taken together, these initiatives produce a robust "fund of funds" for Chugoku.

PANEL 2 DESCRIPTION OF PRIMARY DELIVERY RISKS

1. Credit risk/"counterparty risk"

Buyers must consider the stability of the seller by looking to its credit rating or, if it is an unrated company, to its recent financial documentation. The credit rating is a factor in determining the financial viability of the seller and its ability to deliver firm amounts on schedule.

The credit rating is particularly important if any pre-delivery payments are considered. Private sector buyers – unlike their government counterparts – are usually bound by strict limits to the amount of credit they can offer a company with such a rating as well as limits on the duration of contracts and collateral requirements.

As entities make buy-and-sell decisions based on the expected value of future deliveries, they often discount the quantity of future deliveries expected from individual projects or forward-allowance offers to reflect credit risk. Different sellers will have widely different credit positions, and widely different premiums or discounts based on credit quality can certainly be expected.

2. Country-specific investment risks ("Performance Risk – Country" in Natsource's Delivery Risk Model)

The investment climates of different countries pose very different risks to the buyer of project-based emission reductions. Consequently, buyers can expect forward streams to track against rating agencies' views of the investment climate in the country – or, in the case of a JI deal, this risk can include the countries' ability to comply with requirements to maintain their eligibility to trade under the Kyoto Protocol. Ratings services (Fitch, Moody's, S&P, *The Economist*) all offer absolute and comparative ratings of country risk that are in wide use today.

Purchasers of country obligations and project-based reductions will no doubt price these effects into their decisions as is common practice with country-debt-related instruments today.

3. Country-specific regulatory risks ("Regulatory Risk – Country")

Each host country for emission reduction projects also poses different risks relating to the regulatory approvals, transfers and registration of the emission reductions. Buyers must understand whether the regulatory climate is stable for emission-reduction approvals, tax treatment of transactions and conveyance of rights to the reductions. A country may score highly on investment climate in Section 2 above, but score poorly due to an overly complex approval process. Conversely, a country may score moderately on investment climate, but be viewed more favourably by buyers resulting from having a well-functioning CDM approval system.

4. Technology-specific risks ("Performance Risk – Technology, and Performance risk – Carbon")

Buyers must understand whether the technology involved in the project will work as planned. This is the case with commercial technologies that have been used for lengthy periods of time. Technologies in their infancy that are not in widespread commercial application will not be viewed as favourably and be considered a higher risk by buyers. We assess this in the category of risks as "Performance Risk – Technology", wherein we analyse the operational and commercial features of a project.

Similarly, we use the term "Performance Risk – Carbon" to capture the extent to which creditability, volume of and ownership of ERs is affected by the particular type of baseline that is used for a given technology. For example, based on the specific technology utilised, the project's baseline may be subject to adjustments over time.

As illustrated by this brief description of risks that can plague emission-reduction projects, different project types carry different risk profiles. Whether assessed qualitatively or quantitatively for risk, they can be expected to score differently for their potential to deliver contracted amounts. Buyers must factor in delivery risk, and such considerations as guarantees provided by the seller (for example, a guarantee to deliver eligible compliance instruments in the event of under-delivery), into the price of their purchases of candidate CERs. Similarly, sellers are well served to appreciate the risk profile of their project so that they can develop competitive offers that are consistent with it and will attract buyer interest.

Electricity Supply Board (ESB)

ESB, of Ireland, joined the buyers' pool at its first close, a part of its response to the EU Emissions Trading Scheme (EU ETS). Ensuring that it had exhausted all cost effective internal measures, including increased use of wind energy and efficiency improvements, ESB then entered the buyer's pool and engaged in EUA transactions, both in forward and spot sales over time, to get benefit of average pricing. It sees an important niche for CER purchases: since they are bankable throughout Phase 1 and 2 of the EU ETS, and given their global fungibility, ESB envisioned building a supply of CERs for strategic use over time. ESB will purchase some CERs in multi-year deals of its own, and some through the buyer pool. Importantly, the market intelligence gained in the buyer pool, plus the access to additional volumes and deals coming in through the buyer pool pipeline, enhances its value to ESB.

MARKET CONTEXT

The value of carbon pools relates essentially to their superior performance on price of the compliance unit delivered. This section surveys the market's development on price to offer context for why a purchasing pool for CERs is attractive. The clearest examples appear in Europe, where EUAs regularly trade at higher prices than CERs. The price differentials in Europe relate to the differing risk profiles of the two commodities – CERs carry more risks than EUAs. But given the savings potential in purchasing CERs, plus their superior bankability (EUAs in Phase 1 cannot be banked into Phase 2 in most member states), large companies will purchase CERs as part of their compliance portfolio. The reason is obvious: it is cheaper, so long as risks can be managed cost effectively.

In 2004, trade of a variety of GHG commodities occurred in a variety of distinct GHG markets around the world. In a survey for the World Bank Carbon Group in May 2005, Natsource reported on market activity. The 2004 results showed three key market trends.

1. Trading continued to increase in 2004 (see Figure 3)
Total trading of project-based emission reductions reached approximately 107 million in 2004.

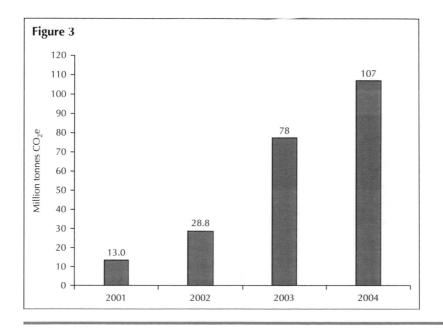

Figure 3

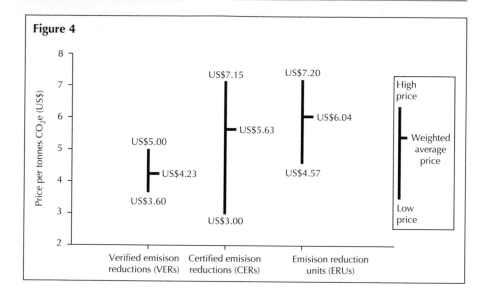

Figure 4

The increases included purchases from private companies in the EU and Japan, plus the Dutch government initiatives and the PCF – but not many of the other national funds that are emerging. In future years, carbon funds and pools will add significant demand to the global market.

2. Prices for compliance-ready project-based reductions are between US$3 and US$7 per tonne (see Figure 4)

Average prices paid for pre-compliance project-based emission reductions were approximately US$3.60 to US$5 per tonne. Higher prices ranging from US$3 to over US$7, were paid when the seller is paid upon delivery of CERs, the commodity created by the CDM. Similarly, ERUs, the commodity created under Joint Implementation, were priced at US$4.57 to US$7.20.

3. EUA prices are commanding the highest market prices

Average prices paid for early trades of 2005 vintage EUAs has ranged from €6.90 to €20 since early 2004. These prices reflect the lower risks of purchasing allowances, lack of potential for delivery failure, assured compliance value and ease of contracting (See Figure 5).

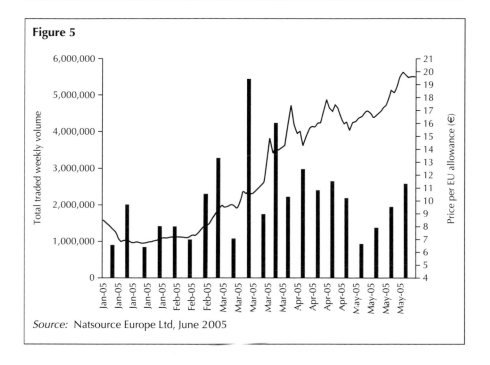

Figure 5

Source: Natsource Europe Ltd, June 2005

Prices of EUAs rose and fell over the course of 2004 with various developments on the National Allocation Plans (NAPs).

❑ if moves were made to strengthen NAPs, prices rose; and,
❑ if developments occurred to weaken the NAPs, prices fell.

But by the end of 2004 other drivers began to appear: temperature and rainfall impacts on power production, as well as shifts in fuel use or pricing (gas prices rose from March to May 2005, so coal generation increased, and allowance sales and prices rose).

In summary, recent market performance illustrates the trends towards compliance and growing interest in low-priced project-based reductions – the trends that provide the underlying fundamentals that make CER/ERU purchases, buyers' pools and carbon fund vehicles attractive as part of a company's compliance strategy.

LINKS BETWEEN PRICE AND RISK
In assessing how to get a fair price in a given transaction, the buyers'-pool participants and their portfolio manager must appreciate the key drivers of carbon prices in the market. As evident from the

previous discussion, price relates to the quality of the asset being offered. Allowances, project-based (CDM, JI) reductions and financial derivatives each carry different prices. Prices in the EUA market have ranged from €6.90 to €13 in 2004 to over €20 in 2005. In the same period, candidate CERs traded at US$3 to US$7 (or €2.43 to €5.69.)

In part, these price differentials reflect the lack of risk of and complication in allowance transactions compared with CER transactions. For the most part, well-established European firms with good credit ratings sell allowances that they are allocated when they are confident that their emissions are performing below baseline levels. No project-related regulatory approvals are required for a trade, so there is minimal risk that they will not be delivered. If they are not delivered, contracts typically impose financial penalties on the seller. Thus, allowance transactions are less complicated and less risky than CER transactions, so the seller receives a higher price.

GREATER RISK OF CERS

In contrast, CER transactions are more complicated and carry greater risk. Project methodologies must be approved and applied to the project, and then the project can be registered – after which financing must be arranged, technology put in place and emissions reductions achieved. Then the CERs can be verified, certified and issued by the CDM Executive Board. Nonetheless, CDM projects have positive compliance attributes, given that they will be usable for compliance until 2012. In contrast, a Phase 1 EUA is usable for emission reduction requirements only from 2005 to 2007.

Market prices are also driven by basic supply–demand dynamics. Traders regularly assess the supply-and-demand picture, most notably five factors:

❏ the level of demand created by the stringency of EU member state NAPs for covered industries;
❏ the emissions implications of weather, fuel use and electricity demand;
❏ the performance of the CDM executive board and methodologies panel in processing and approving CDM projects and its impact in creating adequate supply;

❑ speculation about future events, such as tightening of regulations or emergence of new technologies (this factor can cause severe volatility in spot and medium-term markets and sometimes fundamental shifts in the longer term pricing); and

❑ the amounts and timing of large government purchases, given the growth in government purchasing programmes (Italy, Denmark, Ireland, Spain, etc) which are likely to impact private-sector buyers and market evolution.

Different buyers and sellers will, of course, have widely different perceptions of the likelihood of these factors and current events, all of which will influence their views on pricing.

As discussed previously, prices for CERs also reflect the risk attributes of the counterparty, the project's host country, the technology, the baseline and the regulatory climate. Candidate CERs are subject to delivery risk – the risk that a portion of emission reductions contracted for will not be delivered or usable for compliance with the Kyoto Protocol. Buyers of EUAs, which will be distributed to EU installations in 2005, need to consider credit, or counterparty risk. However, they will not have to consider country- and technology-specific risks associated with CDM or JI transactions.

12

Choices Facing Firms in a CO_2 Cap-and-Trade Emissions Trading Scheme

Charles Donovan; Mustafa Hussain*

Enviros Consulting; Frontier Economics

The EU Emissions Trading Scheme (EU ETS) is a central element in European climate-change policy and is expected to be a primary mechanism by which EU member states will meet their international climate change commitments. By transferring some of the burden of meeting national emission reduction targets to the private sector, the EU hopes to increase the probability of meeting its obligations under the Kyoto Protocol.

The EU ETS is a "cap-and-trade" scheme for reducing CO_2 emissions across all 25 EU member states. The scheme provides a framework for the costs of emission reductions to be allocated among firms in the most economically efficient manner. In this chapter, we describe the choices facing firms in adjusting to a carbon-constrained European economy and identify the characteristics of firms that will emerge as "winners" and "losers" under the EU ETS.

WHAT IS CAP-AND-TRADE?

Cap-and-trade is one of a number of ways in which an emissions trading system can be organised. For example, an alternative mechanism, known as "baseline and credit", was employed in the UK

---

* The views in this paper are the views of the authors, and not necessarily the views of the organisations they are affiliated with.

Emissions Trading Scheme (UK ETS). Under the EU ETS, firms are allocated allowances at the beginning of the compliance period. Each allowance confers the right to emit 1 tonne of CO_2 equivalent greenhouse gas emissions.[1] At the end of each compliance period, the firm must surrender a quantity of allowances equivalent to its CO_2 emissions.[2] The penalty for emitting CO_2 at a quantity above the number of allowances it holds is €40/tonne CO_2 during the initial phase (2005–7) and €100/tonne CO2 in the second phase (2008–12).[3]

The total number of allowances allocated by EU member states sets an economy-wide emissions limit. Provided that the cap is set below the level of emissions expected from all firms included in the scheme, allowances have a market value. As firms are allowed to sell their surplus allowances to other market participants, the cap provides an incentive for firms to profitably reduce emissions by reducing CO_2 emissions and selling the unused rights to emit. Economic theory states that firms should reduce CO_2 so long as the marginal cost of emissions reduction is less than the marginal revenue gained from selling the emissions allowances.

Under the cap-and-trade framework, some firms will reduce emissions and others will choose to purchase allowances. How the firm chooses to act will be determined primarily by the marginal costs it faces in reducing CO_2 and the market price of CO_2 allowances.

WHAT IS THE IMPACT ON THE FIRM?

The introduction of the EU ETS will have two immediate economic impacts on firms. These are:

❏ wealth effects from the allocation of emissions allowances; and
❏ changes in the firm's variable operating costs.

Wealth effect

Each installation owned by the firm and included in the EU ETS will receive an annual allocation of allowances. While EU member states will distribute the majority of their emissions allowances for free, the allowances have an immediate market value. The "free" allocation of allowances therefore acts as a one-off windfall benefit to the firm. The magnitude of this benefit is determined by the quantity of emissions allowances it receives and the market price for allowances. As all firms in the scheme will benefit from the initial allocation, it is not the absolute number of allowances, but rather the amount *relative* to its competitors, that will determine the magnitude of any economic impacts arising from the allocation process.[4]

Change in operating costs

Under cap-and-trade, all emissions are undertaken at a cost. In deciding how to act, firms should compare their own costs of abatement with the market price of allowances. Where the total cost of emissions reductions is less than the revenue gained from selling emissions allowances, firms will abate CO$_2$ emissions profitably. Those that find abatement costs higher than the price of allowances will choose to purchase allowances.

While simple in theory, there are numerous complications in the structure of the EU ETS that will make the determination of future changes in operating costs difficult for firms. A change in the variable costs of production will become evident in two distinct ways:

❏ *changes to the production cost structure*. Even if a firm emits at a level below its initial allocation, it incurs an opportunity cost associated with consuming its stock of CO$_2$ allowances. For this reason, all emissions are undertaken at a cost. The level at which the firm chooses to produce will be determined by the trade-off between the opportunity cost of allowances and the value to the firm of emitting extra greenhouse gases.
❏ *increases in energy input costs*.[5] Any firm that uses energy faces a potential change in the cost of inputs. The most immediate impact will be on firms that use electricity, although consumers in primary fuel markets (such as natural gas) may also face higher costs as a result of the EU ETS. Firms with high demand for energy in their production process will face relatively higher variable costs of production.

An illustration of the economic impacts of the EU ETS on the firm is provided in Figure 1.

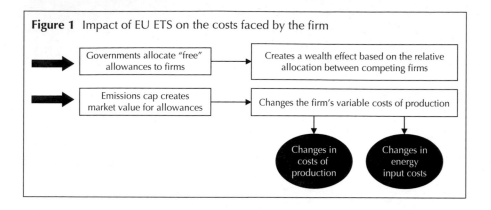

Figure 1 Impact of EU ETS on the costs faced by the firm

WHAT CHOICES DOES THE FIRM FACE?

Firms act to maximise profits. In general, where firms do not exhibit market power and are therefore price takers, they can increase profits by increasing output whenever the market price for its product exceeds its marginal cost of production (including the cost of CO_2). Whenever the market price is less than its marginal cost, profits increase by reducing output. The optimal level of production is therefore at the level of output where the market prices for its goods are equivalent to its marginal costs of production.[6]

Profit maximisation under a cap-and-trade system will require firms to rethink decisions about how, and how much, they produce. Firms affected by the EU ETS must consider whether they should reduce their need to buy emissions allowances (and carbon-intensive forms of energy) or expose themselves fully to cost increases associated with carbon caps and changes in energy prices.

Anecdotal evidence suggests that firms are not fully altering behaviour to respond in a rational way to the incentives being offered under the EU ETS. In particular, they may be valuing allowances as a free resource rather than a resource with an opportunity cost. This can be ascribed to limited experience with market-based policy instruments and regulatory uncertainty surrounding the EU ETS.[7]

Managers must consider carefully the combination of options that can be employed to achieve a level of production that is consistent with profit maximisation. Some of the options available to them are illustrated in Figure 2.

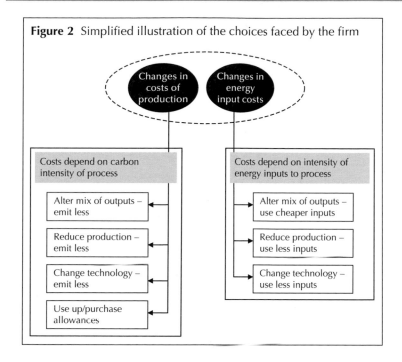

Figure 2 Simplified illustration of the choices faced by the firm

Not all firms in the EU ETS face the same set of choices. The characteristics of the sector in which the firm operates will be an important determinant of optimal firm behaviour. These characteristics include:

❑ carbon intensity of the production process; and
❑ energy intensity of production inputs.

Carbon intensity

The EU ETS will reward firms with the ability to employ less carbon-intensive manufacturing processes. The power-generation sector is an obvious example of a sector where individual plants can achieve a market advantage from improvements in carbon intensity.[8] However, many firms can alter the carbon intensity of production by pursuing one or more of the following strategies:

❑ *altering output mix* – shifting operating expenditures to less carbon-intensive processes from highly intensive ones;
❑ *reducing production* – simply producing less of the good; and
❑ *changing the technology employed* – making capital investment in new manufacturing processes.

In instances where these strategies cannot be employed profitably, a firm has the option to purchase allowances to meet any shortfall. Recent research on how firms make investment decisions under uncertainty (such as when future CO_2 prices can not be accurately estimated) suggests that firms may have a bias towards delaying the implementation of some CO_2 abatement strategies, particularly those involving significant capital investment.[9]

Energy intensity

A number of inputs to production processes could become more expensive under the EU ETS and lead to increased variable costs. Different input costs will fare differently under the EU ETS. Firms will therefore experience different effects depending on the types of input required by their production process.

Energy inputs, particularly electricity, are likely to become more expensive for consumers. The International Energy Agency has estimated that wholesale electricity prices could rise by 21% if the price of allowances under the EU ETS reaches €20 per tonne of CO_2 (see Reinaud, 2004). Under such circumstances, firms that are intensive users of electricity will suffer. Sectors such as cement manufacture and steel manufacture are among the most energy-intensive sectors and most likely to be impacted (see Oxera, 2004).

CAN FIRMS PASS THESE COSTS TO THEIR CUSTOMERS?

The proportion of cost increases that firms will be able to pass through to consumers will depend upon the nature of their output product market. Some firms affected by the EU ETS will be in a much better position to pass through costs than others. The ability to pass through costs will depend upon the following characteristics of their sector.

❑ *elasticity of demand:* Firms in markets where customers are relatively unresponsive to changes in price (are demand-inelastic to changes in price) are likely to be able to pass through a larger proportion of cost increases than firms in markets where customers are highly responsive to changes in price.
❑ *nature of competition:* Firms whose competitors do not face higher costs of the EU ETS (for instance, because they are located outside Europe) will find it hard to pass through higher costs. Firms

selling into product markets with significant levels of international trade face a threat of a reduction in market share if they seek to increase prices.

In general, variable cost increases tend to be passed through more easily in highly competitive markets where retail prices already bear a close resemblance to variable costs. Firms that can pass through a higher proportion of cost increases due to the EU ETS will typically be more profitable; firms that enjoy a wealth benefit and pass through a very high proportion of their costs may actually profit from the EU ETS.

WHAT DO WINNERS AND LOSERS LOOK LIKE?

Table 1 illustrates how the framework developed in this chapter can be applied to a simple comparison between the power generation and aluminium production sectors.

Whether a firm is a *winner* or a *loser* under the EU ETS depends upon the characteristics of the firm and its sector. These factors include the carbon intensity of the sector, the intensity of the use of certain inputs (such as energy) in the production process and the extent to which the firm can pass through higher costs to its customers without losing market share.

Table 1 Comparison between the power generation sector and aluminium production sector

Characteristics of sector	Power generation	Aluminium production
Wealth effect from allowance allocation?	Yes	No
Carbon intensity of process	Depends on the technology used	Irrelevant, as the firm is not a scheme participant
Intensity of energy inputs affected by EU ETS	Depends on the generating technology[10]	High[11]
Elasticity of demand	Demand relatively inelastic	Demand relatively elastic
Nature of competition	Local[12]	Global[13]
Winner or loser?	*Winner*	*Loser*

Firms face a number of choices in how they react to the EU cap-and-trade mechanism. The framework identified in this chapter can be used by managers to help their firms think about the best way to react to a carbon-constrained European economy.

1 Allowances cover CO_2 emissions in the initial phase (2005–7) and wider greenhouse gases in the second phase (2008–12).
2 Regulation is placed upon individual installations owned by the firm.
3 The incentives faced by the firm may alter if the price of allowances rises above the penalty.
4 This is a static analysis that assumes that the market price of the firm's output is unchanged.
5 There may also be other input costs that are affected by the EU ETS.
6 For the sake of completeness, there is a further consideration as to whether the firm should produce at all. The firm should produce whenever price exceeds the firm's average variable costs. Further discussion on the firm's decision to produce can be found in a standard microeconomics textbook.
7 Reinhardt (2000) refers to firms being focused on problem avoidance and risk management rather than on the creation of opportunities made possible by market-based instruments. His view is that, without significant changes in structure and personnel, the full potential of market-based instruments will not be realised.
8 For example, generating plant with lower carbon intensity, such as nuclear- and renewable-fuelled plant, will experience low or no increases in running costs but will still profit from a general rise in the price of electricity. On the other hand, more carbon-intensive generating plant may have more opportunities to alter their use of carbon to profit from the greater amount of free allowances they will receive.
9 This is the "deferral option" identified by de Jong and Walet (2004).
10 Power can be generated from a variety of different technologies. Although all technologies will be energy-intensive in the scientific sense, fossil-fuel generation will using more inputs whose costs have been affected by the EU ETS than, say, wind generation. The firm therefore has the choice of altering its exposure to the effects of the EU ETS through its choice of technology.
11 Electricity is a basic requirement of the primary aluminium production process as it is used to split aluminium oxide into aluminium and oxygen. The firm has little control over its use of electricity as an input to the aluminium production process.
12 Most competitors in the European power market face input cost increase as a result of the EU ETS, which in competitive markets may allow higher costs to be passed to customers without a large loss in market share.
13 Competing firms outside the EU will not face higher input costs as they are not affected by the EU ETS.

REFERENCES

de Jong, and Walet, 2004, *A Guide to Emissions Trading: Risk Management and Business Implications* (London: Risk Books).

Oxera, 2004, "CO_2 emissions trading: How will it affect UK industry", report prepared for the Carbon Trust.

Reinaud, J., 2004, "Emissions trading and its possible impacts on investment decisions in the power sector", International Energy Agency.

Reinhardt, F. L., 2000, *Down to Earth: Applying Business Principles to Environmental Management* (Boston, MA: Harvard Business School Press).

UK Government, 2000, "Climate change – the UK programme", Department of Environment, Transport and the Regions.

13

Banking the Valuation of the Commons

Claire Byers

Fortis Bank

They hang the man and flog the woman
That steal the goose from off the common,
But let the greater villain loose
That steals the common from the goose.

– English folk poem, c 1764

Framing the problem of climate change/global warming/the greenhouse-gas effect, call it what you will, is an intricate one, which requires far-reaching considerations. Many aspects of both "the problem" and any possible solutions do not fall into the traditional remit of environmentalism and, as a result, mitigating climate change can often seem so daunting as to be impossible. It is an issue where seeing the woods from the trees in order to tackle any one of the interrelated issues on its own is notoriously difficult. Yet this is what is being been done, not for the first time, but certainly in the most ambitious way, with the introduction of the European Union Emissions Trading Scheme (EU ETS). The scheme tackles the fact that we're pushing the limits of the natural world's bounty while most economic models still see the environment – or the commons – as being infinitely plentiful.[1] As a result, the environment is not valued in the same way as other goods. The EU ETS changes this by placing a market value on reducing carbon dioxide.

While no one would profess that the scheme is a perfect way in which to tackle the underlying reasons for spiralling anthropogenic emissions, it does go one step towards giving the services and benefits reaped from the natural world as represented by the commons, a value.

With the allocation of European Union Allowances (EUAs) and the valuation of carbon dioxide as a liability, the EU ETS places the onus and the value of reducing emissions – or, in other words, of contributing to improving the commons – on individual companies.

The cap-and-trade nature of the system comes with a strong heritage of effectiveness that has been evidenced through the SO_2 reductions achieved in the US through a similar scheme. Expanding from this, the EU ETS will see trading across 25 countries. With the import of credits from Clean Development Mechanism (CDM) and Joint Implementation (JI) projects (of the Kyoto Protocol) via the Linking Directive, the scheme theoretically allows carbon dioxide to be reduced where it is cheapest. It is the most economically efficient and effective way of reducing emissions and a far cry from the command-and-control policy tactics of yester-year.

EUROPEAN CARBON ALLOWANCES – A NEW ASSET VALUE CREATED

An important aspect of the system is the new asset value created. Using conservative estimates, the total value of the EUAs handed out to companies in Europe will be more than €10 billion per year between 2005 and 2007. The impact of this on the corporate balance sheet and the way it is accounted for will be one of the most important challenges to industry in the coming years.[2] The scheme will not only impact the sectors directly covered under the scheme but, via indirect effects such as the expected increase in power prices (via cost pass-through), all companies and individuals in Europe will be effected by this newly created value.

Furthermore, any asset owned by a company will have a bearing on a potential lender's decision to lend to that company, and EUAs are no different in this respect.

Tracking emissions liability will be a complicated process and will require disclosure of new information by companies to their investors. At this early stage, it is difficult to develop quantitative sectoral data due to the paucity of firm disclosure. However, it is clear that the EU ETS does pose potential earnings impacts.

The greatest carbon risk to shareholder value arises in firms that are in sectors most affected by emissions regulations (steel, cement,

---

PANEL 1 CARBON RISKS TO SHAREHOLDER VALUE

Quantitative risks

❑ Managing the risk that actual emissions exceed the number of EUAs received from the government thereby requiring purchases of EUAs – which have both a cashflow and an earnings impact;

❑ designing a strategy for managing the market risk for buying and selling EUAs;

❑ managing the risk of an earnings impact from higher power prices;

❑ exposure to the need for capital outlays necessary to reduce emissions in an installation; and

❑ failing to be in compliance with the rules of the scheme, necessitating the payment of a fine (€40 per excess tonne of CO_2 emitted between 2005 and 2007, and €100 between 2008 and 2012).

Qualitative risks

❑ Successful monitoring, reporting and accounting management of EUAs and emissions of CO_2;

❑ reputation risk through the process of community stakeholders demanding concrete emissions action from firms and who will increasingly patronise those who can demonstrate such commitment; and

❑ political risk from future regulatory changes and tighter emissions targets.

---

chemicals, energy, building equipment, and pulp and paper sectors) and to those who have not adequately managed carbon risk. The most important of these risks can be categorised as being either qualitative or quantitative as indicated in Panel 1.

Companies can reduce their quantitative risks by adopting strategies similar to the ones at their disposal for managing financial risks. Products like those available in more mature markets are being developed for EUAs to enable firms to hedge their emissions liabilities. Currently, a firm expecting to have an EUA deficit could enter into a forward contract for a fixed volume at a fixed price and delivery, thereby eliminating the price risk and reducing the risk of non-compliance.

As a spot market develops and a reliable index becomes available, a company could hedge their position by swapping a floating carbon permit price for a fixed price using exactly the same principal as is used with interest-rate derivatives. Consider a company

PANEL 2 EUROPEAN STEEL COMPANY

This case demonstrates the earnings impact on a fictitious loss-making European Steel Company using different values for EUAs.

For steel companies, which are both energy- and emissions-intensive, there is a direct correlation between output and CO_2 emissions.

The case assumes that the company in question increases production and as a result its annual emissions exceed its allocated EUAs by 10%. The scenario shows the impact on earnings rising from 2.4% where EUAs trade at €9 rising to 8.1% in the case that EUAs trade at €30. Power prices are not varied in this model yet these variations will also have a strong impact on the earnings.

With impacts on earnings as high as these, it is clear that for an energy- and emissions-intensive producer (such as a steel or cement firm) buying EUAs has the potential to take a material bite out of earnings.

Case 1: Loss-making European Steel Company

EUA allocation, tonnes	10,725,000	10,725,000	10,725,000	10,725,000	10,725,000
Actual ETS emissions	11,261,250	11,261,250	11,261,250	11,261,250	11,261,250
Difference	536,250	536,250	536,250	536,250	536,250
Delta factor	5%	5%	5%	5%	5%
EUA price	9	12	18	25	30
Cost of additional EUAs	(4,826,250)	(6,435,000)	(9,652,500)	(13,406,250)	(16,087,500)
Percentage of sales	–0.1%	–0.1%	–0.1%	–0.2%	–0.2%
2003 op loss	(199,000,000)	(199,000,000)	(199,000,000)	(199,000,000)	(199,000,000)
Adjusted loss	(203,826,250)	(205,435,000)	(208,652,500)	(212,406,250)	(215,087,500)
Earnings impact	2.4%	3.2%	4.9%	6.7%	8.1%

Source: Fortis Bank Equity Research

who has implemented a project that reduces their emissions and would like to sell their additional EUAs while ensuring they receive a certain price for them. In this fixed-for-floating swap construction, the buyer of the swap (the company) agrees to make periodic payments to the seller (usually a financial intermediary) based on a fixed price for a specific quantity of EUAs. At the same time, the seller agrees to make periodic payments to the buyer based on a floating price (the variable market price) for the same quantity of

EUAs. The floating price would be based on a well-known reference price or index for the EUAs, and only a net payment is made at each payment date based on the difference between the floating and fixed prices. This fixed-for-floating EUA price swap enables the buyer of the swap to guarantee that they receive the fixed price for a certain volume of EUAs over a particular period.

Looking further ahead, options and other derivatives are likely to emerge as being the ideal product for protecting against market fluctuations.

As can be seen from the case study in Panel 2, the EU ETS should start to give investors reason to differentiate stocks based on the efficacy of management's handling of EUAs, especially as the price of EUAs rises. Clearly, the firms whose managers have had the foresight to think about the complexity and opportunities of properly managing their emissions and their EUAs (liabilities and assets), and adopt appropriate early strategies, are better positioned. Companies in some sectors may have difficulty coping with cost implications of the EU ETS, but those who are able to adopt appropriate management strategies are the ones that will thrive. In fact, when other factors that impact the profitability of a company are considered – the fluctuation in oil prices and exchange rates, for example – the EUA price and position are just another variable to be managed. The management's degree of proactivity in reporting comprehensive environmental data will speak volumes for its ability to handle this new variable.

Another dimension to valuation of stock is how the management handles carbon risk, from a strategy, communication and operations perspective. Rather than considering the EU ETS as a negative development for their business, companies at the forefront of emissions management treat it as something that sustains existing business and creates new opportunities for competitive advantage. This supports the notion that environmental performance is a proxy for quality of management, and that there is a strong correlation between environmental performance and stock price performance.

DEVELOPING A MARKET TO KICK-START THE FINANCING OF EMISSION REDUCTION PROJECTS

At present, projects that include emission reduction assets are generally going to be economic and financeable without taking into account the value of these reductions. All usual project financing risks apply and the carbon factor is often (although not always) simply the icing on the cake – an additional value taken into account in the best-case scenario.

Projects reducing emissions in installations covered under the EU ETS have two new risks to deal with alongside the traditional definitions of project finance risk. These are the EUA market price and the uncertainties relating to the EUA allocation plans (for companies and installations), especially for the second trading period in Europe (or the Kyoto Protocol period 2008–12 for the rest of the Annex I countries who have ratified the protocol). Dealing with market risks has been discussed in some detail above. In Europe, the risks associated with uncertainties on the allocation plans precludes much of the long-term certainty required for planning and financing projects to reduce emissions since the installation owner simply does not know how many spare EUAs they will have after implementing their project. In the case that a certain return from the EUAs is required in order to make the project profitable, no project will occur until the quantity of EUAs that will be available to sell becomes clear.

The story is more complicated for the CDM, as it raises many concerns as to the additionality of a specific project.[3] Without a reliable market price and a predictable and efficient approval process for these projects through the CDM Executive Board, the risks of price and actually having the credits delivered (delivery risk) make it difficult to fairly value the emission reductions. As a result it is problematic to include them as an income flow in the financing. So, determining additionality remains complex, few credits reach the market, the market for credits remains thin and the confidence needed to boost the whole system falters.

Nonetheless, various innovative initiatives such as carbon funds and facilities have sought to harness the opportunities offered through the CDM and provide price and delivery risk reduction through building a diversified portfolio of emissions credits from different technologies and countries.

Despite the teething problems that currently beset the EU ETS, it is already helping to create a market into which credits from CDM projects can be sold and used for compliance in a regulated system. It is this market that is becoming increasingly transparent and driven by fundamentals (fuel price and weather in particular)

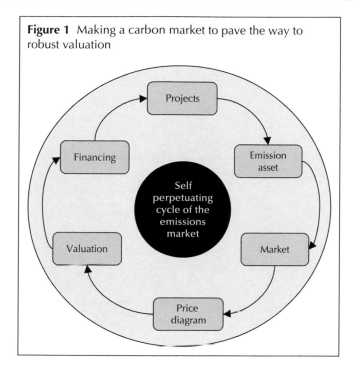

Figure 1 Making a carbon market to pave the way to robust valuation

that will give project financiers the confidence to take emissions credits as an assured form of income.

As Figure 1 shows, increasing confidence in the existence of a market for EUAs and emissions credits drives financing, which reduces emissions. In addition, it spreads the valuation of mitigating greenhouse gas emissions outside of Europe, into other sectors and into gases other than CO_2.

As can be seen from the above discussion, an increasingly liquid and reliable market for emission assets, in combination with long-term political certainty, is needed to kick-start the self-perpetuating cycle that will lead to real emission reductions and the mitigation of climate change.[4] In Europe, the forward market for European EUAs has been active for over two years and in March 2005 more than 15 million tonnes of EUAs were traded, which is 50% more than the total traded in 2004. Several countries now have operational registries and have allocated the EUAs to industry. This first allocation sparked immediate spot trading and several exchanges are already offering cleared forward trading with the spot market set to follow as and when new registries become active. The traded market is expected to grow to €2.5–3 billion in 2005, up from €200 million in 2004.

The EU ETS is certainly an excellent start to creating a market with the depth and liquidity needed to reliably value the reduction of CO_2 emissions. Yet, as can be seen from the case study, accessing this market will remain an issue for the large majority of companies covered under the EU ETS. It is the task of the market makers to

PANEL 3 CASE STUDY: ACCESSING THE EU ETS MARKET – GETTING READY TO TRADE

It seems fairly simple: determine the EUA position in relation to expected emissions, determine whether reductions can be made more cheaply in-house or on the market and buy or sell the difference on the market. Unfortunately, there are several more hoops to jump through to get to the market.

An individual in the company has to be responsible for dealing with the emissions balance, which may mean hiring an EU ETS professional. Regulatory clearance to trade has to be sought (although in most jurisdictions this is nothing more than a check) and transactions have to be tracked in the internal systems. Credit lines and contracts need to be put in place with trading counterparties and the internal balance of the company has to be determined. Taxation issues on the transfer and transaction of EUAs need to be addressed and accounting methodologies finalised.

Having determined the position concerning assets *versus* liabilities (EUAs *versus* forecast emissions of CO_2) through implementing a monitoring and reporting protocol, a strategy needs to be developed in order to approach the market. The price on the forward market has reached intraday volatility of 21% (22 March 2005) so coming to buy or sell on the market at any one given time can present a huge market risk.

In the near future, as the market develops and becomes more liquid, it will be possible to reduce this risk by taking out derivative hedges for a given volume of EUAs with a bank or other trading intermediary.

Finally, to have full access to market data, connections to the exchanges such as the European Climate Exchange and Nord Pool and to the OTC (over-the-counter) brokers, screens have to be put in place requiring concerted systems, IT and legal coordination.

If all this seems like a huge amount of administration for a new business that is not core to the company's operation, it is possible to outsource the entire process via a market access and position management agreement with financial or other intermediaries who have already been through this process.

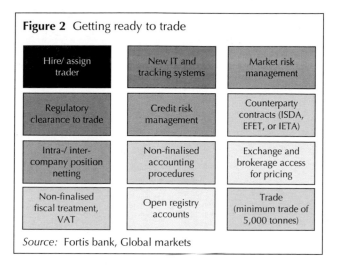

Figure 2 Getting ready to trade

Hire/ assign trader	New IT and tracking systems	Market risk management
Regulatory clearance to trade	Credit risk management	Counterparty contracts (ISDA, EFET, or IETA)
Intra-/ inter-company position netting	Non-finalised accounting procedures	Exchange and brokerage access for pricing
Non-finalised fiscal treatment, VAT	Open registry accounts	Trade (minimum trade of 5,000 tonnes)

Source: Fortis bank, Global markets

ensure that these companies have the access they need in order to assure the integrity of the system as a whole. If companies are unable to bring their EUAs to market or, conversely, to purchase EUAs to cover their emissions liability, the least cost of reducing emissions will not be achieved.

CONCLUSIONS

EU environment ministers have now agreed on ambitious post-2012 climate goals for upcoming international climate negotiations, proposing that greenhouse-gas emissions in developed countries should be reduced by as much as 15–30% by 2020 and 60–80% by 2050. These goals, while non-binding, demonstrate the continued leadership in Europe to tackling the climate issue as well as indicating the requirement for real technological and habitual change. When setting our sights on these ambitious targets, the need for a market mechanism to act as a central valuation system to start managing, preserving and replacing the services provided by the commons becomes clear. Whether valuing the priceless is acceptable from an idealistic perspective, not valuing the commons at all means that they will continue to be degraded, which is most definitely an unattractive prospect.

It remains to be seen how other big emitters in the world will go forward in these discussions, but what is clear is that valuing emissions of CO_2 in Europe alone will not lead to any real mitigation of burgeoning greenhouse-gas concentrations. The system needs to be closed by bringing the rest of the world into this new market. Only in this way will we see a liquid market for emission reductions that makes an impact on stock valuation, forces emitters to address their pollution of the commons and drives finance initiatives. The role for the politicians is clear and, once the regulations are in place, the market makers will drive the cycle to deliver efficient and effective reductions of greenhouse gases.

While the EU ETS is only a tentative step on a long journey towards mitigating climate change, it is an exceptionally ambitious scheme that will pave the way to a worldwide acceptance of market mechanisms to deal with distributed and complicated social and economic problems that degrade the environment.

In the words of Shellenberger and Nordhaus (2004), "Global warming is not an issue that will be resolved by the passage of one statute. This is nothing short of the beginning of an effort to transform the world energy economy, vastly improving efficiency and diversifying it away from its virtually exclusive reliance on fossil fuels."

1   The term "the commons" derives from the 1968 essay entitled "The tragedy of the commons" by Garrett Hardin. The tragedy of the commons is a metaphor for the problem that it is hard to coordinate and pay for public goods – that is, things that belong to everyone and to no one simultaneously. In his metaphor, Hardin represents the commons as a pasture used by a group of people. Each individual owns sheep and has the incentive to put more and more sheep on the pasture to gain, privately. The overall effect when many individuals do this overwhelms the capacity of the pasture to provide food and the sheep cannot all survive.

2   The currently unfinished accounting interpretation of IFRIC3 values EUAs as an intangible asset to be recorded on the balance sheet and emissions as liabilities accounted for in the profit-and-loss account. This difference will lead to volatility in the profitability of a company, which is related to the price of EUAs and not to the performance of the company itself. These fluctuations need to be understood and accepted by investors until such time that an updated approach to accounting for EUAs and emissions is developed.

3   Additionality: Various tools have been developed in order to assess whether a project will emit less than it would do under the "business-as-usual" situation. These include identification of alternatives to the project activity, investment analysis to determine that the proposed project activity is not the most economically or financially attractive, and practice analysis.

4   Emission assets as described here encompasses EUAs, allowances from other similar systems that may emerge, credits from JI and CDM projects or any other asset from the reduction of greenhouse gas emissions that can be used for compliance with a target under a regulated emission reduction scheme.

REFERENCES

Shellenberger, M., and T. Nordhaus, 2004, "The death of environmentalism".

14

Weather Derivatives and Carbon Emissions Trading

Stephen Jewson; Stuart Jones

RMS; Centrica

In this chapter we discuss the European carbon emissions trading market, the weather derivatives market and the potential links between the two. We start by introducing and describing the carbon emissions trading market, and we explore the factors that drive changes in the prices of the allowances traded in that market. We will argue that both supply and demand for allowances is strongly impacted by the weather, creating significant weather risks for those involved in such trading. We then describe weather derivatives and the weather derivatives market. Finally, we discuss how companies exposed to weather risk in the carbon trading market could potentially use weather derivatives to hedge that risk.

The Kyoto Protocol and the Marrakech Accords

The Kyoto Protocol sets legally binding targets to limit or reduce greenhouse gas (GHG) emissions. It also defines three methods by which the cost of limiting GHGs can be reduced. One of these methods is emissions trading. The emissions reductions set in the Kyoto Protocol and the Marrakech Accords add up to a reduction in GHG emissions of more than 5% below 1990 levels by the end of the first commitment period of 2008–12 for Annex 1 (developed-economy) nations.

The EU Emissions Trading Scheme (EU ETS)

The European Union's 8% reduction target is made up of separate targets for each of the 25 member states of the recently expanded

EU. The EU hopes to achieve this 8% target using a number of policy instruments designed to reduce emissions. One of these is the EU ETS. The EU has set up guidelines for how such a scheme should work, and exactly how each member state interprets the EU ETS guidelines is decided by individual national government. The EU are introducing the EU ETS in a two-phase approach. Phase I, which runs from 2005 to 2007, is regarded as a test phase. The time period of Phase II is aligned with the Kyoto commitment period of 2008–12, and during this phase the legally binding agreements of the Kyoto Protocol take effect.

The currency of the EU ETS is a European Union Allowance (EUA) and is equivalent to 1 tonne of CO_2. The basic idea of the scheme is that companies who emit CO_2 will have to cover their emissions either by using allowances allocated to them by their government, or by purchasing allowances from other companies involved in the scheme (that could be in other countries within the EU). Any emissions in excess of the number of allowances surrendered for compliance in a given period will attract a significant fine.

Approximately 46% of all CO_2 emissions across the EU25 are captured under the EU ETS. These emissions come from around 12,500 individual installations, in industrial sectors including power generation, oil and gas, iron and steel, pulp and paper, and building materials.

The significant event was the start of Phase I of the EU scheme itself, on 1 January 2005. The market responded with a big increase in trading activity. At this point, most of the traders are major European energy companies. However, more and more financial institutions are getting involved, attracted by the increasing liquidity and high volatility.

Market fundamentals

What determines the prices of the EU ETS allowances? The emissions market, like any other, is driven primarily by two key fundamentals, namely, underlying fuel prices and weather. We discuss each of these below.

The relation between fuel prices and the price of EUAs

Of the 46% of emissions across Europe captured by the EU ETS, 65% comes from the power-generation sector, so much of the impact of the scheme is on this sector, and much of the influence on prices will come from economic considerations within this sector. The power market in Europe is dominated by four major types of generation: burning coal, burning natural gas, hydroelectric power and nuclear power. Each type of generation has a carbon intensity, defined as how much CO_2 is produced to generate 1MWh of electricity. The carbon intensity of hydro and nuclear is virtually zero. This makes them relatively more valuable in an emissions-trading world. Burning coal and gas, however, generates significant volumes of CO_2. The level of emissions depends on the efficiency of the plant and the exact composition of the fuel, but in general burning coal emits around twice as much carbon as burning gas (0.9 tonnes/MWh *versus* 0.43 tonnes/MWh). Thus the EU ETS makes coal less attractive than before as a source of power relative to gas, and both are less attractive relative to hydro and nuclear.

Nuclear and often hydro generation run as base load, delivering a steady and inexpensive flow of electricity. Unlike coal- and gas-based generation, nuclear in particular cannot respond to rapid changes in demand. Prior to the EU ETS, the decision on which of coal or gas to use to make up the shortfall left by nuclear and hydro and to satisfy fluctuations in demand for power was mainly made according to the relative costs of the two fuels. The prices of these fuels relative to the cost of power are known as the "spark spread" for gas and the "dark spread" for coal. Now with emissions obligations placed on the generation sector, the cost of CO_2 is also part of the decision as to which fuel to burn.

The price of EUAs is determined by supply and demand, and is thus influenced by factors such as the relative prices of the various underlying fuels and generation methods, and, in particular, by the difference between the price of coal and the price of gas. From a theoretical economic point of view one might argue that the price of EUAs should adjust until it reaches an equilibrium at which there is no benefit from switching from coal to gas or vice-versa. If the price were higher than this equilibrium level then one should burn more gas, and if the price were lower then one should burn more coal. The fuel prices are in turn not fixed, but are affected by both demand and a number of fundamentals such as the oil price, foreign exchange rates, freight costs and, of course, the EUA price itself. As a result of this complexity, and the interacting nature of fuel and

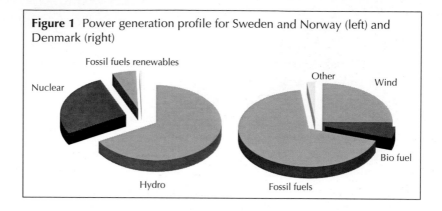

Figure 1 Power generation profile for Sweden and Norway (left) and Denmark (right)

EUA prices, it is not easy to predict in advance what the price of the EUAs will be.

The relation between weather and the price of EUAs

The other factor that is likely to influence the price of carbon allowances is the weather. This is mainly because weather can influence both the supply of and the demand for energy, as we shall see below.

On the demand side, weather conditions determine the usage pattern for energy on a daily basis. A colder-than-average day could lead to an increase in heating load; a wetter-than-average day could lead to an increased lighting load; and a warmer-than-average day could lead to an increase in air-conditioning load. These changes in demand for heating and power then affect power prices, fuel prices and ultimately the price of EUAs. On the supply side the weather has a profound effect on the availability of certain types of power generation, most notably hydropower and wind power.

Different countries in Europe have different configurations for meeting their energy demand, and this affects how weather impacts energy and EUA prices. Also, some groups of countries have interconnectivity that allow them to trade power, while others are reliant solely on their own resources.

As an example of how these effects can work, we consider the Scandinavian region. Within this region, both Sweden and Norway are reliant on hydropower for a considerable percentage of their energy requirements. They also import power from Denmark, which generates that power using wind farms and coal burning. A low precipitation season in Sweden and Norway leads to diminished reservoir levels and places restrictions on the energy that can be produced. This leads to increases in the amount of power imported from Denmark, and hence increases in the amount of coal that Denmark needs to burn. Putting this all together, a dry season in Sweden and Norway can reasonably be expected to lead to an increase in coal generation in Denmark and therefore an increase in emissions and an increase in the demand for EUAs from the Danish generators. This in turn would be expected to increase the price of EUAs, all other things being equal.

We have seen above that the weather is likely to have a large impact on supply, demand and price of EUAs. However, we cannot control the weather. Companies that have exposure to the emissions market are therefore exposed to significant weather risk. How can this exposure be managed? There are various possibilities, including weather derivatives.

WEATHER DERIVATIVES

Weather derivatives are financial products that allow businesses to protect themselves against adverse fluctuations in the weather. Whether the climate is changing or not, they make good financial sense for companies whose revenues are highly weather-sensitive. Indeed, many companies in different industries in Europe, the US and Japan use weather derivatives to hedge their weather risks. The size of the weather market can be judged using figures from the Weather Risk Management Association's annual survey. In 2004 this survey reported a total notional value of trades of nearly US$5 billion. The Chicago Mercantile Exchange also reported more than 20,000 trades.

Weather can both bring benefits and cause harm. The negative effects of weather can manifest themselves in many different ways: a reduction in sales volume, downward pressure on sales prices and, most extremely, property damage and business interruption. Property damage and business interruption can usually be insured against by using traditional insurance products, but weather-related fluctuations in sales volume or price cannot. This is where weather derivatives provide a unique benefit: they allow any exposure to the weather to be hedged, irrespective of the nature of the risk.

The industry where weather hedging is currently most commonly used is the retail natural gas industry. Natural gas sales increase in volumes in a cold winter, and hence the profitability of gas retail companies is very highly (inversely) correlated to temperature. Appropriate weather hedging can reduce this weather exposure to almost zero, allowing predictable and reliable profits from year to year.

Weather derivative definitions

Weather derivative contracts all have the same underlying structure. They are based on:

❑ a weather station;
❑ a weather variable such as precipitation, wind speed or temperature;
❑ an index derived from the weather variable such as average temperature over a season; and
❑ a contract structure.

The contract structure requires a little more explanation. In a *swap* contract two entities enter into a deal on a particular weather index at a negotiated strike level (which is usually close to historical average levels for the index). For typical over-the-counter (OTC) swap contracts, no money changes hands until the end of the deal, and the settlement amount is proportional to the extent to which the weather index lies above or below the strike level. If the index is above the strike then the seller pays the buyer, while if it is below the strike the buyer pays the seller.

Option contracts, while still based on a weather index, are similar to insurance. The buyer of an option pays a premium upfront for the right to buy (call option) or sell (a put option) the swap at a certain strike level, usually a little away from the average. For example, if a call option is structured to hedge against a high index value and the index settles higher than the strike, the buyer receives a payout proportional to how far above the strike the index settles.

The weather derivatives market

The *primary* weather derivatives market consists of banks, reinsurance companies and hedge funds selling weather hedging deals to corporate end-users. It is the engine that ultimately drives the whole of the weather market. Deals in the primary market are often very large, with many millions of dollars in payout possible. They are also highly secretive. The *secondary* market consists of the same companies, and some speculators, trading among themselves. This trading serves the economic purposes of allowing dispersal of end-user weather risk among the traders, and of creating a market with transparent market pricing. It may also allow informed traders to make money from the other participants in the market. Some secondary market trades occur through voice brokers, while others go through the Chicago Mercantile Exchange, which supports trading of monthly and seasonal temperature contracts on fifteen locations in the US, five in Europe and two in Japan.

Weather derivative pricing

How are weather derivative contracts priced? The "price" of a *swap* contract is given by the strike level at which that contract is traded. The "fair" level for this strike is usually taken to be the expected value for the index. Pricing the contract then becomes a question of estimating this expected index, and this is more or less a meteorological question. For instance, before the contract has started one can estimate the expected index using historical weather data, with appropriate treatment of trends. As the contract approaches, seasonal forecasts, which predict whether upcoming seasons will be overall warm or cold or wet or dry, can also be used (particularly in the US). And finally, when pricing in the few days preceding the contract and during the contract itself, weather forecasts may add additional information.

The price of a weather *option* contract is known as the premium. The "fair premium" is usually taken to be the expected payout. The expected payout of the option is estimated using historical weather data, again with appropriate treatment of trends, and maybe with a distribution fitted to interpolate or extrapolate the historical values. The premium an end-user would pay for an option when hedging their risk is likely to be a little above the fair premium to compensate the risk taker for the risk they are taking on. The size of this risk loading will depend on whether the deal is standard or exotic: an option based on temperatures measured in London, Chicago, New York or Tokyo would have a much lower risk premium than

> ## PANEL 1: AN EXAMPLE OF A WEATHER DERIVATIVE
> ABC gas company don't like warm winters because they sell less natural gas. In fact, they can lose up to £10 million in a warm winter relative to an average year. They decide to use weather derivatives to help. They analyse their historical revenues against historical weather and conclude that there is a strong relationship with heating degree days (HDDs) based on London Heathrow from November to March. Because of this they decide to base their weather derivative on heating degree days. This has the added advantage that this is a well-traded index, which means that they are likely to get a good deal because of the price transparency brought by the trading. In the first year they buy a put option, which will pay them if the number of HDDs is low (corresponding to a warm winter). A reasonable estimate of the average number of HDDs at this location and over this period would be around 1,670 HDDs, with a standard deviation of 120 HDDs. ABC decide to hedge themselves from 1,650 HDDs downwards. They buy an option with a "tick" of £50,000/HDD, and a limit of £10,000,000 (this limit corresponds to 200 HDDs below the strike, or 1,450 HDDs). They pay a premium of £2,000,000. When the actual weather comes in at 1,500 HDD they receive a payout of £7,500,000, and hence an overall profit on the weather derivative of £5,500,000. In the second year they sell a swap with a strike of 1,670 HDDs, a tick of £50,000/HDD and limits at both ends of £10,000,000. Again, the weather comes in warm at 1,640 HDDs. They lose money on their business because of the warm weather but pick up £1,500,000 on the weather swap.

an option based on precipitation on a minor location. For certain locations weather option pricing also has elements of the Black–Scholes-type pricing methods common in other derivatives markets. For instance, if a swap contract is being traded heavily and can be used to hedge the option, then it makes sense to price the option using the swap level rather than use an estimate of the expected settlement index.

Temperature trends
We have mentioned above that trends have to be taken into account when pricing weather derivatives. This is because most meteorological data, and especially temperatures, show large trends over the last 50 years. For instance, most temperature data from 50 years ago show values much colder than measurements made today.

These trends are partly due to urbanisation and partly due to global warming. There are two ways that trends can be taken into account when pricing weather derivatives. One can either use averages of only the most recent data (using only the last 10 years is very common) or use much more data (maybe 30 or 50 years) and try to model the trend. Using more data has the advantage that it will give a better estimate of the risk of extreme weather, but is accurate only if the trend can be modelled reasonably well.

In terms of the climate-change discussion, the most interesting aspect of the relationship between temperature trends and weather derivatives pricing is that the prices that one observes in the weather market for temperature derivatives very clearly price-in information about the warming trend. The argument about the size of the warming trend (whatever its cause) is not just an academic one for weather traders: the trend is the most important factor for pricing and millions of dollars stand to be made or lost according to whether you understand the trend. Weather market prices show that traders believe that the trend over the last 30 years is both real and large. Furthermore, the prices are continually adjusting year on year as the trend develops. We believe that the weather market prices for locations such as London and New York give both the most accurate and the most accurately updating estimates of the level of the current climate that are available.

One consequence of climate-change trends may be that weather extremes will become more frequent. This would mean that the need to hedge weather risk will increase, further encouraging growth in the use of weather derivatives.

Weather derivatives and renewable energy

As an example of how weather derivatives can be used, we now discuss how weather derivatives can support renewable-energy projects. In particular we consider wind farms, although similar principles would apply to other (slightly more speculative) sources of renewable energy, such as solar cells and wave energy.

The financial viability of wind farms suffers greatly from the variability of the wind from season to season. There are two possible solutions to this problem, which can be used separately or together. The first is to use geographical diversification: build many wind farms in different places, and hope that the wind will always be blowing somewhere. This may often not be practical, for a number of reasons. The second solution is to use weather derivatives. Weather derivatives can be tailored to the risk in question, and hence can reduce the weather risk greatly, even for a single site. Furthermore, use can be made of weather derivatives even before a wind farm has been built. If a weather derivative is purchased at the same time as a loan is taken out to build the wind farm, then it may be possible to negotiate a better rate for the loan interest on the basis that the revenues from a well-hedged wind farm will be more stable and less risky than those from an unhedged one.

Because wind farms are, by design, often built in remote and isolated areas it is not always easy to get appropriate data on which to base the weather derivative. If there is a nearby weather station, it may be possible to use that. If not, then one can set up a weather station at the location in question. With as little as a year of data it is usually then possible to identify relationships between the wind at the site and the wind at a nearby weather station or group of stations. Assuming that the misfit in such relations is not too large, one can then build a hedge on the nearby station or stations, and the pricing analysis can be based on the longer record of data at those stations. These methods work well as long as the hedging periods are rather long (seasonal rather than daily). This is because the correlations between winds at different locations are much higher over long periods than short periods.

WEATHER DERIVATIVES AND CARBON TRADING
We have discussed the carbon trading market, and concluded that the suppy, demand and price of EUAs traded in that market is likely to be influenced by weather in different parts of Europe. As an example we argued that levels of precipitation in Sweden and Norway could affect prices by changing the demand for coal-generated power in Denmark. Other European weather patterns such as temperature fluctuations in London or rain in Spain, are also likely to be important. As a result of the impact of weather, companies that participate in the carbon market are likely to be exposed to significant weather risk.

We have also described the weather derivatives market, which exists to provide financial contracts that can hedge exposure to weather fluctuations. Putting these two together, it seems that the weather derivatives market may be able to play a significant role in helping companies that trade in the carbon market to hedge their weather risk. What challenges need to be overcome to make that happen? The main challenge is to actually quantify the impact of weather on the supply, demand and price of EUAs. Given the geographical diversity of the EU and the complexity of the European energy markets, the influence of weather on the price of an EUA is a very complex issue that is not yet properly understood. This is a work in progress, but one that will be made much easier once more EUA price data are available. Having quantified the effects of weather on the supply, demand and price of EUAs, designing appropriate weather derivative hedges will be relatively easy. Such hedges could be based on individual locations, or could aggregate a number of the weather effects likely to affect the price of EUAs, such as precipitation in Scandinavia, temperature in the UK and so on.

Weather derivatives could then be used in a number of ways: for example by energy companies who may have to buy more EUAs in some years than others, by financial institutions that sell EUA price hedges, or by speculators in hedge funds seeking an arbitrage opportunity between the carbon, weather and energy markets. In this way, using the weather derivatives market may help to make the fluctuations in the supply, demand and price of EUAs less painful.

SUMMARY

We have discussed the relationships between the weather derivatives market, climate change and carbon trading in the EU ETS. Our main points can be summarised as follows.

❑ The supply, demand and price of allowances in the European carbon trading market is strongly influenced by weather in different parts of Europe, and so participants in this market have significant weather risk.
❑ Weather derivatives exist to allow companies to hedge themselves against weather-related swings in revenues. They are used by firms from a wide range of industries from gas and power companies to restaurants, construction companies and agricultural organisations.

❑ Use of weather derivatives makes good financial sense independently of the issues related to climate change and carbon trading. But there are also several ways that weather derivatives are linked to climate change and the new carbon trading markets.

1) First, climate change may lead to more extreme weather, in which case the need to use weather derivatives to hedge weather fluctuations will be greater than it is now.

2) Secondly, weather derivatives pricing works in such a way that it adapts automatically as the climate changes. This means that even as the climate changes, weather derivatives will remain a cost-effective hedge for weather risk. In fact, the prices on weather derivatives markets may be the most up-to-date and accurate view of the current climate, since they take into account all the available information about climate-change trends.

3) Thirdly, weather derivatives are an ideal tool for hedging the weather risk associated with wind farms, thus overcoming the problem that the revenue from wind farms is highly sensitive to season-to-season fluctuations in the weather.

4) Finally, companies that are exposed to weather risk because of the ETS (either because of fluctuations in supply and demand, or because of fluctuations in price), will be able to use weather derivatives to hedge some of that risk.

15

Verifying Value: The Anchor for the Carbon Emissions Markets

James Anderson

BSI

While the Kyoto Protocol struggled through summits and endless arguments both at industry sector level and intergovernmental and governmental level before being finally ratified, the introduction of the European Union Emissions Trading Scheme (EU ETS) on 1 January 2005, under the auspices of the EU Emissions Trading Directive, became the first pan-European piece of legislation that focused everyone's attention.

Despite the deadlock on future climate-change commitments by the US impacting the United Nations timetable of the Kyoto Protocol, the concept of tradable allowances has by far outweighed the implementation issues surrounding emissions trading. However, verification, as this chapter argues, is the anchor of the carbon markets. The verification of carbon emissions is a key factor in the development and credibility of emissions trading markets, such as under EU ETS and the Kyoto Protocol's flexible mechanisms.

THE UK ETS EXPERIENCE

The United Kingdom became the real pioneer as well as a trend-setter for emissions trading when it launched its UK Emissions Trading Scheme (UK ETS) in 2002. There are three principal features of the UK ETS that have made it a unique financial as well as an environmental venture. First, the bidding process to allocate £215 million of incentive capital to 31 of the top emitters in the UK enthused both company executives and those in the trading arena.

Secondly, the scheme runs for five years and allows underachievers to purchase carbon reduction units to meet their targets while adhering to key global principles such as transparency and consistency. Thirdly, but more importantly from the abatement cost aspect, it did not allow "double-counting". Hence reductions under "business-as-usual" conditions or subject to Integrated Pollution Control cannot be counted for UK ETS reduction targets.

Perhaps some of the other major benefits of such pioneering schemes may be taken for granted. These include capacity building at both regulatory and practitioner level, heightening awareness in the financial trading and prospecting arena, and widening the role of energy and environmental managers. The National Audit Office, which carried out an analysis of the UK ETS, focusing on its cost-effectiveness, concluded that some 66% of the emission reductions were attributable to the UK ETS. Furthermore, it pump-primed the carbon trade economy.

Although the UK ETS is a voluntary scheme, it has all the features of a legislative instrument embodied in a number of supporting framework documents. The most important financial aspect became the registry of verified or tradable allowances kept by the Department of Environment, Food and Rural Affairs (Defra). Some argue that this scheme turned out to be "the big emitters' club", not allowing the medium-sized organisations to benefit from participating into it. The counterargument to this is that most of such smaller industries had already been party to the climate-change levy and relative targets either individually or through their industry sector association.

Our success in verification of UK ETS baselines, annual emissions targets and the overachievement of relative targets in the climate-change agreements helped boost the liquidity and value of tradable allowances. This verification success spanned not only whole-sector group verifications but also included a wide range of large, medium-sized and small manufacturers.

The UK ETS finally agreed bid value of 1 tonne of carbon dioxide equivalent (tCO_2e) settled at about £53 for the 31 companies taking part in the £215 million voluntary market. This has been the highest financial carbon value to date! Such high value elevated the importance of managing, and setting a solid foundation, for the importance of the confidence needed in the market through verification.

The UK ETS acted as a precursor to the EU ETS, the latter being mandatory with a far-reaching and much wider remit in tackling emissions.

Strategically, the cap-and-trade system is much easier for organisations to embrace than any other system. The major deciding factor has always been the average or rising abatement cost of reduction technology, as legislation becomes more integrated and more complex.

The UK ETS market is extremely small in terms of the number of participating companies and the initial bid price is extremely different from regional or national unit prices traded in open markets.

The national allocation plans, introducing national emission caps combined with the EU non-compliance penalty figure of €40 per tonne, were the first stabilising element of the emissions market values with the EU market. For example, BSI so far have verified 190 million tCO_2e with an approximate market value of €1.2 billion. The major factor in the tradability of any allowances is the confidence the traders place on the accuracy and transparency of the reported emission reductions.

VERIFYING VALUE

Verification is a key tool to ensure both financial and environmental integrity. It is the activity that provides the financial and environmental credibility of an emissions trading system. Verification of carbon emissions covers a much wider arena than just auditing financial figures. A company asserting emission reductions is warranted to prove its correct attitude towards how it identifies, monitors, manages and reports its emissions, while it also needs to demonstrate its commitment as well as faithful representation of all facts relating to its greenhouse gases (GHGs). Risks can emanate from a number of areas: errors, omissions or violations.

Verification cannot eliminate or guarantee the elimination of such risks, which may result in misstatements or inaccurate reduction units. Verification, when carried out properly, can greatly minimise the misstatements by identifying and minimising those risks. To arrive at a reliable, active and healthy carbon market we need to instil confidence in a number of circles, namely the market traders, those who purchase and sell, the regulators and the verifiers.

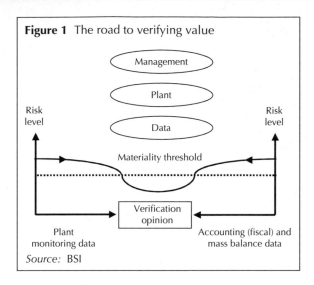

Figure 1 The road to verifying value

Management

Plant

Data

Risk level

Risk level

Materiality threshold

Verification opinion

Plant monitoring data

Accounting (fiscal) and mass balance data

Source: BSI

The verification of carbon emissions is a key factor in the success of emissions trading markets. Operators of installations, or developers of projects, must incorporate the requirement for the verification process within their plans, to ensure time, resource and budget is available. Verification will provide the operators with an independent opinion of the accuracy of reported emissions data. The independence adds confidence, and hence the "perception" held in the market or in those who are very active in the market. Verification has also helped identify operational and management risks that would not have otherwise been identified.

Verification involves a trained team of individuals to conduct an independent assessment of three aspects of the data reporting system. These key areas, assessed during the verification, are the management control of the system, the plant monitoring processes and the accuracy of datasets (see Figure 1). The verification will be conducted against the principles of completeness, consistency, accuracy, faithfulness and materiality. These are often best managed through an acknowledged framework, such as the international environmental management system ISO 14001. Our emissions verification services have evolved from the position of being a recognised expert in the certification of environmental management systems. This has enabled the understanding of key risks associated with

PANEL 1 THE PROCESS

Verification follows a procedure of strategic review to:

❑ understand the emissions profile;
❑ identify any key risk areas for verification;
❑ review reported datasets and evidence; and
❑ peer-review, having an assessor independent of the process reviewing the verification decision.

Accreditation is the process of licensing verifiers to conduct the verification work. A thorough review of the verifier's management system is conducted to ensure the integrity and consistency of their own verification procedure and to ensure that it conforms to agreed guidelines for the schemes within which they operate.

emissions verification, in terms of the management control, plant monitoring and data accuracy.

Emissions trading schemes have greatly contributed to the recognition of much wider stakeholder community than was initially thought of. The financial-sector members such as banks, insurers, underwriters and traders are now very interested in the knowledge of the depth, breadth and the level of complexity or the methodologies utilised for the verification.

The verification process therefore provides the anchor for the trading market. Without transparent data-collection processes and independently verified data, the carbon commodity markets simply could not function. The verifier will unlock the market value of clients' reported emissions data and respective tonnage of carbon, at both entity and project levels. It is the robustness of the accreditation process that verifiers must subject themselves to that ensures confidence in the verification activity.

The UK ETS is based on the key principles of faithful representation, accuracy, reliability, completeness and transparency. In order to ensure that the participants deliver on these key principles, the reporting protocols explicitly define what sources of GHGs are to be included, how emissions are to be calculated, how measurements should be taken, and so forth. Participants need to have their emissions verified by accredited verifiers whose job is to check that the participants have applied the key principles correctly. Given the early-mover advantage of the UK ETS, the most advanced verification is currently being practised in the UK ETS.

FROM UK ETS TO EU ETS

The EU ETS is now providing one of the biggest single challenges in one of the biggest harmonised carbon markets to be formed. The key features of the EU ETS, which directly impact upon and form the financial aspects of this scheme, are (a) the expanse of industries it covers, (b) the parity across the industries it aims to create and (c) the consistency with which emission targets can be allocated, verified and adjusted, if necessary.

The UK baseline verification as a precursor to the annual EU ETS verifications revealed a number of important facts and lessons. Fewer than 15% of the installations in the UK accounted for more than 80% of the total emissions. Just over 3% of the installations were the largest emitters (those emitting over half a million tonnes per year). The degree of confidence in the accuracy of reported data was not directly proportional to the emission size of the installations.

Those installations emitting less than 50,000 tonnes per year, particularly very small ones of less than 10,000 tonnes per year, found it extremely hard to justify the cost of managing and the verification of their emissions in relation to the market value of the carbon.

The EU ETS is planned to run in two phases: Phase 1, 2005 to 2007, for the first set of industry sectors, covering some 14,000 installations across Europe; and Phase 2, from 2008 onwards, and additional industry sectors covering a further 12,000 installations. The issues surrounding the parity warranted by the EU ETS become paramount, bearing in mind the diversity of the industries and the diversity of the way each of these industries operates across the EU member state countries. For example, the allowance caps for two cement factories of similarly sized emissions, one in the UK and one in Spain, may become very similar, but the ability to manage the carbon emissions and to meet the allowance cap may be much higher for a plant built much more recently. This lack of parity is then exacerbated by the unit price of carbon across Europe, which the noncompliant factory has then to purchase. Here, the dilemma persists in price as well as implementation parity (or lack of it). The net result of any such lack of parity would be lack of competitiveness due to abatement cost related to the "best available technology".

Market equilibrium would force the less able installation out of business if that installation cannot be supported by a parent company. Market economics could also force certain difficult-to-modernise industries completely out of the EU boundary – ie, an export difficult emitters out of Europe scenario!

VERIFYING VALUE IN CDM PROJECTS

The other major factor in this market economy is the impact of the "emissions reduction projects" through the Clean Development Mechanism (CDM) of the Kyoto Protocol.

The CDM Executive Board (EB) is taking a strict line on the modalities and procedures in the submission, validation and registration of CDM projects. A number of new methodologies have been rejected and recently the first registration has been recommended for review. The validation process ensures that the plans drawn up for the project are accurate according to the CDM rules and will deliver the emissions savings calculated by the developer. It is the role of the validation/verification body to ensure the accuracy of a project developer's plans and reported data.

In this respect, the validator or verifier is capable of giving confidence to all stakeholders in the process. If a project developer or operator of an installation engages the verifier at an early stage, they are able to provide an interim report on the status of the accuracy of emissions reporting, prior to the compliance period. This "health check" on performance can prevent any surprises during the year-end compliance verification or when the regulator scrutinises final reports.

Interested parties may also be reassured that the correct procedures have been followed by the reporting entity and, from an environmental perspective, that it is actually delivering the emissions reductions. Verification also ensures that parties are dealt with equally and fairly, so that the essential transparency is fed into the market.

The market value of any allowance from any market system will undoubtedly be affected by the CDM projects and verified emission credits. In the latest Conference of the Parties (COP) meeting of the UN, project developers and policymakers have been very frustrated over the slow progress made with the CDM. Ongoing disagreements over "additionality" have fuelled anger over the CDM approval process, currently overly bureaucratic and costly. Furthermore, complaints of regulatory risks have followed the EB's move to reassess the rules for handling industrial gas-abatement projects.

FROM EU ETS TO CDM

The link between CDM and EU ETS is provided through the EU Emissions Trading Directive, called the Linking Directive 2004/101/EC. The EU member states have until 13 November 2005 to emplace legislation in order to implement this directive. The essence of this linking directive is to allow businesses covered under the EU ETS, and subject to controls over their CO_2 releases, to gain credits by investing in projects or by transferring technology that brings about a reduction in greenhouse-gas emissions in another country.

The financial and market implications of CDM project credit values against those credits from facility-level emission reductions are far reaching, since CDM projects can be instigated by any Protocol signatory outside, as well as inside, the EU. The risk of credit value erosion *versus* EU-instigated CDM projects remains high. This can endanger the global applicability and the parity expected of the CDM.

The lack of clarity, exacerbated by the complexities of CDM methodology examination criteria against the requirements of meeting, is putting the success of the wider applicability of emissions trading at risk.

CDM at the outset relies on the project reduction integrity and capability of novel designs. As CDM projects increase, investors become more and more interested in forward sales of carbon-emission reduction units. Provided such CDM projects remain verifiable, the markets of the EU ETS and CDM can interact in a healthy and reliable fashion. This is as yet proving difficult, since the sting in the tail of the CDM projects is the "additionality" burden of proof – that is to say, should the project go ahead, the reductions would not be "business-as-usual".

For CDM projects, validation at the stage of the project design document and verification at the implementation stage play a crucial part in ensuring both credibility and reliability of reduction credits to gain value in the market.

CONCLUSIONS

It is evident that every industry that has a carbon footprint on the planet is now deciding to address its carbon issues. But it will be the economic driver, pushed forward by the trading engine, that will provide enough momentum to accelerate the true management of greenhouse gases and the dynamics of the massively growing trading activity.

To maintain this momentum, both policymakers and legislators must provide clarity and efficiency with which the compliance and approval criteria are managed.

Verification value is a key part of such a process. The verification process therefore provides the anchor for the trading market. Without transparent data-collection processes and independently verified data, the carbon commodity markets simply could not function. The verifier will unlock the market value of clients' reported emissions data and respective tonnage of carbon, at both entity and project levels. It is the robustness of the accreditation process that verifiers must subject themselves to that ensures confidence in the verification activity, and therefore the value of the emissions. Verification by independent and internationally experienced third parties is an essential means of protecting such confidence and credibility.

Section 4

Investor Perspectives

Corporate Carbon Disclosure – The Work of the CDP

Paul Dickinson

Carbon Disclosure Project

Climate change pitches humans against a huge problem – one that will, I believe, test our species, perhaps to the brink of destruction. The potential onset of abrupt climate change could result in staggering loss of life. Addressing the first Carbon Disclosure Project (CDP) launch on 17 February 2003, Sir Derek Higgs (author of the Higgs report on corporate goverance) spoke of the six previous mass extinctions that are identified in the history of Earth and noted the words of the UK's then environment secretary, Michael Meacher, that this is the first time a species has been at risk of generating its own demise. Sir Derek went on to say, "And that's a pretty pertinent point because our hands, all our hands, are on the controls and if we don't exercise those controls appropriately we'll have nobody to blame but ourselves. That's companies, that's governments, but it's also institutional investors. All of us are the real principals in this; the companies are in a sense the agents."

In this chapter, I explain why investors care about climate – and how the CDP is helping them understand company responses with regard to the relatively new, permanent, disruptive phenomena of climate change.

ABOUT THE CDP

The CDP was launched in 2003 with the goal of providing an efficient means for institutional investors to collect and analyse how the world's largest companies are responding to the challenges posed by climate change. The CDP provides a secretariat for the world's largest institutional investor collaboration on the business implications of climate change. CDP represents an efficient process whereby many institutional investors collectively sign a single global request for disclosure of information on greenhouse-gas emissions. CDP then send this request to the chairs of the boards of the FT500 largest companies in the world as measured by market capitalisation. Three hundred of the 500 largest corporations in the world currently report their emissions through the website,[1] and represent 13% of the anthropogenic total.

The CDP is a special project of Rockefeller Philanthropy Advisers, with US IRS 501(c)3 charitable status, for the sole purpose of providing a coordinating secretariat for the participating funders and investors. With massive backing by institutional investors, corporations should feel obliged to respond to the CDP information request, although a surprising number fail to do so.

PANEL 1 LAUNCH OF SECOND CARBON DISCLOSURE PROJECT

Speaking at the launch of the second Carbon Disclosure Project report on 19 May 2004, Sir John Bond, HSBC chairman, stated:

"The fact that investors representing assets in excess of 10 trillion dollars have signed up shows the level of interest in the subject. And the increase in the response rate shows that companies are also taking global warming more seriously. Of course with 40 per cent not responding, there is still a way to go.

As a bank with over 100 million customers around the world, we believe that HSBC has a role to play in formulating a coherent response to the issue of global warming.

Our judgement at HSBC is that climate change represents the largest single environmental challenge this century. It is all the more dangerous because it is such a slow and hard-to-track phenomenon; it is truly the invisible enemy."

Across the Atlantic in New York, at the launch of the same report, Alan Brown, at that time group chief investment officer of State Street Global Advisors, the world's largest institutional asset manager, said:

"Climate Change is evolving into a highly significant environmental risk factor. Combining environmental analysis with traditional financial analysis makes sense given the shifting competitive landscape. Our research suggests that sophisticated analysis of environmental risks generates portfolio outperformance relative to the benchmark."

PANEL 2 THE THIRD CDP INFORMATION REQUEST

The third CDP information request was sent on 1 February 2005 and was signed by more than 150 investors with assets of some US$20 trillion.

The third CDP questionnaire comprised nine questions (see below):

Carbon Disclosure Project (CDP) Greenhouse Gas Emissions Questionnaire

1. General: Do you believe climate change, the policy responses to climate change and/or adaptation to climate change represent commercial risks and/or opportunities for your company?
   - If yes, specify the implications, detail the strategies adopted and actions taken to date.
   - If no, please indicate why.

2. Responsibility: Do you allocate specific responsibility to executive and independent directors for climate change related issues?
   - If yes, what is the title of the person/department/board committee with this responsibility?
   - If no, are you planning on doing so, and if so when?

3. Innovation: What are the relevant technologies and/or processes that can be employed in your company/sector to achieve emission reductions? Have you taken any steps to develop/implement these technologies and do you anticipate being able to profit from their commercialisation?

4. Emissions Trading: Do you have a strategy regarding emerging greenhouse gas emissions regulation and trading initiatives such as the EU Emissions Trading Scheme and the Chicago Climate Exchange?
   - If yes, specify the implications, detail the strategies adopted and actions taken to date.
   - If no, are you planning on doing so, and if so when?

5. Operations (note 1): What is the quantity in tonnes CO_2e of annual emissions of the six main GHGs (note 2) produced by your owned and controlled facilities in the following areas?
   - Globally.
   - Annex B countries of the Kyoto Protocol.
   - EU Emissions Trading Directive.

6. Products and services: Do you estimate the emissions associated with:
   - Use and disposal of your products and services (note 3)?
   - Your supply chain.
   - Other indirect emissions (eg, business travel)
   - If yes, for each of the above, please provide further information.
   - If no, are you planning on doing so and if so when?

7. Emissions reduction: Do you have emission reduction programmes in place?
   - If yes, when were they established and what are the targets? What have been the reductions achieved, the investment involved and the associated costs or savings? Please also detail any targets relating to Questions 6 and anticipated costs or savings.
   - If no, are you planning on doing so, and if so when?

8. Emissions intensity: Do you measure emissions intensity against production, sales or other output measures?
   - If yes, what is your historical and current intensity data? What are your emissions intensity targets?
   - If no, are you planning on doing so and if so when?

9. Energy costs: What percentage of your total revenue is represented by the costs of fossil fuels and electric power?
   (Note 1) Please specify the methodology and boundaries used for measuring emissions eg, www.ghgprotocol.org. Explain if these data are audited and/or externally verified. If responding for the first time please supply data for the last three annual measurement cycles.
   (Note 2) Carbon dioxide (CO_2), methane (CH_4), nitrous oxide (N_2O), Hydroflurocarbons (HFCs), Perfluorcarbons (PFCs) and Sulphur Hexafluoride (SF_6).
   (Note 3) For example, if you are a financial services company, do you take into account the emissions related risks and/or opportunities of the companies you invest in, lend to, or insure.
   The responses to the questionnaire are provided to CDP signatories, and where permitted by respondents, are posted on our website, www.cdproject.net. Furthermore, Innovest Strategic Value Advisors, a New York-based investment research and advisory company, has won the contract to produce a thematic report examining the information provided. The results – alongside a report analysing the responses – are due to be made public at events in London, New York, Tokyo, Paris and Hong Kong in September 2005.
   For corporate responses to previous questionnaires, the CDP reports and a list of signatories, visit www.cdproject.net.

WHAT ARE THE RISKS PRESENTED BY CLIMATE CHANGE?

As noted above, climate change poses a number of challenges to companies. The risks can be summarised under the following categories:

❑ *Adaptation*: This relates to the cost of damage from increased frequency of extreme weather events, the impact on insurance cover and the cost of upgrading infrastructure to withstand new conditions.

❑ *Regulatory*: As governments seek to reduce GHG emissions, companies will bear some of the burden in limits on emissions, or increased taxation of climate-change-causing fossil fuels. The CDP secretariat believe governments will be compelled to reduce GHG emissions to avoid dangerous interference with the climate system. Abrupt climate change must obviously be avoided and emissions reductions to reduce the risk will have to be implemented globally in due course. Great uncertainty, however, surrounds the likely progress of this inevitable process.

❑ *Infrastructure economics*: This relates to the viable future operation of infrastructure such as fossil-fuel-powered electricity-generating equipment, especially where the heat is not captured and used. Taxation and regulation of GHGs may cause such plant to have to be abandoned long before it reaches the end of its expected life span.

❑ *Brand*: There are already strong indications of major corporate brands positioning themselves for a carbon-constrained future. For example, HSBC, a huge global consumer-facing brand, has decided to become "carbon-neutral" at some expense. The UK telecoms giant BT has cut its GHG emissions by 80% since 1991. The footwear manufacturer Nike has also made a public commitment to emissions reduction.

Many companies report to CDP that these factors will have zero effect on them, or do not exist, are unproven or unlikely to occur. The CDP process reports these views as part of a diverse mix of corporate opinions that investors should be aware of.

WHAT ARE THE OPPORTUNITIES PRESENTED BY CLIMATE CHANGE?

The opportunities presented by climate change are not so easily defined, but they may be of far greater financial significance than the risks. Industries that look set to benefit from climate change can be divided into the general categories of adaptation and mitigation.

In adaptation, the UK government alone estimates that improving the country's coastal defences may require between about £22 billion and £75 billion of new engineering by the 2080s. The global market for coastal defences will prove considerable.

At a recent debate in London on climate change, Chris Mottershead, BP's distinguished adviser on energy and the environment, observed that "the world has already accepted it's going to spend sixteen trillion dollars on energy infrastructure in the next thirty years. And that doesn't matter whether you believe in fossil fuels or whether you believe in renewables – the world is already committed to that." There is clearly a huge bounty for companies that can provide energy in a sustainable manner.

New energy technology from wind to wave and solar has already been the subject of multibillion-dollar investments over the last decade. The role of nuclear power in the move to a low-carbon economy forms a part of this complex debate. However, it is very hard to conceive of a credible business case for such an expensive and potentially dangerous technology when the great bounty available from energy efficiency measures remain largely untapped. Building expertise in winning government climate-change-related contracts would seem to be a valuable new competence for engineering companies, from sea walls to home insulation, via renewable energy.

The CDP Web site allows users to access for free the disclosure of responses from more than 300 large corporations. A search function allows users to filter the responses for specific areas of interest. For instance, six companies – Eni, BHP Billiton, Total, Encana, Repsol and ChevronTexaco – mention "geological sequestration" in their submissions to the CDP. Geological sequestration is a fascinating new technology that could prevent hundreds of millions of tonnes of CO_2 from entering the atmosphere. It offers the promise that the world's vast coal reserves could be burned safely. If it works, how much might it be worth?

ANALYSING THE RESPONSES TO CDP

The information collected by CDP is becoming an invaluable source of information to investors. For example, the insurance giant Swiss Re minimise "questionnaire burden" for their clients: where they act as a direct insurer of large corporate companies, their directors, officers and insurance underwriters check with the CDP results for that company's response. This gives a first indication on where these companies stand with regard to climate change and emissions. Only if the companies are not included there, or specifically did not answer, do they follow up with their own questions.

Indeed, the responses can illustrate differences in thinking on climate leadership. Take the CDP responses of Microsoft and Intel. The two firms are in separate, but connected, segments of the same industry, with Microsoft in software, and Intel in hardware and chip manufacturing. Both influence the life-cycle impacts of computer systems around the world.

In its CDP response, Microsoft does not mention any steps that it is taking towards configuring its software in order to minimise energy consumption of computers. The firm's response to the CDP question, "Do you measure the emissions associated with both the use and disposal of your products and services?" is, "Due to the categories of products and services we produce, Microsoft does not quantify emissions and has no current plans to do so."

The stance contrasts starkly with the pioneering attitude of Intel, which recognises that the chips it makes (and that Microsoft software frequently operates), result in substantial GHG emissions: "Intel provides Instantly Available PC (IAPC) technology that reduces the power use to less than five watts when the PC is in 'sleep mode'. If all PCs in the US operated with Intel IAPC, the US Environmental Protection Agency estimates that, over 10 years, IAPC would save the following over the Energy Star standard: 75 Million Metric Tons of CO_2 eliminated."

SUMMARY THOUGHTS FOR INVESTORS[2]

❑ Weather-related natural disasters caused about US$70 billion damage during 2003 (US$18.5 billion was insured). For the first time, climate change was explicitly identified as being a factor. More extreme weather events should be expected in the future, according to leading reinsurers.

❑ The effects of this will be felt in key sectors and commodity markets – notably, the power, energy, insurance, transportation, heavy manufacturing and building/infrastructure industries, and the crude oil, gasoline, grain, soy and wheat markets. The application – and bundling together – of weather derivatives, catastrophe bonds and other environmental financial risk-hedging instruments is turning into a viable, but underutilised, risk-management option for many firms.

❑ Mainstream pension trustees, analysts, bankers, insurers and fund managers have begun to appreciate the implications of climate change and greenhouse gas (GHG) policies in financial terms. No longer can fiduciaries claim to be unaware of what is at stake. Taking climate risks into account is now becoming part of smart financial management. Failure to do so may well be tantamount to an abdication of fiduciary responsibility. FT500 firms can expect to come under greater pressure from shareholders as a result.

❑ Carbon finance is now a reality. Legislation favouring a shift to a low-carbon-intensity economy is now a fact of life for FT500 companies across the EU as well as in many parts of the US, Japan, Australia and Canada. In January 2005, more than 14,000 entities began trading carbon in what promises to be the largest, most liquid carbon market in the world: the EU Emissions Trading Scheme (EU ETS). Approximately 29% of the FT500 companies contacted through the CDP are located in countries that are included in the EU ETS. In the US, more than 20 states have passed or proposed legislation on CO_2 emissions, or have developed carbon registries, sequestration studies and similar measures.

THE FUTURE OF CDP

The CDP process has proved to provide an effective system for gathering information on the GHG emissions of major corporations and likely impact of climate change on investment performance. At the time of writing (April 2005), the CDP secretariat are in discussions with multiple parties regarding expansion of the CDP information requests to a wider group of companies in a larger number of countries. While there are many variables, including the availability of partners and resources to support the work of CDP, the trajectory of CDP is likely to reflect that of the climate change issue itself.

1   http://www.cdproject.net.
2   Source: CDP2 Executive Summary.

17

Investor Collaboration on Climate Change: The Work of the IIGCC

Rory Sullivan; Nick Robins; David Russell; Helen Barnes

Insight Investment; Henderson Global Investors;
Universities Superannuation Scheme; IIGCC

The *prima facie* case for investors to be concerned about climate change is obvious. Climate change is, arguably, the most significant environmental threat facing the planet. It is expected to have significant economic impacts, directly through, for example, flooding and extreme weather events and indirectly through new regulatory or fiscal measures to limit greenhouse gas (GHG) emissions. Virtually all sectors of the economy are likely to be impacted, including utilities, insurance, tourism, property, transport, construction, retail and agriculture/food.

However, the fact that climate change is an important economic and environmental issue does not necessarily mean that investors will take action to address the issue. While it has always been possible to find some institutional investors (fund managers, pension funds) with an understanding of the commercial importance of environmental issues, for the majority these issues have not enjoyed much of a profile. The major exceptions have been those specific situations where an issue has become so obviously financially material that it can no longer be ignored and some action is required. As a consequence, most investor intervention has tended to be reactive rather than proactive.

However, there are signs of change, with a growing number of asset managers and pension funds starting to focus much more of their attention on climate change. This change can be attributed to

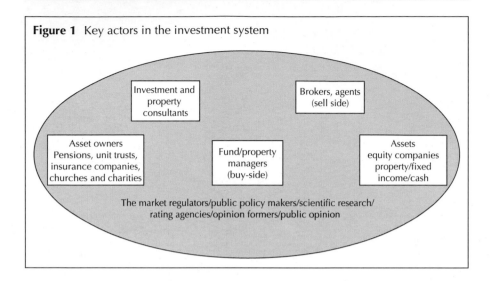

Figure 1 Key actors in the investment system

Investment and property consultants

Brokers, agents (sell side)

Asset owners
Pensions, unit trusts, insurance companies, churches and charities

Fund/property managers (buy-side)

Assets
equity companies
property/fixed
income/cash

The market regulators/public policy makers/scientific research/ rating agencies/opinion formers/public opinion

two factors. The first is the rising awareness among asset owners such as pension funds that issues, such as climate change, if unmanaged, could significantly impact on long-term investment returns (ie, climate change is increasingly recognised as a fiduciary issue). The second is that mainstream asset managers are becoming more attuned to how extra-financial and intangible issues, such as carbon exposure and the implications of climate change, can affect company value and therefore expected returns.

This has led to a number of initiatives where investors collaborate to address market-wide risks associated with climate change. This chapter describes one of the most important initiatives in this regard – the Institutional Investors Group on Climate Change (IIGCC) – with a particular focus on the IIGCC's work on public policy.

ABOUT IIGCC

The IIGCC was convened by the Universities Superannuation Scheme (USS)[1] in 2001 as a forum for collaboration between pension funds and other institutional investors on issues related to climate change[1]. IIGCC's objectives are to identify, promote and demonstrate competence throughout the investment system (see Figure 1), to assess and actively manage the risks and opportunities presented by climate change, and the need for society to transition to a secure climate system. IIGCC seeks to:

- ❑ equip its members with the knowledge and tools to assess, engage and actively manage the investment implications of climate change on the assets they own in order to preserve and enhance the value of these assets;
- ❑ act as a champion for the integration of climate risk into the everyday functioning of the investment community; and
- ❑ communicate to public-policy makers and to the market the importance of a proactive, orderly and efficient transition to a secure climate system, in order to protect beneficiaries and customers from the costs of discontinuous change.

The reason for establishing a collaborative initiative between institutional investors (pension funds and asset managers) was that these organisations are among those with the most to lose if companies and markets are negatively affected by the direct impacts of climate change and/or by sudden political or policy responses to climate change. Given that corporate and investor behaviour could do much to minimise the negative impact of climate change, pension funds and other institutional shareholders also have an important role to play in encouraging proactive corporate responses to climate change and in ensuring that climate change is properly factored into investment decision making.

IIGCC is not intended to substitute for individual fund managers taking action on climate change or to argue that there is a uniformity of investor views on climate change. IIGCC's aim is to leverage the influence of individual organisations and to focus its effort on areas where collaboration provides clear benefits over individual organisations working on their own. The potential advantages of investors working through IIGCC include: greater coverage of companies, sectors and markets; enhanced access to specialist sell-side analysts and senior corporate executives; and providing stronger signals to the market regarding the importance of climate change as an investment issue. One specific advantage of IIGCC is that it helps ensure that companies are not being pulled in different directions as a result of investors failing to coordinate. IIGCC's position on climate change issues is presented in Panel 1, and IIGCC's members – who represent assets of approximately £1 trillion as at the end of April 2005 – are presented in Panel 2.

PANEL 1

IIGCC's position on climate change

IIGCC recognises the growing scientific and political consensus that emissions of carbon dioxide and other GHG are contributing to climate change. IIGCC further recognises that companies and markets face significant risks and opportunities associated with climate change, either indirectly through changes in the regulatory environment or directly through changes in the physical environment.

IIGCC believes that institutional investors and companies will benefit from a greater understanding of these risks and opportunities presented by climate change. Specifically, we believe that, if companies are more aware of the impacts of climate change, this could lead to an increase in the long-term value of our investments.

IIGCC members are aware that as responsible owners, who may have commitments to good practice standards of corporate governance and socially responsible investment, we can play a part in encouraging a proactive response to what is one of the most significant environmental threats to investors, business and society.

Source: IIGCC website, http://www.iigcc.org

IIGCC's activities have focused on company and broker engagement, property investment, trustee training and public policy. IIGCC works with a broad range of national and international stakeholders involved in investment and climate risk (for example, the Carbon Trust,[2] the Investment Property Forum[3] and Upstream[4]) and encourages the development of investor initiatives in other global markets as well as seeking to work with parallel bodies and other investor-led organisations in other parts of the world (for example, the Investor Network on Climate Risk,[5] Investor Group on Climate Change, UN Environment Programme Finance Initiative[6] and the Carbon Disclosure Project[7]).

IIGCC's engagement work to date has covered the construction, aviation and electricity utilities sectors. For each of these sectors, IIGCC has met with companies and relevant brokers, and published investor briefings on how climate change could impact these sectors.[8]

Property

In addition to equities, the IIGCC's work includes consideration of the impacts of climate change on property investments. The aim of the property workstream is to ensure that climate change and its

PANEL 2
IIGCC membership, April 2005

BBC Pension Trust
Bedfordshire County Council
   Pension Fund
BNP Paribas Asset
   Management
CCLA Investment
   Management Ltd
Central Finance Board of
   the Methodist Church
Co-operative Insurance Society
Corporation of London
   Pension Fund
Environment Agency
   Pension Fund
Ethos – Investment Foundation
F&C Asset Management
Generation Investment
   Management
Greater Manchester
   Pension Fund
Henderson Global Investors
I.DE.A.M. – Group
   Crédit Agricole

Insight Investment
Jupiter Asset Management
Local Authority Pension Fund
   Forum
London Borough of Hounslow
   Pension Fund
London Pensions Fund
   Authority
Merrill Lynch Investment Managers
Merseyside Pension Fund
Morley Fund Management
Prudential Property Investment
   Managers
Schroder Investment
   Management UK
Transport for London Pension Fund
Universities Superannuation
   Scheme
West Midlands Metropolitan
   Authorities Pension Fund
West Yorkshire Pension Fund

implications are included in the management and decision-making processes in property investment portfolios. While many architects and property consultants are already aware of the potential gains from good energy management and the impacts of climate change through factors such as flood risk and subsidence, it is probably fair to say that property investors have lagged behind in their consideration of how these factors could impact investment returns. This, when combined with the low turnover rate in property assets, has made the sector a key area of the IIGCC's work. The workstream has built links with leading and influential property industry bodies, in particular, the Investment Property Forum[9] (IPF). IIGCC's objective is to raise awareness in the property investment industry about the implications of climate change on the current and future value of property investments and to specify ways in which it can reduce climate change impacts.

Trustees

To help trustees, the IIGCC, with support from the Carbon Trust, commissioned Mercer Investment Consulting to develop training materials for pension fund trustees on the fiduciary aspects of climate change.[10] The aim of the training materials is to raise awareness among pension fund trustees about the relevance of climate change as a fiduciary issue, and to communicate the opportunities

---

PANEL 3

Questions for investment managers

❑ Have you developed internal expertise in this area? How many of your investment analysts and portfolio managers (across different asset classes) have a reasonable level of understanding around the potential for climate change issues to impact financial risk and return?

❑ Do you have any individual or a group with a dedicated focus on climate change? If yes, how does that group relate to your traditional operations?

❑ Have you made any public statements about climate change as a financial risk? To which asset classes does this extend?

❑ How often are climate-change issues discussed with company management? Are these issues addressed during specific meetings between environmental specialists and management, or as part of your mainstream analyst meetings with management?

❑ What are some of the climate-change-related discussions you've had with company management in the past 12 months?

❑ Do you purchase any external research, or participate in any external networks on this issue?

❑ Is there a process for ensuring climate risks are built into your traditional investment decision-making process? How is this accomplished?

❑ Do you participate in the Enhanced Analytics Initiative (http://www.enhancedanalytics.com), hence encouraging brokers to integrate climate change factors into company analysis?

❑ Are there mandate qualities or particular benchmarks that would encourage climate-change issues to be better incorporated into investment decision making?

❑ Do you collaborate with others to address climate-change risks and opportunities (for example, the IIGCC, the US Investor Network on Climate Risk (INCR), Australian IGCC or the Carbon Disclosure Project)?

❑ Can you incorporate a regular discussion of climate-change analysis into your fund's monitoring reports?

---

that exist for them to address climate change. The training materials provide guidance on how trustees can assess their preparedness to respond to climate change, the exposure of their investments to climate change and the competence of their investment managers to assess and manage these risks to their investments. The materials include a series of questions that trustees can use to evaluate their fund managers' competence (see Panel 3).

Finally, IIGCC's public policy work has sought to ensure that public-policy makers take into account the long-term interests of institutional investors in their decision-making process and responses to climate change.

THE PUBLIC POLICY DIMENSION

IIGCC's view is (as indicated in Panel 4) that climate-change policy is an increasingly important issue for investment decision making and a lack of clarity in public policy will lead to companies excluding (or reducing the importance of) climate change as a factor in their decision making. That is, in situations of policy uncertainty, companies will assume that public-policy makers are not committed to addressing climate change and business decisions will reflect this assumption. As noted in Panel 4, IIGCC emphasises the importance of clear long-term policy targets to provide an appropriate context for investment analysis and for long-term investment decision making.

Without clear long-term targets, investors face two sets of risks. The first is the direct risks of climate change to investments; a failure to respond effectively will increase the risks associated with extreme weather events and other changes in the climate. The second is that, over these timeframes, there is the potential for government to develop and implement policy measures that move towards a low-carbon economy while minimising disruptions to existing business activities (for example, avoiding the need to retire capital stock much earlier than planned). That is, governments need to specify and commit to meeting long-term policy goals, in order for companies to make economically efficient investment decisions that properly incorporate climate change factors. From an investor perspective, policy should be developed and implemented in such a way as to permit this shift in an as efficient manner as possible. This is a view that is also being articulated by companies.

PANEL 4
IIGCC's position on climate change and public policy

Climate change is a product of market failure: the absence of appropriate incentives has led to individuals and companies externalising the costs associated with GHG emissions, generating significant risks to both the global environment and the global economy. As a result, public policy intervention is essential not only to minimise the damage caused by climate change, but also to maximise the opportunities from the transition to a low-carbon economy. Without credible public policy frameworks, companies and their investors will be handicapped in planning how they respond to the climate change challenge. Moreover, a policy framework that fails to take account of the strategic nature of climate change could result in discontinuous change in the future, which would probably be a suboptimal outcome for long-term institutional investors.

Understanding and influencing public policy thus becomes an essential element of an effective investor strategy for enhancing long-term shareholder value in an increasingly carbon-constrained world. IIGCC members believe it is part of their fiduciary duty to their clients and beneficiaries to engage on climate change policy.

We see that investor collaboration (on research, corporate engagement and public policy) will be most effective – and most likely to be seen as credible by analysts, policy makers, companies and other stakeholders such as non-governmental organisations – if it is geared towards achieving a smooth transition to specific policy goals that lead to a low-carbon economy. In the UK (reflecting the work of the Intergovernmental Panel on Climate Change), these goals are currently the 20% (by 2010) and 60% (by 2050) reductions in greenhouse gas emissions proposed by the UK government in the 2003 Energy White Paper.

Source: IIGCC website, www.iigcc.org

The two key objectives of the public policy workstream are: (a) to become better informed of existing and forthcoming public policy developments in order to understand the possible implications for investment strategy across key asset classes, such as equities, bonds and property; and (b) to become more effective at informing policy makers of investors' needs and concerns in order to ensure that policy adequately reflects the long-term financial interests of their beneficial members and clients. As the costs of climate change become progressively reflected in asset valuations (for example, through emissions trading), the IIGCC believes that it is important for

PANEL 5
IIGCC on EU Action on Climate Change Post-2012

We are of the view that the following principles should underpin the EU's work in this area:

❑ Policy certainty over the longer-term is key. One of the challenges presented by the Kyoto Protocol is that it does not provide sufficiently clear direction for policy beyond 2012. This has led to governments establishing policy that focuses on meeting emissions targets for the 2008–2012 period, rather than necessarily considering the longer-term (ie, the need to create sustainable long-term reductions in greenhouse gas emissions). The consequence is that we face the very real risk of a policy and emissions disconnect after the 2008–2012 period, where we are likely to see sharp increases in greenhouse gas emissions and/or draconian policy measures to reduce greenhouse gas emissions, rather than a smooth and staged transition. Therefore, we are of the view that the EU should specify emission targets over the longer term, probably out to 2050 and then set intermediate targets from 2050 back to the present. In this regard, we see the approach adopted by the UK government in its Energy White Paper (ie, a 60 per cent reduction in emissions by 2050) as providing an appropriate model.

❑ Harness renewables and energy efficiency. We are of the view that renewables and energy efficiency should allow the EU to meet its long-term targets, assuming that these are appropriately supported by governments.

❑ The policy approaches adopted should be economically efficient and minimise transaction costs. We recognise and support emissions trading as a particularly important policy measure in this regard. We encourage the EU to broaden participation in the scheme and to ensure that key sectors such as aviation are included as soon as possible.

❑ We support the common but differentiated responsibilities policy approach. We recognise that this approach has been opposed by some governments who have argued for developing countries to more fully engage with climate change issues before they themselves take serious action. We are of the view that a properly focused long-term strategy will be economically advantageous for the EU and will also provide important international leadership through demonstrating the benefits of proactive approaches to climate change.

❑ Developing greater clarity about the likely impacts of climate change. One of the key issues is that it is widely assumed that adaptation costs will not be significant. As investors, our interest is in ensuring that companies in which we invest take proper account of likely changes in the context in which they work. While much of the focus of these discussions has been on government responses such as changing flood defences, etc, less attention has been focused on the implications for companies.

Source: Extract from the IIGCC's submission to the EU stakeholder consultation on EU action on climate change post-2012

investors to be at the heart of the decision-making process that is shaping this critical transition in modern economic life. We have found that climate policy makers are more than willing to meet with investors and to share information on current and future trends in this area.

In relation to engagement on specific public-policy issues, IIGCC has made contributions to or formal submissions on the EU Stakeholder Consultation on EU Action on Climate Change Post-2012 (see Panel 5), the UK's proposed Operating and Financial Review (OFR), the UK Energy White Paper, the EU Emissions Trading Scheme (EU ETS) and the second commitment period of the Kyoto Protocol.

FUTURE DIRECTIONS
Public policy
Until recently investors have been the "missing stakeholder" in climate policy discussions. Not only did investors not engage in policy formulation, but governments did not appreciate the importance of direct interaction with asset owners and managers. Efforts by the IIGCC and others to engage in policy dialogue have now succeeded in raising awareness within the UK government and elsewhere of the critical importance of mobilising the investment community behind a proactive climate strategy. Investors have specific needs and viewpoints that need to be reflected in climate policy alongside the voices of other parts of the financial sector (such as insurance and banking), as well as the wider business community.

The work of the IIGCC (and the emergence of similar initiatives in other international markets) is a clear sign that investors are prepared to send strong messages concerning the long-term direction of

PANEL 6
Insight's approach to climate change and governance
IIGCC member, Insight Investment, expects companies to have:
- ❏ high-level policy commitments on climate change, including commitments to emissions reductions;
- ❏ clearly defined board and senior management responsibilities for climate change;
- ❏ where appropriate, clear links between executive remuneration and corporate performance on climate change;
- ❏ formal systems and processes for managing climate change (for instance, clearly defined responsibilities and accountabilities through the organisation, clear and transparent reporting on GHG emissions and performance);
- ❏ comprehensive inventories of GHG emissions (both directly from operations and activities and indirectly from, for example, the use of the company's products); these inventories should allow historic performance to be assessed and should include projections of likely changes in future emissions;
- ❏ processes for (a) the assessment of greenhouse risks (for example, direct impacts, opportunities and threats from changes in law and policy), (b) identifying, evaluating, ranking and, as appropriate, implementing potential GHG-emissions-reducing actions;
- ❏ specific objectives and targets, including GHG emission-reduction targets; and
- ❏ benchmarking of GHG emissions and efficiency performance against peers.

Source: Insight Investment (2005), Investor Responsibility Bulletin, October to December 2004, pp. 6 7 www.insightinvestment.com/documents/responsibility/ir_bulletin_winter2004.pdf

climate change policy. This may seem somewhat surprising, as it implies that investors will support policy measures that may impose costs on companies or even that investors will act as "advocates" for stronger policy measures. In relation to the former point, policy makers have frequently assumed that the interests of investors and companies are the same. In practice, this is not necessarily the case. Investors need to have regard to the overall effects of the policy and direct impacts of climate change on their portfolios as a whole, and recognise that actions that may be in the interest of an individual company may not be in the interests of investments as a whole. This fits with the concept of institutional investors, particularly pension funds, as universal investors,[11] which argues that large investors, as the holders of a broad selection of different companies and other assets, are often as dependent on the performance of markets or economies as a whole, as much as they are on the performance of individual companies. As policy makers set the parameters for markets, it is therefore essential that investors actively participate in policy discussions. Such an approach also fits with the fiduciary responsibilities of pension funds and other institutional investors to maximise long-term returns – and hence consider issues that could affect fund performance over the longer term.

A further implication is that the messages from investors may run counter to the views of industry lobby bodies. As long-term investors, IIGCC recognise that climate change is not only a critical issue for companies to manage but also presents significant opportunities for companies to innovate and create long-term shareholder value through, for example, the identification of new technologies, through capturing new markets or through avoiding or reducing the need for defensive expenditures (for example, to respond to the increased risks of floods or extreme weather events). Achieving these kinds of benefit requires that public policy on climate change be focused on long-term goals, with the specific policy instruments

---

PANEL 7
Henderson's approach to climate change and corporate practice
Henderson expects companies to integrate climate change into corporate strategy and has identified the following good practice elements:

  i establish a greenhouse gas emissions inventory;
 ii assess corporate exposure to climate change, in terms of both mitigation and adaptation;
iii project future exposure and develop scenarios;
 iv carry out competitor analysis to benchmark with other companies;
  v agree a climate strategy, with clear targets for reducing greenhouse gas emissions;
 vi develop internal capacity;
vii work with suppliers and customers to implement the strategy;
viii engage creatively with stakeholders;
 ix act as an advocate for action on climate change; and
  x report publicly on climate change policies and performance.

Source: Henderson Global Investors, Socially Responsible Investment – Climate Change Position Paper, August 2002

---

being chosen on the basis of their ability to deliver on these goals (their dependability) while also being economically efficient, minimising transaction costs and stimulating innovation.

Individual investors

IIGCC is not intended to be a substitute for activity by individual investment managers. For example, many of IGCC's members also engage directly with companies on the systems and processes that they expect companies to have in place. To illustrate: Insight Investment has issued a list of the governance systems and processes that it expects companies to have in place relating to climate change (see Panel 6), while another IIGCC member Henderson Global Investors has issued a comprehensive position paper in 2002 describing the investment risks and opportunities associated with climate change, setting out its expectations of corporate practice (see Panel 7).

CONCLUSIONS

Investors are starting to look far more closely at the public policy issues around climate change and have an increasing appetite for engaging with government policy in this area. The policy positions being advocated by investors, individually and collectively, are progressive: supporting the establishment of long-term targets, and actively encouraging companies and government to work towards these targets. This is complemented by the messages being sent by investors to individual companies, both on the management systems and processes that investors expect companies to have in place and on the policy positions that investors expect companies to adopt when engaging with the policy process.

Investor engagement with public policy is still evolving. It is, as yet, too early to say what the outcomes will be. However, if sustained, investor initiatives such as IIGCC can only add impetus to public policy efforts to address the challenges of climate change.

---

1 USS published an analysis of the investment implications of climate change in July 2001 (see Mansley and Dlugolecki, 2001) and, subsequently, convened a meeting of interested fund managers and pension funds in October 2001.
2 http://www.thecarbontrust.co.uk/carbontrust.

3   http://www.ipf.org.uk.
4   http://www.upstreamstrategies.co.uk.
5   http://www.incr.com.
6   http://www.unepfi.org.
7   http://www.cdproject.net.
8   The briefing notes are available on IIGCC's website at http://www.iigcc.org.
9   http://www.ipf.org.uk.
10 These materials are available through the IIGCC website.
11 See, generally, Hawley and Williams (2000).
12 Henderson Global Investors (2002), 'Climate Change Position Paper. August 2002' (Henderson Global Investors, London, UK).

REFERENCES

Hawley, J. and A. Williams, 2000, *The Rise of Fiduciary Capitalism* (Philadelphia: University of Pennsylvania Press).

Henderson Global Investors, 2002, "Climate change – SRI position paper", Henderson Global Investors, London, August.

Insight Investment, 2005, *Investor Responsibility Bulletin*, URL: http://www.insightinvestment.com/documents/responsibility/ir_bulletin_winter2004.pdf, October to December.

Mansley, M. and A. Dlugolecki, 2001, *Climate Change: A Risk Management Challenge for Institutional Investors* (London: USS).

18

Climate Change, Investment Risk and Fiduciary Responsibility

Matthew Kiernan

Innovest Strategic Value Advisors

In what is really an astonishingly short space of time, climate change has evolved from a relatively arcane, primarily scientific issue into a rapidly growing *investment* concern for fiduciaries worldwide. This evolution has been driven by the convergence of at least six powerful global "mega-trends":

❑ growing scientific and societal consensus on the extent, potential consequences, and anthropogenic genesis of climate change;
❑ increased evidence that the potential financial consequences of climate change extend well beyond the obvious, energy-intensive industry sectors;
❑ increasingly pervasive, government-led restrictions on green-house gas (GHG) emissions, most prominently through the 2005 ratification of the Kyoto Protocol and the EU's Emissions Trading Scheme (EU ETS).
❑ the recent convergence of the traditional corporate governance agenda with the much less-established "sustainable develop-ment" agenda, accelerating the transformation of climate change from a primarily environmental concern into a *fiduciary* and investment issue;
❑ legal changes to both corporate disclosure requirements and pension fund regulations, essentially broadening the ambit of fiduciary responsibility and thereby increasing the saliency of environmental issues for corporations and investors alike; and

❑ a dramatic, worldwide increase in institutional shareholder concern and activism over climate change, hand in hand with the rise of the notion of "fiduciary capitalism".[1]

These trends have by no means been geographically ubiquitous or uniform within and between countries, but over the past 12–18 months they have achieved sufficient critical mass and momentum to propel climate change squarely onto the mainstream investment agenda. Any time that over 140 institutional investors with more than US\$20 *trillion* in combined assets become sufficiently mobilised to press the CEOs of the world's 500 largest corporations on the subject – via the unprecedented Carbon Disclosure Project – it is fair to say that climate change has now "arrived" as a bona fide, mainstream investment issue.[2]

CLIMATE RISK: THE FIDUCIARY IMPERATIVE

Historically, mainstream institutional investors have, almost without exception, accepted the conventional "wisdom" that the pursuit of corporate "sustainability" – that is, superior performance on environmental and social issues – could be achieved only at the cost of higher risk for investors, lower financial returns, or both. An important corollary of this argument has long held that, since environmental and social factors are, at best, irrelevant to the risk–return equation and at worst injurious to them, fiduciaries should actually be precluded from considering them. It turns out that both the conventional wisdom and its corollary are quite wrong-headed.

The "prudent fiduciary" equation is now inexorably – and quite rightly – being turned on its head. Since there is now growing (if not incontrovertible) evidence that superior environmental performance does improve the risk level, profitability and stock performance of publicly traded companies,[3] fiduciaries can now be seen to be derelict in their duties if they do *not* consider environmental and social performance and risk factors.

Over the past several years, investment legislation in the UK, Continental Europe and Australia has implicitly recognised this, and has created an affirmative obligation on institutional investors to either report on how they are integrating environmental and social factors into their investment strategies or, if not, to explain why not.

On the corporate side, disclosure requirements are undergoing a similar tightening. In the UK, the new Operating Financial Review rules came into effect in April 2005, and place a similar "disclose or explain" requirement on roughly 1,300 publicly traded companies. Similar requirements also exist in France, Germany, the Netherlands and other European countries. In the US, the much-ballyhooed Sarbanes–Oxley Act also required greater disclosure overall, albeit with much less explicit attention to environmental risks.

Climate change, described by both business and government leaders at the Davos World Economic Forum as "the most urgent problem facing humanity", is arguably the "mother" of all such risk factors. Since companies' environmental and financial performance are becoming increasingly intertwined, it follows logically that companies' response – or lack of response – to climate change could have a material bearing on their risk levels and financial performance, and therefore on shareholder value for investors.

The growing international proliferation of organisations of major institutional investors focused on climate risk attests to a growing level of investor awareness and concern. In addition to the global Carbon Disclosure Project, there are several major regional collaborations: the Institutional Investors Group on Climate Change (Europe); Institutional Investors for Climate Change (Australia); and the Investors Network on Climate Risk (US).

The stakes are high indeed. Depending on which sectors companies are in and what their specific risk exposures are, climate change could cost shareholders hundreds of millions of pounds and require major strategic shifts in companies' business models. In a worst-case, yet entirely plausible, scenario, their very survival could be threatened. Recent research has demonstrated that, in some high-impact sectors, even under highly conservative scenarios, as much as 45% of earnings and 35% of total market capitalisation could be at risk from the potential financial consequences of climate change.[4] Yet despite this, City and, in particular, Wall Street analysts continue to ignore or understate these risks as improbable or immaterial.

One recent illustration of the analysts' collective blind spot vis-à-vis climate change was provided by the initial public offering of Xstrata, a Swiss-owned coalmining company being listed on the London Stock Exchange. The initial public offering was led by a top-tier, global investment bank. In the 400-plus-page offering memorandum supporting the underwriting and outlining its investment risks, precisely *one line* was devoted to climate change. Yet within weeks the Japanese government began musing publicly about imposing a carbon tax on imported coal to help combat climate change. In as much as a substantial portion of Xstrata's revenues come from exporting high-sulphur coal to Japan, the market responded by lopping off a full 8% of the company's total market capitalisation, temporarily knocking it out of the FTSE 100 and costing it billions in "automatic" index investment. All this, and investors were given only one line of "analysis" to help them understand and weigh this potential risk. Even today, it is the exceptional City or Wall Street analyst who could distinguish high-risk from low-risk companies with respect to climate change.

SO, WHAT HAVE WE LEARNED SO FAR?

Recent work has led us to a number of conclusions.

1. *The financial impacts of climate change affect a much wider range of industry sectors than previously thought.* It seems intuitively obvious that climate change and carbon constraints would affect such high-impact, energy-intensive sectors as oil and gas, mining, and electricity utilities, and this is indeed the case. Upon closer analysis, however, the impacts on other less obvious sectors, including financial services, tourism, and agriculture, may prove every bit as profound if not more so.

   Indeed, we would argue that climate change is simply the latest and most pervasive manifestation of what might be termed an "Eco-Industrial Revolution" – a global industrial restructuring where the entire basis of competitive advantage is being transformed, with environmental performance in a position of unprecedented importance. As with previous industrial revolutions, the post-Kyoto environment is likely to create whole new classes of corporate winners and losers, and investors and fiduciaries would be well advised to be able to distinguish between the two – preferably, ahead of time! Yesterday's and even today's winners might well be losers in a carbon-constrained world, if they prove incapable of making the necessary strategic and operational adjustments quickly enough.[5]

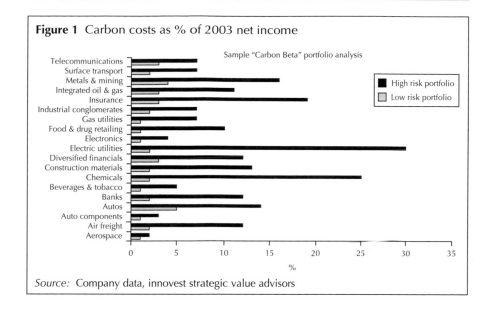

Figure 1 Carbon costs as % of 2003 net income

2. *Risk levels – both among and within industry sectors – can vary dra-matically.* Figure 1 provides a concrete illustration of the vari-ability of climate risk across a number of industry sectors. The two hypothetical global portfolios have *identical* industry-sector exposures, but in each sector I have selected one company with relatively high "carbon intensity" and one low-intensity com-pany. As the chart reveals, the differences are stark, and yet at present few if any traditional investment analysts could assist investors and fiduciaries in identifying which is which.

Even within the *same* industry sector, the risk variance can be extraordinary. For example, recent research on the electricity util-ity sector has revealed variations in climate-driven financial risk exposures among majors of over thirty times! Figure 2 graph-ically illustrates the extent of the inter-company risk variation.

Under such circumstances, prudent fiduciaries simply cannot afford the financial risk of not knowing which company is which.

3. *There is also a wide variance in risk management capabilities.* The variations in companies' ability to *manage* climate risk appear to be just as profound as the risk variances themselves, and are arguably of even greater concern. Recent research for the Carbon Disclosure Project has clearly revealed stark contrasts in the awareness and preparedness levels among chief executives of

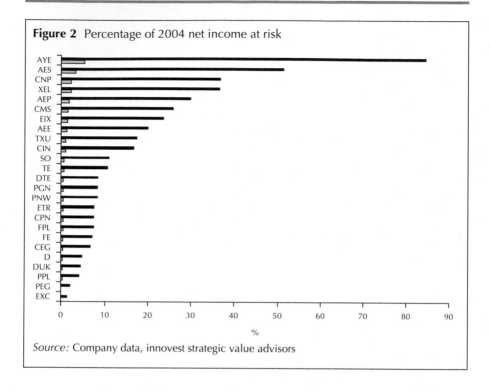

Figure 2 Percentage of 2004 net income at risk

Source: Company data, innovest strategic value advisors

same-sector companies facing essentially the same levels of risk. As we shall see later, major institutional investors are increasingly looking to those differentials as proxies for the overall strategic management capabilities of the companies involved.

4. *It's not all gloom and doom: opportunities abound.* Many "climate sceptics", particularly in the US, tend to view climate change unidimensionally, as simply an unmitigated "black hole" of financial risk and uncertainty. As noted earlier, however, tectonic shifts in the basis of competitive advantage don't create only victims: they also create new opportunities on the upside. With climate change, the three most compelling of these are energy efficiency, investments in "clean technology", and participating in the rapidly growing emissions trading markets. It would take an entire book to begin to do justice to any one of these three sets of opportunities; we will content ourselves here with just a few short comments.

Energy efficiency gains are a virtually inevitable concomitant of virtually any serious and successful effort to achieve significant GHG reductions. The "poster child" for achieving these sorts of benefits is arguably BP. In an environment where some of BP's direct global competitors have argued publicly that significant GHG reductions would be both technically difficult and financially ruinous, by mid-2005 BP was able to cut its GHG emissions by 18% from its 1990 levels, exceeding its own targets several years ahead of schedule. The cost? With an investment of roughly US$20 million, BP estimates it has created savings with a net present value of US$650 million in energy cost savings over three years – a rather impressive return on investment. What is more, BP is by no means an isolated case. IBM has avoided more than 7 million tonnes of CO_2 emissions through energy-efficiency measures, which amounts to more than a 30% reduction in worldwide emissions. The "cost"? A cumulative savings of over US$600 million. DuPont has achieved more than a 70% reduction in GHG emissions vis-à-vis 1990 levels, and estimates that it will save a cumulative US$2 billion in energy costs by the end of this decade.

"Clean technology" can be seen as a second dimension of the opportunity side of the climate-risk coin, and the recent growth of that sector has been impressive indeed. The worldwide market for solar energy, wind energy and fuel cells alone – just a subset of the broader clean-tech market – is already generating US$16 billion in annual revenues as of early 2005. Going forward, China alone expects to install up to 100 gigawatts of new renewable-energy sources by 2020. Industry experts predict a 500% growth of this market worldwide by 2014, to more than US$100 billion (see Clean Edge, Inc, 2005). Emerging opportunities in the clean tech space will be of interest to both pure financial investors and multinational companies seeking solutions to the tightening environmental performance requirements of an increasingly carbon-constrained global economy.

As for the trading of GHG emission credits, suffice it to say that ABN AMRO anticipates a market in Europe along of €45 billion by 2012, the end of the first Kyoto compliance period. Early indications would seem to support that bullish view. Between 2001 and 2003, carbon market transactions more than doubled in volume each year, from 13 million tonnes of carbon equivalent in 2001 to 70 million tonnes in 2003. In 2005, the first three months of the EU ETS saw 25 million tonnes traded, at an average cost of 10 euros per tonne. Once again, the opportunities in this space are of interest both to pure financial investors and to industrial companies seeking cost-effective solutions to Kyoto compliance challenges.

5. *Early movers can gain significant financial and competitive benefits.* Of course, the companies cited in the previous section are all examples of this early-mover advantage. Toyota, Alcoa, Johnson & Johnson, ST MicroElectronics, Canon and BHP Billiton are only a few of the growing list of other examples. Toyota, for example, is currently reshaping its entire corporate strategy around being competitive in a low-carbon global market. Its runaway success with the hybrid automobile Prius is only the first step in a much broader set of initiatives. Like the other companies listed above, Toyota believes that it is creating *strategic* and competitive advantage through being an early mover. And, as of mid-2005, who can argue with it?

"CARBON BETA" – AN INVESTOR'S PROXY FOR MANAGEMENT QUALITY

As we have seen, there is already a rich and growing body of finance literature strongly suggesting that companies with superior overall environmental management and strategic positioning are simply better-managed companies overall, and therefore better risk-adjusted investment candidates.[6] I have argued elsewhere that this is likely to be true because environmental management is becoming an increasingly robust proxy for companies' overall management quality in general (see Kiernan, 2004). Most City and Wall Street analysts consider management quality to be the singly most important determinant of companies' competitiveness and financial performance, although most have yet to "connect the dots" and recognise the link between strategic environmental management and *overall* managerial competence.

Some recent quantitative finance research carried out by State Street Global Advisors (SSGA) would seem to confirm that thesis. SSGA is currently the largest institutional asset manager in the world, with more than US$1.4 trillion under management. The study was conducted by SSGA's Advanced Research Center in Boston in 2005.

In order to isolate and focus on the financial impact of sustainability factors such as climate change, other key financial factors

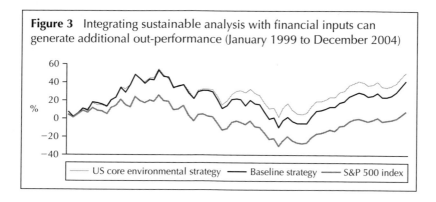

Figure 3 Integrating sustainable analysis with financial inputs can generate additional out-performance (January 1999 to December 2004)

Table 1

Performance results	Cumulative return	Annual return	Cum ex return	Annual ex return	Tracking error	Info ratio	Annual turnover
US core env.	51.21%	7.13%	43.07%	5.88%	4.81%	1.22	102%
Baseline	41.35	5.94	33.21	4.69	5.48	0.86	102
S&P 500 Index	8.14	1.25					

were normalised away, so that there were "no bets" being made on industry sectors, company size, P/E ratios and so on. The only "bets" were on companies with superior sustainability and carbon risk management characteristics, as determined by Innovest.

The result? The hypothetical sustainability-enhanced portfolio outperformed its Standard & Poor's 500 benchmark by 5.88% per year. It *also* added 1.19% to the return of SSGA's core outperformance model, and improved the portfolio's information ratio (balance between return and risk) from 0.86 to 1.22.

Similar results were achieved in a recent study by the head of research of the major Dutch pension fund ABP and his academic colleagues at Erasmus University in the Netherlands. ABP is the largest pension fund in Europe, and one of the three largest in the world. The study has been published recently in a leading academic finance journal (see Bauer *et al*, 2005).

Given the sophistication of both studies' methodologies (and the impressive pedigrees of their authors), it is difficult if not impossible to dismiss the results or to explain the outperformance using traditional financial factors. My hypothesis, instead, is that the focus on sustainability simply provided a powerful signal about the overall management quality of the firm – a perspective not captured by traditional financial analysis. If this is correct, then there is every reason to believe that companies with superior climate strategies will command even larger premiums going forward as regulatory and competitive drivers have been greater impacts.

Climate change could be viewed as the *ultimate* proxy for overall management quality. Climate change has all the ingredients of a supreme test of management capability: enormous financial stakes; massive regulatory and market uncertainty over long time horizons; global impacts with significant regional and even national variation; and multiple and conflicting stakeholder demands. As a general proposition, therefore, we would argue that any company in a high-impact industry sector that can manage the risks and opportunities of climate change better than its competitors is likely to be a better-managed, more agile, forward-looking company – full stop.

INSTITUTIONAL INVESTORS ON THE MARCH

Since the late 1980s, shareholder activism has played an increasingly important role in attempts to influence the quality of companies' corporate governance. More recently, this increase in shareholder activism has coincided with, and been augmented by, two other powerful investment trends: the dramatic increase in the proportion of company shares held by institutions, and the rapid growth in the attention paid to corporate social responsibility and sustainable development issues.

We have already noted the emergence of new coalitions of institutional investors concerned with climate change. The largest of them, the Carbon Disclosure Project, is a global effort. Other significant but regional initiatives are under way in Europe and Australia. Even in the US, ostensibly one of the last bastions of climate change denial, significant institutional investor activity is under way through the Investor Network on Climate Risk, whose numbers control over US$2 trillion in investable assets.

It is also tempting – but somewhat misleading – for international observers to interpret the relative lack of leadership and activity on climate change in Washington as evidence of overall lack of governmental concern in the US. This would be dangerously misleading: in the US today, the real action is at the state level. California,

New York and Connecticut, among other states, have pursued an aggressive compaign of engagement with major corporations. As of mid-2005, claimate change to be the most rapidly growing catagory of shareholder resolutions in the US, and these motions are securing approval rates of 35% and above.

But the activities of US state governments in this area go well beyond the mere filing of shareholder resolutions. In 2004, eight US state attorneys general actually filed formal lawsuits against five of the largest power companies in the US, demanding reductions in their GHG emissions. Several have also threatened to sue their own federal government, in an attempt to force the US Environment Protection Agency to regulate GHGs as harmful substances. Perhaps most significantly of all, the Investor Network on Climate Risk virtually doubled in size in May 2005, and now includes more than 20 US institutional investors, most of them state pension funds.

THE NEXT FRONTIER: NEW INVESTMENT STRATEGIES

As we have seen, institutional investors worldwide are beginning to translate their concerns over the financial risks of climate change into aggressive shareholder engagement with their portfolio companies. What is somewhat surprising, however, is the relative absence of institutions taking their concerns to the next logical level – asset allocation strategy, stock selection and portfolio construction. To date, very few of even the most proactive public-sector institutions have adopted concrete investment strategies that utilise climate risk analysis as an explicit input into actual security selection and portfolio construction. There is already compelling evidence that such analysis can identify both hidden investment risks *and* companies with superior strategic management, yet very few have so far taken advantage.[7]

North American institutions have been particularly conspicuous by their absence in this regard. At the time of writing, however, this appears about to change. Two of the three largest pension funds in the country, CalPERS and CalSTRS (California public employees and teachers) have together committed nearly a billion US dollars to "environmentally enhanced" investment strategies. The State of Vermont is displaying similar leadership. It is to be hoped that other major institutional investors will follow suit, both in the US and elsewhere. Once corporate executives and boards of directors begin to see that their performance on the climate file *directly* affects the cost and even the availability of capital, one can reasonably expect them to redouble – or, in some cases, initiate – their efforts at GHG reduction and mitigation.

Before that day fully dawns, however, the capital markets will need to undergo some fundamental, structural changes. Despite much talk about the evils of "short-termism", virtually all of the key actors in the investment value chain continue to be motivated, assessed, and compensated on the basis of their *short-term* performance. Pension fund trustees generally judge their money mangers on the basis of – at most – a three-year performance cycle, and are frequently prone to jettison them even before that if their performance falters. The pension fund consultants who advise the trustees and help them choose their money managers have in general done little to promote longer-term mandates and perspectives.[8] Money managers in their turn are almost invariably compensated on a short-term basis, and can easily be dismissed or reassigned by their company supervisors if their short-term results are poor. And corporate executives are focused like lasers on "making their quarterly numbers". Woe betide companies and their management teams who disappoint the all-important analysts' expectations: the market generally metes out swift and often savage retribution.

Thus we have a self-reinforcing "conspiracy of short-termism" among all of the key actors in the capital markets. That in turn produces an ironic and perverse result: the very institutions (such as pension funds) whose liabilities to their beneficiaries and investment horizons are *long*-term in nature are impelled towards investment strategies that are driven by *short*-term performance imperatives.

Under such circumstances, it is little wonder that persuading trustees, analysts, money managers and consultants to address longer-term issues such as climate change has been prodigiously difficult – there is a fundamental mismatch in investment horizons. Sadly, there are no "magic bullets" to alleviate the problems of short-termism: it will require an entire constellation of measures: greater transparency regarding corporate risk levels, tougher securities listing requirements from stock exchanges, and different and clearer mandates from the *owners* of major companies – the large institutional investors themselves. Above all, it will require a major *attitudinal* shift – one towards an ethos that recognises that critical sustainability issues such as climate change *do* have an increasingly strong bearing on companies' competitiveness and financial performance.

As we saw earlier, there is a growing body of evidence from the strong performance of a new generation of sophisticated "eco-enhanced" investment funds that explicitly address climate risk. One only hopes that this evidence will be taken seriously *before* the last vestiges of the polar ice cap disappear!

1   The term "fiduciary capitalism" was most widely popularised in Hawley and Williams (2000).
2   The Carbon Disclosure Project is a London-based not-for-profit initiative, which is currently in its third year of operation. The CDP institutional investor signatories have now sent letters to the chief executives of the world's 500 largest publicly traded companies for three years in a row. Over its three-year life, the volume of institutional assets supporting the disclosure request has grown by nearly 500%. Company response rates have also increased. Innovest Strategic Value Advisors serves as the chief technical advisers to the project.
3   See, for example, Bauer *et al* (2005); Gluck and Becker (2005); Cowe (2004); Panmure (2002); Forum for the Future (2002); UBS Warburg (2001); Bank Sarasin (1998, 1999); European Federation of Financial Analysts (1996).
4   See, for example, the Carbon Disclosure Project's major report: *Climate Change and Shareholder Value in 2004*, which was written by Innovest Strategic Value Advisors.
5   Two recent reports by the World Resources Institute provide compelling scenarios of the potential competitive impacts of climate change on companies in the oil and gas sector and automobile manufacturing sectors. See World Resources Institute (2002, 2003).
6   See Note 3.
7   There are, however, some conspicuous exceptions: in the Netherlands, the major pension funds ABP and PGGM, in Sweden the AP7 and AP3 funds, and in the UK, the pension fund of the Environment Agency.
8   One welcome exception was provided in 2003–4 by an innovative competition in the UK sponsored by the Universities Superannuation Scheme and the consultants Bacon and Woodrow. The competition was for a hypothetical 30-year, US$30 billion asset-management mandate, and received some excellent and innovative responses. While there appears to be growing sympathy in the consultant community for longer-term mandates, examples on the ground are still virtually unknown.

REFERENCES

Bank Sarasin, 1998, "Environmental shareholder value".

Bank Sarasin, 1999, "Sustainable investments".

Bauer, B., *et al*, 2005, "The Eco-efficiency premium puzzle in the US equity market", *Financial Analysts Journal*.

Clean Edge, Inc, 2005, *Clean Energy Trends 2005*.

Cowe, R., 2004, "Risk, returns, and responsibility", Association of British Insurers.

Dlugolecki, A. and M. Mansley, 2005, "Asset management and climate cange", Technical Report #20, Tyndall Centre for Climate Change Research.

European Federation of Financial Analysts, 1996, "Sustainability and financial analysis".

Forum for the Future, 2002, "Sustainability pays".

Gluck, K. and Y. Becker, 2005, "The impact of eco-efficiency alphas", *Journal of Asset Management*, January.

Hawley, J. and A. Williams, 2000, *The Rise of Fiduciary Capitalism*, (Philadelphia: University of Pennsylvania Press)

IRRC, 2005, "Environment: Global climate change".

Kiernan, M., 2004, "Sustainable development", in George Dallas (ed), *Governance and Risk* (New York: McGraw Hill).

Panmure, W. L. B., 2002, *More Gain Than Pain: SRI Sustainability Pays Off*.

UBS Warburg, 2001, "Sustainability investment: The merits of socially responsible investing".

Section 5

Sector Developments

19

Climate Change and the Automotive Industry – Impact on Companies' Value*

Philipp Mettler

SAM Research AG

Climate change, of which global warming is one manifestation (see Figure 1), has the potential to become a significant issue for the automotive industry. Climate-change policies are already in place in several major automotive markets and appear likely to spread, forcing OEMs (original equipment manufacturers) to lower the carbon emissions profile of new vehicles. However, this will not only cause higher costs for the industry, but also offer the potential to increase market shares and profitability for the successful companies.

The purpose of this chapter is to help investors to make better-informed decisions regarding automotive stocks in the light of emerging carbon constraints policy measures designed to mitigate climate change by limiting emissions of carbon dioxide (CO_2) and other greenhouse gases. The chapter explores how carbon constraints in global automotive markets may affect the value of 10 leading automotive companies until 2015, a timeframe in which major technological and policy changes are likely to occur.

In this chapter we look at the value drivers of car manufacturers and try to evaluate how they will be affected by carbon constraints. We shed light on the policy framework of the most important car markets while showing the main lower-carbon technologies that are

* This chapter is based on the report "Changing Drivers – The impact of climate change on competitiveness and value creation in the automotive industry", which has been produced by SAM Group (SAM) in collaboration with the World Resources Institute (WRI).

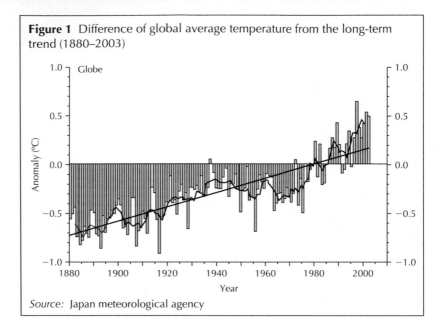

Figure 1 Difference of global average temperature from the long-term trend (1880–2003)

Source: Japan meteorological agency

expected to be developed between now and 2015. Next we try to quantify the impact of carbon constraints on competitiveness and companies' value (the analysis comprises 10 leading OEMs). And lastly, we conclude with the main findings and recommendations.

DRIVERS FOR CAR MANUFACTURERS

The value model for the automotive industry can be split into two sections. The tangible value drivers consist of the supply/demand situation (the cyclicality), the available and used production capacity (which is also linked to the cost structure) and the model policy. In addition to them, a number of intangible value drivers – such as brand, innovation and product quality – are increasingly viewed as important sources of competitive advantage (see Figure 2). Intangible assets may represent a substantial part of an OEM's market value.

The automotive industry is highly capital-intensive. In order to compete, OEMs must achieve either significant economies of scale or operate in a market niche (such as luxury cars), which in turn raises barriers to entry and exit. The combination of generally low sales growth and high entry/exit barriers ensures market rivalry and competitive pressure within the sector. This manifests itself in

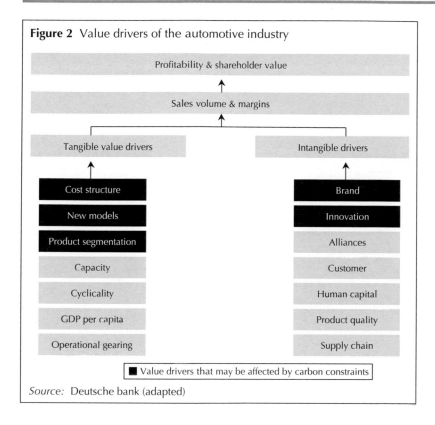

Figure 2 Value drivers of the automotive industry

Profitability & shareholder value

↑

Sales volume & margins

↑

Tangible value drivers	Intangible drivers
Cost structure	Brand
New models	Innovation
Product segmentation	Alliances
Capacity	Customer
Cyclicality	Human capital
GDP per capita	Product quality
Operational gearing	Supply chain

■ Value drivers that may be affected by carbon constraints

Source: Deutsche bank (adapted)

excessive additions to overall capacity, as each OEM tries to recoup large fixed costs and to gain market shares through higher sales volume. The result is global production overcapacity, currently around 20–25%, which puts pressure on pricing and margins, and leads to a return on capital employed below its cost. An important means of securing, at least temporarily, an advantage is through innovation (such as new models and technologies).

Carbon constraints will complicate existing industry dynamics. The following drivers (see Figure 2) are some of the ways in which carbon constraints could affect key value drivers, positively or negatively.

Brand: As homogenisation of vehicles increases, OEMs compete more and more on non-manufacturing factors such as brand. Environmental quality can be an important component of brand, and being viewed as a leader on climate change could enhance brand value.

Innovation: Maintaining innovative capacity is critical in the automotive industry as new models and technologies are a source of differentiation and competitive advantage. Leadership in lower-carbon technologies could translate into first-mover advantages of stronger pricing power and higher margins.

New models: The development and launch of new models is key for staying in the business. Failure to address carbon constraints at this early stage could compromise a new platform's long-term viability in markets that subsequently require reduced carbon emission.

Product segmentation: OEMs that depend on market segments featuring carbon-intensive (fuel-inefficient) vehicles, such as SUVs (sports utility vehicles) may be more exposed to emerging carbon constraints. Diversification into lower-carbon-intensive segments could diminish profitability if it is just done through the move to smaller vehicles instead of the introduction of new technologies.

Cost structure: Carbon constraints will raise costs across all stages of the business, from R&D and design to production. Nevertheless, some OEMs may gain competitive advantage by either facing lower cost increases than their competitors or increasing market shares.

A successful business strategy in a carbon-constrained market will be one that can maintain or enhance profitability from sales of progressively less carbon-intensive vehicles. The management challenge will require both minimising the risks and capitalising on the opportunities noted above (schematically shown in Figure 3).

Not only are OEMs at different positions today with regard to this challenge, but the direction of immediate business plans may be inconsistent with moving to a more sustainable position. The management of OEMs has therefore to incorporate carbon reduction plans into the business and ensure that they are aligned with traditional profitability goals.

CLIMATE-CHANGE POLICIES

As part of international efforts to tackle climate change, several of the world's major automotive markets are adopting policies to reduce vehicle-related CO_2 emissions. With the bulk of automotive-related CO_2 emissions occurring during vehicle use (see Figure 4), fuel economy and CO_2 emissions standards offer the best prospect

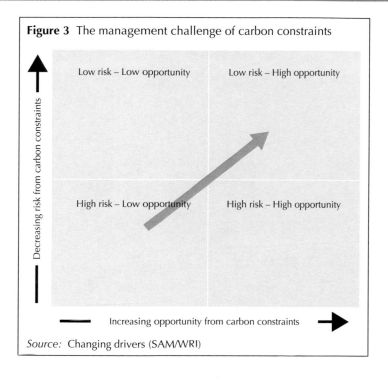

Figure 3 The management challenge of carbon constraints

Low risk – Low opportunity

Low risk – High opportunity

High risk – Low opportunity

High risk – High opportunity

Decreasing risk from carbon constraints

Increasing opportunity from carbon constraints

Source: Changing drivers (SAM/WRI)

for reducing vehicles' contribution to climate change. This type of "carbon constraint" is already emerging in the following markets.

❑ In the EU, a dialogue between regulators and the automotive industry trade association (Association des Constructeurs Européens d'Automobiles, or ACEA) inspired a voluntary commitment from the industry to reduce CO_2 emissions from passenger cars by 25% by 2008 to a level of 140 g CO_2/km. The commitment extends to JAMA and KAMA, the Japanese OEM and Korean OEM associations respectively. Depending on early progress, ACEA may extend the target to 120 g CO_2/km by 2012. This tougher objective will be substantially more difficult and costly to meet than the 2008 one, because it might require the hybridisation of the drive-train and more dramatic shifts in the product portfolio. According to EU member states' data, in 2002 the average CO_2 emissions from ACEA's new vehicle fleet was 165 g CO_2/km (petrol-fuelled cars: 172 g CO_2/km; diesel-fuelled cars: 155 g CO_2/km). This is in line with the 2003 intermediate

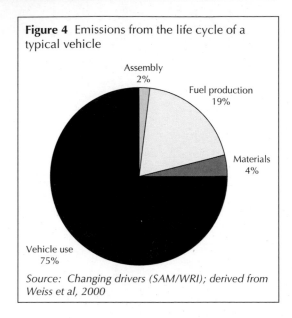

Figure 4 Emissions from the life cycle of a typical vehicle

Assembly
2%

Fuel production
19%

Materials
4%

Vehicle use
75%

Source: Changing drivers (SAM/WRI); derived from Weiss et al, 2000

target range of 165–70 g CO_2/km. Compared with 2001 this represents a reduction of 1.2% in new vehicle emissions. In order to reach the 2008 target, OEMs will have to accelerate the annual reduction rate compared with the rate achieved since 1995.

❑ In Japan, new legislation requires fuel-economy improvements in cars of 23% beyond 1995 levels by 2010. Specific targets vary with vehicle weight but the lowest level is 125 g CO_2/km.

❑ To date, the US has taken no comparable action to regulate vehicle emissions in response to the climate-change challenge. The long-term Corporate Average Fuel Economy (CAFE) programme has held standards unchanged through the 1990s, and made them slightly stringent only two years ago. In April 2003, CAFE standards for light trucks were raised from 268 g CO_2/km to 249 g CO_2/km by 2007. Fuel economy levels for cars remain fixed at the 201 g CO_2/km level first set in 1990. Moreover, Congress has repeatedly rejected bills proposing higher fuel economy standards. However, a 2002 Californian law seeks to regulate vehicle CO_2 emissions for cars and light trucks. The regulations will go into effect in 2006, but will give OEMs until 2009 to comply. Though not a national law and still subject to challenge in court, this initiative could have profound implications for OEMs as other states, most notably New York, might follow California's lead. In addition to this, there is an increasing number of non-governmental initiatives (for instance, www.idontcareaboutair.com).

❏ A key issue for the industry is whether emerging automotive markets will embrace carbon constraints as part of their development. Although mature automotive markets still account for over two-thirds of global vehicle sales, emerging markets will account for most of the growth in the industry in the coming years, given the pace of urbanisation and population growth.

The above-mentioned developments suggest that concern about climate change will exert a significant influence over the industry in the next decade. Companies well positioned to handle these constraints will find themselves with a competitive advantage over those unable to adapt to new market conditions and rules.

LOWER-CARBON TECHNOLOGIES

In carbon-constrained markets, OEMs will have to produce vehicles that emit less carbon while continuing to create value for shareholders. To meet carbon constraints, OEMs can turn to a wide range of "lower-carbon technologies", some of which could transform the industry in terms of competitive advantages.

These technologies vary in terms of their carbon-reduction potential and the degree to which they can penetrate the market within the next 10 years. Incremental technologies added to the standard gasoline-ICE (internal-combustion engine) have achieved significant carbon savings up to 35% compared with a 1996 reference vehicle (see Figure 5). CO_2 savings from fuel cells are sensitive to the choice of the fuel.

The main lower-carbon technologies that are expected to be developed between now and 2015 can be grouped into four main categories:

❏ incremental technologies (including advanced gasoline-ICE technologies);
❏ diesel (or compression-ignition) technology;
❏ hybrid technology; and
❏ fuel-cell technology.

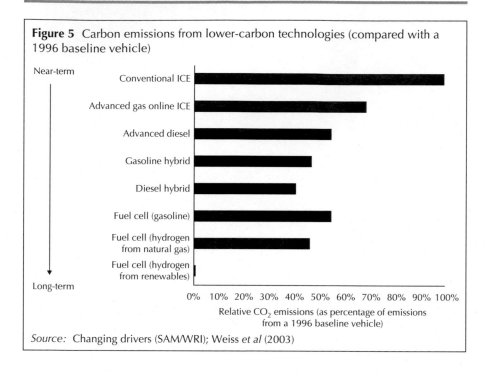

Figure 5 Carbon emissions from lower-carbon technologies (compared with a 1996 baseline vehicle)

Near-term

Conventional ICE

Advanced gas online ICE

Advanced diesel

Gasoline hybrid

Diesel hybrid

Fuel cell (gasoline)

Fuel cell (hydrogen from natural gas)

Fuel cell (hydrogen from renewables)

Long-term

0% 10% 20% 30% 40% 50% 60% 70% 80% 90% 100%

Relative CO_2 emissions (as percentage of emissions from a 1996 baseline vehicle)

Source: Changing drivers (SAM/WRI); Weiss *et al* (2003)

While incremental technologies (transmission technologies, weight reduction, direct fuel injection, drag reduction and so on) may play a significant role in helping OEMs to meet carbon constraints, they offer little scope for the companies to derive a specific competitive advantage. On the other hand, while fuel cells may deliver few actual carbon reductions through 2015, they represent a major and potentially disruptive advance in the automobile's evolution that could reward technology leaders with competitive advantage. Hybrid and diesel technologies lie somewhere between these extremes, offering both the prospect of CO_2 reductions through 2015, and potential for brand differentiation and competitive advantage (see Figure 6).

The internal-combustion engine is likely to continue to be the dominant platform through 2015 across all markets, with scope for diesel to grow further in the European market and to penetrate the US market. Facing carbon constraints, many OEMs will steadily "hybridise" their product portfolio over time, coupling electric motors and batteries with both gasoline and diesel engines.

The whole development is complicated by the uncertainty over which technology option(s) will become the market standard(s).

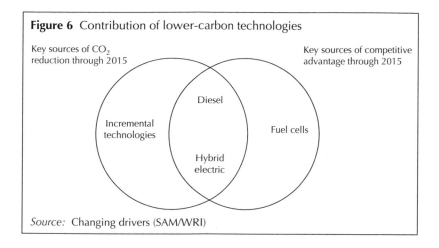

Figure 6 Contribution of lower-carbon technologies

Key sources of CO_2 reduction through 2015

Key sources of competitive advantage through 2015

Diesel

Incremental technologies

Fuel cells

Hybrid electric

Source: Changing drivers (SAM/WRI)

Therefore, OEMs face not only the R&D challenge of producing lower-carbon technologies, but also the management challenge of applying the right innovation strategy. To control expenditures, many OEMs are now engaged in research partnerships and alliances around lower-carbon technologies.

RISKS AND OPPORTUNITIES FOR OEMS

With respect to the growing carbon constraints on the automotive markets, a key challenge is for sector investors and OEM managers to quantify the impact of carbon constraints on competitiveness. The analysis comprises 10 leading OEMs: BMW, Daimler-Chrysler (DC), Ford, General Motors (GM), Honda, Nissan, PSA Peugeot Citroën (PSA), Renault, Toyota and Volkswagen (VW). The geographical focus is the US, EU and Japanese markets, which together account for nearly 70% of global sales. The time period analysed is from 2003 to 2015.

CURRENT CARBON PROFILES OF OEMS

By measuring the "carbon intensity" of current sales and profits, it is possible to assess each OEM's initial exposure to emerging carbon constraints. All else being equal, OEMs that earn a relatively large proportion of their profits from carbon-intensive segments will find carbon constraints more challenging. Differing consumer preferences and regulatory attitudes to carbon constraints across major markets must also be taken into account.

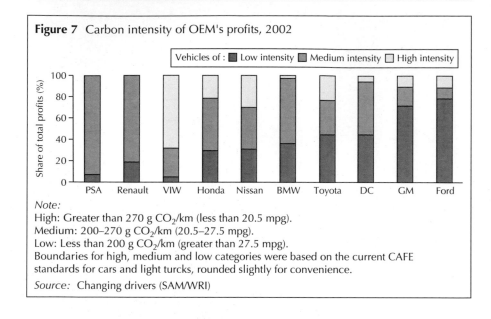

Figure 7 Carbon intensity of OEM's profits, 2002

Note:
High: Greater than 270 g CO_2/km (less than 20.5 mpg).
Medium: 200–270 g CO_2/km (20.5–27.5 mpg).
Low: Less than 200 g CO_2/km (greater than 27.5 mpg).
Boundaries for high, medium and low categories were based on the current CAFE standards for cars and light turcks, rounded slightly for convenience.
Source: Changing drivers (SAM/WRI)

OEMs are differently positioned to respond to the challenges of carbon constraints. This is because of differences regarding:

❑ segment mix (for example, more sales of light trucks in the case of Daimler-Chrysler than of VW)
❑ carbon intensity of models (SUVs, for instance, emit much more CO_2 than smaller and lighter cars – but on the other hand have a higher margin); and
❑ geographic distribution of sales (for example, Ford and GM are much more exposed to the US than PSA and Renault).

The structure of each OEM's product portfolio largely determines its current "carbon intensity of profits" (see Figure 7).

The carbon intensity of profits provides only a snapshot of where OEMs find themselves at a certain point in time and says little about how OEMs can, and will, respond to carbon constraints. The following three sections will be more forward-looking. First, we estimate the costs for OEMs in order to meet the higher fuel economy standards in 2015 (see "Value exposure assessment"). Second, we try to assess the management ability to capitalise on their investments in lower carbon technologies (see "Management quality assessment"). And, at last, we translate the previous findings into changes of discounted EBIT (earnings before interest and taxes), a foundation for financial valuation in the sector (see "Aggregate results and valuation implications").

VALUE EXPOSURE ASSESSMENT

In all three main automotive markets – the US, EU and Japan – governments have committed to higher fuel economy or CO_2 emission standards in the coming years. These standards will require OEMs to make potentially costly changes to vehicle specifications and sales mix. The costs incurred by each OEM will vary depending on its product portfolio and on the costs of achieving CO_2 reductions for different vehicle types.

Using a risk-assessment methodology developed by the World Resources Institute (WRI), we estimated the cost that each OEM will incur to meet the carbon constraints by 2015. In the analytical model, each OEM is assumed to have access to three main lower-carbon technologies – incremental technologies, diesel and hybrid technology (fuel-cell technology is ignored because it is unlikely to contribute to actual CO_2 reductions before 2015). The model calculates the lowest-cost combination of technologies that an OEM must add to its vehicle fleet while taking into account uncertainties about the future regulatory environment (via weighted scenario analysis regarding different levels of carbon constraints that may emerge by 2015) as well as the market penetration rates of diesel and hybrid technologies. I would like to point out that the costs to comply could be much higher than stated here as they rise disproportionately with tougher standards.

Because OEMs' product mixes differ with respect to carbon-intensity levels, the costs incurred in meeting new standards will vary quite a bit across the industry (see Figure 8).

Availability of diesel and hybrid technologies differs by market. Moreover, for hybrid and diesel technology, we assume that manufacturing costs vary among OEMs according to level of expertise with these technologies.

While production costs will increase as a result of the carbon constraints, OEMs could see returns on these costs in the following ways:

❑ some OEMs have to spend less than others, and so should become more price-competitive in the marketplace and enjoy higher sales; and

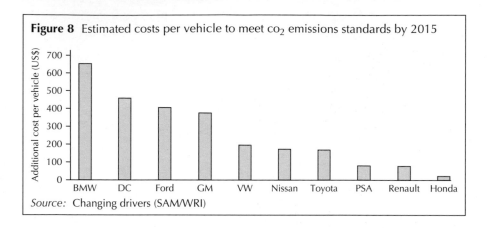

Figure 8 Estimated costs per vehicle to meet CO_2 emissions standards by 2015

Source: Changing drivers (SAM/WRI)

❑ consumers might put some value to the fuel savings and, therefore, at least some of the additional costs could be recovered.

MANAGEMENT QUALITY ASSESSMENT

We identify diesel, hybrid and fuel-cell technology as key sources
for future competitive advantage. Besides the development of these
technologies, OEMs have also to commercialise, market and mass-
produce these technologies in order to reap the full rewards.

The analytical framework we used to assess lower-carbon management quality is based on a management competence model
developed by SAM Research (see Figure 9).

By combining scores across technologies, we derive an overall
score for lower-carbon strategies for each OEM (see Figure 10, horizontal axis). Toyota, Daimler-Chrysler, and Renault-Nissan appear
to have the strongest current management quality with regard to
lower-carbon technologies.

Besides the overall strength, an OEM's current strategy with
regard to carbon constraints may be more or less robust (or balanced) across alternative-technology pathways. While most
European OEMs display a strategic bias towards diesel, US-based
OEMs focus on fuel-cell technology. Toyota and Honda show most
bias towards hybrid technology. Renault-Nissan stands out among
OEMs as having one of the more balanced carbon strategies,
reflecting the alliance's strategic fit and competitive potential.

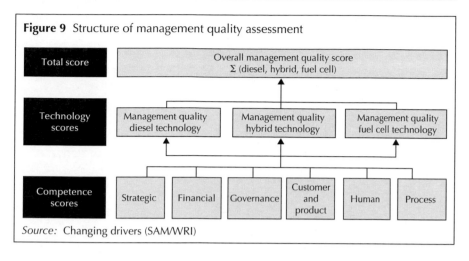

Figure 9 Structure of management quality assessment

Source: Changing drivers (SAM/WRI)

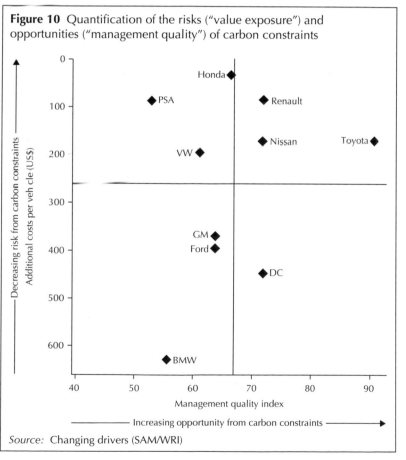

Figure 10 Quantification of the risks ("value exposure") and opportunities ("management quality") of carbon constraints

Source: Changing drivers (SAM/WRI)

AGGREGATE RESULTS AND VALUATION IMPLICATIONS

The combined results of the "value exposure" and "management quality" assessments are illustrated in Figure 10. Risks are presented in terms of average additional cost per vehicle (lower costs are better). The upside strategy opportunities are expressed as a qualitative score between 0 and 100 (higher scores are better). OEMs in the top right quadrant can be considered "lower-carbon leaders" with below-average exposure to risks and above-average management quality with regard to lower-carbon technologies.

Several findings are of note:

❏ OEMs vary considerably with respect to both value exposure and management quality – this indicates that carbon constraints have the ability to influence the competitive balance within the industry.

❏ Honda has the lowest-value exposure to carbon constraints, while Toyota emerges as the clear leader on carbon-related management quality with a strong position in all three technologies that will be key for long-term competitiveness.

❏ Renault and Nissan are also strongly positioned with better-than-average management quality scores and lower-than-average expected costs from carbon constraints.

❏ BMW stands out as having the greatest-value exposure, though this may be somewhat misleading. As the company produces almost exclusively premium (high-cost, high-price) vehicles, it has greater ability to pass on costs to consumers than other OEMs.

A key challenge for analysts is to determine the implications of these findings for shareholder value creation. Consequently, we translated the results of the "value exposure" and "management quality" assessment into changes of forecasted EBIT for the period 2003 through 2015.

We started with the base EBIT forecast for the period, which reflects important differences in OEMs' fundamental business performance. For example, some OEMs, such as GM and Ford, are expected to see slower-than-average sales growth in the coming years. Additionally, some OEMs, such as BMW and Toyota, are expected to retain higher EBIT premiums because of such factors as brand and quality. We then added the results of our "value exposure" and "management quality" assessment in the form of EBIT. This adjusted EBIT was then discounted back to the base year (2003) in

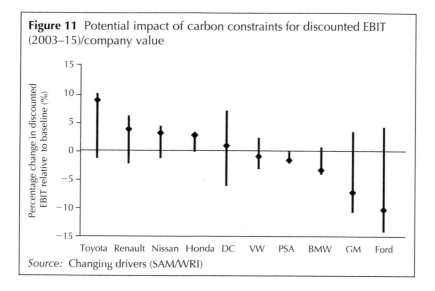

Figure 11 Potential impact of carbon constraints for discounted EBIT (2003–15)/company value

Source: Changing drivers (SAM/WRI)

order to figure out the difference to the present value of the "original" EBIT forecast.

Figure 11 shows the range of possible effects on EBIT, in terms of percentage changes from business-as-usual EBIT projections. The upper limits reflect the results from the "management quality" assessment alone, while the lower limits are the results from the "value exposure" assessment alone. The points indicate our estimate of the combined impact of both assessments on EBIT.

In Table 1 we illustrate how important the right strategy – in terms of future products and therefore pricing power as well as cost control – for the valuation of the company is (company value = present value). A small change in the long-term EBIT margin (for example, due to the product strategy) can make quite a difference for the value of the company which can have further implications.

CONCLUSIONS

❑ Emerging carbon constraints could significantly impact the competitive landscape of the automotive industry, primarily through pressure to increase the fuel economy of CO_2 emissions intensity of vehicles.

Table 1 EBIT margin and company value

EBIT Margin	3.0%	4.0%	5.0%	6.0%	7.0%	8.0%	9.0%
Sales	100.0%	100.0%	100.0%	100.0%	100.0%	100.0%	100.0%
Depreciation	4.5%	4.5%	4.5%	4.5%	4.5%	4.5%	4.5%
EBITDA	7.5%	8.5%	9.5%	10.5%	11.5%	12.5%	13.5%
EBIT	3.0%	4.0%	5.0%	6.0%	7.0%	8.0%	9.0%
Tax 30%	0.9%	1.2%	1.5%	1.8%	2.1%	2.4%	2.7%
Investments	6.0%	6.0%	6.0%	6.0%	6.0%	6.0%	6.0%
Free Cash Flow (Margin)	0.6%	1.3%	2.0%	2.7%	3.4%	4.1%	4.8%
Present value (PV)	10.3	22.3	34.3	46.4	58.4	70.4	82.4
Price/Earnings Ratio	4.9	8.0	9.8	11.0	11.9	12.6	13.1
Sales as % of Ev	10.0%	22.0%	34.0%	46.0%	58.0%	70.0%	82.0%
EV/EBIT	3.4	5.6	6.9	7.7	8.3	8.8	9.2
EV/EBITDA	1.4	2.6	3.6	4.4	5.1	5.6	6.1

Assumptions: growth rate = 3%; WACC = 9%, tax rate = 30%; no debt
Source: SAM Research

❑ Carbon constraints are already in place in major automotive markets. An indication of growing pressure in this area is the fact that more than 60% of global vehicle sales in 2002 occurred in countries that have ratified the Kyoto Protocol.
❑ OEMs are differently positioned to respond to the challenges or carbon constraints. This is because of differences regarding:
  ❑ segment mix;
  ❑ carbon intensity of models; and
  ❑ geographic distribution of sales.
❑ Lacking transparency makes it difficult for stakeholders to get a clear picture regarding the actual position and future strategy of the automobile companies in terms of CO_2 emissions (required research-and-development costs as well as capital expenditure).
❑ In the short term, carbon constraints could present the industry with new cost burdens that vary among OEMs. Some of these costs could be recouped by price premiums if more consumers were to account properly for fuel cost savings, though this tendency varies from market to market.
❑ In the mid- to long-term, carbon constraints will also create opportunities by raising the competitive edge of companies who have introduced fuel-efficient technologies. Toyota stands out as

the best positioned on these issues overall while GM and Ford could face the largest impact on market valuation.

❏ The cost of complying with continuously tougher standards rises disproportionately.

❏ While the findings refer primarily to carbon constraints, they also shed light on how OEMs may perform in response to other pressures that would lead consumers or regulators to value fuel economy more highly.

❏ Indeed, in the case of an energy shock, the demand for fuel-efficient vehicles might even accelerate the impacts described in this chapter.

❏ The findings may also offer insight into the relative performance of OEMs in key emerging markets (such as China), where fuel economy might be valued for non-carbon reasons. Low average income and crowded cities may steer consumers to smaller, more efficient vehicles.

Overall, environmental considerations for the automotive industry (carbon constraints, etc) are very likely to receive a prominent place within the valuation and stock selection framework of investors over the years to come. This also implies that companies have to become more open and publish a roadmap that shows how they are going to achieve the goals, including the costs involved.

20

Climate Change Policies and Energy Intensive Industry

David Pocklington, Richard Leese

British Cement Association

GOVERNMENT AND INDUSTRY

With its focus on energy-intensive industry, current climate-change policy is inevitably dependent on the "deep pockets" of industry generating a "technical fix", rather than the encouragement of attitudinal or structural changes. Industry participation is a vital component of government-initiated regimes, since much of the essential technical information lies at plant or company level. Sector-specific issues are an important consideration, but across manufacturing industry there is a high degree of commonality in the areas that are of major concern.

In the development of UK schemes, government engaged with industry through plenary meetings with pan-industry representation and bilateral meetings with individual sectors or industrial organisations. Industry in turn formed its own groups with which to develop common positions. Similarly, analysis of responses to the European Commission consultation on the EU Emissions Trading Scheme (EU ETS) revealed a high degree of convergence of the views within industry (see Pocklington, 2002).

ENERGY-INTENSIVE INDUSTRY AND CLIMATE CHANGE

The Integrated Pollution Prevention and Control (IPPC) regime has provided a convenient, if undiscerning, vehicle for applying CO_2-reduction measures to energy-intensive processes in both UK[1] and the EU[2] schemes. These include the manufacture of iron and steel, paper, cement, lime, ceramics, chemicals and glass. However, such an approach necessarily restricts the ambit of the controls and the potential carbon dioxide reductions.

Energy-intensive industry is largely dependent on the burning of fossil fuels either directly within the process or indirectly through electrical energy supplied to the process by the electricity generators, another energy-intensive process. To date, most attention has been paid to the reduction of carbon dioxide, which accounts for approximately 85% of the UK's greenhouse gas emissions, and a smaller percentage of their total global warming potential.

Energy costs

The impact of climate-change controls is a function of three factors: dependency of the process on energy; principal energy source(s); and extent to which market conditions affect the energy cost. Energy represents about 35% of the cement industry's variable costs, and this provides a strong driver for improved performance even in the absence of mandatory CO_2-reduction measures. The introduction of climate-change controls/emissions trading adds a further component to the overall cost of energy, and its impact is dependent upon the level of this cost in comparison to the three factors above.

While high-added-value products will be able to absorb much of the costs of carbon abatement, this is not the case for low-value products such as cement. Compared with other materials, cement has the highest carbon dioxide emissions per unit of profit/turnover. Coal has traditionally been the dominant fuel in cement making, and its replacement with "waste-derived" fuels is an important means of offsetting these high costs.

OPPORTUNITIES TO REDUCE CARBON DIOXIDE

For manufacturing processes, the reduction of carbon dioxide emissions is governed by the laws of physics and chemistry, and can be achieved *only* through:

❏ switching to energy sources that do not generate carbon dioxide;
❏ improving the efficiency with which the primary energy is generated, transmitted and used;
❏ improving the efficiency with which energy is used; or
❏ reducing the demand for energy.

The energy efficiency of physical processes can be improved through plant and process design, by maximising the heat transfer to the process and minimising the heat losses. However, for processes involving a chemical reaction, there is an additional requirement of delivering sufficient energy to ensure that the reaction proceeds at the required rate – that is to say free energy and kinetic requirements must be satisfied. These chemical criteria are determined by the thermodynamics of the process and cannot be changed.

Some manufacturing operations involve mineralogical transformations that release carbon dioxide ("process CO_2"), in addition to CO_2 emissions from the fuel source ("fuel CO_2"). Cement manufacture is dependent upon the decomposition of limestone, $CaCO_3$ ("calcination") for the production of cement clinker, and approximately 60% of the total CO_2 emissions from the cement kiln are "process CO_2" and only 40% arise from the fuel.

Ongoing improvements

Energy-intensive industry is continually seeking to reduce energy consumption and improve its energy efficiency/reduce CO_2 emissions. Worldwide, the cement industry is responsible for approximately 5% of anthropogenic CO_2 emissions, but within the UK the contribution is 1.8%.

Fossil-fuels such as coal, coke and petroleum coke account for over 90% of the fuel used in UK cement kilns, and the replacement of these with waste-derived materials provides an important means of reducing CO_2 emissions, in addition to other significant environmental benefits. The use of waste-derived material in cement kilns is an efficient means of recovering their energy content, which would have been lost had the waste been landfilled, or generated CO_2 in an incineration process.

Materials used include used oils and solvents, used tyres, pelletised sewage sludge, meat and bone meal, packaging and refuse-derived fuel. In 2001, 4.37 million tonnes of these materials were used in European cement kilns, saving 3.5 million tonnes of coal and yielding significant reductions in stack emissions.

The development of replacement fuels has been more marked in mainland Europe, where the average level of substitution was

12.2%.[3] Many countries burn extremely high levels of waste-derived fuel:

- ❑ >80%, Netherlands;
- ❑ >40%, Switzerland, Austria;
- ❑ >30%, Belgium, France, Germany, Norway;

But in the UK this is below 10%.

The low use of these materials in the UK reflects the restrictive controls imposed by the extra-statutory Substitute Fuels Protocol (SFP), which involve significant expenditure and time delays. Typically, the time involved in gaining permanent authorisation under the SFP for a new fuel is 15–30 months (see House of Commons, 2001–2) and cost £1–2 million, with trial costs adding a further £600,000 to £800,000. In France, permits are given in around 7 months.

New plant

In contrast with other energy-saving options, the installation of new, energy-efficient plant and/or the shifting of production to large, modern, efficient kilns requires substantial investment. The development cycle (from planning to full-scale operation) for plant in the energy-intensive sector is many years and within the cement industry is about 7 years, see Table 1. This is longer than each phase of the EU ETS. Once installed, cement plant will have an operational lifetime of 30 years or more.

Within the UK, the cement industry is engaged in a £400 million programme of investment in new plant. As parts of larger international groups, UK cement companies must compete for funding of capital projects within the parent company on an international basis, and any "gold plating" of European legislation or additional national controls provide strong disincentive for investment in UK projects.

Advanced CO$_2$ management approaches

An analysis of the cement industry in 2002 by the World Business Council for Sustainable Development (WBCSD) indicated a world-wide potential to reduce CO$_2$ emissions by approximately 30% by 2020 using conventional approaches such as those described above.

Table 1 Cement development cycle and the Kyoto agreement

1998	1999	2000	2001	2001	2003	2004	2005	2006	2007	2008	2009	2010	2011	2012
							Kyoto Phase I			Kyoto Phase II				
Development cycle for 2005 start														
	Development cycle for 2007 start													
		Development cycle for 2008 start												
							Development cycle for 2012 start							

In order to deliver CO_2 reductions of 60% or more by 2050, the industry must explore a number of advanced CO_2 management approaches, and three potential options are: the use of non-limestone-based binders; production of cement and electrical energy on hybrid cement-energy facilities; employment of carbon capture and sequestration.

DOMESTIC MEASURES
The UK's ratification of the Kyoto Protocol on 31 May 2002 committed it to a 12.5% reduction in greenhouse gas emissions on 1990 levels by 2008–12. Additionally, the government set a medium-term goal of reducing carbon dioxide by 20% by 2010. The Royal Commission on Environmental Pollution recommendation of a 60% reduction in carbon dioxide emissions by 2050 has been incorporated in its Energy White Paper and into the revised UK Climate Change Programme, published in 2004.

UK Climate Change Levy
The UK Climate Change Levy (CCL) (see Pocklington, 2001) applies to the industrial and commercial use of certain prescribed fuels: electricity; natural gas as supplied by a gas utility; petroleum and hydrocarbon gas in a liquid state; coal and lignite; coke, and petroleum coke.

Energy-intensive processes that agree to reduce carbon emissions or improve energy efficiency are given an 80% discount to the Levy. The European Commission has examined the scheme and ruled that this and other exemptions from CCL taxation are not deemed to be State Aid.[4]

PANEL 1 CASE STUDY – THE WORLD BUSINESS COUNCIL FOR SUSTAINABLE DEVELOPMENT CEMENT SUSTAINABILITY INITIATIVE

Ten global cement companies accounting for a third of the world's cement production have been working on a US$4 million study to highlight key sustainable-development issues. Its findings on climate change issues are summarised in Table A.

Table A Potential actions for climate protection

Recommendation: Establish corporate carbon management programmes; set company-specific and industry-wide medium-term CO_2 reduction targets; and initiate long-term process and product innovation

Potential actions	Responsibility	Time frame
1. Establish a CO_2 emissions baseline and mechanisms to enable cost-effective emission reductions.	Cement companies working collaboratively	short term
Develop and implement a standardised cement industry CO_2 accounting protocol, which allows companies to establish emissions baselines and to track and report future progress.	Independent review by NGOs, Governments	
2. Set challenging emission-reduction targets and state them publicly.	Cement companies	short term and medium term
Establish goals and adjust them over time as technology and management techniques advance.	(Note: industry-wide and company-specific targets should be set)	
3. Cooperate with stakeholders to develop government policies, product standards and market practices that remove barriers to: (1) the sale of innovative (but safe) cement products with lower embodied CO_2 emissions, and (2) the use of appropriate waste fuels that reduce lifecycle CO_2 emissions.	Cement companies Cement associations standard-setting bodies government regulatory agencies non-governmental organisations	short term and medium term

Table A contd.

Potential actions	Responsibility	Time frame
Encourage industry associations to support such policies. Develop government liaison function related specifically to climate issues within individual companies.		
4. Explore prospects of reducing CO_2 emission reduction costs through emissions trading or offset schemes.	Cement companies governments	Short term
Investigate cost of controlling CO_2 using various options, and compare control costs among plants and between cement industry and non-cement emission sources.	Other industries	
5. Cooperate with governments, customers, suppliers and competitors on pre-competitive R&D projects that develop low-carbon products and processes.	Cement companies Government agencies customers	short term, medium term and long term
Initiate a major R&D effort focused on long-term, cost-effective CO_2 reductions. Work collaboratively to lower the risk and hasten the development of breakthrough innovations.	Suppliers academia	

The revenues raised are "recycled" to business through reduction in the employers' National Insurance contribution payments (NICs), and additional government support for energy-efficiency measures. However, for many businesses within the CCL Agreements scheme, the CCL payments exceed the NIC reduction by a substantial amount. Furthermore, employers outside the scheme also benefit from this reduction, regardless of their energy efficiency/CO_2 emissions.

UK Emissions Trading Scheme (UK ETS)

The UK ETS began in March 2002 and was the world's first economy-wide greenhouse gas trading scheme. Thirty-one organisations entered the scheme as "direct participants" (DPs), and voluntarily agreed to emission-reduction targets under a "cap and trade" scheme. Over the life of the scheme (2002–6) they are expected to make $11.88\,MtCO_2e$ reductions against 1998–2000 levels, in return for a total of £215 million in incentive payments (see NERA, 2004).

Participants of the UK Climate Change Agreements were permitted to participate and buy UK ETS allowances to meet their CCLA targets, thus providing an opportunity for risk management. In addition, they could also sell any over-achievement of their CCLA targets, once this has been converted into the currency of the scheme (carbon) from the currency of the agreement (often energy efficiency).

DPs achieved emission reductions of $4.64\,MtCO_2e$ in the first year of operation and about 5.2 million tonnes CO_2e in the second. The scheme was criticised at its commencement for generating "hot

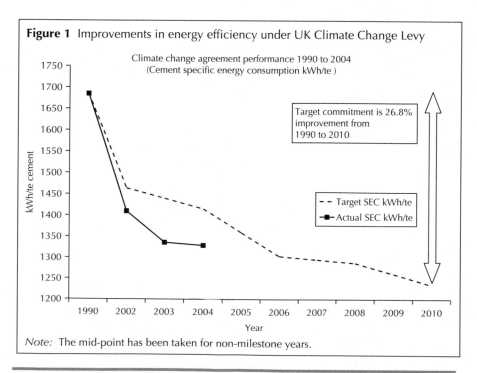

Figure 1 Improvements in energy efficiency under UK Climate Change Levy

Climate change agreement performance 1990 to 2004
(Cement specific energy consumption kWh/te)

Target commitment is 26.8% improvement from 1990 to 2010

- - Target SEC kWh/te
—■— Actual SEC kWh/te

Note: The mid-point has been taken for non-milestone years.

air" through issuing allowances for reductions achieved by clo-
sures or from other measures.

In 2004, the resulting surplus of emissions allowances and
low market price in the UK emissions market prompted the
Department of Environment, Food and Rural Affairs (Defra) (see
Defra, 2004d) to request DPs for a further "voluntary" commitment
to emissions reduction, with the threat of a formal retirement of
credits. Six major companies in the DP scheme pledged further
reductions totalling 8.9MtCO$_2$e. This intervention in the market
sent the wrong signals to operators, particularly as this event took
place in November 2004, when plans were being drawn for the
implementation of the EU ETS.

INTERNATIONAL MEASURES
EU Emissions Trading Scheme
The EU has been in the forefront of advocating emissions trading
and in April 2002 approved the Kyoto Protocol, committing the
Community to an 8% reduction in greenhouse gas emissions.

Other European initiatives, such as the voluntary agreement
with the automotive industry for the reduction of CO$_2$ emissions
from new vehicles (see Pocklington, 2000), were already in place
and delivering results, while others such as energy taxation[5] had
not been as actively pursued.

Key elements of the Emissions Trading Directive (ETD) are:

❑ a mandatory regulatory framework for permitting CO$_2$ emissions through the IPPC scheme;
❑ commencement in 2005 of a selected group of "energy-intensive
   industries", including electricity generators but excluding the
   direct emissions of the chemicals industry;
❑ a "cap and trade" system for installations, based on absolute levels of CO$_2$ emissions; and
❑ a penalty for exceeding allowances, initially €50/tonne CO$_2$, or
   twice the average market price for allowances, whichever is the
   higher.

A separate commission decision gives guidance on monitoring and
reporting,[6] and a "Linking Directive"[7] amends the ETD to permit the
use for credits from Joint Implementation and Clean Development

Mechanisms (flexible mechanisms for making CO_2 savings in other countries).

Allocation of carbon credits

The Emissions Trading Directive required each member state to submit its National Allocation Plan (NAP) for the first phase of EU ETS (2005–7) to the European Commission for approval by 31 May 2004. In the UK, Defra commissioned National Economic Research Associates (NERA), to undertake a study (see NERA, AEA Technology and SPRU, University of Sussex, 2003) into the potential alternative allocation methods.

A draft UK NAP was approved by the Commission in July 2004, which included a total Phase I allocation of 736 MtCO$_2$ with 30.4 Mt allocated to the cement industry. Allocation was made by Defra via a two-stage process – initially to the sector and then to installations based on historical emissions. Historical-emissions data were supplemented by other factors – CCA targets, growth factors and new-entrant reserve contribution factors – to yield sector allocations for the first phase. For growth assumptions, the cement subsector was included in the minerals sector rather than the construction sector, whose performance is directly linked to cement usage.

LESSONS LEARNED

The UK CCL scheme is now into its fifth year, and the interim targets for 2002 and 2004 have been satisfied by all major participants.

Both this and the UK ETS have given government and industry valuable experience in the operation of controls in this area and in the trading of carbon credits through a UK registry. However, the continuation of these schemes in parallel with the EU ETS places an unnecessary burden on its participants.

The implementation of the EU ETS was similarly complex, and during the approximately 12-month timescale there were about 20 formal consultations and a similar number of informal consultations with companies or sector associations or through the UK Emissions Trading Group.[8] These consultations continued post-implementation.

Where significant expenditure is required to meet targets such as those in the EU ETS, industry needs the *certainty* of the detailed legislative regime that will be in place, and the *time* in which to plan and install the requisite plant. The implementation of the first phase of the EU ETS failed spectacularly on both counts. The fact that some "trading enthusiasts" within UK industry have decided to opt out of the first EU ETS phase is indicative of the problems.

There is general agreement within industry that emissions trading is the preferred means of achieving reductions in greenhouse gas emissions, although it is clear that the current system is beyond the scope of SMEs. However, industry as a whole is currently responsible for approximately 35% of the UK's greenhouse gas emissions[9] and only a fraction of industry falls within current agreements – the 44 agreements under the UK Climate Change Levy cover approximately 60% of UK manufacturing and within the EU ETS only about 46% of European industry is included.

Even with adequate time and certainty, GHG reductions of 60% or more by 2050 cannot be delivered by industry-focused schemes using current technology. Industry has begun to consider the technology it will need to achieve these higher levels of reduction, but to be effective these must be incorporated by equal efforts from other stakeholders. The UK's 2005 Climate Change Programme review (see UK Government, 2004) provides an opportunity to minimise the resource intensiveness of the current policy, simultaneously shifting the burden to a more even balance between industry and public by considering the "whole-life" benefits of products such as cement and concrete in thermally efficient buildings.

TEN POINTS FOR PRACTITIONERS

1. Climate change is a global issue and only unrestricted multilateral action will be effective in reducing its effects.
2. Climate-change measures demand a holistic approach that maximises synergy between industry, public, governments and climate. Whole-life product benefits and costs must be factored into climate-change policy measures.
3. Industry prefers market mechanisms such as emissions trading over taxation as a means of delivering cost-effective emissions reductions.

4. Multinational trading schemes generate unfair competition within industry sectors unless there is a common allocation methodology.

5. Domestic, industry-focused measures can give rise to "emissions shift" from regulated to non-regulated countries.

6. Policy measures must recognise the physical/chemical constraints on delivery, and match their timing with the investment, design and construction cycles.

7. Any new GHG measure must take full account of existing policy measures.

8. Early engagement by industry with policymakers is necessary to highlight specific industry issues.

9. Legislators should consider more fully the short-term direct and indirect costs to industry.

10. "Conventional technology" is unlikely to deliver the required GHG reductions, and radical new approaches are required.

1   The Finance Act 2000 restricts the UK CCL scheme to the "energy-intensive" processes, covered by the Pollution Prevention and Control Regulations.

2   EU Directive 2003/87/EC establishing a scheme for greenhouse gas emission allowance trading and amending Council Directive 96/61/EC on IPPC.

3   CEMBUREAU data for 2001.

4   Community Guidance on State Aid for Environmental Protection, 2001/C 37/03, OJ (2001) C37/1, 03.02.01.

5   Proposal for a Council Directive restructuring the Community Framework for the Taxation of Energy Product on 12 March 1997, the COM(97)30 final.

6   EU Monitoring and Reporting Guidelines: Commission decision of 29.01.04 establishing guidelines for the monitoring and reporting of greenhouse gas emissions pursuant to Directive 2003/87/EC of the European Parliament and of the Council.

7   Directive 2004/101/EC of the European Parliament and of the Council of 27 October 2004 amending Directive 2003/87/EC, establishing a scheme for greenhouse gas emission allowance trading within the Community, in respect of the Kyoto Protocol's project mechanisms.

8   An independent non-political sounding board with members from companies, traders, brokers and consultants, and with representatives from DEFRA and the DTI.

9   According to Defra projections for 2005, business and industry will account for 51.7 MtC and 11.4 MtC out of the UK total of 178 MtC.

REFERENCES

Defra, 2004a, "EU emissions trading scheme – partial regulatory impact assessment", January.

Defra, 2004b, "EU emissions trading scheme UK national allocation plan 2005–2007 – regulatory impact assessment", May.

Defra, 2004c, "EU emissions trading scheme announcement on the revised UK cap – questions and answers", 27 October.

Defra, 2004d, "DEFRA welcomes voluntary changes to the UK emissions trading scheme", URL: http://www.defra.gov.uk/news/2004/041130b.htm.

Gilbert, A., J-W. Bode, and D. Phylipsen, 2004, "Analysis of the national allocation plans for the EU emissions trading scheme", August.

House of Commons Environment, Food and Rural Affairs Committee, 2001–2, "Hazardous waste", Eighth Report of Session 2001–2, HC 919.

NERA, 2004, "Review of the first and second years of the UK emissions trading scheme", Report, August.

NERA, AEA Technology and SPRU, University of Sussex, 2003, "Alternatives for implementing the UK's national allocation plan: A report for the department for environment, food and rural affairs", London, URL: http://www.defra.gov.uk/corporate/consult/eu-emissions/annexa.pdf, 11 August.

Pocklington, D. N., 2000, "Environmental law and management", **12**(2), p. 60.

Pocklington, D. N., 2001, "The UK climate change levy – innovative but flawed", *European Environmental Law Review*, **10(7)**, p. 220.

Pocklington, D. N., 2002, "European emissions trading – the business perspective", *EELR* **11**(7), p. 210.

UK Government, 2004, "Review of the UK climate change programme", consultation paper, December.

21

Best Practice in Strategies for Managing Carbon

Abyd Karmali

ICF Consulting

There are now compelling commercial and reputational reasons for companies to take a proactive approach to managing their emissions of greenhouse gases (GHGs). This chapter summarises emerging best practices in this nascent field of corporate strategy from work undertaken with dozens of leading companies. It defines the management of carbon as a holistic, systematic and analytically rigorous thinking about the impact of GHG emissions on strategy, asset values, investments and the commercial activities of the firm. A key lesson is that companies seeking to develop their strategies should first analyse their value-at-stake under a variety of scenarios from current and emerging policies to reduce carbon emissions. Companies that exhibit best practices are delivering measurable financial value through integrating climate change considerations into their short-term and long-term thinking and capitalising on new opportunities to bring new no- and low-carbon products and services to market.

The rapid emergence of the carbon market has significant commercial and reputation impacts for companies. It provides a strong rationale for taking a proactive approach to designing and implementing strategies to manage their emissions of GHGs. Over the past decade, ICF Consulting has worked with approximately 50 companies among the Global Fortune 500 to help develop climate change strategies that are aligned with broader commercial and corporate responsibility strategy. This chapter distils some of the emerging best practices in managing carbon emissions.

First, however, it is important to have a working definition of carbon management. We define the management of carbon as *a holistic, systematic and analytically rigorous thinking about the impact of GHG emissions on strategy, asset values, investments and the commercial activities of the firm.* This thinking is important for any organisation striving to derive maximum value from their carbon assets, or, conversely, appropriately manage their carbon liabilities at least cost, whether the goal is developing credible GHG emissions estimates in response to voluntary reduction targets or a strategy for participating in emission trading, such as through the EU Emissions Trading Scheme, where significant financial value is now being exchanged on a day-to-day basis.

To develop a robust strategy, each company first needs to *assess its true value-at-stake from carbon constraints over different time periods.* Our experience advising companies entering the EU Emissions Trading Scheme has identified that companies often make two fundamental errors when considering the commercial and competitiveness impacts. Both tend to lead to an overestimation of the impacts of carbon constraints.

The first error is that impacts of the EU ETS are often considered in isolation from other industry trends or regulations, thus muddying the baseline against which impacts are being measured. For example, the baseline scenario for the European steel sector must consider that profit margins have recently improved thanks to soaring demand for steel from China in 2004 and that this will likely be followed by a softening in steel prices as the market adjusts. As another example relating to measurement of the indirect impacts, the spread between prices of gas and coal in Europe is a key influence in determining wholesale electricity prices and indeed EU Allowances (EUA) (see ICF Consulting, 2003). One must therefore include analytically consistent long-term scenarios for fuel forecasts when setting the baseline against which impacts from the EU ETS are measured. Put another way, every equilibrium price of EUA has an associated feasible set of prices for fuel that reflect implied demand for gas and coal.

The second error often made is that impacts of the EU ETS must consider both positive and negative impacts resulting from an increased scrutiny that companies place on GHG emissions and strategic management of emissions (or "carbon management"). For example, through developing its own internal emissions trading

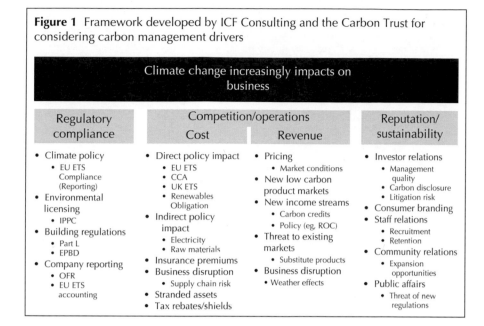

Figure 1 Framework developed by ICF Consulting and the Carbon Trust for considering carbon management drivers

Climate change increasingly impacts on business			
Regulatory compliance	**Competition/operations**		**Reputation/ sustainability**
	Cost	**Revenue**	

• Climate policy
  • EU ETS
    Compliance
    (Reporting)
• Environmental licensing
  • IPPC
• Building regulations
  • Part L
  • EPBD
• Company reporting
  • OFR
  • EU ETS
    accounting
	• Direct policy impact
	  • EU ETS
	  • CCA
	  • UK ETS
	  • Renewables
	    Obligation
	• Indirect policy impact
	  • Electricity
	  • Raw materials
	• Insurance premiums
	• Business disruption
	  • Supply chain risk
	• Stranded assets
	• Tax rebates/shields
		• Pricing
		  • Market conditions
		• New low carbon
		  product markets
		• New income streams
		  • Carbon credits
		  • Policy (eg, ROC)
		• Threat to existing
		  markets
		  • Substitute products
		• Business disruption
		  • Weather effects
			• Investor relations
			  • Management
			    quality
			  • Carbon disclosure
			  • Litigation risk
			• Consumer branding
			• Staff relations
			  • Recruitment
			  • Retention
			• Community relations
			  • Expansion
			    opportunities
			• Public affairs
			  • Threat of new
			    regulations

scheme and setting internal emission reduction targets, BP has identified more that US$650 million of energy efficiency savings. Our experience with other emissions trading schemes also reiterates the point that, when a value is placed on emissions, there is a strong incentive to innovate and undertake structural change that leads to overall lower costs of compliance.

As summarised in a recent research paper (see Wordsworth, Kwartin and Karmali, 2004), there are *three broad categories of climate change drivers impacting business value.* These are *regulatory compliance, competitive position* and *reputation considerations.* We illustrate these in a framework developed for considering commercial and competitiveness impacts on UK companies (see Figure 1) as part of the Carbon Trust's Carbon Management Programme.

Under regulatory compliance, companies in the UK must maintain their compliance with the EU ETS as well as environmental licensing requirements, building regulations and new corporate reporting requirements such as the Operating and Financial Review (OFR), which mandates companies to publicly disclose and have their board of directors sign off on a statement of material environmental and social risks.

This suggests that the EU ETS may ultimately have a financial impact on many companies in both the trading and non-trading sectors as the value of emission allowances and rising costs of key production inputs such as electricity are incorporated into production costs. As a consequence the EU ETS has the potential to change the competitive landscape of many sectors. It should be emphasised at the outset that, while the EU ETS will often result in a net increase in a company's production costs, implications for competitiveness will, however, not necessarily be negative. And, as mentioned above, the impacts from the EU ETS need to be considered distinct from other factors and market trends affecting each sector. The implications for the international competitiveness of national industries and key domestic companies will depend on three key factors:

❑ price elasticity of demand;
❑ the volume of the manufacturing supply base (and substitutes) that will be impacted by the EU ETS; and
❑ the relative emission and electricity intensities of producers in each affected market.

PRICE ELASTICITY OF DEMAND

All affected companies will find it desirable to increase prices to reflect the cost or opportunity cost of emission allowances and rising electricity purchase costs under the EU ETS. Clearly, however, companies will be able to increase prices only if the desired price increase will not have a significant impact on their competitive position. The critical factor, therefore, is the responsiveness of customer demand to changes in price (price elasticity of demand). As a first step it is therefore necessary to identify whether or not the competitive position of an industry as a whole will change if prices increase by examining the price elasticity of demand.

For industries exposed to limited price elasticity of demand it can reasonably be concluded that players will be able to increase prices without any serious adverse impact on their competitive position. For example, because 93% of international production of cement does not cross borders, some although not all producers in the cement sector will experience limited competitive impacts. For all other industries, it will be necessary to consider the volume of the market supply base that will be affected by the EU ETS.

VOLUME OF SUPPLY BASE AFFECTED BY THE EU ETS

If the majority of producers of a particular product (and substitute products) fall outside the scope of the EU ETS (for example, fall below the size threshold or have operations outside the EU), it can be broadly concluded that production costs may rise among European producers, while those of their competitors remain static. In such circumstances the competitive implications for the affected industry are likely to be negative. If, on the other hand, the majority of producers fall within the scope of the EU ETS, it will be necessary to consider the relative emission and electricity intensities of manufacturers within the industry.

RELATIVE EMISSION AND ELECTRICITY INTENSITIES

The EU ETS will have implications for the relative competitive position of European companies, both in domestic markets and vis-à-vis competitors within the EU and in some cases outside the EU. In either case, for industries that fall within the trading sector, the impact of the EU ETS on competitive position will be determined by the relative emission intensities (tonnes CO_2e emitted per unit of production) of different players. All companies will find it desirable to increase prices by the emission intensity of each unit output multiplied by the market price of emissions. This is because, for each unit of output, either they will be required to pay for the allowances embodied in that product or they will forgo the ability to sell a surplus allowance to the scheme. As a consequence, players with relatively low emission intensity may experience an improvement in their competitive position to the detriment of those with higher emission intensity.

Similarly, for industries that fall outside the trading sector but who are expected to experience a significant increase in electricity purchase costs, the impact of the EU ETS on competitive position will be determined by relative electricity intensities (kWh of electricity consumed per unit of production) of players and regional differences in the expected change in electricity prices (in the case of entities that compete with players located in different EU member states). Clearly, players with relatively low electricity consumption levels and with operations in regions expected to experience relatively low increases in final electricity prices will benefit to the detriment of others.

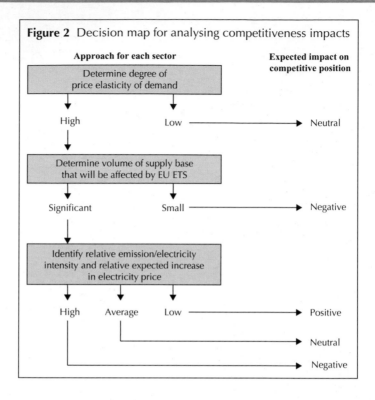

Figure 2 Decision map for analysing competitiveness impacts

Approach for each sector

Expected impact on competitive position

Determine degree of price elasticity of demand

High   Low ————————————→ Neutral

Determine volume of supply base that will be affected by EU ETS

Significant   Small ————————————→ Negative

Identify relative emission/electricity intensity and relative expected increase in electricity price

High   Average   Low ————————————→ Positive

————————————→ Neutral

————————————→ Negative

The decision map for assessing the projected competitiveness impacts from the EU ETS is summarised in Figure 2. As the framework that we outlined in Figure 1 indicates, various other factors are at play in inducing behaviour to reduce GHG emissions among companies in the EU. Some of the positive impacts that we have noted, from companies by whom we have been engaged, is an increased desire to accelerate energy efficiency options and consideration, under more positive economics, of options such as owning one's own dedicated electricity generating plants and combined heat and power (CHP) production.

Another best practice in carbon management is that, given the indirect impacts on companies resulting from carbon constraints, *companies need to develop an enhanced ability to assess accurately the impacts on the energy markets consistent with the fundamentals of longer-term supply and demand for carbon.* Various modelling approaches are commercially available to enable this in a cost-effective manner. Our

Table 1 Relative importance of commercial impacts

Sector	Quantified value at stake (%EBIT)	Relative importance of driver category			
		Regulatory	Cost	Revenue	Reputation
Utilities	10–40%	Low	High	High	Medium
Manufacturing	2–5%	Medium	High	Low	Low
Chemicals	5–10%	High	High	Low	Low
Pharmaceuticals	1–2%	Medium	Medium	Low	Medium
Materials & metals	10–20%	Medium	High	Low	Low
Food & drink	5–10%	Low	High	Low	Low
Property	1–2%	High	Low	Medium	High
Retail	1–2%	Low	Medium	Low	Medium
Banking and financial services	<1%	Low	Low	Medium	High
Transport	2–5%	Low	Medium	Medium	High

integrated planning model (IPM) is one of the world's most widely used power market models and employs a dynamic linear optimisation approach to assess forward price curves and impacts on asset valuation from variations to emissions, fuel costs and other key factors, whether policy, technical or economic.

To project prices most accurately, renewables targets, national and plant-level decisions on the Large Combustion Plant Directive and expected changes in transmission capacity need to be reflected in scenarios. IPM also captures the quite specific impacts of the national allocation plans (NAPs). One of the key insights that IPM has revealed is that sizeable new-entrant reserves and certain types of closure provision will dampen any price increase.

Our experience to date across various sectors summarised in *Table 1* illustrates the *relative importance of the commercial impacts and driver categories.*

Utilities are clearly the sector with the most potential value-at-stake. Among other sectors, steel and aluminium companies face potentially high impacts, based on the competitiveness of product markets and the material impacts of electricity price increases. While the financial services sector is not directly impacted by the EU ETS, the indirect costs and opportunities could be significant. Our experience suggests that the most forward-looking companies in the sector are exploring the carbon footprint of their project finance and portfolio lending activities and in some cases examining the feasibility of launching new climate-friendly products and services.

Now that the Kyoto Protocol has come into force, *companies must approach the strategic management of GHG emissions as they would any other asset or liability on their corporate balance sheet*. This leads to several more lessons.

Leading companies such as Anglo American plc have begun to *incorporate a price for carbon into their mainstream investment planning through adjusting their investment appraisal protocols*. Most business leaders have embraced the likelihood that carbon emission constraints will become a reality and actively manage the concomitant likely impacts upon corporate performance and shareholder value. Regardless of the fate of the Kyoto Protocol after 2008–12, the trend in recognition among the world's leading companies that policy-makers will likely require action to reduce GHG emissions is marked, and efforts will continue post-2012.

Many companies have responded prudently by taking measures to enhance their understanding of the nature and magnitude of the risks and opportunities they may face under different policy outcomes. For example, Norsk Hydro ASA employs scenarios to develop a robust picture of the fundamentals driving supply and demand for carbon over different periods relevant for new power plants.

Any unilateral investment decision that a company makes to reduce its emissions needs to be couched within a robust business strategy. Furthermore, it must be commercially justified in terms of the investment's impact on shareholder value. In some industries, carbon is inextricably interwoven with other strategic drivers. In the energy sector, for example, comprehensive carbon management strategies cannot be properly developed without a thorough understanding of the pressures and opportunities existing in the wider energy marketplace. That is, to be successful, an effective carbon management strategy must be an integral part of an overall corporate business strategy.

In other cases, carbon management strategy can be used to develop a leadership position in a given industry. For example, HSBC Group is identifying options to support its stated commitment to be the first Global Fortune 500 company to take a carbon-neutral position.

To maximise shareholder value, companies need to use *a three-pronged strategy to manage carbon risks*. First, companies should incorporate GHG emissions considerations into core business strategy. Any asset divestiture, any acquisition and all operating plans should consider impacts on GHG emissions. Due diligence to support proposed financial transactions should now examine the impacts of GHG emissions and other environmental parameters on asset values. The International Finance Corporation, the largest lender to companies in emerging markets for example, uses GPAT, an innovative tool to help it assess potential GHG emissions liabilities in its lending portfolio.[1]

Second, companies can implement in-house projects to reduce GHG emissions such as fuel switching, increasing energy efficiency and simultaneously reducing operating and energy costs. For example, companies in the wood products sector, such as International Paper, are identifying opportunities to increase use of biomass-derived energy and, in some cases, earn carbon credits. At some point, however, a company's supply curve of emission reduction opportunities becomes quite steep. Each company has its own marginal abatement cost curve, which reflects its own portfolio of assets, choice of technology and fuels, and cost structure.

The third element of the strategy involves the manipulation of the abatement cost curve by either securing emission reduction opportunities off-site through domestic programmes or the so-called Kyoto Mechanisms, that is to say the Clean Development Mechanism (CDM) and Joint Implementation (JI).

One of the first two CDM projects to have their methodology approved in July 2003 was the Salvador da Bahia project, a landfill gas management project undertaken by the French company Suez's subsidiary in Brazil. This project, along with other pioneering projects, demonstrates several valuable lessons for those seeking to earn carbon credits through CDM.

Case Study: Lessons learned from CDM projects
Companies need to understand the fundamental importance of additionality and the reputation risks attendant from paying

insufficient attention to the environmental integrity of their proposed CDM projects.

Companies need to differentiate GHG emissions data risks that exist at the corporate and project levels.

Companies need to undertake due diligence prior to completing transactions involving the reduction of GHG emissions.

We tackle each of these in turn.

Additionality: This has been the most analytically thorny issue facing CDM project developers. A review of the project methodologies that have been submitted to the CDM Executive Board leads to a conclusion that the most common reason for methodologies being rejected by the methodology panel is a failure to appreciate the importance of additionality by adhering to the guidance provided by the Marrakech Accords. Some companies have created unwanted attention to themselves by proposing projects that lack the environmental integrity that the CDM tries to ensure.

GHG emission data risks: Credibility and technical integrity are the critical elements of a GHG emissions inventory. For both corporate inventories and emission reduction projects, the quality of a GHG protocol, monitoring, and verification provides the basic integrity of any GHG emissions trading market. Indeed, the relative cost of applying credit enhancement tools to GHG transactions reflects the market demand for robust emissions data.

In 1999, the global energy company BP commissioned a team to develop the first-ever corporate GHG emissions protocol, consistent with international financial and accounting standards. Table 1 summarises one of the key lessons that emerged in this activity, namely that often the perception of the most material GHG emissions data risks can be quite different from the reality.

Due diligence: Companies need to undertake a "market acceptance" due diligence prior to devoting resources to developing any GHG emissions reduction projects. Essentially, this exercise serves to ensure that the attributes of emissions savings are of a nature that represents value to potential carbon investors. We are concerned that our clients should not invest in a process to monitor, verify and certify emissions reductions, only to discover subsequently that those reductions do not comply with the requirements of the market and, as such, represent little value to the wider investment community. The number of failed project methodologies that have been

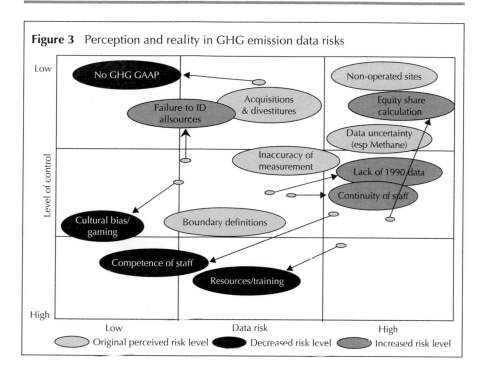

Figure 3 Perception and reality in GHG emission data risks

proposed to the CDM Executive Board is testament to the fact that a lot of resources are still being devoted to poor-quality projects. We have developed a CDM screening tool to assist clients in prioritising their CDM efforts and avoiding unnecessary expenditures on in-house or consulting resources.

CONCLUSIONS

Recent meetings of the World Economic Forum in Davos, Switzerland, have concluded that climate change will pose a challenge for senior executives for many years to come. Our experience with numerous leading companies confirms that systematic carbon management presents excellent opportunities for companies to derive strategic advantage. Given the scale of commercial impacts in some sectors and the value that forward-looking companies are creating through strategic management of carbon, companies should continue to refine their analysis of competitiveness impacts using the frameworks identified above.

Our experience suggests that the companies exhibiting best practice in managing commercial impacts are those that now include the price of carbon in their investment planning analyses and those that recognise the financial value created from setting up processes to facilitate company-wide management of carbon emissions, allowances and project-based carbon credits.

Key: Initial assessments of perceived risk (light grey) often change dramatically as more experience is gained, with some perceived risks increasing (dark grey) while other risks decrease (black).

1   GPAT was developed by ICF Consulting for IFC in 1998–9 and is now shared by other regional development banks.

REFERENCES

ICF Consulting, 2003, "The European carbon market outlook".

Wordsworth, A., R. Kwartin, and A. Karmali, 2004, "The carbon trust's carbon management program: description and evaluation of pilot phase results", ACEEE Paper 206.

22

Aviation and Climate Change: Can Emissions Trading Deliver a Solution?

Andrew Sentance, Andy Kershaw

British Airways

Aviation is currently a small contribution to manmade climate change, but has the potential to grow significantly in the future. According to the Intergovernmental Panel on Climate Change (IPCC), aviation contributes approximately 3.5% to total anthropogenic climate change.[1] However, the IPCC's central estimate projects a fourfold increase by 2050, using relatively conservative forecasts for the future growth of aviation. Against a background where some policymakers are identifying a 60–70% cut in carbon dioxide emissions, this creates a major challenge for the aviation industry.

In this chapter, we explore the contribution that emissions trading can make to addressing this issue. The chapter is divided into three main sections. The first sets out the background – and describes aviation's current and projected climate change impact. The second section reviews the case for emissions trading as a key mechanism for addressing the most clearly identified impact of aviation – carbon dioxide emissions. The third section discusses the potential development of emissions trading within aviation, and reviews BA's experience within the UK Emissions Trading Scheme (ETS), as well as the potential for integrating aviation into the EU ETS.

THE AVIATION CONTEXT

The climate-change impact of aviation falls into two parts: (a) the contribution to global CO_2 from aircraft burning fossil fuels; and

(b) other effects in the upper atmosphere, linked to ozone generation, methane reduction and cirrus cloud formation.

The most authoritative report on the impact of aviation on climate change is the study by the IPCC (1999). This showed that aviation was responsible for about 2% of carbon dioxide emissions – the most important greenhouse gas – and around 3.5% of manmade global warming in total.

According to UK government estimates, aviation emissions of carbon dioxide are about 5% of the national total (though this figure is sensitive to the method used for allocating international emissions). The total contribution of aviation to climate change is likely to be higher – though there is great uncertainty surrounding the scale of the non-CO_2 effects.

The importance of fuel efficiency

Our industry takes its environmental responsibilities very seriously and particularly its contribution to climate change. Aircraft fuel efficiency per passenger kilometre has improved by over 70% in the last 40 years and is expected to increase at a rate of around 1–2% per annum going forward. This might absorb half of the emissions due to the expansion of the sector. While air transport's overall contribution to emissions is small in absolute numbers, industry growth is likely to cause an overall increase in emissions in the long term. Given this, the industry is committed to finding effective and proportionate measures to limit aviation's climate impacts.

Airlines can therefore make a contribution to reducing global warming by buying fuel-efficient aircraft and operating them efficiently. British Airways has set itself a target for raising fuel efficiency by 30% in the period 1990–2010. We have made around three-quarters of the improvement already and we are therefore on track to meet the target. British Airways also aims to reduce its contribution to global warming through its ground operations. We have set ourselves the target of raising the energy efficiency of our UK buildings by 2% per annum.

THE KYOTO PROTOCOL

In the Kyoto Protocol, nation states committed themselves to greenhouse-gas reductions between 1990 and 2008–2012. Emissions from domestic aviation are covered by the Kyoto targets, but international aviation emissions are excluded because of difficulties in deciding how the emissions should be allocated between countries. Article 2.2 of the Kyoto Protocol requests that "the parties included in Annex I shall pursue limitation or reduction of emissions of greenhouse gasses not controlled by the Montreal Protocol from aviation and marine bunker fuels, working through the International Civil Aviation Organization and the International Maritime Organization, respectively".[2]

The Kyoto Protocol has now come into force and is an important framework of reference for policymakers, especially in the UK and Europe, where there is strong political commitment to reducing greenhouse-gas emissions. However, the United States has not ratified the treaty. This creates difficulties for global aviation – as around 60% of passenger kilometres worldwide involve a journey either within the US or to/from a US destination.

Global warming effects in the upper atmosphere

In addition to carbon dioxide emissions, aviation also contributes to other effects in the upper atmosphere, linked to ozone generation, methane reduction and cirrus cloud formation. The scale of these effects is dependent on the time and place of flights and the prevailing weather.

Designing measures to take these issues into account is difficult until there is a clearer scientific basis. A combination of instruments is likely to be needed to address these upper-atmosphere effects, combining technical standards and operational changes. There may be a role for economic instruments, but it will be inefficient and ineffective for one country or region to act in isolation. The main emphasis in the short term should be on research to better understand these effects and how they might be mitigated.

EMISSIONS TRADING – THE WAY AHEAD

Based on historical and forecast growth rates, fuel efficiency improvement will be insufficient to prevent the growth of carbon dioxide emissions from aircraft. This has led some to suggest that the growth of the industry be restricted in some way, relative to the likely growth trend of 3–4%. A number of environmental campaigning groups have argued for large increases in taxation of air travel to achieve this.

However, punitive tax policies of this sort would be socially and economically undesirable, requiring significant rises in the cost of air travel and a reduction in the economic benefits it brings. Instead, British Airways believes that the way forward is not to artificially limit the industry's growth, but to ensure that, if aviation does increase its emissions, this rise is funded by cuts in other sectors. This can be achieved by incorporating aviation emissions within an ETS.

In an ETS, the overall total of emissions are capped and companies must hold permits to cover their emissions. Each company receives an allocation of emissions. If it wants to exceed that allocation, it must buy excess permits from companies emitting less than their allocation.

Under such an emissions trading regime, the market will determine the cost of carbon necessary to meet the agreed target. Unlike a tax, where the level of tax needed to achieve the environmental objective is unclear, the overall cap – enforced by a system of permits – ensures that the required emissions reduction is achieved.

Another advantage of emissions trading is that it works with the grain of incentives, combining a "carrot" alongside the "stick". Assuming a grandfathered system of allocation, firms that achieve the biggest reductions can gain by selling their permits into the market. This reinforces the financial incentive for investing in technology that will enhance emissions reductions.

While there are some risks attached to emissions trading, these pale into insignificance when we consider the alternatives – which are generally based on punitive taxes and charges. Taxation applied to emissions, fuel usage or directly to air travel would not only be bad for the economics of our industry, it would also be bad environmental policy. A tax that doubled the cost of aviation fuel – costing airlines and their customers US$50 billion a year – would cut less than 0.5% off the growth rate of air traffic over a 30-year period. We are daily reminded of the ineffectiveness of a tax-based approach on the roads in the UK and the rest of Europe. Very high motor-fuel taxes have not prevented the continued growth of traffic and emissions and the associated problems of congestion.

But is emissions trading a feasible approach for aviation? British Airways has experience of emissions trading through its participation in the UK voluntary scheme. Our experience is that trading is a workable approach and need not be excessively costly.

UK AND EU EMISSIONS TRADING SCHEMES

As a signal of its commitment to emissions trading, and to gain experience of this approach to limiting greenhouse gas emissions, British Airways has joined the UK ETS. Because international aviation emissions are not included in the agreed Kyoto caps, the scheme can include only our domestic services and UK ground energy sources.

British Airways initially made a commitment to reducing the emissions covered by the scheme by 12.5% over five years. This commitment has recently been increased to 19%. By 2004, BA had achieved a 23% reduction in its carbon dioxide emissions covered by this scheme, compared with the 1998–2000 baseline. (See Panel 2 for further details of our involvement with the UK ETS.)

The 2003 Air Transport White Paper committed the UK government to pursuing emissions trading as the main policy mechanism for limiting global-warming impacts from aviation. (As noted earlier, about half of the potential growth in emissions could be averted through endogenous efficiency improvements). The UK government will pursue the inclusion of intra-EU aviation CO_2 emissions into the EU ETS from 2008.

British Airways is keen to work alongside the UK government and the European Commission to ensure that emissions trading can be introduced for European aviation without distorting international competition or imposing unreasonable cost burdens on airlines.

To avoid competitive distortions, the EU ETS should initially apply only to flights that operate fully within the EU. Also, aviation

---

PANEL 1 CRITERIA FOR LINKING AVIATION WITH EMISSIONS TRADING SCHEMES

1. Avoid market distortions
Any scheme must be applied to minimise competitive distortions within the EU, between EU and non-EU carriers, and between transport modes. A harmonised approach to allocation and target setting should be sought for aviation. All operators on a particular route must be covered by the scope of a scheme.

2. Focus on CO_2 for emissions trading
Emissions trading is a suitable instrument for CO_2 and other Kyoto greenhouse gases but not appropriate for addressing the upper atmospheric effects of aviation. Technology standards for NOx emissions and prioritisation of atmospheric research are appropriate policy responses for aviation's non-CO_2 effects.

3. A long-term strategy to include aviation CO_2 within the international policy framework
Any regime created for EU aviation CO_2 should be developed as a first step towards a global approach. Design should be consistent with the ongoing work of the ICAO to include aviation in global emissions trading.

4. Seek simple approaches to the particular circumstances of aviation
Air service operators should be the trading entity. Initial allocation should be a free allocation. Targets should reflect high marginal abatement costs in aviation. International and domestic regimes should be harmonised as far as possible. Aviation should have the broadest possible access to emissions allowance markets.

should not be forced to comply with standards that differ from those for other industries. The suggestion that its targets should be more stringent because of other, less well-understood, effects in the upper atmosphere should be resisted. These effects need more research before evaluation of potential policy mechanisms can be undertaken. However, emissions trading is unlikely to be an effective way to tackle them.

The method used to distribute allowances to airlines may have significant implications for competitiveness. Distortions would occur if the approach adopted for Phase I of the EU ETS were applied to aviation, whereby each member state applies its own interpretation of the EC Directive and determines allocation and emissions targets at the national level. Given the mobile nature of aviation emissions and the provisions of the European Open Aviation Area, whereby EU air carriers are free to operate air services between any two points in the EU, it is essential that a harmonised EU-level approach to allocation and target setting be adopted for aviation.

The fact that international aviation emissions are excluded from the national caps agreed at Kyoto is another potential obstacle to

PANEL 2 BRITISH AIRWAYS' INVOLVEMENT IN THE UK ETS

British Airways believes that the best long-term mechanism for ensuring that aviation takes account of its carbon dioxide emissions – which add to global warming – is through international emissions trading.

In 2001, we joined the UK ETS, covering emissions from our domestic air services and UK properties, to gain practical experience of emissions trading across business and financial institutions. The scheme is based on voluntary commitments to reduce CO_2 emissions over the period 2002 to 2006, for which the government offers an incentive payment.

The UK ETS is the first cross-industry, national greenhouse-gas emissions trading scheme. The scheme began in 2002, with 32 companies pledging to cut emissions of greenhouse gases by 11.88 million tonnes of CO_2 equivalent before the end of 2006. BA's initial target was a reduction of 12.5% per annum by 2006 on a 1998–2000 baseline.

There are penalties for not achieving the annual target: no incentive payment for the year in question; £30 per tonne for each excess tonne of CO_2; and a reduction of allowances for the next year of 1 tonne per tonne of excess CO_2. Excess allowances can also be "banked" and offset against emissions in later years.

In the first three years of the scheme we have achieved a reduction of 23% relative to the 1998–2000 baseline. We have therefore significantly overperformed relative to our target, though BA is not alone in achieving bigger reductions than expected. In the first two years of the scheme many participants achieved emissions cuts beyond initial expectations, leading to a surplus of emissions reductions allowances in the UK emissions market. Following discussions with the UK Department of Environment, Food and Rural Affairs (Defra), six companies – including BA – have now offered to increase their emission reductions. BA will now be targeting an emissions reduction of around 19% by 2006.

British Airways has built up valuable experience of emissions trading by participating in the UK voluntary scheme. This experience benefits our business in several ways. The concept of emissions trading helps focus the minds of management on the importance of environmental improvements, and our involvement in the scheme has greatly raised the profile of emissions reduction with BA's senior management. Our network planners and managers of our property portfolio are already taking into account the "external cost" of emissions in their planning. We have also gained valuable knowledge on how to gather and report emissions data. And our practical understanding can help us influence the framework for future trading schemes.

including aviation in the EU ETS. In the long term, the solution should be to ensure that international aviation emissions are not excluded from post-Kyoto international negotiations on climate change. In the short term, it should be possible to devise a mechanism that allows international aviation emissions to be included in emissions trading without distorting the schemes that are in place.

None of the issues associated with linking aircraft emissions with the EU ETS should be insoluble. British Airways is committed to building support and assisting policymakers in developing practical solutions – to ensure aviation plays its full part in the global drive to reduce greenhouse gas emissions and stabilise the global climate.

We also support the continuation of discussions within the UN ICAO to establish a clear international framework for the involvement of aviation in emissions trading worldwide. The successful incorporation of aviation into an emissions trading regime within the EU could be extremely helpful in persuading more sceptical nations, notably the United States, that this is the right approach globally.

CONCLUSIONS

For CO_2 emissions, British Airways has consistently supported the participation of aviation in an open emissions trading scheme as the most economically efficient and environmentally effective way of ensuring aviation reflects the cost of these emissions. Under such an emissions trading regime, the market will determine the cost of carbon necessary to meet the agreed target. Unlike a tax, where the level of tax needed to achieve the environmental objective is unclear, the environmental objective is assured by the overall cap on emissions.

Another advantage of emissions trading is that it works with the grain of incentives, combining a "carrot" alongside the "stick". Assuming a grandfathered system of allocation, firms that achieve the biggest reductions can gain by selling their permits into the market. This reinforces the financial incentive for investing in technology that will enhance emissions reductions.

As a signal of its commitment to emissions trading, British Airways has joined the UK ETS. We support the inclusion of aviation emissions into the EU ETS, as long as this can be achieved without significantly reducing the international competitiveness of the European airline industry on the global stage. We are also active in supporting the development of emissions trading in the ICAO and other international forums. However, the participation of aviation in an open global emissions trading regime is complicated by the Kyoto treatment of emissions from international bunker fuels, which has the result of excluding international aviation emissions from the global caps that have been agreed for the current commitment period. This difficulty would be avoided if aviation were fully included in post-Kyoto emissions reduction commitments from 2013.

While the EU or other governmental authorities may be under pressure to introduce new taxes and charges as an "interim solution", or as a supplementary measure, this pressure should be resisted. In particular, unilateral measures taken in the UK or at EU level outside of any agreed international framework for aviation risks serious damage to the competitiveness and sustainability of our domestic aviation industry.

1   See IPCC (1999). The IPCC used a metric called *radiative forcing* to describe the warming of the earth from a wide range of different climatic effects. However, debate continues over the appropriateness of adding up best estimates of radiative forcing to determine the global temperature response of aviation.
2   Kyoto Protocol to the United Nations Framework Convention on Climate Change, 1997.

REFERENCES

IPCC, 1999, "Aviation and the global atmosphere".

23

Insuring Climate Change: Implications for the Insurance Industry

George Walker; Charles Crosthwaite Eyre; Alan Punter

Aon Re Australia; IRMG, Aon Ltd; Aon Capital Services Ltd

This chapter provides a review of the likely impacts of anthro-pogenic climate change on the insurance industry and the reactions of the industry to any such consequences. In this chapter the insurance industry is assumed to encompass primary insurers, reinsurers and the brokers that serve these. The first half of the chapter is an overview of the salient characteristics of the insurance industry in regard to the likely impacts and its response to date. The second half of the chapter is more speculative, looking at the possible implications for the insurance industry as the world begins to both adapt to the expected changes in climate and implement policies to mitigate the amount of climate change. Anthropogenic climate change is seen as posing both threats and opportunities to the insurance industry, but the overall impact over the next 30 to 50 years is likely to be much less than that of demographic and political changes.

THE INSURANCE INDUSTRY

The present-day insurance industry had its origins about 400 years ago. Since then it has demonstrated an ability to adapt itself to the major social and business changes that have occurred during this period, including the Industrial Revolution and the major demographic, economic and political changes that followed it. It has also shown itself to be very resilient to major shocks or catastrophes such as the 1906 San Francisco earthquake, Hurricane Andrew in 1992, the destruction of the World Trade Center in 2001 and the four Florida hurricanes in 2004, each of which gave rise to unprecedented costs that significantly impacted the structure and operations of the insurance industry. This resilience and capacity for adaptation to changing circumstances and experience should ensure that the insurance industry will cope successfully with the predicted effects of anthropogenic climate change.

Insurance policies are classified as *life* or *non-life*. Life assurance policies make payments to dependents in the event of the death of the insured. Non-life or general insurance policies provide financial compensation in the event of the insured party suffering the loss or physical damage to an asset (for example, from a hazard such as fire or theft) or incurring a legally enforced liability arising as a result of being deemed part or fully responsible for financial loss or injury borne by another party (such as an employee or a customer). The total worldwide insurance premiums in 2003 were estimated at US$2,947 billion, of which US$1,672 billion were for life business and US$1,275 billion were for non-life business (see Swiss Re, 2005).

THE PRINCIPLES OF INSURANCE AND INSURABILITY

The main principle of insurance depends on being able to pool a number of risks of financial loss from prescribed hazards so that the volatility of the risk to the individual contributor to the pool (the policyholder) from financial loss is significantly reduced – a fixed and known premium replacing variable and unknown losses. This reduces the amount of "spare" capital required by each policy-holder to safeguard against the risk of sustaining above-average or major unexpected financial losses.

Ideally to be insurable the risks must meet certain criteria – they must:

1. be large in number;
2. be relatively uniform in characteristics;
3. be small in size;
4. be independent in occurrence;
5. have random occurrence;
6. have no moral hazard;
7. have affordable premiums; and
8. have low management costs.

Some commercial and industrial risks fail these simple criteria because of their variability in size, especially at the larger end. Another class of risk that can stretch these simple criteria are those known as *catastrophe risks*, which arise from geographically large hazards such as earthquakes, hurricanes, floods and severe storms, potentially giving rise to large numbers of individual losses from the one event, thus breaking the requirement for independent occurences. Both of these can greatly increase the volatility of the overall risk to an insurance company, increasing the capital that an insurer would need to protect itself against the risk of insolvency. To reduce this volatility, insurance companies tend to only retain a portion of these risks, ceding the remainder by way of reinsurance, or excluding them.

A characteristic feature of reinsurance is sharing of risk on a global scale, through international reinsurance companies only accepting a portion of the risk ceded by individual insurance companies, and through the sharing of risk between reinsurance companies in a process known as *retrocession*. As a result of this the whole insurance and reinsurance industry is in effect an integrated global financial pool. This gives the industry its remarkable resilience.

CLIMATE CHANGE AND INSURANCE INDUSTRY RESPONSE TO DATE

Although the industry has been slow to react as a whole, there has been increasing attention devoted to the issue of anthropogenic climate change by individual companies, individuals within companies, and industry associations. Outcomes include:

❑ The sections in the Intergovernmental Panel on Climate Change (IPCC) reports on the impact of climate change on the financial industry;
❑ The United Nations Environmental Program Financial Initiative (UNEPFI) to look at the role of financial institutions in mitigating greenhouse-gas emissions and adapting to the effects of climate change.[1];
❑ Major US and British studies on the impact of climate change on the insurance industry (see Mills, Lacompte and Peara, 2001; Dlugolecki, 2004).

Much of this has been driven by the huge increase in insured losses from natural hazards in recent years, as shown in Table 1, and a perceived threat to the insurance industry from a further increase in

Table 1 Natural catastrophes, aggregate losses by decade

Decade	1950–9	1960–9	1970–9	1980–9	1990–9
Number of events	20	27	47	63	91
Economic losses $bn	44.9	80.5	147.6	228.0	703.6
Insured losses $bn	–	6.5	13.7	26.8	132.2
Insured losses as % of economic losses	–	8%	9%	13%	19%
Multiple over previous decade					
Number of events	–	1.35	1.74	1.34	1.44
Economic losses	–	1.79	1.83	1.54	3.09
Insured losses	–	–	2.11	2.10	4.59

Source: Munich Re, 2005

these losses as a result of more frequent and/or more severe weather events occurring as a result of anthropogenic climate change.

Note that the catastrophe losses in Table 1 include those caused by earthquakes, tsunamis and volcanic eruptions, but the majority of the events and associated cost of losses are due to weather-related risks, principally windstorm and flood. The major feature of this table is the step change in the cost of losses from the 1980s to the 1990s after a number of decades of relatively uniformly increasing losses. Some commentators have attributed this to anthropogenic climate change but the natural behaviour of random extreme hazard events is by far the major influence. This is compounded by the combination of demographic changes and the huge growth in real wealth, which has resulted in exponential growth of insured values in hazard-prone regions. It is significant that, although there is a growing gap in absolute financial terms between insured losses and overall economic losses, the ratio of insured losses to overall losses is increasing as a result of an increasing proportion of property being covered by insurance in the world.

Of greatest significance to the current issue is that change from the 1980s to the 1990s is greater than any rate of increase predicted in the next 30 to 50 years by climate-change predictions – and the industry has coped with it. There were problems, but overall the insurance industry has coped with these property catastrophe losses, which came on top of other major problems due to liability, primarily from asbestos claims. Apart from the integrated global nature of the industry, one of the reasons that the property insurance industry has been so adaptable and resilient is that much of its activity is focused on annual risk, with most insurance policies being taken out one year at a time. This means that insurance and reinsurance companies have the ability to annually renegotiate premiums and policy conditions in the light of recent loss experience. Additionally, following extreme losses, the insurance and reinsurance industry has demonstrated the capability to raise more capital due the higher resulting premiums.

Addressing the problems arising in the large losses in the last 15 years, and adapting to the changes in perceived risk that have followed, has been a much higher priority to the industry in the last few years than concerns about something that might happen in the next 30–50 years. However, the changes made have almost certainly made the industry much more resilient to any changes in weather-related property insurance risks that may arise from the predicted climate change.

ADAPTATION RISKS – GENERAL INSURANCE
Adaptation to climate change assumes that, despite international policies being developed to limit the production of greenhouse gases, it is too late to prevent some warming of the atmosphere, and consequently the global community will need to adapt to any resulting changes in the climate that will be induced.

Much of the media coverage on the effect of climate change on weather hazards focuses on predictions that many hazards will increase in both frequency and intensity. It is commonly implied that, far from being risks, these changes are certainties; but this represents a big misunderstanding of scientific opinion. Currently there is a high level of uncertainty about the changes in frequency and intensity of weather hazards that will result. Almost certainly the risks will vary from one location to another, and in many places the chance that some hazards may decrease in intensity may be higher than the chance that they will increase. In Australia for example the level of losses from tropical cyclones over the past 40 years has decreased in real terms, despite demographic changes that suggest they should have increased even if climatic characteristics had stayed constant, and as losses from severe storms have done so.

This highlights the complexity of the issue with the hazard risks associated with climate change differing greatly from one region to

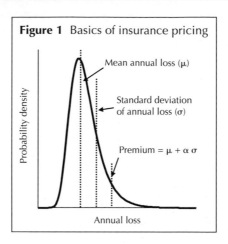

Figure 1 Basics of insurance pricing

another, and the insured risk being also very dependent on local approaches to mitigation of the hazard impact and the scale of the risk. Consequently, the impacts on insurance will vary geographically, thus making generalisation of the issues difficult. What may be important to the insurance industry in one country may be a non-issue in another. This will create a particular problem for reinsurers, who will need to understand all the local and regional nuances of the issue.

Underlying it will be some fundamentals, of which a critical one is pricing. The basics of insurance pricing are shown in Figure 1 (see Walker, 2003). The premium rate depends on both the mean annual risk and the spread of uncertainty or volatility generally measured by the standard deviation. Climate change will impact on both of these, the mean may increase or decrease. At this point in time there is not very much consensus within the scientific world of the likely mean impact of anthropogenic climate change on insured hazards at regional and local level, but there is a high level of uncertainty. Consequently, unless countered by additional mitigation of the hazard impact, in general premiums should now include a component to reflect this uncertainty, a component that should change with time as the uncertainty decreases and the mean effect becomes better known. Since increased volatility implies an increased need for capital it will affect this as well.

For the general property insurance industry the tools exist for efficiently handling these changes, the impact of which is likely to be small relative to the impact of demographic and political changes, particularly in the developing world. Increasing wealth and the associated increased penetration of insurance in China, for instance, over the next 30 to 50 years could have a much bigger impact on the global general property insurance market. China is also one of an increasing number of developing countries that are looking to providing some form of national insurance against disasters. By increasing the spread of insurance, these could have a positive effect on the industry, as they will tend to increase the geographic spread of catastrophe insurance, thereby reducing the volatility of insured losses at global level. However, even though it will increase the size of premium pool, it will also increase the capital requirements of the reinsurance market. Because these schemes will be primarily social in purpose they may also need input from governments in the form of guarantees or subsidies, leading to the need for some form of partnership between governments and the insurance industry as already exists in some countries, where affordability and insurability are difficult to satisfy simultaneously (see Gurenko, 2004).

Much more uncertain is the impact on the insurance industry of risks arising more indirectly from adaptation to climate. Climate often plays a significant role in the economic activities of communities, especially those in which agriculture and tourism make significant contributions, and increasingly in those where water is becoming a scarce resource. Predicted changes in local climate can have major implications for decision making in these communities. These will bring opportunities for new products but also threats.

The threats arise due to the possibility of latent risks, particularly on the liability side, which are largely unrecognised at present but could be activated indirectly by consequences of anthropogenic climate change. One of the biggest problems for the insurance industry during the last 30 years has been the growth of the so-called "compensation culture" (see Aon, 2004). If significant losses arise to significant groups of people or organisations in the future that are perceived as being the result of faulty decision making or negligence when the possible consequences of climate change were considered to be well known, then the circumstances exist for potential major claims on the insurance industry. Ultimate liability may depend on insurance policy wordings being written now, and interpreted by a judge or jury in 30 years' time. The insurance industry has learned much from its experience over the last 20 years, but latent claims remain a threat, precisely because the industry is conservative and not good at identifying new risks to itself and predicting the long-term effect they may have in respect of accumulated liability claims.

ADAPTATION RISKS – LIFE AND HEALTH INSURANCE

Because life insurance is long-term it is inherently less resilient to change than general insurance. However, in general, because it is based on an assessment of risks from past experience, with continuing improvements in living conditions and healthcare, life insurance has generally been seen as a low-risk profitable business. The exception was the fixed pensions side of the industry, where declining interest rates and lower investment returns in combination with a significant increase in life expectancy caused some significant problems. As a consequence, the risk component of this sector has effectively been removed, and it has become largely an investment-based savings sector, with pensions linked to savings and investment conditions, and transferable to dependents in the event of death. This means the insurance side is becoming more dependent on pure life insurance, which is primarily a function of mortality. If there should be a reversal in the historic mortality trend, the life insurance sector could face a severe threat. The death of 30,000 people who died in the summer of 2003 in Europe has been attributed to the extreme heat wave and climate change. They were mainly elderly, but what if changing climatic conditions resulted in conditions more amenable to the development and spread of major global pandemics that had more impact on the middle-aged?

CLIMATE CHANGE MITIGATION RISKS

One of the areas in which there has already been an active response within society to the problems raised by anthropogenic climate change is the mitigation of the risks arising from climate change by reducing the level of change through stabilisation of the level of greenhouse gases in the atmosphere. This is already having a big impact on industries traditionally associated with the production of greenhouse gases such as the energy industry and big industrial users of energy.

The primary initiative has come through the United Nations Framework Convention on Climate Change (UNFCC) and its Kyoto Protocol, signatories to which have agreed to cut overall emissions of greenhouse gases from 1990 levels by agreed amounts by 2012. Although the US and Australia have not ratified, most industrialised countries have, and are now developing policies to achieve their emissions targets. A typical policy approach has been the imposition of a carbon tax on emissions or energy consumption or by capping emissions above a prescribed annual limit. In the case of emission caps, this liability can be met by purchasing emission allowances from a company whose emissions are within the limit set, or by purchasing emission reductions or offsets from approved projects in the case of forestry sequestration. The development of this market in emissions trading introduces new forms of risks, some of which may provide opportunities for insurance-related products and solutions.

In a related area, Kyoto will inevitably shift energy generation towards renewable resources that are by definition less reliable and predictable. This means that, whereas today the significant demand driver for energy is weather, in future increasing percentages of generation capacity and supply will also be weather-dependent, making both demand and supply weather-dependent. This will increase the volatility of earnings, which the insurance and weather derivatives markets will seek to mitigate.

There will also be new political risks in that policies to incentivise investment mean a significant part of the revenue stream may be policy-dependent. Governments are still feeling their way in terms of the implementation of the Kyoto Protocol. There are no precedents, so it is inevitable that there will be a degree of trial and error in the development of appropriate regulation.

Providers of professional environmental audit and verification services – or *operational entities*, as they are known under the Kyoto Protocol – will be responsible for verification and certification of corporate compliance as well as emission reductions against baselines in projects within the Clean Development Mechanism (CDM).[2] Errors and omissions arising from this activity could result in significant liability claims. These providers are required to be accredited by the UNFCC, and this accreditation will depend on their having adequate financial protection or insurance in place against these risks.

THE ROLE OF THE INSURANCE INDUSTRY IN MANAGING CLIMATE-CHANGE RISKS

Where the risks are of a traditional form, then the insurance solution may be little different from what is provided now. In general, weather-related catastrophe risks will probably be in this category. A possible change could be a demand for longer-term policies in relation to mortgage lending on property to ensure cover over the term of the mortgage.

The insurance industry is also experienced in handling liability risks. The major problem for the insurance industry will be assessing the risk, as past experience provides no guide to risks that will only surface in the future. For the industry this is likely to be primarily an issue of policy wording.

The risks associated with the emissions market may need new risk transfer and financing products designed for the purpose. Traditional property and casualty insurance may not be suitable, with recourse being made to alternative forms of financial risk transfer and risk financing. The past 20 years has seen considerable developments in this area, often utilising capital markets solutions, including:

❏ finite insurance;
❏ weather hedges;
❏ insurance-related derivatives; and
❏ catastrophe bonds.

While generally not competitive with traditional insurance for normal insured risks, these alternatives have found application in some specialist areas where traditional insurance has limitations. A traditional aspect of insurance is that the insurance is provided against the risk of a loss, and it is the potential loss that is being indemnified. A characteristic feature of these alternatives is that they are often not directly related to the actual loss that is experienced, but are more designed to provide compensation if a prescribed event occurs, which has the potential to cause loss. As a consequence, instead of the insured risk being the potential loss, which is often difficult to estimate in advance, and sometimes even more difficult to assess when it occurs, the insured risk is the physical event itself that can be more reliably assessed. Other benefits include less moral hazard and a more efficient claims process.

Another important area where insurance might be able to provide a measure of protection relates to the liability for carbon such reversals due to mortality of trees in sequestration projects, as a result of unforeseen natural events such as fire or pest attacks.

RESEARCH NEEDS

Insurance is a quantitative financial approach to risk management. It can work efficiently only if there is good quantitative information on the risks, and the tools are available to use this information. During the last 20 to 30 years, the insurance industry has developed some very powerful tools to assist with decision making regarding premiums, policy conditions, capital management, reinsurance purchasing, claims management and solvency. These include dynamic financial analysis and catastrophe loss modelling. These will need further development, but this will be of limited value until the underlying risks of climate changes, particularly at local and regional level, are better understood.

CONCLUSIONS

1. The global insurance industry is very robust, having demonstrated great resilience to sudden shocks, and adaptability to change, over the past 400 years.
2. While the most direct impact will be the effect on catastrophe insurance, its response to unprecedented insured catastrophe losses over the past 15 years gives some confidence that it will adapt and cope with any additional demands on it due to climate change.
3. It will require partnerships between the insurance industry and governments to develop effective insurance solutions to growing weather-related risks in many developing countries where commercial insurance is not yet well established.
4. Risks arising from anthropogenic climate-change adaptation and mitigation may provide opportunities for new markets for insurance-related solutions to financial risk management.
5. The emergence of a totally new market in emissions trading, estimated to be worth €35 billion by 2010,[3] and the fact that carbon will now be an element of both the balance sheet and

profit-and-loss, will lead to its being considered in insurance claims adjustment as well as risk financing options.

6. Latent liability risks that may be exposed by changing the attitude of society to the consequences of climate change pose a possible threat to the insurance industry from anthropogenic climate change.

7. An increasing risk of global pandemics arising from climate change could pose a threat to the life insurance industry.

8. Computer-based tools developed in recent years can be expected to play an increasing role in developing insurance-related solutions to the risks generated by anthropogenic climate change as scientists develop a greater quantitative understanding of these risks.

1 See www.unepfi.org.
2 The CDM is the flexible mechanism by which projects in non-Annex I countries can deliver compliance instruments to Annex I countries.
3 ABN Amro, London, April 2005

REFERENCES

Aon, 2004, "Compensation and blame culture – reality or myth?", URL: http://www.aon.co.uk.

Dlugolecki, A., 2004, "Achanging climate for insurance: A summary report for chief executives and policy makers", Association of British Insurers, June.

Gurenko, E. N. (ed), 2004, *Catastrophe Risk and Reinsurance: A Country Risk Management Perspective,* (London: Risk Books).

Mills, E., E. Lacompte, and A. Peara, 2001, "US insurance industry perspectives on global climate change", Laurence Berkeley National Laboratory, MS90-400, US Department of Energy, February.

Munich Re Group, 2005, "Annual review: Natural catastrophes 2004", URL: http://www.munichre.com.

Swiss Re, 2004, "World insurance in 2003", sigma no. 3/2004, statistical appendix updated February 2005, URL: http://www.swissre.com.

Walker, G. R., 2003, "Pricing of catastrophe risk", in N. R. Britton (ed), *Catastrophe Risks and Insurability,* (Sydney: Aon Re Australia).

24

Protecting Your Carbon Asset: Risk and Insurance in the Greenhouse Gas Markets

Christopher Walker, Brian Thomas

Swiss Re

Swiss Re has been active in assisting the development of the greenhouse-gas (GHG) emissions reduction market for a number of years. Our prominence emanates from an early expression of concern about the effects that climate change will have on our businesses.

In a way, insurance companies have been in the climate business for a long time. Insuring against large losses has made insurers very attentive to the risks from weather. Indeed, it was these risks that prompted Swiss Re to pay attention to climate change. However, our position on climate change has made us a nonconformist compared with the majority of our peers, since, in general, the insurance industry still suffers from two broad fissures on the issue of climate change.

The first split divides Europe and the US. In Europe, there is more awareness of the issue and some pockets of activity on emissions constraints; in the US, there is scant awareness and only nascent activity. A similar gap divides the European reinsurers – particularly Swiss Re and Munich Re – from the primary insurance companies. The large reinsurers view climate change as a reality, and therefore a matter of strategic business importance, perhaps more than any other segment of the financial services industry. Meanwhile, the primary insurance companies are biding their time.[1] They cite three reasons, not all of them consistent. They maintain that climate issues are:

1. *manageable,* arguing that climate change will be progressive, allowing risks to be underwritten with the option of adjusting premiums as and when necessary;
2. *irrelevant,* because reinsurers, as opposed to primary insurers, bear most of the risk for catastrophic events; and
3. *unclear,* because the scientists have not yet proved that extreme weather events are demonstrably increasing in frequency and severity.

The big reinsurers believe these three reasons for procrastination are untenable. Climate change cannot be expected to develop in a gradual way: the prehistoric record shows many instances of abrupt climate change (see National Academy of Sciences, 2001). Secondly, reinsurers are well ahead of insurers in assessing their catastrophic liability, and now limit their aggregate exposures tightly, to well below the maximum economic damage potential.[2] Finally, a strong scientific consensus on the reality of human-induced climate change has emerged. Over the near term, natural climate variability will continue to complicate the debate on trends. But, even if some cause-and-effect relationships are not yet fully established scientifically, we advocate the precautionary principle: climate change has the potential to generate enormous harm and damage to human health, the environment and the economy.

We face a future of potentially worsening chronic risks that could threaten our global prosperity and wellbeing. We are likely to see more extreme swings of weather, more frequent and severe storms and greater damage. There are obvious impacts to people's property and livelihoods from windstorms, flooding, heat waves and other effects of a changing climate. To cite just one source, the California Energy Commission points out that in California this will translate into hotter days, additional smog, sea-level rise and a 15–30% reduction in surface water available for California's cities and farms.

Shifting climate patterns can take lives and pose major public-health dangers. Disease vectors and mortality rates may also show hitherto unexpected links with climate change. And, importantly, the ecosystems that underlie the economy are feeling the stress also, and are in danger of deteriorating further. Climate-change-induced deforestation and soil erosion could devastate entire regions, jeopardising our food supply and agriculture, along with wildlife on land and off our shores.

Clearly, such developments would impact all insurance lines of business, not just property. They also threaten the insurance industry's investment portfolios, whether through impaired returns or increased operating costs. Reinsurers like us are making business decisions based on climate change prediction, adjusting their management practices and product offerings. The likely responses to projected increases in losses range from price increases and primary cover changes, to more difficult reinsurance terms and withdrawal from high-hazard areas.

Insurance can and should play a crucial role in grappling with these broad societal issues. We anticipate risks by trying to understand them before they come to pass, and developing financial tools to deal with them. As such, we foster confidence in the markets. Climate change is a complex phenomenon that is nonetheless amenable to mitigation. With a forward-looking attitude, we can help create conditions that will make the transition to a post-Kyoto world much easier and more predictable. The reinsurance industry is not a monolith in its approach to climate change. Munich Re concentrates on climate modelling work, while Swiss Re is committed to facilitating GHG reductions. Swiss Re sees a potential large market for GHG-related insurance products (or, more accurately, adaptations of existing product lines to the GHG issue) and financial risk management services.

CORPORATE GHG RISK MANAGEMENT

There is a further risk management dimension: the liability regime associated with carbon. Swiss Re believes that soon all industries will be operating in a carbon-constrained future. We have seen how asbestos went from a widely used industrial material to an exponentially ballooning liability that has bankrupted entire industries. If the industries affected had begun managing their liability when knowledge of the risk first appeared, the liability crisis with asbestos might have been greatly diminished. We may be at an early stage in this process with climate change. Certainly, from an insurance point of view, proactive management by companies of the risks posed by emissions constraints would be ideal. However, anticipating issues and their potential to develop into insurance claims is a two-way street, and insurers also need to be proactive in anticipating potential claims such as the treatment of European Union Allowances (EUAs) under business interruption policies.

PANEL 1 CLIMATE CHANGE IN THE BOARDROOM – DIRECTORS' AND OFFICERS' LIABILITY CONCERNS

Dealing with climate change has been brought to the boardroom by a combination of post-Enron world disclosure requirements and the activism of shareholders seeking transparency and proactive risk management of long-term issues. This was the premise of the Carbon Disclosure Project (CDP), now backed by financial institutions representing more than US$20 trillion in assets under management. From 2003, the project has written to the world's 500 largest corporations asking for the disclosure of investment-relevant information concerning their GHG emissions. In 2003, the CDP study found that, while 80% of CEOs acknowledge the importance of climate change as a financial risk, only 35–40% were actually taking action to address the risks and opportunities. This apparent lack of risk mitigation is a concern. Simultaneously, shareholder activism has moved into the realm of the institutional investor community such as pension funds. In 2004, more than 25 shareholder resolutions related to climate change were filed in the United States. As a result many companies have voluntarily agreed to analyse and report the potential impact of GHG emissions constraints on their business in return for the withdrawal of the resolutions. Three multinational banks, for instance, have agreed to voluntary reductions of their operational GHG footprint as well in relevant lending and investment activity.

Directors' and officers insurance' – potential liability exposure
In this context, Swiss Re concluded that an exposure potentially exists within our directors' and officers' insurance (D&O – professional liability insurance for senior management) portfolio. Companies not preparing for or complying with climate-change-related regulations could create personal liabilities for directors and officers, posing a significant risk to insurers, because GHG-related shareholder litigation is a distinct possibility. We are attempting to address our concerns by considering a company's responses to the CDP. If it is inadequate, we issue the company a questionnaire upon new or policy renewals. The purpose at this point is not at this time to exclude cover, rather:

- ❏ to act as a guide post for risk assessment and underwriting;
- ❏ to educate our clients to a significant risk; and
- ❏ to determine effects on insurability, coverage and costs (premium).

RISK MANAGEMENT FOR CARBON CREDITS

From an insurance point of view, the regulation of emissions via flexible market mechanisms serves as a potentially efficient risk management tool. Carbon is a risk, and managing it through emissions trading and offsets can help move it from a company's liability column. Prior to the European Union's Emissions Trading Scheme (EU ETS) and the entry into force of the Kyoto Protocol, risk management surrounding emissions exchanges in the market consisted of:

❏ for the purchasers: small-volume buys from a number of sellers – to limit counterparty exposure;
❏ for the sellers: maintenance of a surplus emissions reduction reserve to reassure buyers; and
❏ other risks, such as political risks and risks that Kyoto would not come into law, which were left with the buyer

With EU ETS and Kyoto's becoming law, more sophisticated risk transfer products that complement the use of the market mechanisms are developing. Today, in general, insurable and or hedgable risks in the GHG market are:

❏ price;
❏ volume;
❏ financial credit;
❏ operations and equipment; and
❏ weather.

Continuing to be difficult to insure are traditional political-risk issues such as nationalisation and confiscation, particularly within the Clean Development Mechanism (CDM) or for Joint Implementation (JI) projects in countries from the former Soviet Union. What compounds GHG-related risk is the potential for wilful default on the part of the project developer who has sold future streams of Certified Emissions Reductions (CERs) but now wilfully defaults due to better price options from another party. The developed-country buyer will have little recourse outside of attempting to enforce a contract in a local developing-country court. Managing this risk will become increasingly important as CERs become a fungible currency post-2008. Finally, almost impossible for commercial insurers to risk-manage are the potential risks

PANEL 2 CONDITIONS FOR INSURABILITY

To be insurable, an event or activity must meet four conditions. These conditions do not always occur, but, if they are ignored too persistently, an insurance company (or industry) will not be sustainable. These conditions, which are all interrelated, are as follows.

❏ *randomness*: The time at which the insured event occurs must be unpredictable, and the occurrence itself must be independent of the will of the insured. Thus many infectious diseases are not insurable as such, because they break out exponentially.

❏ *assessability*: The probability and severity of losses must be quantifiable to facilitate the calculation of premiums and the potential extent of loss occurrences.

❏ *mutuality*: Numerous persons exposed to a given hazard must join together to form a risk community in which the risk is shared and diversified.

❏ *economic feasibility*: Private insurers must be able to charge a premium that is commensurate with the risk, and the premium must be affordable to buyers.

A functioning emissions trading market can improve the insurability of carbon assets and liabilities in general. When carbon has a value that can be traded, that helps assessability. Informed and accurate pricing is essential to insure or hedge exposures. Because historical data patterns are lacking, forecasting capabilities need to be developed on the basis of market intelligence and experience gained over time. The entire trading market introduces an aspect of mutuality, as all participants in the market have a strong interest to maintain the order and liquidity of the market. And, of course, trading revenues can add to the overall economic viability of a market.

around how the Kyoto Protocol is implemented. Items such as changes in implementation legislation, the value of credits in the event of a collapse of the Protocol itself, and whether the CDM Executive Board will approve a project baseline are currently outside any risk appetite of commercial insurers.

THE CARBON-CONSTRAINED FUTURE

Obviously, a GHG market is emerging, and we have entered into a risk dialogue with clients so that we can develop appropriate solutions as they make decisions in a carbon-constrained future. This is really a question of how we can complement the market mechanisms. As the Kyoto Protocol evolves, the development of CDM and

JI offset projects opens new opportunities to apply familiar technical, operational and construction covers in novel ways and to new
technologies. However, for a market in GHG emissions to emerge,
the right regulatory infrastructure needs to be in place. For example, there must be clearing mechanisms to reliably transfer the carbon credits from buyer to seller.

Swiss Re is an industry pioneer in identifying and incorporating
risk and capital management procedures related to climate change
and a carbon-constrained future. We were the first to dedicate a
business unit (in 2001 called Greenhouse Gas Risk Solutions) to
deal with the risk and opportunities emanating out of constraints
in GHG emissions. It acts as a hub for these issues on business
development and focuses on several relevant activities centred on
the transfer of emissions reductions. Whether for voluntary or
compliance reasons, the transfer of emissions reductions presents
risks to the participating counterparties revolving around credibility, standards and assurance of delivery.

At Swiss Re we are working on the following solution areas.

❑ Structured GHG derivatives and insurance products to facilitate
   trading. Puts, calls, delivery guarantees are some of the examples.
❑ End-user derivative products by packaging together risk management services to suit individual client needs such as combined weather/GHG derivatives centred on the potential impact
   that precipitation, wind and temperature have on the amount of
   emitted/credits created, thus allowing our clients the potential
   for options to cover losses, monetary damages or replacement
   emissions reductions.
❑ Providing clearing and portfolio management mechanisms to
   facilitate emissions reduction projects and trading.
❑ Insuring construction, technical and operational risks of projects
   such as on- and offshore wind farms, thereby improving the risk
   profile for financiers and enabling them to proceed.
❑ Assisting GHG emission reductions through the development
   and distribution of investment vehicles aimed at institutional
   investors. In general, these vehicles will provide financing for
   renewable and energy efficiency projects throughout Europe.
   Fund investors may receive additional return from the sale of
   emissions reductions acquired in the financing of the projects.

VOLUNTARY MARKETS

It is still early, but companies in all industries are already beginning to grapple with carbon constraints. They are assessing their climate-change exposure, looking for opportunities presented by climate change, benchmarking against other companies, setting up formal lines of accountability and seeking the reputational value of climate-change engagement. For voluntary GHG reduction commitments, the same risks surround the purchase of emissions offsets, credibility, standards and assurance of delivery. Swiss Re is attempting to assist companies entertaining voluntary commitments (particularly those outside of current regulatory scope, reach or absence, such as the US via the Footprint Neutral programme).

FOOTPRINT NEUTRAL

Swiss Re has embarked on a public–private partnership with the United Nations Development Programme to catalyse the development of markets in ecosystem services as well as enable companies to voluntarily offset their environmental footprint by supporting projects that offset greenhouse gases, protect biodiversity, enhance water quality and/or promote community development.

Footprint Neutral is an evolutionary approach to addressing the planet's sustainable development challenges, by proactively engaging companies, consumers and municipalities in addressing climate change and ecosystem degradation. Footprint Neutral works closely with companies and municipalities to design a programme that addresses their unique environmental priorities. The programme provides several options for participation.

❏ *company offsets*: A company can offset all or part of its greenhouse gas footprint.
❏ *customer offsets*: A company can market "Footprint Neutral" products, which include a small premium to offset a product's greenhouse gas emissions.
❏ *employee offsets*: A company can offer employees the opportunity to contribute to offset projects, creating a shared offset goal for both corporate and employee contributions.
❏ *municipality offsets*: Local governments may offset the GHG emissions of their own activities and operations, or facilitate offset programmes targeted to citizens or local companies.

Footprint Neutral provides companies with a portfolio of projects that not only offset greenhouse gas emissions, but also provide multiple environmental benefits – protecting biodiversity, enhancing water

---

quality and promoting community development. The programme offers a robust project portfolio enabling companies to address global and local sustainability challenges through a single programme.

Footprint Neutral is dedicated to providing voluntary offsets of the highest quality and the programme's project standards will ensure the selection of the most credible and high-impact offset projects. By channelling offsets through the programme, and drawing on the expertise of the programme's partners and management staff, companies will achieve significant leverage in the quality, scope and impact of its strategic sustainability activities. Footprint Neutral is anticipated to be launched during the autumn of 2005.

CONCLUSIONS

This brings me to three final observations. First, there are too many disjointed scientific bodies, international agencies and nongovernmental organisations addressing the issue of climate change. To achieve maximum impact, these efforts must be consolidated, mainstreamed and engineered to build one upon the other. The sheer scale of the issue demands nothing less.

Second, this is an urgent global problem, and not one owned by any political party or point of view. Governments and supranational organisations must set ambitious goals and devise regulations that supply business with long-range clarity about emissions targets, and provide incentives for reaching them. Stop/start markets caused by regulations such as the Wind Production Tax Credits in the US, which have only a two-year lifespan, are conducive to neither long-term secure financing nor financial market attention.

Third, good deeds and charity are just not enough. Government alone cannot do it. This is ultimately an economic issue. The business community and particularly the financial and insurance sectors must recognise and become engaged in the significant opportunities to be found in developing products and solutions. Managing the changing landscape of risks in the next decades requires public–private collaboration on an international scale.

---

1 These two gaps are not hard and fast. Many UK and Japanese insurance companies are formulating policies on climate change, some as part of a wider public commitment to sustainable development. However, of the top 15 US underwriters, only one company explicitly

identifies climate change within its corporate literature, while a handful are studying the link between tropical storms and climate.

2   In fact, reinsurers pay close attention to all emerging risk areas such as nanotechnology, genetically modified organisms – the list is extensive.

REFERENCES

National Academy of Sciences, 2001, "Abrupt climate change", Washington, DC.

Swiss Re, 2004, "Tackling climate change", Switzerland.

Section 6

Global Developments

25

CDM Financing and its Practice – An Asian Perspective

Kyoko Tochikawa, Mari Yoshitaka, Junji Hatano

Mitsubishi Securities

With the entering into force of the Kyoto Protocol in February 2005, interest in the Clean Development Mechanism (CDM) has increased substantially. However, there is still little understanding of the exact nature of the assistance and implications for their projects. This chapter discusses the basic role of the CDM in financing, accompanied by a brief description of the steps and costs involved in the CDM application process.

This chapter also introduces subsidies offered by the Japanese government as one example of public funding availability. Lastly, it looks at several real projects and describes the different ways in which CDM assistance made the projects possible.

ROLE OF CDM IN PROJECT FINANCING

The CDM's well-known objective is to enable Annex I (industrialised) countries to meet part of their greenhouse gas (GHG) reduction obligations through the implementation of GHG-reducing projects in non-Annex I (developing) countries, at the same time as assisting sustainable development in those non-Annex I countries.

From a purely monetary perspective, this means that the CDM enables Annex I countries with high per tCO_2 reduction costs to meet part of their obligations at a fraction of the cost of achieving the reductions domestically. To non-Annex I countries, the CDM presents an opportunity to attract both public- and private-sector investment from Annex I countries to environmentally and socially sound projects.

How CDM will assist project financing

So how exactly does the CDM fit into project financing? There are many ways to finance projects in developing countries. When project developers seek financing for a project, their options include public financing, such as official development assistance (ODA), grants, subsidies and export finance, as well as commercial financing, such as bank loans and equity investment. Many projects that have GHG-reducing effects fortunately have access to these funds and from at least an investment perspective, do not necessarily need the assistance of the CDM.[1] More often than not, the flow of funds does not extend to smaller project developers attempting to introduce innovative and often expensive projects. It is pertinent to note that innovative technologies are not only expensive, reducing the project returns, but also present a higher real and perceived risk. It is to the latter type of projects that the CDM aims to provide a means of finance.

The CDM is specifically aimed at helping those projects that cannot be implemented without it, whether it is due to investment or other barriers.

Here, the effect of the CDM on project returns and investor behaviour will be briefly discussed.

Price of CERs

Of obvious importance is the price of CERs. The CDM is a market-based mechanism where the price of CERs is determined by supply and demand. It is possible that an unregulated flow of "hot air" from Russia[2] and the potential flooding of the market from fluoro-carbon destruction projects[3] would see a heavy fall in the overall carbon market price, including CERs. In the following analysis, the conservative figure of US$5 per tCO_2 will be used.

The effect of CERs on project returns

As a simple example, let us take a renewable, fuel-based power-generation project such as wind, small hydro or biomass. According to the consolidated methodology for grid-connected electricity generation from renewable sources,[4] the emission reduction from such a project stems from the displacement of fossil fuel-based grid electricity with the project's carbon-neutral electricity. For a 20 MW power plant generating about 140,000 MWh of electricity annually, and assuming the CO_2 emission factor of the grid to be $0.6 tCO_2/MWh$, the project will be responsible for reducing approximately 84,000 tCO_2 annually. Sold at US$5 per tCO_2, the CERs will increase cashflow by US$420,000 for each year of the crediting period.[5] As a result, the equity IRR for this project will increase by 4.7%,[6] enough in many cases to make the difference between implementation and non-implementation. If the CERs are traded for US$10 per tCO_2 instead, the increase in equity IRR will be even more pronounced, at 9.4%.

PANEL 1 EFFECT OF CERS ON PROJECT RETURNS (SIMPLIFIED)

Capital cost: US$30 m (equity US$9 m; rest in bank loan)
Electricity generation: about 140,000 MWh of electricity annually.
Assuming the CO_2 emission factor of the grid to be $0.6tCO_2/MWh$, Annual CO_2 reduction will be 84,000 tCO_2 annually (140,000 MWh $\times$ $0.6tCO_2/MWh$).

Scenario 1:
Sold at US$5 per tCO_2, the CERs will increase cashflow by US$420,000 for each year of the crediting period.[7]
Equity IRR increases by 4.7% (US$420,000 ÷ US$9,000,000).

Scenario 2:
Sold at US$10 per tCO_2, the CERs will increase cashflow by US$840,000 for each year of the crediting period.[8]
Equity IRR increases by 9.4% (US$840,000 ÷ US$9,000,000).

The effect of CDM status in attracting investors

Notwithstanding the inherent high risk of many CDM projects, the CDM status often attract those public and private investors interested in acquiring CERs. These investors could be government agencies looking to acquire CERs for their country, companies with an obligation to reduce emissions or brokers and trading companies. These investors either act purely as CER purchasers, pre-negotiating the volume and price of CERs, or become equity investors to the project with a view to acquiring their percentage, if not all or a greater percentage, of the CERs.

Another group of investors are those who aim to heighten their corporate image by associating themselves with CDM projects, with their greater recognition as environmentally and socially oriented projects. These companies usually already have a portfolio of such projects, and want to expand it to include CDM projects. These companies are somewhat more selective in terms of the nature of the project, and tend to look for those projects that have a visible positive environmental or social impact, such as renewable energy, energy efficiency and afforestation/reforestation.

It is interesting to note that, at this early stage of the CDM, some of the larger and wealthier companies are allocating significant amounts of resources into projects with unspectacular returns, purely to gain CDM experience and expertise. There is still a small window of opportunity for early movers on the project development side to take advantage of this.

REQUIREMENTS OF THE CDM

For a project to qualify under the CDM, it must go through a process set by the CDM Executive Board. The following is an outline of the main requirements.

Project design document

The project design document (PDD) is the central document in the CDM process. It shows information necessary to determine whether the project meets all criteria and shows the CER calculations and the monitoring methodology. Under the CDM rules, the PDD must be released for public comments during the project's assessment period, called "validation". The PDD is prepared by the project proponents or CDM consultants.

New baseline and monitoring methodologies

The PDD must apply baseline and monitoring methodologies that have been approved by the CDM Executive Board. The methodologies determine the methods for the calculation of emission reductions and for the monitoring of the project to ensure that it results in a real emissions reduction. If there are no methodologies applicable to a project, the project proponents or their consultants will need to prepare a new methodology application. This adds significantly to the time and cost. At present, there are only 22 approved methodologies, mainly for renewable energy and landfill gas projects.

Host and investor country approvals

As the CDM is based on bilateral or multilateral cooperation, a CDM project is required to obtain both the *host* (non-Annex I) and *investor* (Annex I) country approvals through their respective *designated national authorities* (DNAs).[9] While obtaining approval from the sponsor country is relatively straightforward and quick, the host country approval process tends to be more complicated and lengthy as the DNA checks, among others, the project's environmental performance as well as its contribution to the country's sustainable development. It is advisable to approach DNAs at an early stage in project development.

Validation

Validation is essentially an audit of the contents of the PDD and the CDM merits of a project by an independent third party, or *Designated Operational Entities* (DOEs).[10] The DOE will interview various stakeholders as necessary to confirm the content of the PDD. It also involves a mandatory release of the PDD on the UNFCCC Web site for public comments over a 30-day period. When the DOE draws a favourable conclusion on the project, it will forward the PDD, its validation report, and investor country approvals to the CDM Executive Board for registration.

Registration

Once the project applies for registration, the CDM Executive Board will consider the project at its meeting. Unless there are three or more requests for review, the project will be registered as CDM.

Monitoring

The input variables necessary for the calculation of emission reductions are to be monitored after project implementation and recorded according to the monitoring methodology given in the PDD.

Verification, certification and issuance

The DOE verifies the monitored data and certifies the emission reductions. The CERs are issued by the CDM Executive Board based on the verification/certification.

Costs of CDM financing

Due to the various requirements under the CDM, project proponents wishing to apply for CDM status will incur additional transaction costs. Significant costs are involved in the preparation of a PDD, preparation, if necessary, of new baseline and monitoring method-ologies and payment to a DOE for validation. In addition, the feasi-bility study may have to be expanded for the CDM component of the project. While some developers have the expertise and resources to produce the PDD and methodologies in-house, many rely on CDM consultants. Without exception, all must pay the DOE. It is noted most if not all of these costs are incurred and payable prior to registration and CER delivery.

Registration fees, which are set according to the estimated amount of emission reductions, are payable to the CDM Executive Board. After project implementation, CDM costs, including moni-toring costs and verification costs, are payable to the DOE.

Estimates of CDM transaction costs range from US$100,000 to $250,000 for regular-scale projects.[11] Estimated major costs for a regular scale CDM project are:

Preparation and review of the project[12]	US$25,000
Project Design Document and Monitoring Plan[13]	US$55,000
(Additional costs incurred where a new methodology is required)	
Validation[14]	US$25,000
Registration fee[15]	US$15,000 – US$30,000
Monitoring and verification	US$10,000 per year

As can be seen from the above, significant costs are incurred in the CDM process. To minimise the burden, developers should explore the possibility of applying for funding programmes offered by various governments, and also partnerships with CER investors. This is elaborated on below in the context of the Japanese govern-ment and investors.

ESTABLISHMENT OF BASELINE AND MONITORING METHODOLOGIES FOR RENEWABLE-ENERGY PROJECTS

The PDD must apply baseline and monitoring methodologies already approved by the CDM Executive Board. As examples, we will introduce two approved methodologies.[16]

It is noted that the CER calculations provided in the PDD are only estimates based on projections. The actual number of CERs

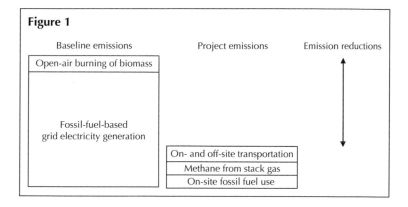

Figure 1

generated by the project will be based on actual monitored data collected after project implementation.

Grid-connected biomass power generation that avoids uncontrolled burning of biomass (AM0004)

The project is designed to use, for electricity generation, biomass that would otherwise be burned in the open air or left to decay. It will reduce anthropogenic GHG emissions by displacing fossil fuel-based electricity generation with GHG-neutral biomass electricity generation. In addition, the project will curb methane emissions from open-air uncontrolled burning of rice husk.[17] The baseline and project emissions are summarised in the figure below.

The formulas used are straightforward and largely based on Intergovernmental Panel on Climate Change (IPCC) factors. Taking the example of a $20\,MW_{net}$ biomass power plant supplying 130,000 MWh of electricity annually to the grid, the resultant total emission reduction is in the order of 80,000–90,000 tCO_2e per year.[18] Displacement of grid electricity comprises the large majority of this.

An important issue for biomass power generation projects is their potential for "leakage", which is a project's indirect contribution to an *increase* in GHGs. For example, a project may source biomass from a supplier who, before the project, sold some of the biomass to the surrounding community for use as fuel in their homes. By taking away their source of supply, the project may divert users of this fuel to a fossil fuel. To ensure that leakage does not occur, AM0004 requires a macro analysis of biomass supply and demand.

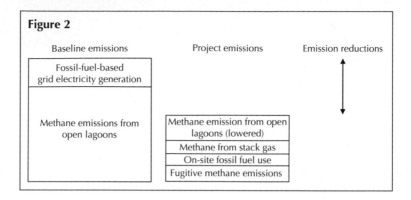

Figure 2

Methane extraction from organic wastewater treatment plants for grid-connected electricity (AM0013)

This project involves the installation of a closed anaerobic system that will produce and collect methane-rich biogas from wastewater generated at a palm oil mill. The wastewater will be diverted from the mill's existing wastewater treatment system, an open lagoon system under anaerobic conditions, into a closed anaerobic digester. The collected biogas will be used to produce renewable energy. By extracting and capturing biogas in a closed digester, the project will reduce methane emissions that would have occurred in the existing open lagoon. In addition, the use of the collected biogas as fuel for electricity generation will displace grid electricity and its associated emissions.

As with AM0004, AM0013 relies on IPCC formulas and values in the absence of localised data. The emission reduction projection for a 1.0–1.5 MW capacity power plant destructing methane (biogas) is in the order of 48,000 tCO$_2$e per year,[19] where the avoided methane emissions from open lagoons is the significant emission reduction component.

The salient feature of the methodology is the comparison between theoretical baseline emissions and the actual monitored amount of methane destruction. This is different from simple activities concerning landfill gas-collection projects, which do not introduce a change in the methane generation process, and can hence rely solely on monitored amount of methane destruction for an accurate emission reduction estimate. As AM0013 is designed for projects that change the methane generation process, it conservatively requires that the lower value of the theoretical and actual values be used for the emission reduction calculations.

SUPPORT PROGRAMMES BY JAPANESE GOVERNMENT AND OPPORTUNITIES WITH JAPANESE STAKEHOLDERS

It is widely known that Japan will not be able to meet its Kyoto commitment through domestic measures alone. The resource-poor country had already largely implemented efficiency measures prior to the Kyoto Protocol, making further domestic emission reductions costly. The Japanese government therefore plans to achieve 1.6% of its 6% reduction target through the Kyoto mechanisms. Without US participation in Kyoto, this is expected to make Japan the single largest buyer of CERs.

There are many support programmes offered by the Japanese government to project developers through which it hopes to ultimately help procure carbon credits for Japan. Two institutions are prominent in the area of CDM. They are the New Energy and Industrial Technology Development Organisation (NEDO) under the Ministry of Economy, Trade and Industry (METI) and the Global Environment Centre Foundation (GEC) under the Ministry of Environment (MOE). Each offers two programmes for the CDM, one that funds part of the CDM transaction costs, and another that subsidises part of a project's capital cost. The subsidies are not ODA.[20]

Support of CDM transaction costs

Both GEC and NEDO provide similar subsidies to cover the costs of the feasibility study and PDD production. The programmes require the applicants to be Japanese companies together with a local partner.

Due to the growing interest in the CDM, there is strong competition for the grants. The two institutions slightly differ in the types of project that they subsidise. GEC favours waste management projects while NEDO funds primarily energy-related projects. In addition, the CER performance of the project, in terms of the volume generated compared with project size and investment will be taken into account.

The GEC/NEDO subsidies for the support of transaction costs can be combined with the subsidies for capital costs described below.

Support of capital costs

Both GEC and NEDO offer grants to finance a project's initial investment in exchange for the project proponent's agreement to transfer the project's CERs to the Japanese government. The grants essentially allow project proponents to sell all or part of their project's CERs with significant upfront payment. This is different from normal CER purchase agreements, where payment occurs in the future as CERs are delivered, after project commencement. Even when an upfront payment is negotiated, a hefty discount is required.

For reasons of budgetary classifications, the grants take the form of a subsidy for the initial investment, instead of a straightforward purchase agreement. The grants are capped at ½ of the initial capital investment. It is not tied to purchasing Japanese equipment.

As an example, we will take the NEDO programme and discuss it in connection with a hypothetical renewable-power project, where the initial equipment investment is in the order of US$20 m. This will mean that the cap for the project is US$10m.[21] The project may be expected to generate CERs of approximately 50,000 tCO$_2$e annually, or 350,000 tCO$_2$e over seven years, which is worth a total of US$1.75 m at current prices of US$5/tCO$_2$e. Should this project qualify for the NEDO funding, it is likely that the developer will negotiate a grant in the order of US$1.75 m in return for transferring all of the CERs generated by the project. It is noted that the cap of US$10m will come into effect only for those CDM projects such as methane collection and utilisation that have a high CER generation–investment ratio.

The GEC and NEDO programmes are attractive despite the complicated and time-consuming administrative process. As with the subsidies for the transaction costs, these grants will be accorded only through a Japanese entity.

CER investors and other stakeholders

Many Japanese firms, notably power companies, are interested in investing in CDM projects either as equity investors or a CER purchaser. While not always the case, a large number of these companies will have resources available to take over the lengthy and costly CDM process, either through in-house expertise or by hiring outside consultants.

Another active Japanese player is the Japan GHG Reduction Fund (JGRF). Inaugurated in 2004, JGRF, through Japan Carbon Finance Limited (JCF), will become one of the largest buyers of CERs. The Japan Bank for International Cooperation (JBIC), as the principle proponent of, and largest shareholder in JCF, is interested in facilitating the implementation of high-quality CDM projects.

One possibility a project developer may wish to pursue is to seek JBIC debt finance for part or all of a project in return for the project agreeing to sell CERs to JCF. This arrangement would be a package deal comprising debt financing and regular purchasing agreement for payment against delivery.

IMPLICATIONS OF THE CDM

While the CDM is not an all-encompassing solution for project developers and investors alike, there are undoubtedly many benefits. Some of the implications of this mechanism are given below.

For project developers:

❑ *Future cashflow.* The CERs are traded in hard currencies and can be treated as cashflow, increasing project returns. The more attractive returns can also help to attract debt or equity financing.
❑ *Exposure to potential investors.* The CDM process is a very public one, giving the project developer a platform to highlight the project's credentials to CDM investors. The project will be viewed by a wide range of investors after, say, a successful methodology application or public comments during validation.

For investors:

❑ *Increased project returns.* Notwithstanding the focus given to the benefit to the developer from additional revenue, it is important to note that equity investors also benefit from the increased returns.
❑ *Environmental performance.* The CDM gives investor companies an opportunity to improve their corporate environmental performance in a cost effective manner.

❑ *CERs.* Companies in Annex I countries that have or expect to have emission caps will have a means to offset their emissions by acquiring CERs. This allows companies to achieve their target at a lower price than carrying out domestic measures.

PANEL 2 LANDFILL GAS RECOVERY PROJECT IN THE PHILIPPINES

The project involves landfill gas collection and electricity generation at a landfill in the Philippines capital of Manila. The landfill gas is to fuel a 1.0 MW capacity generator, which will produce electricity to be sold to the grid.

The project reduces GHG emissions by capturing and destructing methane (biogas) that would otherwise be emitted into the atmosphere. By using the methane for grid electricity generation, the project will also reduce emissions from fossil-fuel-based power plants in the grid. The emission reduction ranges from approximately 75,000 to 7,000 tCO_2e per year.[22]

Due to the perceived risks associated with the use of a technology new to the country, it has proved difficult to obtain loans for the project. The developer expects to fund the project either by itself or together with equity partners, based on the higher financial performance from CER sales. An international financial institution has expressed some interest in funding the project as part of its corporate social responsibility as the project is considered to have a large positive social impact.

PANEL 3 BIOMASS POWER PROJECT AT A PALM OIL MILL IN MALAYSIA

The project uses biomass waste from the palm oil milling process – empty fruit bunches, fibres and shells – as fuel for grid electricity generation. The biomass will be sufficient to fuel a generator of about 6 MW.

By displacing grid electricity with the project's biomass-fuelled electricity, the project leads to an emission reduction of approximately 25,000 tCO_2e annually. The project is also eligible to claim emission reductions for avoiding methane from decaying stockpiles, which will increase CERs by 55,000 tCO_2e/yr to a total of about 80,000 tCO_2e annually.

The developer for this project has been in talks with Japanese equity investors interested in acquiring CERs. They are also considering taking advantage of the GEC/NEDO subsidies for capital costs.

PANEL 4 METHANE RECOVERY PROJECT FROM WASTEWATER TREATMENT AT A PALM OIL MILL IN MALAYSIA

The project involves the installation of a closed anaerobic system that will produce and collect methane-rich biogas from palm oil mill effluent (POME) generated at a palm oil mill. The POME will be diverted from the mill's existing wastewater treatment system, an open lagoon system under anaerobic conditions, into a closed anaerobic digester. A 1.5 MW generator is also to be installed and will use the collected biogas as fuel to produce renewable energy.

The project will reduce methane emissions from the lagoons as well as CO_2 emissions from fossil-fuel-based electricity generation. Total emission reductions are expected to be in the order of 48,000 tCO_2e per year. The additional revenue from the sale of CERs is expected to increase the project's IRR, which is projected to be a low 7.7% in the absence of the CDM, to a level acceptable to investors.

After the approval of the AM0013 methodology, prepared in connection with this project, the developer for this project was approached by potential CER purchasers and equity investors.

1 A project may still require the assistance of the CDM even where it has sound financing. For example, a government may be suspicious of unfamiliar and innovative projects but will see the CDM status of a project as an implicit endorsement from an internationally recognised authority such as the UNFCCC.

2 The fall in economic activity in Russia and many other Eastern European countries has led to a natural decrease in GHG emissions in those countries as compared with the 1990 base year. This gives those countries a large reserve of "emission reductions". Most of these countries are eligible for Joint Implementation (JI) and will generate Emission Reduction Units (ERUs), another form of carbon credit.

3 Fluorocarbons have a global-warming potential of several hundred to more than 10,000 times that of CO_2.

4 See http://cdm.unfccc.int/EB/Meetings/015/eb15repan2.pdf.

5 The crediting period is chosen from either (i) 7 years with the option of renewal up to a total of 21 years or (ii) 10 years only.

6 This is a simplified calculation, assuming that the project life and CDM crediting period have a similar time span. If, however, the project lifetime is, say, 20 years while the project's crediting period is only 10 years, then the increase in IRR will be lower.

7 See note 5.

8 Ibid.

9 In its meeting on 19th May 2005, the CDM Executive Board will be asked to allow CDM eligibility to extend to so-called unilateral projects involving the host country. Under such projects, no Annex I country buyer is identified prior to registration. DNAs in some countries such as Malaysia specifically require project participants to show there is Annex I country involvement in their project and this will need to be reviewed.

10 Designated by the UNFCCC.

11 See "Estimating the Market Potential for the Clean Development Mechanism: Review of Models and Lessons Learned", PCF*plus* report, 2004.

12 See http://carbonfinance.org/docs/ProjectCyclePresentationMarch2004.ppt.

13 Ibid.

14 Ibid.

15 The full list of registration fees is available at: http://cdm.unfccc.int/Projects/pac/howto/CDMProjectActivity/Register/regfee.pdf.

16 Both methodologies were prepared by Mitsubishi Securities on behalf of the project proponents.

17 The methodology conservatively sets the baseline as open-air burning. The emission reductions will increase significantly if the baseline is dumping instead.

18 Estimate based on Thai electricity grid. The figure will be different depending on the characteristics of the grid that the project is connected to – lower for grids with greater hydro representation, and higher for those with greater coal-fuelled plants, etc.

19 Based on the characteristics of the Bumibiopower Methane Extraction and Power Generation Project, for which the original methodology was prepared.

20 The CDM must not result in a "diversion" of ODA. ODA involvement in itself is not prohibited.

21 Based on current cap of ½ for the fiscal year 2005 programme.

22 The dumpsite is required to close several years into the project, resulting in a decline in methane generation.

26

CDM and Renewable Energy in China

Lu Xuedu; Li Junfeng; Song Yanqin; Liu Yingchun

Tsinghua University; Chinese Renewable Energy Industries Association; Energy Research Institute of National Development and Reform Commission; Building Capacity for CDM in China

The use of renewable energy resources plays a key strategic role in maintaining a balance between energy demand and supply in China. The Chinese government has therefore consistently promoted renewable-energy development. China's use of renewables in 2003 accounted for 15% of the nation's total energy consumption. Comparison with other nations shows that China has climbed to the top position globally both on the total utilisation of renewables and on the proportion of renewables in the overall energy use.

NATIONAL DEVELOPMENT TARGETS

Due to the fast increase of the energy demand, total power installation by 2020 is expected to amount to about 1,000 GW. Such a big increase creates great potential for all types of power technologies, including renewable energy. The specific targets for renewable energy include the following: by 2010, the installed capacity of small-scale hydropower, wind power, biomass power, geothermal power and power generated by solar energy will reach about 60 GW in total and account for about 10% of China's total installed power generation capacity; by 2020, the installed capacity for power generated by renewable energy will reach about 121 GW, accounting for about 12% of China's total installed power generation capacity. It must be emphasised that the achievement of such targets would rely heavily on all of kinds of measures, including investment, economic instruments and technology development.

BIOMASS
Resource availability

China's main biomass resources are agricultural waste, waste from the forestry and forest product industries, and municipal waste, all with large potential. Agricultural waste is widely distributed and includes crop stalks, waste from the processing of agricultural products and manure from livestock farms. With the implementation of China's Natural Forest Protection Programme (which includes logging bans and logging reductions over much of the nation's natural forests) and its Sloping Cropland Conversion Programme (which calls for the conversion of much of the nation's sloping cropland to trees and grasses), it is expected that the amount of waste from the forestry and forest product industries will increase substantially. Perhaps 60% of the municipal waste could be used in landfill methane applications. Finally, "energy crops" are a biomass energy resource with the potential for commercialisation, for example, rapeseed and other edible oil plants and some native plants, such as sumac, Chinese goldthread, and sweet broomcorn could yield over 50 million tonnes of liquid fuel annually, such as ethanol and bio-diesel.

Current development status

At present, biomass energy resources in China are utilised mainly through conventional combustion technologies. Biomass gasification, biomass liquefaction and biomass power generation technologies, however, are gradually being developed. China has already established two large ethanol fuel production bases, with a total annual production capacity of more than a million tonnes. Production of bio-oils in China has reached about 50,000 tonnes annually. Biomass power generation in China, with an installed capacity of almost 2,000 megawatts (MW), consists mainly of combined heat and power (CHP) in sugar mills and power generation using rice husks.

Potential projects for CDM

Grid-connected power generation will be one of the ideal CDM (Clean Development Mechanism) projects in China, based on bagasse co-generation, straw and stalks, wood residuals, urban refuse and landfill, and sized at MW level. The grid-connected project potential will range from 10 to 15 GW in total by 2020. Biomass for distributed power is another potential CDM priority. Village-sized (from 10 kW to about 100 kW) biomass gasification-for-power application are widely deployed in Germany and other north European countries and are now being demonstrated in some rural areas of China. It is projected by 2020 or beyond, there will be about 5 GW distributed biomass for power around China.

SMALL-SCALE HYDROPOWER
Resource availability
The potential total capacity of small-scale hydropower is 125 GW, including sites in more than 1,600 counties (or cities), 65% in Southwest China. The Chinese government has announced policies to support small-scale hydropower.

Current status and development potential
At present small-scale hydropower stations, with an installed capacity of 30 GW, represent about 20% of the total projected potential capacity. By 2030, China's small-scale hydropower resources will be almost fully developed, with a capacity of 100 GW and accounting for about 10% of China's total installed power capacity at that time. Most is grid-connected technology.

Potential CDM projects
Most of the potential CDM projects of small hydro-power projects are located in the western part of China. Currently, there are two CDM projects developed. One is in Gansu and another one in Yunnan. Based on the additionality analysis, distributed small hydro-power has higher priority for CDM, together with some special small hydro-power for the purpose of fuel substitution. The total capacity of these is estimated to be 10–15 GW. The grid-connected small hydro-power can also be an option for CDM.

WIND POWER
Resource availability
Land-based wind resources represent a potential power generation capacity of 253 GW. Ocean-based wind resources represent a potential of about 750 GW, so that the total estimated wind power potential of China is about 1,000 GW.

Current status and development potential

By the end of 2003, total grid-connected installed capacity of wind power in China was 560 MW, making China tenth in the world in terms of wind-power capacity. Aside from grid-connected installations, China also has about 200,000 standalone small-scale wind turbines (with installed capacity of 25 MW) that provide electricity to households in remote areas. Most experts believe that the total installed grid-connected wind-power capacity will be about 30–40 GW by 2020 and more than 100 GW after 2030. Distributed wind power by 2020 will be no more than 1 GW.

Potential CDM projects

Almost all of the wind projects are suitable for CDM because of the very high cost. By 2020, the wind project potential for CDM will be from 20 GW to about 40 GW, or even more.

SOLAR ENERGY
Resource availability

The total solar radiation hitting China's land area annually is equivalent to about 170 billion tonnes of coal equivalent (tce). Areas on the Qinghai–Tibetan Plateau receive the largest amounts of solar radiation in all of China.

Current status and development potential

Currently, the main use of solar energy in China is the supply of hot water to urban and rural households. The cumulative installed capacity of solar water heaters is now more than 50 million square metres of collector area. In 2020 and 2050 total installed capacity could reach 200 million and 500 million square metres respectively, with the potential to conserve 120 billion kWh in 2020 and 300 billion kWh in 2050. Potential reductions in peak power loads resulting from these installed capacities would be 80 GW (2020) and 200 GW (2050). Photovoltaic (PV) technology is the main technology used in China for the generation of electricity from solar energy. At present, China's installed capacity of PV systems is over 50 MW, of which about 50% is used to supply electricity to the residents of remote rural areas. Grid-connected solar power is under development worldwide. The Chinese Solar Energy Society estimates that by 2050 there will be 1,500 to 2,000 GW of grid power capacity using rooftop and desert-based installations. Distributed solar power will be mainly for the use of electricity supply for remote application, with a potential capacity of 1–2 GW.

Potential CDM projects

All solar PV projects are suitable for CDM. In the case of solar collector systems, due to the commercialised market development status, it is hard to define the baseline for the hot-water supply system as a CDM project. From the greenhouse gas (GHG) reduction point of view, the solar collector application has a great contribution to make. Therefore, new methodologies should be developed to enable the solar collector to be selected as CDM-eligible.

OTHER RENEWABLE ENERGY

The Chinese government has been paying close attention to the development and utilisation of other renewable-energy resources, such as geothermal resources, ocean energy sources and hydrogen. Geothermal pumping technology, in particular, has already begun to play a meaningful role in building energy conservation in China. In general, geothermal and ocean energy will become good candidates for CDM throughout China.

CDM AND RENEWABLE ENERGY

Grid-connected applications will take the majority of the CDM projects in the future and distributed ones will be supplementary.

Grid-connected technology

Renewable grid-connected power comes mainly from wind, small hydro and biomass with some solar power. The total potential of grid-connected power generation for CDM will be about 40–60 GW by 2020, among which wind is 20–40 GW, biomass is 15 GW and small hydro power is 20 GW or more. The average size of grid-connected renewable power installations is 1–50 MW, except solar rooftop, which is from 5 kW to 1 MW. Based on current practice, grid-connected technologies would be the mainstream of CDM project.

Off-grid technology

Currently, solar PV and small wind turbines in remote areas are the majority of distributed renewable energy. For CDM, mini and micro hydro-power, as well as off-grid biomass for power, will take the lead in future distributed power generation, with a potential 15–20 GW in total by 2020. The other major off-grid systems are solar collectors for hot-water supply and biogas technologies. Solar collector could replace about 100 TWh to 200 TWh of electricity by 2020 and biogas could replace about 40 million tonnes of coal. The major difficulties of distributed technologies to be developed as CDM are:

❏ *smaller size*: The capacity of distributed technologies is from 10 W to several kW. In contrast, a grid-connected system is generally over MW level.
❏ *high cost*: in general, distributed technology will be high-cost for energy production, compared with grid-connected technologies. Taking wind, for example, the total investment of grid-connected technology is about US$800 per kW, whereas the off-grid system will cost about US$4,000 per kW.
❏ *difficulty in monitoring*: Due to the large and remote area of the distribution of the off-grid system, the cost of monitoring a CDM project will be very high.

PROJECT FINANCING

Since most of renewable-energy technologies are not commercialised, financial tools are necessary to support their development. This section will discuss the current situation of renewable-energy project financing and the importance of CDM in the financing of the renewable-energy sector.

Government-grant financing

Government financing comprises direct investment and government concession programmes, which play very important roles in renewable energy development both worldwide and in China. Currently, the Chinese government's direct investment in renewable energy is more than 2.5 billion RMB yuan or US$300 million, mostly into distributed technologies such as household biogas, small hydropower and PV. The typical government direct-financing project for renewable energy is the programme for village power (Song Dian Dao Xiang). In order to promote the commercialisation of wind power, the Chinese government has adopted the concession approach.

ODA support for renewable energy

ODA support plays an important role, especially in the distributed renewable-energy technologies. To cite the Bonn Renewables Declaration, the policy options related to developed countries are as follows.

Increase funding for renewable-energy R&D: IEA member governments allocate only 8% of their energy research and development funding to renewable energies. Here governments have an opportunity to strengthen renewable energies by reversing the ratio of funds allocated for renewables *versus* those provided for conventional-energy R&D. Demonstration projects in cooperation with the private sector should be encouraged as well.

Focus bilateral and multilateral development assistance on catalytic funding of renewable energy programmes: Capacity building and catalytic financial leverage to extend energy services from renewable-energy sources are key priorities. They should be provided in parallel with the creation and extension of micro-finance schemes that target consumers and small-scale businesses. Governments must take care to encourage, rather than undermine, the development of markets through the use of such subsidies, particularly with regard to renewable-energy technology exports to developing countries. Public–private partnerships are a successful means for developing such markets and should be further expanded.

Promote renewables through export credit agencies (ECAs): The public promotion of exports through the provision of credits or guarantees by ECAs can help mobilise private financing for renewables. ECAs should become more active in building industry awareness about renewable-energy investment opportunities. Specifically, it is essential to establish standardised and simplified procedures for small-scale projects so as to reduce transaction costs. It is also essential to encourage long-term contract durations for renewables (say at least 15 years) and more flexible modalities (for example, flexibility in repayment terms, liberal treatment of local costs) to suit the variety of renewable-energy projects.

Table 1 ODA support in solar PV marketing in China

Programme	Source	Total	Approach	Time schedule
Renewable-energy development	GEF	US$25.5 m	Sales subsidies and technology innovation support	2002–7
Salk-road brightness programme	Netherlands	US$10.5 m	Household subsidies	2002–6
Village power	Germany	US$23 m	Set up village power system	2003–5
Village power	Canada	US$2 m	Training and demonstration	2003–5
Village power	Japan	US$4.6 m	Demonstration and testing centre support	1998–2002

ODA plus export credit guarantees (from ECAs) were the major financing approaches in the development of renewable-energy projects, especially in wind power. Before 1998, about 70% of wind turbines were installed with the support of ODA/ECA money, which mainly came from Denmark (more than 100 MW), Germany, the Netherlands and Spain.

International financial institutions

Since 1990, the World Bank (WB) has approved nearly US$4 billion as loans, credits, grants and equity for alternative energy (including large hydropower in that definition). About US$500 million went to China, mainly for large hydro-power. Cumulative Asian Development Bank (ADB) lending to China as of 31 December 2003 was US$13.62 billion, of which about 16% was for energy. However, very little of that was renewable-energy investment. Currently the WB and ADB have started to conduct renewable-energy financing with the support of the Global Environment Facility (GEF).

The China Renewable Energy Development Project: This is an international cooperation project of the National Development and Reform Commission (NDRC) and the World Bank, with grant financing provided by GEF. The project aims to establish sustainable markets for wind and PV technologies in order to: (1) supply electricity in an environmentally sustainable way; and (2) increase access of isolated rural populations and institutions to electricity services It will install about 20 MW grid-connected wind and 10 MW solar PV household systems. The total investment is about US$50 million with US$30 million of GEF grant and US$20 million of WB loan.

The China Renewable Energy Scale-up Programme: This was designed by the Chinese government in cooperation with WB and GEF. The programme supports renewable-energy policy development and investment, and aims to: (1) assess renewable energy resources in China; (2) learn from the experiences of developed countries in developing renewable energy; (3) research and formulate policies for the development of renewable energy in China; and (4) on the basis of pilots, gradually achieve scale-up of renewable-energy power generation, so as to provide cost-effective and commercialised renewable energy to China's electric-power market. The total budget for this programme is US$366 million, of which US$141 million is GEF grant, US$100 million WB loan and the rest from the Chinese government and investors.

ADB Renewable Energy Technical Assistance Project: The ADB project was originally a 78 MW project that got downsized to 20. The objective of the project was to accelerate the growth of large-scale, grid-connected, wind-power development in China by developing a policy/regulatory mechanism to compensate utilities for the price difference between wind-power and grid average price. It also aimed to train utilities on market-oriented wind-power tariff methodologies. The total installation is 21 MW and the total investment about US$24 million, of which ADB loan was US$11.5 million, GEF grant US$1.8 million, and the rest equity and local bank loan. Eventually the beneficiary decided not to take the loan from ADB, because the procedures were too complicated and a local commercial bank loan was available, with a reasonable interest rate and much simpler procedures.

FDI for renewable energy

There are very few FDI projects available in China and the incentives for renewable-energy development are unclear. A successful investment project for wind was made by one Dutch company – Nuon. The 24 MW wind-power project on Nan'ao Island was China's first fully commercially developed and financed wind-power project and has been in operation now for more than eight years.

Commercially based investment

This comes from the commercial banks and private investors. The commercial banks' involvement in renewable energy started with ODA and other bilateral and multilateral financial support because, under Chinese regulations, all ODA money must go through a local commercial bank for co-financing. Even with about 10 years' experience, the national commercial banks still believe that renewable energy development is very high-risk. Before 2003, there were almost no private investors involved in renewable-energy project development, especially in wind and other high-cost technologies. This situation started to change after the wind concession programme, since the government guaranteed the purchase price of electricity for 30,000 hours.

Roles of CDM in renewable energy

From the total-investment point of view, CDM plays a limited role in the development of renewable energy. However, from the cash-flow point of view, the income of sales of Certified Emission Reduction credits (CERs) would be about 30% to 50% of the project profits. That could be sufficient to make a project profitable, and therefore enable it to happen. Take one government-approved CDM project for example, the Huitengxile wind farm project. CDM money is only about 10% of the total investment. However, the sales of CERs would be about US$300,000 per year, double the annual profit of the project. In conclusion, the CDM's ability to reduce investment risk is limited, but, as soon as the project financing available, the sales of CERs will be an important economic instrument to support the project implementation and operation.

RENEWABLE-ENERGY POLICY IN CHINA

General description of renewable-energy policy

The discussion in this section will focus on legislation, national planning and economic incentives, which include taxation deduction, investment subsidy and other instruments.

Policy and legislation

The Chinese government has attached great importance to the development and utilisation of renewable energy for many years. In the 1980s, renewable energy was part of the plans for the development of rural energy and rural electrification. In 1994, the Ministry of Power issued recommendations for wind power, and in 1999 the Chinese government issued several policy recommendations on promoting the development of renewable energy. In 2003, the government began to formulate its Law for Renewable Energy Development and Utilisation, with the goals to: (1) confirm the important role of renewable energy in China's national energy strategy; (2) remove barriers to the development of the renewable-energy market; (3) create market space for renewable energy; (4) set up a financial guarantee system for the development of renewable energy; and (5) create a social atmosphere conducive to renewable energy. In February 2005, the National People's Congress ratified the law and it will enter into force on 1 January 2006.

At present, the Chinese government is in the process of formulating its Medium- and Long-term Energy Development Strategy and Plan to 2020. The basic principles relating to renewable energy are as follows.

❑ support the harmonious development of society, the economy and the environment, with priority on achieving a basic level of comfort for all citizens through technologies such as PV, small hydropower and other renewable-energy technologies, which can resolve the basic needs for electricity in rural areas. This principle also calls for improvement in the quality of energy used by rural residents, which can be achieved through biomass energy technologies, particularly biogas technology, which can promote the development of ecological agriculture and organic food products.
❑ stress should be put on the development of small-scale hydropower, solar water heaters, geothermal heating and other renewable-energy technologies that are already competitive. The share of renewable energy should be raised as rapidly as possible, so as to make a strong contribution to the adjustment of China's energy consumption mix.
❑ The commercialisation of new and developing renewable-energy technologies should be promoted actively. In particular,

wind power and biomass power generation, for which resources are vast and commercialisation prospects good, should be promoted through measures to stimulate market demand, technical progress and manufacturing capability so as to basically realise full commercialisation and large-scale application by 2020.

❑ long-term technical progress should be integrated with short-term development and utilisation. Renewable-energy technologies that have both a market at present and great potential for the future should be actively developed. PV technology should be developed so as to serve in speeding up the realisation of rural electrification in the short term and to gain experience for large-scale grid-connected PV in the future. Ethanol, gasoline and bio-diesel technologies should be developed through pilots and demonstration projects in the short term to establish the necessary basis for future large-scale development and supplement China's oil supplies.

Specific targets for renewable energy, include the following: by 2010, installed capacity of small-scale hydropower, wind power, biomass power, geothermal power and power generated by solar energy of 60 GW or 10% of China's total installed power generation capacity; by 2020, 121 GW, or 12% of China's total installed power generation capacity.

Economic incentives

Although there is no comprehensive financial incentive system for the development of renewable energy in China at present, government support has been provided for a long time. In the 1990s, with the emphasis on sustainable development, the technologies receiving support were extended from small hydropower, biogas and fuel wood saving stoves to wind power, solar energy – including PV power – and biomass utilisation technologies and so on. The types of support changed from supply subsidy to tax reduction or exemption, preferential price, credit guarantee, etc. These measures have contributed greatly to renewable-energy development in China. However, to reach the ambitious targets mentioned above, these measures are not systematic and strong enough. Therefore, it is necessary to seek other measures, including CDM, to promote renewable-energy development. The major financial incentives in existence are as follows.

Subsidies

Subsidies from central and local government are one of the most popular economic incentives. The following are the major ones:

❑ *Management support*: This mainly refers to operating expenses and other expenses of renewable energy managerial institutions in central government. There are about 100,000 staff for the management and R&D as well as training, equipment certification, inspection and so forth for renewable-energy development, especially for rural energy application. The total administration cost was about US$240 million.

❑ *R&D*: Central government subsidises R&D on key renewable-energy technologies through NDRC and the Ministry of Science and Technology (MOST) as well as local government. For example, R&D funds on renewable energy offered by MOST during the Ninth Five-Year Plan period will be US$7.2 million.

❑ *Investment subsidies*: The Department of Resource Conservation and Utilisation (DORCU) provides low-interest loans of about US$14 million each year to support industrial development of renewable energy. The Ministry of Water Resources (MWR) provided low-interest subsidies of about US$ 36 million for small hydropower development. The government also provided interest subsidies (50% of commercial bank loan interest) to some renewable energy projects.

Taxation

Based on collection and distribution rights, tax can be classified as central government tax, local government tax and shared tax. Following the implementation of the new tax-sharing system introduced on 1 January 1994, taxation in China can be classified as shown in the Table 2. A favourable rate of VAT can be applied to some renewable energy, such as wind, biomass and small hydropower.

Custom duties

To be consistent with the international market, import customs duty has been decreased to 23% on average. Although there is no specific government document that clearly specifies low customs duty rates on renewable-energy products, the main components of

Table 2 Classification of taxation in China

Items	VAT	VAAT (value-added annex tax)	Income tax
General	17%	8% of VAT	33%
Biogas	13%	8% of VAT	15%
Wind	8.5%	8% of VAT	15%
Landfill gas	0	0	

wind turbines, wind turbines themselves, and PV modules all enjoy favourable customs duty rates. (Customs duty exemption depends on whether the equipment is considered high-tech.)

Potential impact of the Renewable Energy Law

The Renewable Energy Law will come into force from 1 January 2006. The main purpose is to remove barriers to renewable energy, with a feed-in tariff and supplementary measures of Renewable Portfolio Standard. However, due to backward infrastructure – especially weakness in manufacturing and technology innovation – additional technologies and financial incentives will still be needed.

There is a national commitment that China is serious about sustainable development. However, since the total energy production is huge, currently renewable electricity in China is about 5% in the overall energy supply mix. Even in 2020, the planned renewable capacity will still be less than 12% of total electricity plant. The CDM Executive Board has ruled that such policies or laws, except enforced implementation, should not be taken as a baseline. In addition, the technology and financial barriers still exist, and so the additionality condition for CDM projects should still be applicable.

CDM-related policy

CDM is one of the important tools for promoting the development of renewable energy by introducing technology and investment from advanced countries. The National CDM Board ("the Board") reports to the National Coordination Committee on Climate Change ("the Committee"), and a national CDM project management centre will be established under the Board. The NDRC and MOST serve as co-chairs and the Ministry of Foreign Affairs (MOFA) serves as vice-chair of the Board. The Board will consider and approve CDM projects by checking the participation require-ments, project design documents, CER price, issues related to funds and technology transfer, sustainable development effects of the project, and so on. The Board will also report and make recom-mendations on general matters relating to national CDM policy.

In the June 2004 Interim Measures for Operation and Management of CDM Projects in China, priorities were given to energy efficiency improvement, development and utilisation of new and renewable energy, and recovery and utilisation of methane and coal bed methane. The Board has formally approved two projects, the Inner Mongolia Wind Farm Project and the Beijing Landfill Gas Project.

CONCLUSIONS AND RECOMMENDATIONS
Conclusions
Renewable energy has great potential for CDM projects in China, especially in the power sector. By 2020 100 GW can be developed as CDM projects, with total CER potential of 210 million tonnes of CO_2.

More renewable-energy projects can be expected under CDM in the near future. The current organisational structure involving the Designated National Authority and other supporting ministries, national committees, secretariats, boards and so on works very well. However, it is not so clear to outsiders like the private sector and civil society. Awareness building is needed to inform the private sector of how and whom to approach for submitting a CDM project.

From the international point of view, the CDM market at this moment is limited because several major developed countries have not yet ratified the Kyoto Protocol. From the management view-point, the methodology and the approval procedures for CDM pro-jects in the United Nations Framework Convention on Climate Change (UNFCCCC) system should be improved to meet the need for large numbers of CDM projects, both in China and in the world.

Recommendations
Coordination between different stakeholders is very important to promote CDM project development, especially between the project owner and the consulting company. More local consult-ants and consultancy companies would help to reduce the cost. International organisations should organise more workshops and

training programmes to do case studies and capacity building for developing-country experts and stakeholders. In addition, a CDM community or club could be developed for people to seek more opportunities for cooperation.

The Interim Measures for the Operation and Management of CDM Projects in China lack clarity on some issues of concern to potential project owners. For example, it is stated that the CER benefits belong to both the Chinese government and the enterprises, but the ratio of distribution of benefits is not prescribed. It also says all the benefits go to the enterprises and it is not retroactive. Without a clear statement on how the benefits are treated, potential project owners, especially for high-cost projects that rely on the CER benefit, are unwilling to proceed. Hopefully a clearer policy will be available soon.

Only four international designated operational entities (DOEs) have been approved by the Board to do validation or verification. More DOEs should be approved by the Board, especially local ones to reduce the transaction cost.

For some projects, especially in rural areas, the project owners are too poor to cover the upfront transaction cost before getting the CER receipts. Some foreign organisations might take the risk of unsuccessful CDM projects and cover the transaction cost, in return for getting the CERs at lower prices.

Improving the establishment of baseline methodologies would be helpful, and it will simplify the baseline study and determination process.

For capacity building, the following actions should be taken:

❑ development of detailed regulations for CDM implementation;
❑ identification of typical projects that would most likely meet CDM requirements;
❑ development of national/regional/sectoral CDM strategies;
❑ development of China's CDM Project Database;
❑ development of a national CDM training strategy, with industry and experts at the provincial level as the major targets and qualified Chinese experts as the main trainers;
❑ facilitation of the establishment of a National CDM Project Management Institute; and
❑ help for selected organisations to apply for Operational Entity status.

CASE STUDY INNER MONGOLIA WIND-FARM PROJECT

Early in 2002 this project was approved by the Committee. From 2002 to 2004, the project experienced many changes, and National Development and Reform Commission (NDRC) and the National CDM Board have provided consistent and strong support to this project. The Huitengxile Wind Farm is located within the Inner Mongolia region. Inner Mongolia is one of the main power generation bases for the North China grid. The total capacity installed in Inner Mongolia is about 4,330 MW, and most of the power capacity is from the coal-fired power plant supplied locally. The project involves the installation of 22 turbines, providing a total of 25.8 MW. The site has an excellent wind resource and also benefits from a strong transmission system nearby, as it is close to one of the main power generation bases for the North China Power Grid. The project will generate approximately 60 GWh per year, which will be sold into the Inner Mongolian Western Grid on the basis of a power-purchase agreement (PPA). In addition, the total CERs to be delivered from 2004 to 2011 will be 54,136 tonnes of CO2.

The specific goals of the project are to:

❑ reduce greenhouse-gas emissions in China compared with a business-as-usual scenario;
❑ help to stimulate the growth of the wind-power industry in China;
❑ create local employment during the assembly and installation of wind turbines, and for operation of the wind farm; and
❑ reduce other pollutants resulting from the power generation industry in China, compared with a business-as-usual approach.

Baseline identification and methodology

The Huitengxile Wind Farm Project supplies electricity to the Inner Mongolia Western Grid, which is part of the North China Power Grid. The operating margin is determined by the entire generation mix of the North China Power Grid, excluding its zero-emission sources, which are hydro and some wind. For 2002, the Operating Margin emission factor was $0.949\,tCO_2/MWh$.

The build margin is approximated by the most recent 20% of the generating units built, and 92.47% of this new capacity was coal-fired power plant, with the remainder being zero-emission sources. For the baseline a weighted build margin emission factor of $0.879\,tCO_2/MWh$ is calculated.

As in the El Gallo Project, the operating and build margin emission factors are given equal weighting. This means that the baseline scenario is a situation where the Huitengxile Wind Farm Project displaces a set of generating units approximating the existing capacity on the North China Power Grid (100% coal-fired generation excluding zero-source units) and defers or delays coal-fired units that are currently planned to cope with electricity sector expansion.

Lessons learned

Since Huitengxile Wind Farm Project is a pioneer project, many valuable lessons can be drawn from the implementation of this project. The critical success factors were as follows.

❏ first of all, the company understood the CDM concept and was willing to share the risk.
❏ secondly, all the participants of the project enjoyed a very close working relationship. This is key for a successful implementation.
❏ thirdly, they checked frequently with the government authorities to make sure the project and its implementation followed the rules and the sustainable criteria set up by the government. They kept close contact with the methodology panel when there was no approved methodology available. They found that the duration of the project could be shorter when they could follow the approval methodology.
❏ fourthly, the company appointed staff to follow this project through from the very beginning. This is very important for consistency.
❏ finally, they found if necessary to consult a lawyer on the content of the CERPA to avoid unnecessary risk and unfair clauses.

REFERENCES

ADB activities in China, www.english.people.com.cn, 2005.

Li Junfeng and Shi Lishan, 2004, "Renewable energy outlook", Bonn Renewable Energy Conference, June.

Li Junfeng and Song Yanqin, 2004, "Overview of renewable energy development in China", EU – China workshop of CDM and renewable energy development, September.

Lin Wei, et al, 2004, PDD report of Huitengxile Wind Project, December.

Lu Xuedu, et al, 2005, CDM in China (Tsinghua University Press).

Saghir, J., 2003, "The Role of the World Bank Group in Renewable Energy and Energy Efficiency", Renewable Energy and Energy Efficiency Partnership Launch Meeting at Merchant Taylors' Hall, London, October.

Li Junfeng, et al, 2004, "The system design of renewable energy law", China Day at Bonn Renewable Energy International, June.

Song Yanqin, et al, 2003, "Renewable energy potential project for CDM", progress report of United Nation Foundation CDM -building project.

Zou Ji, et al, 2003 "Basic Needs Analysis of CDM capacity building in China", progress report of United Nation Foundation CDM capacity-building project.

27

Making Climate-Change Investments in Emerging-Market Countries

Mark Goldsmith, Ben McKeown

with a significant contribution from **Susan Pritchard***
Actis Capital LLP

Although investment in the climate-change space in the developed world is becoming mainstream, there has been relatively little investor interest in this area in the emerging markets.[1] This chapter examines the reasons for this lack of investment and considers the drivers that are likely to lead to greater investment in the future.

INTRODUCTION

The growth in the use of renewable energy for power-generation purposes looks set to continue over the next decade. While much of this growth has been in the OECD countries, the use of renewable energy in the emerging markets is rapidly gaining momentum, and is forecast to increase exponentially over the same time period.

In addition, carbon trading is becoming an important mechanism internationally, with huge potential as a new source of capital for the implementation of energy projects worldwide. Economic models estimate that, once fully developed, the carbon-trading market could reach billions of US dollars per year.

Therefore, one would expect many exciting opportunities to be opening up in the emerging markets for financial investors. However, while there are interesting investments to be made in this sector, making commercial investments in the climate-change arena in the emerging markets is a complex and challenging proposition.

---

* This chapter is dedicated to Susan Pritchard, who tragically died in a car crash following the completion of her research in this area for Actis.

Table 1 Key drivers favouring climate-change projects

Key drivers	Issues that have significantly impacted driver
The emergence of climate change as a global political issue	❏ Stockholm declaration 1972 ❏ World summit UNFCCC 1992 ❏ Kyoto Protocol 1997 ❏ European Trading System and Linking directive 2004 ❏ Kyoto Protocol ratification 2005 ❏ G8 presidency focus 2005
Rising costs of conventional fuels	❏ Yom Kippur war 1973 ❏ Iran/Iraq crises 1979–80 ❏ Increasing global oil capacity constraints ❏ Step change in energy demand from growing economies, China and India
The increasing cost competitiveness of renewable energy technologies	❏ Wind: design and technology improvements ❏ Biomass: technology improvements ❏ Geothermal: more efficient and productive resource exploration and characterisation ❏ Solar: improved components volume manufacturing ❏ PV: technology improvements and sales
The implementation of favourable policy frameworks in several key markets	For example in: ❏ 1981, Denmark committed to generate 10% of their electricity from wind by 2000 ❏ 1992, India introduced various fiscal incentives for renewable energy ❏ 2002, the government of Brazil announced the PROINFA programme to support the establishment of renewable energy electricity production ❏ 2004, China indicated it would generate 10% of its power through renewable sources by 2010

In this chapter, we share our experiences and the lessons learned when considering and making "climate change" investments in the emerging markets.

THE OPPORTUNITY DRIVERS IN RENEWABLE ENERGY

There are several opportunity drivers that have led to a substantial increase in projects relating to climate change, particularly in the power generation sector (see Table 1).

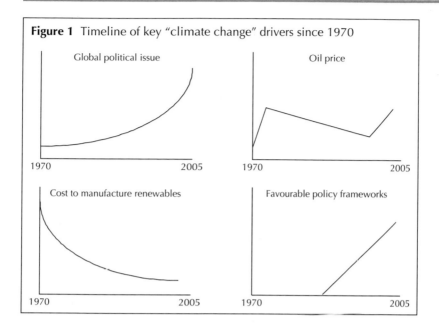

Figure 1 Timeline of key "climate change" drivers since 1970

Figure 1 illustrates how each of these key drivers has developed over the last 35 years. While there has been steadily increasing pressure from the political and policy framework drivers, it is only in the last couple of years that all four drivers have been positively aligned.

ARE RENEWABLE-ENERGY TECHNOLOGIES COST-COMPETITIVE?

The cost-competitiveness of renewable energy compared with conventional fuels is rapidly improving, with enormous advances being made in the design and efficiency of renewable-energy technology. If external costs (such as polluting the atmosphere) are included, the cost of renewable energy compares favourably with conventional sources of energy (Figure 2).

The relative competitiveness of renewable energy and conventional power generation depends to a large degree on the local resources: for example, renewable energy is unlikely to be competitive in a country that is rich in fossil-fuel resources. However renewable energy can be cost competitive especially in countries that rely heavily on high-cost diesel imports.

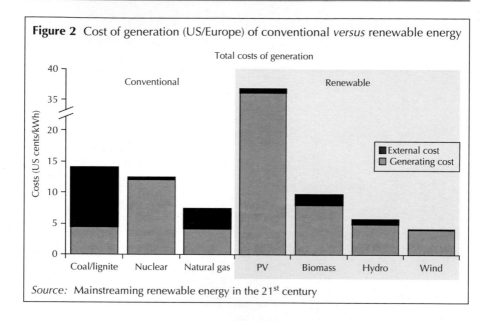

Figure 2 Cost of generation (US/Europe) of conventional *versus* renewable energy

Source: Mainstreaming renewable energy in the 21st century

In addition, renewable-energy projects may qualify for Certified Emission Reductions (CERs) and policy frameworks can have the effect of stimulating the development of renewable energy even if it is not the cheapest available source.

The developing world is less likely to pay a premium in order to encourage use of renewable resources. However, the least cost is not always the preferred route, as this can result in a greater exposure to other risks such as security of energy supply and price volatility. In addition, the rising costs of fuel imports can have a significant negative impact on a country's trade balance.

Renewable energy is characterised by high upfront installation costs and low annual costs, because the fuel is free or cheap compared with fossil fuels (see Table 2).

With the possible exception of onshore wind and landfill biomass, the installed capital cost of conventionally fired power plants (about US$700/kW) is significantly lower than the upfront costs associated with power generated from renewable sources. This differential in installation costs is further magnified in the emerging markets, where the cost of capital is generally higher to reflect the perception of increased risk in these markets.

Table 2 Summary of installed capacity costs for renewables

Category		Installed capital cost (US$/kW installed)
Biomass	Energy crops	2,900
	Landfill	900–1,000
Geothermal		2,000–2,500
Small hydro		1,500–3,500
Solar	Thermal	2,900
	PV	22,000–35,000
Wind (onshore)		900–1,200

Source: WEC (2004), Renewable Energy Projects Handbook

The competitiveness of the mainstream renewable energy technologies can be generalised as follows:

Wind

Wind is often now a commercial alternative to other sources of power, depending upon the alternatives available to the host country, with the average cost of a turbine for a high-wind environment falling from about US$7.2/kW to about US$3.4/kW (EWEA 2004 Wind Force 12) in the last 15 years. In Central America and the Caribbean, wind power is competitive with imported diesel or natural gas.

Biomass

As with wind, biomass power generation does have the ability to compete with conventionally fired power generation in certain locations. This is illustrated by a study on the use of local sugar cane in Belize to generate electricity, where power is produced at about US$8.5/kWh compared with the least cost alternatives from diesel and gas generators in the range of about US$14–20/kWh (KWOK 2003, Belize Sugar Cane study).

Mini-hydro

It costs approximately US$2 million per MW to install a small run of river hydro plant. As many of these projects are only 1–2MW in size, small hydro can be unattractive for financial investors unless projects can be bundled into a single financing package.

Solar

Despite enormous design improvements, solar is generally not yet commercially competitive with alternative sources of grid-based power. However, it can be used effectively in off-grid locations where the cost of connection outweighs the premium for solar energy. In such cases, off-grid PV, with generation costs of around US$20–40/kWh, frequently competes with unreliable diesel generators or kerosene.

Geothermal

A benchmark development cost for geothermal is difficult to predict, because there is substantial variability associated with the considerable geological uncertainties of geothermal projects.

Ocean

Wave and tidal stream technology is still in the development trial stage and is not yet commercially viable.

WHICH EMERGING-MARKET COUNTRIES OFFER THE GREATEST OPPORTUNITIES?

Many renewable energy projects and all greenhouse-gas abatement projects depend upon the revenue stream from the sale of CERs in order to attract investment. Hence it would be expected that countries with well-developed Clean Development Mechanism (CDM) processes would be attracting the most investment. There are several countries in South America and Asia that appear to have reasonably developed CDM processes in place (Table 3).

Figure 3 illustrates the number of country recommendations we independently received in a limited survey of market participants.

Brazil and India clearly come out higher in both CDM process development and market-participant recommendation for investment. There is also a general correlation between how well countries' CDM processes have developed and the market participants' recommendations. However, China, where the CDM process is still in its infancy, was viewed very favourably for investment by the market participants.

As a result of this preliminary research, climate-change investment in Brazil, China and India is considered in more detail.

Table 3 Countries with best potential for climate-change projects

Country	Kyoto signature	DNA* active	CDM application	Projects reported	S&P rating	Projects validated
Brazil	x	x	7	32	B+	27
China	x	x	1		BBB+	1
Colombia	x	x	3		BB	3
Costa Rica	x	x	1	5	BB	2
Ecuador	x	x	1		CCC+	1
Egypt		x	1		BB+	1
India	x	x	10	100	BB	13
Indonesia			3	30	B	
Jamaica	x	x	1		B	1
Korea	x	x	1		A−	
Malaysia	x	x	1	15	A−	5
Mexico	x	x	1	10	BBB−	5
Nicaragua	x	x	1	10		2
Panama	x	x	1	3	BB	2
PNG	x		1		B	1
South Africa	x		1	3	BBB	1
Thailand	x	x	3	32	BBB	2
Vietnam	x	x	1	17	BB−	2

*Designated National Authority

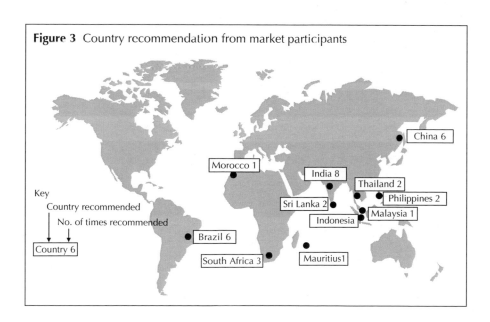

Figure 3 Country recommendation from market participants

China 6

Morocco 1

India 8

Thailand 2

Philippines 2

Sri Lanka 2

Malaysia 1

Indonesia 1

Key

Country recommended

No. of times recommended

Country 6

Brazil 6

South Africa 3

Mauritius1

Table 4 Potential for renewable energy in Brazil

Renewable-energy source	Potential (MW)	Authorised (MW)	Under construction (MW)
Biomass	9,800	3,000	500
Small Hydro	5,300	300	54
Wind	143,000	6,400	n/a

Source: Poppe M 2004, Brazil MME

Table 5 Resource potential for renewables in China *versus* 2010 targets

Renewable-energy source	Potential	2010 target	2010 target as % of potential
Biomass	300 mtce	17 mtce	5.7
Geothermal	6.7 GW	55 MW	0.8
Small hydro	90 GW	27.9 GW	31
Wind	253 GW	3 GW	1.2

Source: Li *et al* 2003, REEEP paper

Brazil

Brazil is the largest energy consumer and carbon emitter in South America and has been a strong supporter of renewable energy. Brazil is endowed with plentiful renewable-energy resources (see Table 4), which complement the existing heavy dependence on large hydro, with wind and biomass primarily available in the dry season.

China

China is the world's second largest energy consumer and emitter of CO_2 emissions. Renewable energy accounted for 19% of Chinese power generation in 2001, including large hydro projects such as the Three Gorges Dam. Table 5 details the targets set for energy from renewables by 2010 and highlights the enormous potential that will remain untapped.

With its diverse industrial base, China also offers opportunities for GHG emission reduction as well as energy-efficiency and

Table 6 Renewable-energy potential in India

Renewable-energy source	Gross potential (MW)	Technical potential (MW)	Exploited to date (MW)
Biomass	n/a	19,500	540
MSW	n/a	2,500	70
Small Hydro	15,000	10,000	1,450
Wind	45,000	13,000	1,870

Source: India MNES undated

fuel-switch opportunities to reduce CO_2 emissions. For example, in the chemical sector, the opportunities for HFC and N_2O abatement include 10 HFC plants.

India

In 2001 India was the world's fifth largest emitter of CO_2 and the second largest in the CDM universe behind China. India accepted the Kyoto Protocol in 2002. India enjoys considerable natural resources for renewable energy (see Table 6). In addition, solar programmes are being developed to bring power to rural communities not served by the grid.

During the five-year plan ending 2007, India plans to add another 1,500MW of wind and 700MW of biomass capacity, which, assuming conservative development costs of US$1,000/kW and 70% leverage, indicates an equity demand of US$660 million from these two sectors alone.

WHAT DIFFERENCE DO CARBON CREDITS MAKE?

CERs offer a source of revenue hitherto unavailable to renewable energy and GHG-abatement projects. However, there is no certainty at the start of the project that CERs will be approved and therefore the transaction costs incurred in development may never be recouped. Projects that follow the methodology approved by the CDM Executive Board are less likely to incur this risk.

The impact of CER to the return on an investment varies significantly between different types of climate-change project. The impact of CER sales on project internal rates of return (IRRs) for different renewable energy types is given in Table 7.

Table 7 The impact of carbon credits on project IRRs

Renewable-energy type	Impact on project IRR (based on world bank data)
Hydro, wind, geothermal	0.5–2.5%
Forest and crop residues	3.0–7.0%
Municipal solid waste	5.0–15.0%

Source: Bishop 2004, Carbon Finance

Table 8 Carbon revenue per MWh renewable-energy generation

Fuel displaced	Generic emissions factor (tCO_2e/MWh)	Carbon revenue at US$4/$tCO_2e$ (US$/MWh)
Gas	0.50	2.00
Coal	0.85	3.40
Diesel	1.00	4.00

Source: Bishop 2004, Carbon Finance

The size of the CER market is undetermined, and early development has been underpinned by the EU Emissions Trading Scheme (EU ETS). With the Kyoto Protocol coming into effect the market will increase in size and market uncertainty should decrease. Price is currently determined by a small number of buyers who have been willing to invest to develop the market. Sellers can eliminate the risk of future price fluctuations and failure to find a buyer by negotiating a forward sale contract prior to the financial close of the project.

In greenhouse-gas abatement, only methane is likely to offer a strong pipeline of projects above the critical size. However, there are attractive joint-venture opportunities to develop a portfolio of projects for the destruction of gases such as HFC and N_2O. These gases have a high global-warming potential and their destruction generates a correspondingly high volume of CERs, resulting in equity IRRs of 30–100%. The carbon intensity of the fuel that is displaced determines the volume of CERs generated, which translates into the amount of CER revenue achievable (see Table 8).

Table 9 Investor expectations of climate-change projects

Investment category	Return requirements	Other considerations
Corporate or strategic investors	Medium–high	May invest for reasons other than purely financial returns (for example, to secure a flow of carbon credits)
Developmental institutions	Low	Focus on a developmental agenda rather than a purely commercial agenda
Financial investors	High	Focus primarily on the target financial returns, the risks and potential downside related to such a project

WHAT DO INVESTORS LOOK FOR IN CLIMATE-CHANGE PROJECTS?

There is a lack of funds allocated to financing climate-change projects in comparison with the quantity of funds committed to the purchase of emissions credits generated by a project. This is especially the case in the emerging markets, where only a few significant renewable-energy projects have been successfully financed.

When identifying investor requirements, it is useful to differentiate between the different classes of investors who may be involved (see Table 9):

Key issues for a private equity investor are as follows.

Returns: Returns to private equity, or quasi-private equity investors will typically be made up of two components: (i) the yield they can expect throughout the investment life, and (ii) the return they can expect upon exiting the investment (typically after 5–7 years). Project returns can often be geared up by third-party debt to meet the return hurdles of financial investors.

Management: The quality of the investee company management team is of paramount importance as financial investors typically do not expect to have day to day operational control of the entity in which they invest.

Solid business fundamentals: In order to assess the expected returns of an investment, financial investors will typically scrutinise the underlying business carefully, carrying out extensive due diligence and assessing the future potential of the company or project. In the case of renewable-energy projects this will typically include careful analysis of the anchoring power-purchase agreement (PPA) and the creditworthiness of the offtaker, such as a state electricity company.

Exit: The ability to recycle investment funds is also important and most financial investors focus on exiting an investment within a pre-determined timeframe, typically 5–7 years. An important part of the pre-investment evaluation process, therefore, is the assessment of the exit prospects for an investment that may be achieved through a sales process (a sale or listing of the investee company) or through structuring the deal to achieve an exit through self-redemption, or some type of put option.

Deal structuring: Deal structuring is important with investments usually being made through an array of financial instruments. Typically an investment will be structured to reflect how returns to the investor will be generated, to provide some degree of downside protection, and to reflect the anticipated exit process.

Deal pipeline: Research indicates that there is a sufficient and diverse pipeline of eligible projects in the emerging markets, which would meet the investment criteria of a financial investor. The best renewable-energy opportunities are identified in on-grid wind, biomass and small hydro projects, which provide a higher level of offtaker creditworthiness, while still ensuring acceptable target returns.

What makes climate-change investments in the emerging markets attractive and what doesn't? A SWOT (strength, weaknesses, opportunities and threats) analysis provides a useful framework around which to analyse an emerging-market renewable-energy investment strategy (see Table 10).

MAKING THE INVESTMENT HAPPEN – PRACTICAL TIPS

Despite the increased level of interest in the renewable-energy sector, there has been little investment in the emerging markets in this sector. However, given the considerable power deficit of many developing countries there is significant opportunity for investment in this area, and an increasing number of investment opportunities. During our research over the last two years, we have learned some valuable lessons (see Table 11).

Table 10 SWOT analysis for renewable-energy investing in the emerging markets

Strengths	Weaknesses
❑ Renewable energy is becoming more cost-competitive, especially if externalities are considered	❑ Renewable energy is not believed to be "mainstream" by the investment community
❑ Many of the underlying technologies (wind, biomass, solar, and so on) have a proven track record	❑ Absence of a reliable long-term reference for resource data such as wind speed, solar radiation and hydrology in some emerging markets
❑ The creation of carbon trading systems has provided an additional source of hard-currency cashflows	

Opportunities	Threats
❑ Many countries in the developing world have a power deficit	❑ Offtaker (for example, state electricity company) payment risk, and unenforceable offtake agreements
❑ Fluctuations in prices of fossil fuels and the desire of large power consumers to lock in the cost of power to reduce risk of unfavourable price movements	❑ Changes in policy frameworks or legislative support could make renewable-energy projects less attractive
❑ Huge untapped potential	❑ Project risks including engineering procurement contract (EPC) and operation and maintenance (O&M) risk
❑ Realisation that renewable energy is often viable on a standalone basis	❑ Business integrity issues associated with permitting & awards of contracts

Source: Adapted from Rabo India, "Renewable energy: A bankers perspective"

Table 11 Practical tips

General	Offtake
❏ Consider a climate-change investment with the same degree of scrutiny as any other investment in the emerging markets ❏ As with any other investment, make sure there is a fully thought-out business plan ❏ It is important to analyse RE investments in same manneras conventional power projects ❏ Try to find investments that are past the bank feasibility stage ❏ Consider financial structuring and insurance possibilities for mitigating some of the risks	❏ Don't rely too heavily on CERs to make the investment viable – there appear to be many organisations chasing CERs ❏ If the project is to be anchored on a power-purchase agreement, make sure this is agreed before spending resources on detailed due diligence ❏ Be wary of favourable tariff regimes significantly higher than competition – there could be pressure to reduce tariffs in the future

Location	Operational
❏ Don't invest in places where you do not have good contacts on the ground ❏ Be aware of local politics and how the political climate can change during the lifetime of an investment	❏ Climatic variability is real–it is important to get as much historic and representative measurement data as possible ❏ When considering biomass projects it is to take into account transportation costs & the impact of oil price fluctuation on fuel costs ❏ With biomass, take into account how the cost of agricultural waste (such as rice husks) can increase once vendors are aware of the potential value ❏ Be aware of the impact on returns of unplanned maintenance and operational downtime

CONCLUSIONS

We believe that, through careful selection and review, it is possible for financial investors to execute attractive investments in the climate-change space in the emerging markets. However, given the inherent risks associated with any investment in the emerging markets, it is vital that favourable renewable energy policy framework commitments made by governments continue to be supported. In addition, investments in the climate-change space in the emerging markets are likely to receive considerably more investment when the mainstream investment community becomes more comfortable with carbon-trading processes such as the CDM.

1   In the context of this chapter, "emerging markets" do not include any Central or Eastern European transition countries.

28

The Clean Development Mechanism in Sub-Saharan Africa: Left Out but not Left Behind

William Greene

africapractice

The Clean Development Mechanism (CDM) is the only part of the Kyoto Protocol that confers directs benefits to developing countries. Its objective is to enable companies and governments to meet part of their greenhouse-gas (GHG) reduction obligations required under the European Emissions Trading Scheme (EU ETS) or the Kyoto Protocol through investing in GHG offset projects within developing countries. At the same time the CDM is intended to provide new sources of finance and environmental technology transfer for the sustainable development of poorer Kyoto signatories, and there are none poorer than those in sub-Saharan Africa.

However, at the date of writing, not one of the four projects registered with the CDM Executive Board was based in sub-Saharan Africa (SSA). In a region where roughly 40% of the population live below the US$1 a day absolute poverty line and where many are highly dependent on unsustainable and inefficient sources of energy (such as deadwood, charcoal and coal), the near-complete absence of CDM project activity raises important questions about its role as a mechanism for catalysing sustainable development in poorer Kyoto Protocol signatories.

This chapter asks why sub-Saharan Africa is failing to take advantage of the CDM, what are the consequences and what donors, international agencies and nongovernmental organisations (NGOs) are doing about it. It shall be argued that in the medium- to

---

PANEL 1 THE CDM: FROM PROJECT TO PROFIT

One of the key stipulations of the CDM, called the "additionality test" is that the GHG reductions created by a project must not have occurred as part of "business-as-usual situation". This is to prevent commercial investors acquiring carbon credits from their regular activities, thus flooding the carbon market and creating abnormal profits on what would in essence be free money.

Each tonne of CO_2 or CO_2 equivalent (CO_2e) that is prevented from entering the atmosphere is then converted into a Certificate of Emissions Reduction (CER), which is tradable under the ETS or International Emissions Trading Scheme.[1]

For companies that invest in CDM projects or that draw up purchasing agreements for the resulting credits, the CDM represents a highly innovative but poorly understood means of generating cheap carbon credits. Furthermore, once a company has banked the credits they have the option of either using them to meet their own emission targets or selling them at a profit via the ETS. To give an indication of the margins involved for traders in CERs, the average cost of CER, depending on the stage of the project in which the CDM finance is put forward, is between €3 and €6 per tonne CO_2e. The price of one tonne of CO_2e on the ETS, as of May 2005, was €19.6, entailing an on paper profit of approximately 650%.

[1]The IETA will become active during the first commitment period of the Kyoto Protocol and is intended for governments only.

---

long-term, sub-Saharan Africa in particular holds great promise for such projects because of its potential to supply cheap carbon credits whilst simultaneously serving as a means for corporations (especially those with investments in Africa) to demonstrate their environmental and social responsibility. In conclusion, a rallying call is made to private investors to pay more attention to the business opportunities available though the Clean Development Mechanism.

The problems besetting CDM in Africa can be broadly categorised as: (i) those resulting from the complex modalities and procedures of the CDM approval process, which neglects to take into account the technical and administrative capacity of sub-Saharan African governments; (ii) those resulting from unfavourable conditions within international political economy and the African investment climate. In other words, we look at how sub-Saharan Africa has been "left out" in the design of CDM and consequentially whether it has been "left-behind" when it comes to attracting new CDM projects. References will be made to three African projects already in the CDM pipeline:

❑ Richards Bay Waste Wood for Coal Project, South Africa;
❑ TransAlloys Silico-manganese smelter, South Africa; and
❑ Bujugali Dam Project, Uganda.

The first two projects are being developed by the natural resources company, Anglo American; the third by the World Bank.[1]

LEFT OUT – AFRICA AND THE MARRAKESH ACCORDS
The main "modalities and procedures" for the Clean Development Mechanism were hastily negotiated during the 10th Conference of Parties (to the kyoto Protocol) in Marrakesh, 2001. The so-called "Marrakesh Accords" define a stringent set of procedures and legislate for the creation of multiple new institutions before a CDM project can qualify for Certified Emissions Reductions. For most Sub-Saharan Countries, meeting these stipulations is a near impossible task. Here we look at three major stumbling blocks facing CDM project developers in the region.

To start with, we look at the bureaucratic and logistical hurdles that must be addressed by governments and CDM project developers in Africa.

Designated national authorities
An important part of the accords states that developing-country signatories must establish a *designated national authority* (DNA), which is responsible for confirming that (a) the government is *voluntarily* allowing a CDM project on its territory and (b) the project activity complies with its sustainable development objectives.

CDM projects cannot be submitted for registration without a fully established DNA, an accomplishment that has been achieved in only two countries in SSA: South Africa and Uganda. Other countries such as Ghana, Nigeria, Tanzania, Senegal, Cote D'Ivoire and Madagascar have introduced the relevant legislative framework and even designated the relevant offices but have yet to gain the capacity to fulfil all of their duties under the modalities and procedures of the CDM.[2]

The absence of a DNA does not, however, preclude the initial development stages of a CDM project and a number of carbon funds and private investors have been working on CDM in countries without fully fledged DNAs. Problems arise only when there are unscheduled delays in the establishment of a new DNA – something that occurred recently in South Africa (see the case study in Panel 2).

PANEL 2 CASE STUDY: CDM IN AFRICA WITH ANGLO AMERICAN

By Ian Emsley Anglo American

Anglo American is a natural-resource company, focused on mining but also including industrial minerals, pulp and paper in more than 30 countries. Most of the operations are energy-intensive, giving rise to carbon emissions from fossil fuels and other sources of 31 mtCO_2e in 2004.

A study concluded in 2003 that potential carbon liabilities for the company amounted to a compliance risk (the expected cost of compliance with carbon regulation in developed countries) of US$5–25 million per year and market risk (that is, the projected negative impact on coal sales arising from carbon regulation) of US$35–71 million by 2012. To offset potential carbon liabilities, the survey of assets pointed to possible carbon savings in the order of 2.75 mtCO_2e/year, thereby potentially more than offsetting the compliance risk and creating a tradable asset. While the financial rewards of carbon abatement will be relatively clear for those operations included in the EU Emissions Trading Scheme, the rewards that could flow from the CDM are less obvious, face greater risks and require greater managerial input if they are to be realised.

Richards Bay Biomass Project

Two CDM projects are under development at the Anglo American pulp and paper mill at Richards Bay in South Africa. The first and earliest project (referred to as the Biomass Project) involves the substitution of waste wood for coal as a boiler fuel, thereby saving CO_2 emissions from the combustion of fossil fuel as well as methane emissions from the decomposition of wood in landfills. The savings amount to 116 ktCO_2e/year. The project is categorised as "small-scale" and is eligible for the simplified modalities and procedures available from the CDM Executive Board. Despite these simplified procedures, project development has not been straightforward. There has been a lack of clarity regarding project boundaries. This is of critical importance to the eligibility of the project as small-scale. Failure to obtain small-scale status would have required the submission of a new methodology with all the costs and uncertainties involved in that process. The project also faced uncertainties arising from the lack of South African regulatory infrastructure, in particular the DNA and the procedures that it will apply.

Defining sustainable development criteria

The Kyoto Protocol's modalities and procedures are silent as to the exact meaning of sustainable development, permitting considerable discretion for host countries to put forward their own criteria. As yet, however, only South Africa and Uganda have robust sustainable-development methodologies in place, against which CDM projects can be assessed. Critics have argued that the lack of transparent criteria is resulting in central and municipal governments in Africa submitting projects to DNAs with dubious environmental benefits. Without transparent, easily available criteria to comply with, many of these projects are rejected by the DNA.

Consultation process

Local community consultation is a core component of the CDM modalities and procedures but can be a lengthy, time-consuming process. The exigencies of African geography, infrastructure and local culture make it even harder for non-local project developers to effectively gauge public opinion, even when there is a genuine intention to do so.

In the case of the Bujugali dam project, allegations have been made by a number of civil society groups in Uganda that the consultation process was far from transparent. Although the company developing the project had a number of village meetings, complaints were made to the DNA that relevant project documentation was either unavailable or not translated into the local dialect, preventing local leaders and civil society groups from properly assessing the impact of the project.[3]

Status of ratification of kyoto protocol

All countries wishing to participate in a CDM project activity must first ratify the Kyoto Protocol. However a vast majority of African countries (28) have yet to ratify and many of them, even large-scale producers of hydrocarbons, do not consider treaty ratification as an immediate requirement.[4] The continent's largest oil producer, Nigeria, did not ratify the treaty until as late as December 2004, and three major African crude oil producers – Gabon, Algeria and Angola – have yet to even accede to the Protocol.

The above evidence suggests that the bureaucratic and administrative components of the CDM are proving a serious challenge for many SSA governments. This should come as no surprise to donor governments since for hard-stretched African governments, scarce resources are likely to be spent on the provision of tangible social services and poverty-alleviation programmes rather than the implementation of environmental treaties with few obvious or immediate benefits. Indeed, an EU sub-Saharan Africa CDM Capacity Building Programme showed that many African governments had only limited awareness of the purpose or benefits of Kyoto Protocol ratification and CDM (see Synergy, 2003). As a consequence, only wealthier, middle-income countries can afford to implement the bureaucratic and institutional changes necessary for compliance with the Marrakesh Accords.

LEFT BEHIND? – CDM IN AFRICA AND THE INTERNATIONAL POLITICAL ECONOMY

Even if African governments are aware of the potential benefits, and strive to develop DNA capacity, how much should they expect to gain in terms of CDM investment and revenue from the sale of Certified Emissions Reductions (CERs)? Accurate predictions of revenue flows from CDM are very difficult to make since the details of most projects are commercially sensitive. The only alternative is to look at the economic demand factors behind CDM and how they relate to sub-Saharan African.

International competition for energy investments

Those developing countries with the highest demand for new sources of energy are most likely to attract new power projects and thus new opportunities for CDM activities. According to the International Energy Agency, the fastest growth in energy demand is expected to be in Asia and Latin America, comprising just under half of global energy usage by 2030, up from roughly 30% today (China alone will account for around 20% of global energy usage).[5]

Feeding the demand for energy in these regions is economic growth, with manufacturers and heavy industry driving the process, again opening up new opportunities for CDM activity. Theoretically, worldwide demand for CERs for the first commitment period (2008–12) could be met by large-scale energy and end-of-pipe industrial projects in Latin America and Asia alone. In Africa, energy demand is set to double over the next 25 years but will still comprise only 10% of total world energy supply by 2030. This means that if trends in economic growth and power consumption continue it is highly unlikely that Sub-Saharan Africa will become a key source of CERs from CDM projects within the first commitment period. To counter this, government energy policies of the kind currently being implemented in South Africa can play a part in stimulating commercial investment in new, sustainable power sources (and hence the possibility for CDM projects). And in the long term, post 2012, there is the distinct possibility that rising GHG emissions and energy consumption in middle income countries will mean that many of them will be allocated GHG emissions targets of their own. This would play straight into the hands of poorer Kyoto signatories, so long as the CDM continues.[7]

Poor investment climate

Sub-Saharan Africa receives only 2% of global FDI, and, as expected this is largely reflected in flows of CDM project finance (UNCTAD, 2004 and Niederberger *et al*, 2005). Again, with the exception of South Africa, much of sub-Saharan Africa suffers from a poor investment climate. Economic and political instability (due to unstable local currencies, strength of democratic institutions, un-predictable taxation and corruption) are a constant bane for governments and investors. High perceptions of risk can also increase the cost of loans, meaning that finance for CDM projects in Africa is often prohibitively expensive, when compared to equivalent investments in Asia or Latin America.

Liquidity and maturity of the international carbon market

Due to the aforementioned risks, it is crucial that CDM investors and carbon brokers can rely on the international carbon market to remain relatively stable and to have a ready supply of buyers for CERs derived from CDM projects. The case of TransAlloys shows how important this factor is. Sadly however, the price of carbon on the largest carbon exchange, the EU ETS has fluctuated wildly since its inception in January, 2005. From a starting price of around €8 in January, Emission Reduction Units (ERUs – the standard tradable unit of carbon in Europe) jumped to €15 in the space of a few days in March. It has since fluctuated between €13 and €19 but the

---

PANEL 3 CASE STUDY: TRANSALLOYS

TransAlloys is a silico-manganese smelter in South Africa. The intention is to retrofit the existing plant with more energy-efficient furnaces. An agreement has been reached with the environmental finance company, EcoSecurities, to pay for their share of development costs, which include the development of a new methodology, by the pre-assignment of a share of the CERs. In this case, the expectation of a healthy future market for CERs was critical to EcoSecurities' decision to carry the expenses involved with bringing the carbon-saving aspect of the project to account. A new methodology was submitted to the executive board in January and the project is expected to generate carbon savings of 98 ktCO$_2$e/yr.

---

lack of liquidity (measured in the number and speed of transactions completed daily) means that making any kind of price related predictions is virtually impossible.

A further danger lies in the fact that there are a large number of ERUs ready to flood the market from countries in central and Eastern Europe. This situation is already effecting the CDM market as buyers of ERUs play the waiting game, hoping that the price of ERUs drops significantly as opposed to investing in CDM projects. If the long-awaited flood does finally wash over the ERU market and prices plunge accordingly, African CDM projects, which already face significant risks and higher transaction costs could become unprofitable (World Bank, 2005).

CONSEQUENCES

At an international policy level, Africa's difficulties in attracting CDM projects call into question the CDM's very purpose as an innovative mechanism for the (clean) development of poorer Kyoto signatories. For most African countries, Kyoto is barely worth the paper it is written on. The material consequence of missing out on this potentially major source of development finance is to impede the ability of sub-Saharan Africa to wean itself off unsustainable sources of energy and ultimately to jeopardise the attainment of the UN Millennium Development Goals (see IIED, 2004).

At an industrial level, losing out on CDM will slow the transfer of environmental technology to African fossil fuel power stations, chemical plants and GHG generating factories, with the consequence of continued risks to human health through poor air quality. At a local community level, the global effort to combat ongoing dependence on unsustainable sources of fuel such as charcoal and wood from old-growth forests will be hampered by the fact that CDM could help fund local renewable energy projects such as solar or wind power generation. CDM credits from carbon sequestration could also serve directly to reduce deforestation and/or encourage sustainable forestry.

THE INTERNATIONAL RESPONSE

How have governments, donors and multilateral organisations responded to the dearth of CDM in Africa? We have already seen how the emissions trading system could survive quite healthily without projects from Africa. Yet we have also seen that Africa is the continent that needs this kind of investment most. The international community has responded with a range of initiatives to kick-start investment in CDM in Africa. Some of these aim at easing the bureaucratic burden, others at increasing the value of African CERs and others still at providing ready sources of finance and expertise for CDM project development. Some of the most important initiatives are discussed briefly below.

Simplified modalities and procedures for small-scale CDM projects

Seeing that most of SSA (except South Africa, which derives most of its energy needs from coal) can boast only limited industrial development and, correspondingly, very low GHG baselines, the potential for large-scale energy and "end-of-pipe" CDM projects is low. Recognising this, the World Bank's Community Development Carbon Fund (CDCF) lobbied the UNFCCC for a new set of modalities and procedures for small-scale community-level projects. Now all projects that are:

❑ renewable-energy projects with a maximum output capacity up to 15 MW;
❑ energy-improvement projects that reduce energy consumption by up to 15 GWh per year; and

❏ other projects that reduce GHG emissions and directly emit less than 15 kt of CO_2 annually.

can be classified as "small-scale" and escape much of the burdensome CDM application process.

The simplified procedures also permit the "pooling" or "bundling" of projects up to the threshold set out above. A portfolio of small projects may thus be submitted for approval and registration, reducing transaction costs even further and enabling very small-scale but locally beneficial CDM projects to qualify for CERs.

Small-scale project funds

In an effort to pilot the introduction of bundled small-scale projects, the CDCF was established alongside the larger, more commercially oriented Prototype Carbon Fund as part of a drive by the World Bank to be a trail blazer in the in the nascent Kyoto project market. Both the CDCF and PCF are piloting small-scale projects in Africa although none are yet ready for submission to the Executive Board. The CDCFs mandate is well suited to the goals of poverty alleviation in Africa since it takes a multi-stakeholder approach by "providing finance linking project developers seeking carbon finance with governments, NGOs and companies seeking to improve the livelihoods of local communities and obtain verified emissions reductions".[8]

Gold standard

A number of governments and NGOs led by the World Wide Fund for Nature (formerly the World Wildlife Fund) have been collaborating to create a "premium market" for CERs from CDM and Joint Implementation (JI) projects. They have designed a form of analytical framework, which aims to simplify some the approval process relating to consultation, additionality and sustainability. Called the "Gold Standard", it can only be affixed to all those projects that have satisfied the stringent environmental, social and economic sustainability criteria in the "Gold Standard Design Document". Africa has great potential for these projects, yet it remains to be seen whether buyers of CERs on international carbon markets will place a price premium on Gold Standard CDM.

Capacity building for CDM

A number of bilateral and multilateral development agencies, including United Nations Environment Programme and the European Commission, have implemented capacity-building programmes for CDM within Africa. Some NGOs such as *South*South*North* have undertaken major CDM information dissemination exercises targeted towards project developers and potential investors wishing to better understand the procedures and modalities for CDM approval (see Panel 4).

CONCLUSION – BRINGING BUSINESS ON BOARD

This chapter has argued that Africa has been both left out and, to a large extent, left behind by the CDM. International development donors and NGOs have recognised the challenges posed by the CDM for Africa. Clearly, there is a need for government to set out CDM expectations in the context of national delivery of set sustainable development goals, including setting sustainable-energy strategies – including the development of policies that are "loud, long and legal".[9]

However there is one constituency that could and, arguably, should work harder to provide research and support for African CDM. This constituency is the private sector, in particular carbon funds, CDM brokers and responsible international businesses with GHG targets (voluntary or compulsory). The business case for

---

PANEL 4 NEPAD BUSINESS GROUP AND AFRICAPRACTICE TO PRODUCE "GUIDE TO CDM IN AFRICA"

In order to stimulate a greater number of CDM projects in Africa, the International Finance Corporation (IFC) have teamed up with the consulting firm africapractice to produce a comprehensive investors guide for businesses, carbon funds and project developers. The guide will map out the contours of the carbon market in Africa, highlighting new opportunities for CDM projects and showing how donors and the private-sector organisation are working to remove some of the obstacles to an expanded CDM market. The guide will be available in September 2005 and is set to generate significant publicity at the NEPAD pre-G8 Summit and the UNEP Finance Initiative's Roundtable in New York.

CDM in Africa is simple: it can be both profitable and fulfil stringent sustainable business reporting guidelines.

By scouting out and investing in new CDM projects, be it from landfill to energy in South Africa, sustainable foresty projects in Uganda or reduction of gas flare reduction in Nigeria, these international companies can give a clear demonstration of business acumen in terms of meeting their obligations under emissions trading schemes. By investing in CDM projects, international companies, especially these already working in Africa, can actually use CDM to diversify their revenue streams whilst simultaneously demonstrating their corporate environmental responsibility. For the executive industries, the case of Anglo American shows how businesses can easily combine these two important tasks.

Another potential area for the expansion of CDM is its use as a component of local economic development projects and/or other social development programmes that aim to offset the negative impacts of a large-scale commercial ventures (such as a new mine or oil/gas project). This type of project work, which might qualify for the streamlined small-scale project application procedure, would enable companies to gain carbon credits at the same time as meeting the requirements of their Social and Environmental Impact Assessments.

Wherever there is a significant commercial gain to be had from CDM, companies could use their financial muscle to lobby African governments and development organisations to help foster institutional capacity and/or encourage them to ratify Kyoto. In turn the international community needs to do more to make the CDM more private sector friendly. Simplifying the application process and giving some early indication as to what to expect post 2012 are the most important steps that need to be taken here. Further simplification of the CDM process and guidance on regulations beyond 2012 is also required (see UNEPFI, 2005).

Until this happens and until the CDM market grows and matures accordingly it is important to bear in mind wider opportunities for climate-change mitigation projects outside of the CDM. Voluntary schemes[10] can help companies offset carbon emissions through forestry projects (carbon sequestration)[11] and local community work, which contains a carbon-offset element. Renewable energy, energy efficiency and climate change *adaptation* projects (building of sea defences, irrigation schemes and insurance) could also contribute significantly to sustainable economic growth and the prevention of climate change.

1   For a full list of UNFCCC approved CDM methodologies pertaining to African projects see: http://cdm.unfccc.int/methodologies/PAmethodologies/approved.html.
2   See http://cdm.unfccc.int/DNA, April 2005.
3   CDM Watch, Bujugali.
4   See http://unfccc.int/essential_background/kyoto_protocol/status_of_ratification/items/2613.phpfor up to date list of countries acceded, approved, accepted or ratified the Kyoto Protocol.
5   The continuation of emissions trading system post 2012 is a matter for climate change nego-tiators to decide at the forthcoming COPs. To date there has been no indication that the CDM will be scrapped although it will probably be radically re-designed.
6   IEA Key World Energy Statistics (2004), p 51.
7   In Madagascar for example, 85% of forest cover has been removed due to pressure from human population growth (see Jolly and Fukuda-Parr, 2000).
8   See http://carbonfinance.org/cdcf/home.cfm
9   See chapter 3 in this book by Kirsty Hamilton.
10 Such as Climate Care UK (http://www.climatecare.org) and Plan Vivo (http://www.plan-vivo.org).
11 Whilst the United State Federal Government remains outside the Kyoto Protocol, voluntary cli-mate change mitigation projects in Africa could become a major source of development finance in the near future as responsible US companies strive to be reduce their carbon footprint.

REFERENCES

Synergy, 2003, "CDM for Sustainable Africa – Capacity Building for Clean Development Mechanism in Sub-Saharan African Countries Final Report", URL: http://www.rgesd-sustcomm.org/CDM_AFRICA/PDF/1st_Report-CDM_Africa-D1.pdf

Chandler, S., et al., 2002, "Climate change mitigation in developing countries", Pew Centre on Global Climate Change.

IIED, 2004, Up in Smoke: Threats from and Responses to the Impacts of Global Warming on Human Development (IIED: London).

Jolly, R. and S. Fukuda-Parr, 2000, Human Development Report 2000, United Nations Development Programme (New York: Oxford University Press).

Niederberger, A. and R. Saner, 2005, "Exploring the relationship between FDI flows and CDM potential", Transnational Corporations, 14(1).

UNCTAD, 2004, "Trade and development report".

UNEPFI, 2005, "Finance for carbon solutions", CEO Briefing, UNEP, France.

World Bank, 2005, State and Trends in the Carbon Market (World Bank: Washington, DC).

29

The Spectre of Liability: Part 1 – Attribution

Myles Allen*

Oxford University

"Climate change is an issue of justice as much as of economic development."

UK Chancellor Gordon Brown
G8 meeting of environment and
development ministers, 15 March 2005

"You get justice in the next world: in this world you have the law."

William Gaddis, *A Frolic of His Own*

What might happen if it all goes horribly wrong? Not with the climate itself, but with intergovernmental efforts to reduce green-house-gas emissions. Given the parlous state of post-Kyoto negoti-ations, one might expect this question to come up rather often, but it features surprisingly little. Supporters of the Kyoto process object to such doom-mongering as potentially self-fulfilling, undermining emerging markets in greenhouse-gas emission permits. Many opponents of Kyoto tend to package their views with a sanguine conviction that climate change will turn out not to be nearly as bad as current projections suggest (see Lomborg, 2001), so that heroic efforts to reduce emissions will either turn out to be a waste of money or (their favoured option) simply will not happen.

*This work was supported by the UK Department of Environment, Food and Rural Affairs and the US NOAA/DoE Ad Hoc International Detection and Attribution Group, but all views expressed herein are the responsibility of the author. I am grateful to Christoph Schär of ETH Zurich and Gerd Jendritzky of the German Weather Service for permission to reproduce Figure 1, and to Peter Stott and Dáithí Stone with help with Figure A in Panel 1.

I will focus instead on the fourth quadrant of this two-by-two contingency table. What if climate change progresses along the lines of the current best-estimate forecasts and yet political negotiations on emission reductions continue to stall? Much as we would like to believe that policy is informed by science, it would be naïve to suggest this gloomy scenario is inconceivable. Factors entirely beyond our control, such as another successful terrorist attack, or a couple of large volcanoes causing a temporary downturn in global temperatures, might move the climate issue off the political agenda for a decade. What would happen if the politicians wash their hands of this issue altogether?

The answer, of course, is that we don't know. I will argue, however, that the largest short-term downside risk of a complete and terminal breakdown of intergovernmental negotiations on greenhouse-gas emission reductions may not be to the environment at all, but to the energy industry and thence to the global economy. Ironically, those who lobbied hardest against US and Russian ratification of the Kyoto protocol may be those who would lose most and first were the process of negotiated emission reductions to break down entirely. The reason is impact liability.

THE DISTRACTION OF "DANGEROUS CLIMATE CHANGE"

Article 2 of the United Nations Framework Convention on Climate Change (UNFCCC) commits the parties to (or at least aspire to) "stabilise atmospheric concentrations of greenhouse gases at levels that avoid dangerous anthropogenic interference in the climate system". The ongoing debate over what constitutes "dangerous climate change" is almost entirely focused on dramatic, large-scale events such as massive ecosystem loss, disruption to the thermohaline circulation or collapse of ice sheets that are not expected to occur until at least 50 to 100 years' time. Given the inertia of the climate system, anything expected on timescales much shorter than 50 years was almost certainly already unavoidable in 1992, and hence cannot, by definition, be what the framers of the UNFCCC meant by the "dangerous climate change" that they were trying to avoid (see Oppenheimer and Petsonk, 2003).

Admirable though the long-term perspective of the UNFCCC might be, it does tend to distract attention from the very substantial costs of climate change that are likely to emerge in the next couple of decades, which will almost certainly be dominated by much more prosaic issues such as the changing risk of adverse weather events. Most integrated-assessment (IA) studies (coupling climate-change models with impact models and economic models) suggest that the net effect of climate change on output (gross world product, or some other aggregate measure of global welfare) on these time-scales will be small, and possibly even positive (see Pearce, 2003; Tol and Downing, 2000). There are, however, significant disparities in costs, with certain sectors and regions beginning to lose out much sooner than others. Moreover, IA studies do not explicitly consider the impact of climate change on asset prices, except in so far as prices are assumed to reflect future output efficiently, while their treatment of non-monetary losses such as pain, suffering and disruption remains highly controversial. It is possible that such non-monetary losses and asset devaluations may dominate the cost of climate change over the next couple of decades, and represent the most "dangerous" aspect of the problem for present-day emitters.

The reason for this is our increased understanding of what is happening. Advances in climate modelling will eventually make it possible to factor changing weather risks into asset prices. Indeed, for properties affected by coastal erosion, for example, this may already be happening, as purchasers recognise that increased erosion rates in some regions may not be a cyclical phenomenon but part of an accelerating secular trend. This is not to suggest that all the necessary science has been done. The risks that have most potential impact on asset prices and intangible losses are those due to extreme weather, which is notoriously difficult to monitor and model. If a building or irrigation system has been designed to withstand a 100-year storm or drought, the increasing risk of what used to be a 200-year event will affect its value, not the changing risk of a 20-year event.

Two factors affect the risk of extreme weather: changes in the shape of the distribution of weather variability (how much the weather varies from year to year around the mean background climate), and changes in the mean climate itself. In general, current climate models do not predict substantial changes in weather variability in the next few decades, though this remains an area of considerable debate.

In contrast, a relatively small change in the mean climate of a particular weather variable, in the absence of some compensating change in the shape of the distribution, has a very substantial impact on the probability of extreme events. For example, the small (0.5°C) increase in mean European summer temperatures that is attributable to human influence has had relatively little impact on the probability of a warmer-than-normal summer. This background warming has, however, substantially increased the risk of a heat wave comparable in magnitude to that which occurred in 2003 (see Panel 1). The reason is very simple: consider the analogy of a loaded die. If you load a die to double the odds of a six, you quadruple the odds on a "double-six", octuple the odds on a "treble-six" and so on. The more unlikely the event, the more impact the loading has on the odds.

The high consensus on short-term changes in mean climate means the coming decade will almost certainly see a substantial reassessment of extreme weather risk. Residential, commercial and agricultural properties that have been designed and priced on the basis of historical weather risk will need to be revalued because weather risks are changing on timescales shorter than the lifespan of many of these assets. Many property owners will lose out. Others, of course, will gain, but, if we assume that historical weather risk information has been used efficiently in asset pricing to date, the losers will outnumber the winners.

In many cases the loss will be subtle and intangible, but often the loss will be all too tangible, as changing flood risk renders residential properties unsaleable, or changing drought risk makes agricultural land uneconomic. This could turn out to be the largest peacetime case of manmade wealth destruction the world has ever seen. Crucially, since asset prices respond to perceived risks, not actual losses, it may take only a handful of iconic events, such as the 2003 European summer heat wave, to trigger a rapid global asset price adjustment.

Substantial financial losses are therefore likely to occur over the next decade or two that are ultimately attributable to climate change. Moreover, as the process is only just beginning, these are the decades in which people will be most at risk personally from climate change because we have not yet learned the art of continuous adaptation that will be necessary in a climate undergoing a substantial secular trend. The 2003 European heat wave, for example, cost more than 20,000 lives, in large part because both individuals and health systems simply did not know how to cope with an event that was almost certainly unprecedented in 800 years. Even more intense heat waves are expected in the future, but it is to be hoped that Europe will learn that the historical record is no longer a reliable guide to weather risk, and adapt accordingly. The lessons will be learned soon, and they will be painful.

What is uncertain is whether those who suffer these losses will realise how much manmade climate change has contributed to their loss (there will always be confounding factors) and seek to obtain any form of redress from those responsible. Of particular interest to present-day vendors and users of greenhouse gas precursors (principally fossil fuels) is whether any of these costs and losses might eventually, through civil litigation or otherwise, be passed on to them. A number of cases are already under way,[1] but so far these are primarily focused on establishing principles or on injunctive relief, where the remedy being sought is either a simple acknowledgement of responsibility or some action to reduce emissions. So far, no one has grasped the nettle of actually suing for compensation for damage caused by climate change or the costs of adaptation. Are they ever likely to do so, and would they have any chance of succeeding? Many social, legal and political questions bear on the outcome: this chapter will focus on the scientific issues.

ATTRIBUTION OF WEATHER EVENTS TO CLIMATE CHANGE

Since many readers will find the idea of anyone's being held liable for adverse weather events highly implausible, I will outline in some detail the science behind quantitative causal attribution of specific weather events to externally driven climate change. I will focus on the meteorological problem of relating atmospheric greenhouse-gas concentrations to changes in weather-related risk. The problem of establishing how specific emissions contribute to changing atmospheric composition is also challenging, but in some respects conceptually more straightforward, particularly for well-mixed greenhouse gases such as carbon dioxide. I will use the European heat wave of the summer of 2003 as a motivating example, but the focus will be on the attribution methodology rather than details of this particular event.

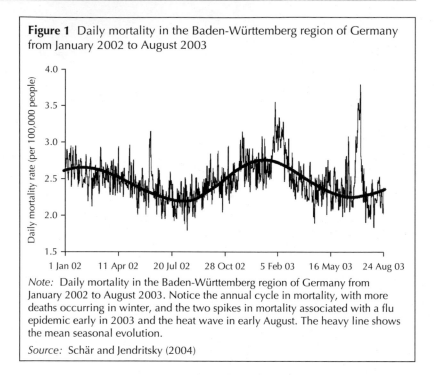

Figure 1 Daily mortality in the Baden-Württemberg region of Germany from January 2002 to August 2003

Note: Daily mortality in the Baden-Württemberg region of Germany from January 2002 to August 2003. Notice the annual cycle in mortality, with more deaths occurring in winter, and the two spikes in mortality associated with a flu epidemic early in 2003 and the heat wave in early August. The heavy line shows the mean seasonal evolution.

Source: Schär and Jendritsky (2004)

The summer of 2003 brought sustained, exceptionally high temperatures to large areas of Europe, with some regions of France experiencing average temperatures over 10°C higher than the average for 2000, 2001, 2002 and 2004 over the first 20 days of August (see Schär and Jendritsky, 2004). This heat wave, and the accompanying drought, is estimated to have caused more than US$10 billion in agricultural losses continent-wide, almost entirely uninsured, and more than US$1.6 billion in losses from forest fires, primarily in Portugal. Even more seriously, the heat wave has been blamed for between 22,000 and 35,000 excess deaths across the continent.

The spike in mortality in early August is clearly visible in Figure 1, against the background annual cycle of mortality in the Baden-Württemberg region of Germany, which is relatively far from the geographic centre of the heat wave. At its peak, the heat-related mortality exceeded that due to a substantial influenza epidemic occurring earlier in the year. To some extent such mortality spikes represent a "harvesting" effect on particularly vulnerable elderly

THE SPECTRE OF LIABILITY: PART 1 – ATTRIBUTION

groups, with subsequent reductions in mortality. Ongoing studies indicate, however, that the heat wave was associated with a significant loss of life years.

This event was almost certainly unprecedented at any time in the past 500–800 years (see Luterbacher *et al*, 2004; Schär *et al*, 2004), leading to considerable interest in the question of whether it might be related to climate change caused by anthropogenic greenhouse gas emissions (see Meehl and Tebaldi, 2004; Stott, Stone and Allen, 2004). If such damage had been associated with some other form of manmade pollution, such as a toxic chemical release, then the civil courts would undoubtedly become involved in efforts to secure compensation for victims and their relatives. This raises the question of whether civil liability might be a way of redistributing the costs of the most acute impacts of climate change, and potentially a mechanism for internalising climate-related risks into current cost-benefit calculations regarding the use of fossil fuels (see Allen, 2003; Grossman, 2003; Allen and Lord, 2004).

The immediate meteorological trigger of the heat wave was a persistent anticyclone over northwest Europe (see Black *et al*, 2004) or possibly two anticyclones, one related to conditions over the Indian Ocean in June and a second to more local drivers in August. There is at present no evidence that increasing greenhouse gases has made such weather patterns more prevalent. The question that needs to be asked, therefore, is whether human influence on *climate* may have increased the risk of such a naturally occurring *weather* pattern causing, instead of a pleasant warm summer, an unprecedented and devastating heat wave.

"CLIMATE IS WHAT YOU EXPECT, WEATHER IS WHAT YOU GET"

The World Meteorological Organisation (WMO) defines climate as the "average weather" and its variability experienced over an extended period of time, generally of the order of 30 years. For a rigorous treatment of causation, however, we need to be more precise: the WMO definition appears to rule out by definition a sudden climate change taking place on a timescale significantly less than 30 years, making it hard to discuss the short-lived influence of a volcano, for example.

The "weather" experienced on a particular day or in a particular year is the actual temperature, rainfall and so forth that is observed over that day or year. The "climate" is the "expected" weather, and variability therein, that we would predict for that day or year given perfect knowledge of the properties of the atmosphere–ocean system and external drivers such as levels of greenhouse gases and solar and volcanic activity, but without knowing what the weather is doing at any particular time. Crucially, climate does not depend on the actual state or rate of change of the system, only on the properties of the underlying system and its external drivers such as levels of greenhouse gases or solar and volcanic activity affecting it (see Palmer, 1999).

Non-specialists may find the analogy of a tangled ball of string helpful. Imagine plotting the observed daily-average temperature, rainfall and cloud cover for a particular location as points in a three-dimensional space. If we connect successive days, a line emerges, wrapping around itself in a tangled mess. If we observe long enough, however, we realise that the overall properties of the tangle are quite predictable, even if the actual temperature, rainfall and cloud cover on a given day are not. For example, in summer, high temperatures are expected to occur more often when cloud cover is low, so the tangle is not a simple ball, but elongated in specific directions: this is the "climate attractor". Edward Lorenz, the father of modern chaos theory, summed up the distinction: "Climate is what you expect, weather is what you get" (see Lorenz, 1993).

Defined in this way, the climate response to external drivers is perfectly predictable, since it emerges from the properties of the atmosphere–ocean system, not the particular chaotic trajectory we happen to observe. This is a significant advantage over the WMO definition. Although 30-year-average global mean temperature is relatively predictable given sufficient knowledge of external drivers and the climate system's response, the total number of floods occurring in Boscastle (a village in southern England that experienced a devastating flood in 2004) over a 30-year period is not. Although we are accustomed to thinking of global mean temperature as a measure of climate, the actual value recorded is simply an aggregate of weather observations, just like the number of floods in Boscastle, and hence depends on the chaotic evolution of the weather. The observations provide an indication of the values of relevant climate variables, but they are not identical to them. In these two examples, the climate variables are the expected global temperature and expected number of Boscastle floods. That is, the average temperature or number of floods we would obtain if we were able to "re-run" the whole earth–atmosphere system an infinite number of times, allowing it to explore its full range of chaotic variability.

The risk of a flood or heat wave occurring in any given year in that hypothetical infinite ensemble of possible worlds is a perfectly predictable function of the properties of the system, levels of greenhouse gases and so forth (see Stott *et al*, 2000). Whether or not a flood or heat wave actually occurs in 2003 is an unpredictable function of the weather. Crucially for the issue of liability, a single tonne of carbon dioxide emitted in 1990 has a perfectly predictable (albeit small) impact on the climate (expected weather, or heat wave risk) of 2003, even though its impact on the actual weather of 2003 is, thanks to the chaotic nature of the system, completely unpredictable.

The distinction between weather and climate is important because it is often argued that it is impossible in principle, because of the chaotic nature of the weather, to associate a particular weather event with externally driven climate change. At its crudest, this argument often degenerates into the line "if a similar event happened in preindustrial times, the current one cannot be blamed on global warming" (see Soon *et al*, 2003). This line of argument betrays a basic misunderstanding of the distinction between weather and climate. The mere fact that an event could occur naturally does not exclude the possibility that human activities can significantly increase the risk.

"CLIMATE IS WHAT YOU AFFECT, WEATHER IS WHAT GETS YOU"

It is also unreasonable to argue, as some commentators appear to have done, that the victims of the 2003 heat wave "should have seen it coming: after all, it happened 900 years ago" (although there is no positive evidence that it did happen 900 years ago). In an efficient and well-informed society, both socioeconomic practices and capital infrastructure will be adapted to the range of climate variability experienced over a typical lifetime. Hence it tends to be "extreme" weather events ("unprecedented in living memory") that are responsible for the bulk of weather-related damage. In the case of the European heat wave, for example, absolute temperatures were higher in southern France than in the Paris region, but social practices and architecture were better adapted in the south to extreme heat, so the death toll was significantly lower. To update Lorenz's quotation for the 21st century, *climate is what you affect, weather is what gets you.*

In general, the smaller the spatial scale and shorter the timescale considered, the more important the distinction between weather and climate. An example of the kind of impact that might be responding to changes on much longer timescales and larger spatial scales would be the decline of snow water availability in the northwestern US (see Mote, 2003). But even here the distinction between weather and climate must be understood: meltwater availability varies naturally, and actual losses would typically result from some tolerance threshold being breached in a particular year. Hence the only well-posed question remains to what extent human influence on climate may have contributed to the risk of that threshold being breached: the actual amount of snow water we get in any particular year also depends on the weather.

A change in climate can itself result directly in financial losses when the losses in question result directly from changes in weather-related risk, rather than from events that actually occur. If a risk increases (of coastal erosion, say) and properties lose value as a result, that loss can be directly attributed to the change in risk, or the climate change itself, rather than to a particular weather event that may have been made more likely by that climate change. This assumes, however, a perfectly well-informed and rational market response to changing risk. In practice, asset prices are strongly affected by recent events, and hence still dependent on the chaotic vagaries of the weather.

In summary, climate change does not itself cause damage directly, since "climate" is, properly understood, the unobservable weather attractor. It is *weather* events that do damage, but these can be made more or less likely by climate change.

PANEL 1 THE EXAMPLE OF THE 2003 EUROPEAN HEAT-WAVE

Stott, Stone and Allen (2004) (hereafter SSA) examined the role of human influence in the 2003 European summer heat-wave, the first concrete application of "probabilistic attribution" to an actual weather event. In principle, this involves comparing the frequency of occurrence of such a heat-wave in two large "ensembles of possible worlds," including and excluding human influence. First, this requires a definition of the event in question, which must not be tailored too closely to what actually occurred to avoid what is known as the "prosecutor's fallacy". For this reason, SSA define a "2003-like" heat wave as temperature anomalies over the full Southern European region exceeding a threshold of 1.6°C above the average for 1961–90 (ie, warmer than the second warmest summer on record, in 2001), even though the actual temperature anomaly over this region in 2003 was 2.3°C.

The figure compares observed June–August temperatures averaged over the region of interest with temperatures simulated from a climate model driven with both human and natural external influences and with human influence removed. Notice how year-to-year

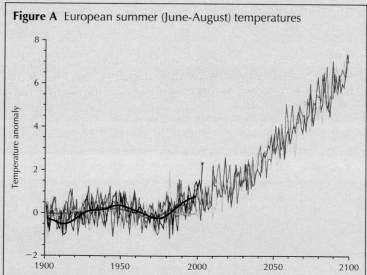

Figure A European summer (June-August) temperatures

Note: European summer (June-August) temperatures, observed (thin black line) and simulated by a model driven with the combination of human and natural external influences (grey lines). Heavy solid line shows smoothed observations, heavy dotted line shows smoothed simulations including all factors, and heavy dashed line with human influence removed. Adapted from Stott, Stone and Allen (2004).

variability is well captured by the model, including "spikes" like that of 2003, and does not seem to be changing substantially over time. This makes things much easier (the impact of any external driver on mean summer temperatures is much easier to establish than any possible impact on the shape of the distribution), but is probably only valid for simple quantities like large-scale temperatures, not local rainfall.

SSA assessed the magnitude of human influence on European summer climate by taking the output of their climate model and scaling the responses to human and natural external influences up and down until the scaled versions of the model were no longer consistent with observations of European summer temperatures over the 20th century.[i] They then assumed they could add year-to-year variability back onto the scaled simulations. This approach provides a method of synthesising an ensemble of possible models without explicitly running them. They concluded human influence had warmed background summer temperatures by around $0.5 \pm 0.2°C$, with relatively little warming due to natural influences.

Crucially, this approach assumes that, before any comparison is made with observations, all values of anthropogenic and/or natural warming are equally likely, so an equal chance of greenhouse-induced cooling as warming. Although such an outcome is highly unlikely on physical grounds, it is here ruled out by the record of observed summer temperatures, not by any model simulation.

Having synthesised distributions of summer temperatures with and without anthropogenic influence for a range of "possible models" of varying degrees of likelihood, SSA then compute the relative risk of summer temperatures exceeding a 1.6°C threshold. On this analysis, the most likely value for the fraction of risk attributable to past human influence on climate is around 0.9, or, equivalently, that the overall summer warming caused by past human influence on climate has increased the risk of summer temperatures exceeding the 1.6°C threshold by around a factor of ten. There is a high level of uncertainty in this estimate, but a fraction attributable risk of less than 0.5 can be ruled out as unlikely at the 10% level. Hence SSA conclude it is very likely that human influence on climate increased the risk of the 2003 heat wave by a factor of at least two, with the most likely increase in risk considerably greater than two.

[i]Stott, P. A., D. A. Stone and M. R. Allen, 2004, "Human contribution to the European heatwave of 2003", Nature, 432, 610–614.

1   See http://www.climatelaw.org/cases for more details.

REFERENCES

Allen, M. R., 2003, "Liability for climate change", *Nature*, **421**, pp. 891–2.

Allen, M. R. and R. Lord, 2004, "The blame game", *Nature*, **432**, pp. 551–2.

Black, E., *et al*, "Factors contributing to the summer 2003 European heatwave", *Weather*, **59**, pp. 217–23.

Grossman, D. A., 2003, "Warming up to a not-so-radical idea: Tort-based climate change litigation", *Colombia Journal of Environmental Law*, **28**, 1–61 (2003).

Lomborg, B., 2001, *The Skeptical Environmentalist* (Cambridge University Press).

Lorenz, E., 1993, *The Essence of Chaos* (University of Washington Press: Seattle).

Luterbacher, J., *et al*, 2004, "European seasonal and annual temperature variability, trends, and extremes since 1500", *Science*, **303**, pp. 1499–1503.

Meehl, G. and C. Tebaldi, 2004, "More intense, more frequent, and longer lasting heat waves in the 21st century", *Science*, **305**, pp. 994–7.

Mote, P. W., 2003, "Trends in snow water equivalent in the Pacific Northwest and their climatic causes", *Geophysial Research*, Letters, **30**, DOI 10.1029/2003GL0172588.

Oppenheimer, M. and A. Petsonk, 2003, "Global warming: the intersection of long-term goals and near-term policy", in D. Michel (ed), *Climate Policy for the 21st Century: Meeting the Long-Term Challenge of Global Warming* (Washington, DC: Center for Transatlantic Relations).

Palmer, T. N., 1999, "A nonlinear dynamical perspective on climate prediction", *Journal of Climate*, **12**, pp. 575–91.

Pearce, D., 2003, "The social cost of carbon and its policy implications", *Oxford Review of Economic Policy*, **19**, pp. 362–84.

Schär, C., *et al.*, 2004, "The role of increasing temperature variability in European summer heatwaves" *Nature*, **427**, pp. 332–6.

Schär, C. and G. Jendritsky, 2004, "Hot news from Summer 2003", *Naturei*, **432**, pp. 559–60.

Soon, W., *et al*, 2003, "Reconstructing climatic and environmental changes of the past 1000 years: a reappraisal", *Energy & Environment*, **14**, pp. 233–96.

Stott, P. A., *et al*, 2000, "External control of 20th century temperature by natural and anthropogenic forcings", *Science*, **290**, pp. 2133–7.

Stott, P. A., D. A. Stone, and M. R. Allen, 2004, "Human contribution to the European heatwave of 2003", *Nature*, **432**, pp. 610–14.

Tol, R. and T. Downing, 2000, "The marginal costs of climate changing emissions", Institute for Environmental Studies, Free University of Amsterdam.

30

The Spectre of Liability:
Part 2 – Implications

Myles Allen*

Oxford University

"Somehow, somewhere, someone's going to pay."
California Governor Arnold Schwarzenegger,
Commando

Following on from the previous chapter, which discussed the science behind causal attribution of specific weather events to externally driven climate change, this chapter poses the challenges for the legal community and possible implications for estimating the overall cost of climate change, or the "social cost of carbon".

THE CHALLENGE FOR THE LEGAL COMMUNITY

For the vast majority of damaging weather events, we will never be able to prove beyond reasonable doubt that "but for" human influence on climate, that event would not have occurred. Fortunately for those adversely affected, however, the law takes a more flexible and pragmatic view of the questions of cause and effect, accepting that a "material increase in risk" may be the appropriate test to apply in certain circumstances (Allen and Lord, 2004). If it could be shown that, comparing populations of possible worlds with and without human influence, the event in question occurred more than twice as often in the population that allows for human influence, a

*This work was supported by the UK Department of Environment, Food and Rural Affairs and the US NOAA/DoE Ad Hoc International Detection and Attribution Group, but all views expressed herein are the responsibility of the author. I am grateful to Peter Cox of the UK Met Office for the data used in Figure 1 and to Peter Roderick, Stephen Jewson, Rory Sullivan, Kenny Tang, Tamsine Green and the reviewers for significant improvements to this and the previous chapter.

court might conclude, on balance of probability, that a "but for human influence" test had been passed.

David Grossman, in an excellent article on the legal aspects of the climate-change issue (Grossman, 2003), makes a strong case that assessments of relative risk are likely to be admissible, through the precedent of epidemiological cases such as smoking and lung cancer. He summarises: "... plaintiffs who rely on epidemiological evidence must show that, more probably than not, their individual injuries were caused by the risk factor in question, as opposed to any other cause. This has sometimes been translated to a requirement of a relative risk of at least two."

Assessments of relative risk will always be subject to some uncertainty, but this uncertainty can be quantified. In the case of the 2003 European summer heat wave, Stott, Stone and Allen (2004) concluded we were over 90% confident that human influence had increased the risk by a factor of at least two, while, on the balance of probability, we would assess that human influence had increased the risk by six to ten. There is a clear parallel with so-called "toxic tort" cases, so the courts have experience of dealing with this kind of information. Exactly what numbers the courts will require before concluding that a "material increase in risk" had occurred remains to be seen, but there appear to be no insurmountable theoretical obstacles.

Grossman surveys a number of other issues relating to the feasibility of those adversely affected by climate change seeking compensation from those responsible through the civil courts. An obvious issue is the multiplicity of potential defendants: it could be argued that every resident of the planet bears some responsibility for the problem of global warming, and that no single entity has contributed more than a few per cent of historical emissions. Clearly, if the courts decide that liability for the environmental consequences of burning fossil fuels applies solely at the point of use, then the class of potential defendants becomes impossibly broad. On the other hand, under the right jurisdiction, a court might well conclude that joint and several liability applies all the way along the product chain, since the use of carbon-based fuels must, given present technologies, result in the release of greenhouse gases (GHGs). In this case, a very substantial fraction of historical GHG emissions can be attributed to products used or sold by only a few dozen easily identifiable major companies. Many of these are of course government-owned or -controlled, and often have operated as the implementation arm of national policy, so it would not be a simple matter to seek redress. Besides that, there are other large sources of GHGs – including agricultural methane and deforestation – for which responsibility is much more broadly distributed, but carbon dioxide is certainly the largest cause for concern.

A closely related issue is how responsibility might be apportioned over time. Because of its atmospheric lifetime, emissions of carbon dioxide continue to impact the climate for many decades. This clearly raises questions both about the feasibility of tracking down past emitters and the foreseeability of harm, particularly for emissions made before climate change was considered a serious issue. Current rates of carbon dioxide accumulation mean, however, that emissions made relatively recently contribute a substantial fraction of the anthropogenic perturbation. Figure 1 shows, based on a very simple carbon cycle model, how carbon dioxide levels are currently increasing under a conventional emissions scenario, and how they would have evolved had emissions stopped in 1990. Post-1990 emissions are "to blame" for the (shaded) difference between these two curves. By the 2020s, more than half the anthropogenic increase in carbon dioxide (relative to the pre-industrial level of 275 parts per million by volume (ppmv)) will be due to post-1990 emissions.

A very different picture to that presented by Figure 1 would be given by considering the temperature change attributable to these two carbon dioxide concentration paths. Since many impacts scale with temperature change, it could be argued this would be the most appropriate metric for apportioning responsibility over time, but it introduces the additional complication that the time-scale of temperature response (and hence the relative importance of recent versus historical emissions) is poorly constrained by data. At the nation-state level, the relative contribution of different emitters is reasonably insensitive to the choice of metric, consideration of non-linearities and so forth (Trudinger and Enting, 2005). At the individual company level this might be much more of an issue, since companies' relative emissions vary on much shorter time-scales than nation-states'.

Grossman also considers a number of other legal issues, such as the standing of potential claimants and defendants, and concludes that none are necessarily insurmountable. Perhaps the most pertinent

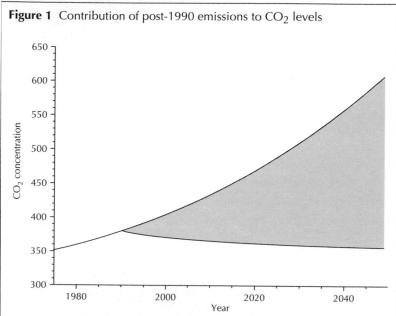

Figure 1 Contribution of post-1990 emissions to CO_2 levels

Note: Upper line shows the evolution of carbon dioxide levels in parts per million by volume (ppmv) to 2050 under a typical, relatively high-growth, baseline scenario, while the lower line shows how concentrations would have evolved had emissions ceased in 1990. The shaded region shows the contribution of post-1990 emissions to enhanced carbon dioxide levels, and any resulting changes in weather-related risk, over the coming decades. Given that preindustrial carbon dioxide levels are approximately 275 ppmv, by 2030, almost two-thirds of the excess carbon dioxide in the atmosphere will be due to post-1990 emissions under this scenario

Source: Peter Cox, UK Met Office

issue at present is pre-emption: the political and/or legal question of whether governments will (or legally can) move in, either to pre-empt all civil liability claims or to cap the total liability at some relatively arbitrary figure. The precedent of the nuclear industry, for example, suggests that any such cap would be relatively low, so any such pre-emption would effectively draw the sting from the issue of impact liability.

A further complication is that civil liability is not the only basis upon which a court can order payments to be made for damage. An alternative approach is under human rights legislation – for

PANEL 1 PRE-EMPTION?

There are signs of a trend in many jurisdictions towards pre-emption, although this is clearly not an issue politicians wish to discuss in public: for example, the European Commission's environmental liability Directive of 2004 explicitly advised that regulation was a more appropriate vehicle than civil tort law for internalising costs of transnational pollution to which large numbers of actors contribute, of which climate change is an obvious example. Note, however, that this provision for a "compliance with permit" exemption from liability in the 2004 directive is expressed as a discretion given to a member state – it is not mandatory, and member states have until 30 April 2007 to decide what degree of exemption to offer, if any. Any such decision would itself be open to challenge at both national and European levels.

More importantly, the fact that the European Commission's liability directive expressly mentions the possibility of exemption from liability, but the carbon trading directive does not, could suggest that the latter does not pre-empt civil liability. Moreover, the member states' legal systems are far from homogeneous on this issue – it is more difficult to establish that regulation pre-empts liability in common law countries such as the UK and Ireland than in "civil" law systems, meaning those essentially derived from Napoleon.

Given the very substantial implications of the decision on how to pay for the costs of adaptation to or compensation for the negative impacts of climate change, it is extraordinary how little political attention this issue receives. Whether a holder of an emission permit under the European carbon trading scheme is thereby exempted from civil liability for any negative consequences of that emission could have profound financial consequences, not only for Europe's companies, but for any citizen of a member state who happens to own a home in a flood plain. Yet this decision, even if it has not been taken already, is effectively being discussed behind closed doors, out of the public arena.

example, the Inuit are currently bringing a case against the US government under human rights law, and although they have said that they will not be seeking compensation in that case, compensation for breaches of human rights is common and well understood. Human rights compensation is usually ordered against governments, so such cases would represent less of a direct risk to private-sector GHG emitters.

Part of the responsibility for the lack of public debate about "who pays" may lie with the environmental movement itself. Emphasising that "climate change is an issue that affects us all" has obscured the fact that it is likely to affect some of us very considerably more than others. Where the issue of differential vulnerability is discussed, it tends to be entirely at the level of poor countries *versus* rich countries, rather than unlucky citizens *versus* lucky citizens. A major contributor to this failure of communication must be the level of aggregation that is typically used in estimates of the overall cost of climate change, or the "social cost of carbon", which we discuss next.

DETERMINING THE SOCIAL COST OF CARBON

Suppose that the science of attribution continues to firm up as it has done over the past decade. Suppose, further, that the climate continues to change as the overwhelming consensus of scientists, including critics of the Intergovernmental Panel on Climate Change, expect it to change over the coming decades. And suppose, finally, that intergovernmental negotiations over emission reductions run into the sand, such that the mitigation regime that emerges has no discernible impact on the problem and hence cannot be argued to pre-empt civil tort law. How large could the eventual bill become?

Estimates of the so-called social cost of carbon (SCC), or the net present value of the aggregated impacts of emissions based on integrated assessment models, vary enormously, ranging from under US$10 to over US$200 per tonne for the marginal cost of present-day emissions. This range reflects differences in valuation methods for the impacts of climate change and the rate at which these impacts are discounted over time (see Clarkson and Deyes, 2002).

Much of the sensitivity of the SCC to valuation methods arises because of the inherent difficulty of valuing damages that are expected to occur many decades into the future, in a socioeconomic context very different from today. Estimates of the cost of climate impacts in the distant future are inevitably highly contingent on baseline assumptions about economic and technological development, success in adaptation and consequent vulnerability. Even more fundamental problems arise if SCC calculations attempt to allow for the risk of irreversible climate discontinuities, such as the collapse of the West Antarctic Ice Sheet. The cost of such global catastrophic events, and how they are risk-weighted and discounted to the present day, can easily dominate any estimate of the SCC, but placing a monetary value on such developments is clearly problematic. Most early attempts to quantify the SCC neglected these discontinuities altogether, but attempting to quantify the overall "cost" of climate change while neglecting its most catastrophic potential impacts is also unsatisfactory. In general, the shorter the timescale considered, the less arbitrary the valuation because the easier it is to express future damages in terms of present-day costs, and the less likely are any such discontinuities. Major uncertainties remain even on relatively short timescales, particularly regarding the role of adaptation.

Uncertainty in long-term impact valuations feeds into the second key problem in determining an appropriate SCC: agreeing on a discount rate for future damages. Overall discount rates (including the long-term per capita growth rate) greater than ~4% have been reported, (Tol and Downing, 2000), to yield relatively low estimates of the net SCC (<US\$10 per tonne). The reason is that, in some impact-assessment models, the overall economic impact of climate change on 10–20-year timescales is positive, due primarily to the positive impact of CO_2 fertilisation on agricultural productivity, although the true magnitude of this fertilisation effect remains controversial. If a discount rate is used that effectively wipes out more than 90% of costs incurred more than 50 years into the future, the SCC is inevitably highly sensitive to the balance between these putative short-term gains and much larger longer-term losses.

A third imponderable in calculations of the SCC is the role of equity: should impacts on poor countries be given greater weight than impacts on rich countries because of differences in the marginal utility of the monetary units of value gained or lost? Including some form of "equity weighting" can change estimates of the SCC by a factor of three or more, and there is little consensus on how, or even whether, to do so (see Clarkson and Deyes, 2002).

Commentators on the SCC have recognised the link between the issue of equity weighting and the "polluter pays" principle. Indeed, Clarkson and Deyes (2002) explicitly state "equity weighting goes some way to incorporating the full impact of our emissions on others into our policy making, which is in line with the polluter pays principle." In stark contrast, David Pearce (2003) argues, controversially, against this principle on the grounds that global warming should not be considered "special" simply because the damage is the responsibility of the rich countries.

Pearce's arguments, like those of Lomborg (2001), make sense if we consider the climate-change problem to be one of global resource allocation, essentially to be determined by central planning. If more lives are saved by providing safe drinking water than reducing greenhouse-gas emissions, then the beneficent central planner should allocate resources accordingly. These arguments are not relevant to the issue of liability. Today's GHG emitters do not have a legal liability to provide clean drinking water to the world's poor, but they may, under the polluter-pays principle, be liable for the harm done by their emissions. Addressing the issue of liability requires a very different approach to determining the social cost of carbon, in which losses and gains are kept separate rather than being aggregated in a single overall net economic impact. Current tools for estimating the SCC are very likely not up to this task, so there is clearly considerable work to be done.

QUANTIFYING POTENTIAL LIABILITY

In contrast to these imponderable philosophical issues in quantifying the SCC from the perspective of the central planner, the question of quantifying potential liability looks attractively straightforward. First, discounting by present-day (and historical) real cost of capital means that any calculation of potential liability will automatically be dominated by risks over the next few decades (both directly, and through their impact on asset prices), so the thorny issue of costing collapsing ice sheets does not arise. Second, only negative impacts need be considered, which tend to be less controversial, since no one will sue for the right to repay unsolicited benefits of climate change. And third, the issue of equity arises only in purely practical terms, regarding the kinds of awards that courts in different jurisdictions are likely to make and their predilection for taking the circumstances of the plaintiffs into account in computing damages.

How large might the bill become? Discounting by the actual cost of capital would put it at the lower end of current estimates of the SCC, since higher estimates depend on the use of low or time-varying discount rates. This might, on the other hand, be outweighed by the fact that short-term benefits can be neglected in the liability calculation and that some plaintiffs might also sue for adaptation costs. Moreover, the impacts considered in typical

PANEL 2 CHALLENGES IN QUANTIFYING LIABILITY

The first challenge is entirely practical: the risks most likely to result in climate damage claims are precisely the infrequent, high-impact events that are most demanding for climate-change modelling. Modelling the impact of external drivers on the extreme tails of the distribution of weather variability is not impossible, but probably beyond the capabilities of most current models used for climate change projections. But this is a purely practical issue. We can already simulate many of these events in forecast-resolution models: it is simply a question of adequate computing and model-validation resources to extend this to the climate problem. The fact that many of these events may be difficult to predict in conventional weather forecasting does not rule out our being able to quantify the impact of external drivers on their overall risk of occurrence, at least at the level of precision in relative risk that is likely to be required by a court.

Second, having quantified changes in extreme weather risk, an assessment of liability would need to quantify the likely impact of these risks both directly, should the events in question occur, and indirectly, through the impact of changing risks on asset prices. Again, this is difficult, but not impossible, particularly given the extensive data available on the pricing of weather risk and the fact that the assessment would focus on the next few decades, over which differences between emissions scenarios have a relatively minor impact. Crucially, one could look to past precedent to assess what impacts should be included, such as whether to focus on physical damage, purely monetary losses or whether to include some assessment of "pain and suffering". Again, unlike the SCC calculation, this boils down to predicting what future settlements might be, not simply an expression of the investigators' ethical convictions about issues such as the importance of intergenerational or international equity.

Third, there is the crucial question of what awards for compensation might actually be made, which would presumably be only a fraction of total net losses if the courts decide only to entertain claims in which human influence contributed a substantial fraction of the risk in question, and how awards would be divided up between prospective defendants. Extensive information exists about past practice in nuisance and product-liability tort law, so again the basis for an estimate exists. Determining from what date courts might conclude a "foreseeable harm" test would be passed, and hence the date from which emitters begin to bear responsibility for the consequences of their emissions, is also clearly a problem.

So, while substantial challenges remain, these look considerably more tractable than agreeing the "correct" long-term discount rate to use in SCC calculations or the "correct" treatment of the issue of equity.

integrated assessment models used to estimate the SCC are dominated by estimated losses in output, and do not in general allow for all forms of extreme weather risk or consequent losses due to devaluation of assets. So a best-guess estimate in the low tens of dollars per tonne of carbon, with some risk of much higher liability, is not inconceivable.

What could present-day emitters do about it? Conventional liability insurance is ruled out, since the risk violates several of the basic principles of insurability, most obviously the fact that risks are not differentiated between prospective policyholders. If climate change turns out to be large, or the courts turn out to be enthusiastic implementers of the polluter-pays principle, all policyholders will lose out simultaneously. On the other hand, the spectre of a large and open-ended liability could have a serious impact on the ability of current energy companies to raise long-term capital, so there will clearly be a demand for some kind of securitisation of the risk or for government underwriting. If only governments had the nerve to refuse to underwrite, and to leave it to the securities market to price this risk, we would obtain, for the first time, a genuinely apolitical, market-driven social cost of carbon: it would be fascinating to see where that price would end up.

SHOULD ENVIRONMENTALISTS BE ROOTING FOR KYOTO?

Climate change is often cited as a paradigmatic example of market failure. The climatic impacts of GHG emissions occur decades to centuries after the emissions occur. These impacts are far from uniform, with different sectors, countries and natural systems having very different vulnerabilities, and there is, if anything, a negative correlation between responsibility for present-day emissions and vulnerability to climate impacts (see Hohne and Harnisch, 2002). So it is taken for granted that the only solution is either a mandatory cap-and-trade system, as favoured by the signatories of the Kyoto Protocol, or heavy government intervention in technology research and development in order eventually to steer energy markets away from fossil fuels, as favoured by many of the Protocol's critics, or some combination of the two. Everyone agrees that the only possible solution is for governments to determine the "optimal" emissions path towards stabilisation and to intervene in the operation of the free market to guide us towards it. Is there really no other way of dealing with this problem?

The following is speculation (or a "scenario", if you prefer): it is highly unlikely to happen, for obvious political reasons, but I am throwing it out as something to think about, no less implausible right now than the idea of a politically negotiated stabilisation of carbon dioxide levels below 450 ppmv.

Suppose governments representing a significant fraction of the world economy (some Group of Eight member states, for example) were to stand up and acknowledge that they could not agree on a definition of "dangerous climate change", never mind the appropriate course of action to avoid it that would be acceptable to the world's largest emitters. Instead, they were simply going to accept that the climate change is inevitable, with a significant likelihood of substantial losses. The response, no doubt, would be loud protests from environmentalists and quiet sighs of relief from the fossil-fuel lobby.

Suppose, however, these governments were to go on to say that, having admitted defeat, it was now incumbent on them to address the issue of who should pay the inevitable costs of adaptation to climate change. The notion that the victims should pay is unjust and ultimately untenable, while a taxpayer-financed bailout or government-administered compensation fund would almost certainly be highly inefficient (since any link between emissions and their externalities would remain up to the politicians). Instead, having established that the normal political cycle simply does not fit a problem like climate change, the politicians would undertake to retire from the scene. In particular, they would not pre-empt individuals, corporations or nation-states that can demonstrate, to the satisfaction of a civil court, that they have been adversely affected by climate change from seeking redress from those who have benefited from the extraction and burning of the fossil fuels responsible.

A handful of ground rules would be required, for example that liability for the consequences of burning fossil fuels should apply from the point of extraction unless an equivalent volume of carbon is verifiably sequestered. This would be necessary to provide a credible course of redress, since identifying contributors at the point of use is clearly infeasible. An overall formula for apportioning responsibility would also be required: for well-mixed greenhouse gases on timescales over which interactions between sources, sinks and the climate response are small (which is the case over the next few decades for carbon dioxide) this could simply be based on fractional contribution to the perturbation on the global energy budget at the time the damage occurs, which is approximately proportional to emissions discounted by the rate at which that greenhouse gas is taken up by natural sinks (see Figure 1). Fractional contribution to temperature change might reflect contributions to risk more accurately, at the expense of greater complexity.

A date would need to be agreed after which climate change was deemed "foreseeable": this could be 1990, or it could be the date of this "Stalingrad moment" when political negotiations to avoid dangerous climate change finally acknowledge failure. Liability for the consequences of emissions prior to that date could be limited to a taxpayer-financed compensation fund: although some victims would no doubt wish to seek additional compensation from historical emitters, whether they should succeed would be up to the courts. But (and this would be the hard part) liability for the consequences of emissions made after that date would rest with those who sold or burned the relevant fossil fuel. Having acknowledged they could not arrive at an effective regulatory regime that would avoid dangerous climate change, governments would need to make a credible commitment not to limit their own emitters' liability, no matter how ugly it gets, and to force their trading partners to do the same to avoid unfair competition.

Initially, claims against current emitters would be small, with the vast bulk of liability being attributable to historical emissions. But this would soon change: by the late 2020s, more than half the excess carbon dioxide in the atmosphere will be due to emissions made after 1990. The sums have not been done, but it is just possible that the prospect of an open-ended liability that would raise its head every time the weather turned nasty anywhere in the world for the next century would be sufficiently daunting for present-day fossil-fuel extraction and major power-generation companies that they would move as rapidly as possible to complete geological sequestration, passing the cost along to the consumer.

The result would be a substantial increase in energy prices, which would no doubt be traumatic for the world economy. But, unlike Kyoto itself or any currently plausible follow-up protocol, it would achieve stabilisation relatively rapidly. If stabilisation at 450 ppmv or below really is desirable, as many studies suggest it is, then the question that should be asked is not whether such a market-driven liability regime would be traumatic for the world economy, but whether it would be more or less traumatic than the kind of heavy-handed demand-management required to achieve a 450 ppmv target by the conventional approach.

There are obvious objections to a private-sector, litigation-based approach to internalising the social cost of carbon: transaction costs (legal fees and so on) are high; the process is slow and the outcome often arbitrary; well-heeled and well-organised litigants tend to do disproportionately well, so such a system would be far from progressive, and so forth. All of these objections could equally be made to the current approach based on internationally negotiated emission targets. My point here is not to advocate one approach over the other, but to discuss what might happen if the negotiated approach collapses or stalls altogether. Will those adversely affected by climate change stoically put up with their lot, or will they seek redress against those who benefit from the extraction and use of fossil fuels, arguably the most profitable large-scale activity mankind has ever come up with?

Obviously, for present-day producers and users of fossil fuels, the prospect of relatively modest emission reductions mandated by a cap-and-trade regime that is constrained by politics to be relatively painless is infinitely preferable to the chaotic prospect of litigation. While it would be difficult to argue that the Kyoto Protocol itself pre-empts liability, this may well become an issue in the negotiation of any follow-up treaty. No doubt the collectivist instincts of many in the environmental lobby will favour a regulatory approach over a free-for-all in the courts, so they might well be inclined to accept pre-emption in exchange for a few extra percentage points off the emission target. But they should think carefully before doing so: do not play this card too early, it could be the Joker.

REFERENCES

Allen, M. R. and R. Lord, 2004, "The blame game", *Nature*, **432**, pp. 551–2.

Clarkson, R. and K. Deyes, 2002, "Estimating the social cost of carbon emissions", GES working paper 140, London, HM Treasury.

Grossman, D. A., 2003, "Warming up to a not-so-radical idea: Tort-based climate change litigation", *Colombia J. Environ. Law*, **28**, 1–61 (2003).

Höhne, N. and F. Harnisch, 2002, "Calculating historical contributions to climate change – discussing the 'Brazilian Proposal' ", *Climatic Change*.

Hohne, N. and J. Harnisch, 2002, "Evaluating indicators for the relative responsibility for climate change – alternatives to the Brazilian Proposal and Global Warming Potentials", in *Non-CO2 Greenhouse Gases*, NCGG-3, (Milpress: Maastricht).

Lomborg, B., 2001, *The Skeptical Environmentalist* (Cambridge University Press).

Pearce, D., 2003, "The social cost of carbon and its policy implications", *Oxford Review of Economic Policy*, **19**, pp. 362–84.

Schär, C. and G. Jendritsky, 2004, "Hot news from Summer 2003", *Nature*, **432**, pp. 559–60.

Stott, P. A., D. A. Stone, and M. R. Allen, 2004, "Human contribution to the European heatwave of 2003", *Nature*, **432**, pp. 610–14.

Tol, R. and T. Downing, 2000, "The marginal costs of climate changing emissions", Institute for Environmental Studies, Free University of Amsterdam.

Trudinger, C. and I. Enting, 2005, "Comparison of formalisms for attributing responsibility for climate change: Non-linearities in the Brazilian Proposal approach", *Climatic Change*, vol. **68**, no. 1–2, pp. 67–99(33).

COMMENTARY

Richard Lord Q.C.

One of the best-known English legal maxims, in the days when Latin was still respectable, was *"ubi ius ibi remedium"* or "where there is a right, there is a remedy". Tort lawyers think along slightly different lines: where there is a wrong, there is a remedy. Whether GHG emission at historic, current or projected future levels is a "wrong" and if so whether it should attract a legal remedy is the subject of much debate.

Myles Allen's message in this chapter is simultaneously informative and provocative. On a scientific level he provides an analysis supporting the important conclusion that inherent variability of weather is no answer to causal links between GHG emissions and extreme weather events. On the contrary, there is strong evidence that GHG emissions have significantly increased the probability of occurrence (and thus the frequency) of such events. On a more general and controversial level, Allen throws down the gauntlet both to regulators and those who oppose regulation, with the spectre of litigation on a massive scale as a feasible long-term consequence of failure of regulation.

It is generally accepted that the law of tort is a "blunt tool" when used in the public domain, and the debate has already started as to whether it has any role in relation to climate change, which, say some (including actual and potential defendants!), should be the exclusive preserve of public international law and a regulatory approach. Nevertheless, the concept of compensation based on "fault" is not only underpinned by basic moral principles but also well entrenched in the Anglo-American legal systems. It provides a basic safety net for those whom society considers deserving of redress. Its protagonists point to its potential power to concentrate the corporate minds of the emitters, as well as the ponderous nature of the alternative by way of attempts at international regulation.

Allen focuses on the "fourth quadrant" situation where climate change-related damage, whether by way of property damage/devaluation or death/disease, has become significant, and (almost by definition) regulation has been either too little or too late. The latter situation is very possible given the time lag between emissions and their effect and the fact that regulation is currently driven by what is politically possible rather than rational assessment of what is necessary to avert predicted damage.

In conceptual terms the legal building blocks necessary to make a case for "impact liability" are already in place – the most basic one being the principle of X's liability, subject to certain conditions being fulfilled, to compensate Y for damage caused to Y or Y's property by X's actions. The issue is whether, and if so when, the facts will support the invocation of such a principle. In Allen's "fourth quadrant" scenario (and thus necessarily in the medium/long term) it is entirely feasible that GHG emitters will face credible claims for compensation on a large scale, and the increasingly sophisticated detection and attribution techniques that Allen and others have pioneered make this ever more realistic. Perhaps the surest indicator that this is the case is not the fact that writs have already started flying, but that "litigation risk" is one of the factors now influencing share price not only in traditionally vulnerable sectors such as the tobacco industry, but also in the energy sector. It is only the very brave or the very foolish emitters or investors who will discount this factor altogether.

COMMENTARY

Andrew Dlugolecki

The idea that governments *would* (or *should*, or even *could*) allow the legal system to set limits on greenhouse-gas emissions through the medium of liability is fanciful. Nevertheless, the threat of litigation, particularly in the USA where the tort system has developed in a plaintiff-friendly way, is a useful weapon in the environmentalists' armoury, because it is damaging to corporate image and expensive in management time.

Myles Allen considers three major questions in terms of practicability (that is, *could* governments do this?): *attribution*, *quantum*, and *allocation* of liability for damages.

On *attribution*, Allen argues that the technical difficulties may soon be overcome, and that it may be possible to quantify the manmade contribution to specific events, such as the European heat wave of 2003. Heat waves are the easiest phenomenon to address, because climate models are in reasonable consensus over temperature predictions, and also we can reconstruct historical temperatures in some regions with some accuracy for 500 to 1,000 years. Even then there may be difficulties. Meteorologically speaking, the 2003 summer was the product of two different circulatory patterns, one in June associated with the Indian Ocean, and one in August associated with the Atlantic. A seeker for truth would wish to know how unusual those were, and how unusual their combination – which we cannot do.[1] When it comes to precipitation or storminess, science is still far from consensus on predictions, and the historical data for calibration are just not there. Thus attributing actual damage is too difficult. At the same time, sea-level rise, which is a truly catastrophic risk, will be modest over the next few decades, and so would not fall into the net of action over the next couple of decades, which Allen focuses upon.

Allen considers *quantum* under two heads: actual damage and potential damage. In considering how to count potential damage, Allen underestimates the quantum of lost value through economic blight: already the Heinz Center reports that around US$500 million per year is lost from US property values due to coastal erosion. Such damage has not arisen from a single event, but rather from anticipation of a pattern of events. Such damage might be a better prospect for action than actual, single-event damage.

A key issue is, who can claim for potential damage that has *not* been crystallised today into lower property values or lost economic opportunities? Future losses may affect unborn people, while on the other hand social and economic mobility is such that it would be difficult to argue that current residents in an area are the ones who will be affected by future events in that area. One approach to this is to act through corporate entities such as cities, which *are* permanently located in an area, with real economic interests. They may not be able to act on behalf of individuals, but they do have quantifiable economic bases, for example property tax, which would be affected by extreme events and anticipation of changing climatic patterns. This avenue is currently being explored in the USA (see "Current non-compensatory litigation on climate change" below).

In the third issue, *allocation* of damages, Allen tries to limit the problem of multiple sources of emissions by focusing on "the few" responsible for manufacturing or extracting fossil fuels. This runs contrary to recent practice in product liability legislation, where literally anyone in the supply chain can be held liable, and so it is unlikely to be adopted. Even the few parties under this definition are considerable in number, and would probably be able to resist the argument that they should pay damages in full and recover from other responsible parties, given that there was no collusion. Any single party would be responsible for much less than 5% of fossil-fuel-derived emissions. In fact perhaps 25% of the conventionally assessed anthropogenic driving force on climate is *not* from fossil fuels, but from other activities, such as agriculture.[2] Furthermore, by around 2020 developing countries will be responsible for more than half of the emissions, particularly from coal, so seeking damages there would hardly serve the redistribution of wealth. Regarding Annex 1 entities, even they have limited resources, and in the ultimate could simply seek bankruptcy status to avoid liability.

On the question of whether governments *should* go the route of liability, the answer is surely no. The legal system is a slow and uncertain process. The transaction costs (legal fees) can be high, and, as we have seen above, it would be very inefficient in terms of actually recovering a satisfactory proportion of the damages for injured parties because of the enormous practical problems. Also, the legal system is not capable of recovering non-financial damage such as species loss. In fact, there are very real alternatives to "business-as-usual", such as adoption of more efficient technologies, and government-sponsored R&D into alternative energies. These will have very significant co-benefits such as energy security and cleaner air, so the likelihood is that they *will* be adopted, anyway, regardless of climate change.

The possibility of obtaining insurance against liability for damage caused by greenhouse-gas emissions is rightly rejected by Allen. It would be impossible: the risks are so large, ill defined and correlated across those creating emissions, that no insurer would ever contemplate it. Indeed, Swiss Re has announced that it will check carefully to avoid inadvertent exposure to risk through contracts that cover corporate directors and officers for negligence: if their companies are not addressing climate change responsibly then cover could be restricted or withdrawn.

Finally, on the question of whether governments *would* go the path of private liability, again the answer is no. They are in many cases directly involved in the business of fossil fuel and would not submit tamely to indictment. Even more, fossil fuels are a critical source of tax revenue. There is absolutely no chance that they would kill off this "golden goose" as suggested by Allen. Realistically, also, energy companies wield huge influence in the corridors of power, and so would easily be able to nip political support for private liability in the bud. A curious side issue is that, under Article 4.7 of the United Nations Framework Convention on Climate Change, matters regarding damage caused by climate change in developing countries are linked to problems caused by emissions limits, so that OPEC countries would stymie compensation for damage unless compensation for lost oil revenue was available! This underlines the complexity of the compensation issue.

Current non-compensatory litigation on climate change[3]

One approach is to attack the process of creating emissions, rather than pinpoint actual damage. On 22 August 2002, Friends of the Earth, Greenpeace and the City of Boulder, Colorado, launched a suit against two federal agencies, Export-Import Bank and Overseas Private Investment Corporation, for lending illegally more than US$32 billion to fossil fuel export projects without assessing their contribution to climate change, because the environmental-impact assessments did not consider that possibility. Oakland, California, has now joined the plaintiffs, who are all citing potential impacts in USA as their cause (see Climate Justice Network).[4]

Most recently, a group of American states is seeking legal restrictions on the operations of major power utilities, on the basis that they pose a prospective threat, not that they have caused actual damage. This would be based on the premise that emissions are a common nuisance (Revkin, 2004). Naturally opinions vary about the desirability and likelihood of success of such an action. A survey of six legal experts suggested that this approach was not likely to succeed in legislatures where regulations to control emissions had been enacted and companies were in compliance (see Climate Group, 2004).

A third type of action has been lodged by Germanwatch against the German government seeking disclosure of information relating to the carbon intensity of energy projects financed by the privately owned German export credit agency Euler Hermes.

---

1 It may be argued that, if large-scale attribution is possible, then the details do not matter. This is unrealistic – damage happens at a local level, and defendants would seek any argument to divert attribution. An interesting example arose after the October 1987 "hurricane" in southeast England. There was a depression at exactly the same time,

which caused significant damage in North Wales and Ulster, and reinsurers successfully argued that these were two different events, so that damage could *not* be aggregated across them both.

2 An interesting variation on the theme of contribution to climate change is raised by recent scientific research on the first agricultural revolution, which started around 5000 BCE. Land clearance and overexploitation in, for example, Mesopotamia may have caused the global temperature to rise 18C before the Industrial Revolution started around 1750. Thus, modern-day emitters could claim that their contribution to climate change should be measured relative to *all* anthropogenic activity, not simply the preindustrial baseline. That would of course roughly halve their contribution in the next two decades.

3 Derived from Association of British Insurers' study of Climate Change, 2004.

4 www.ejcc.org.

REFERENCES

Climate Group, 2004, Interview Series, URL: http://www.theclimategroup.org, 12 September.

Revkin, A., 2004, "New York City and 8 states plan to sue power plants", *New York Times*, 21 July.

Index

A

Activities Implemented Jointly (AIJ) 90
Allen and Lord (2004) 373, 381
Allen (2003) 373
Alternative Investment Market (AIM) 19
Aon (2004) 287
Asian Development Bank (ADB) 326
Assigned Amount Units (AAUs) 52
Association des Constructeurs Européens d'Automobiles (ACEA) 231
Association of South East Asian Nations (ASEAN) 43
Awerbuch (2004) 27

B

Bank Sarasin (1998, 1999) 223
Bauer *et al* (2005) 219, 223
Bishop (2004) 346
Black *et al* (2004) 373
Black–Scholes-type pricing methods 172
"business-as-usual" 15, 184
buyers' pool 129–30, 132, 136, 138, 141

C

cap and trade
  markets 65
  systems 118
Carbon Disclosure Project (CDP) 189, 191, 296
Certified Emission Reduction credits (CERs) 52, 81, 91, 130, 328, 340
Certified Emission Reduction Unit Procurement Tenders (CERUPTs) 89
Chugoku Electric 136
Clarkson and Deyes (2002) 386–7
Clean Development Mechanism (CDM) 26, 52, 66, 77, 89, 117, 120, 129, 156, 183, 267, 289, 297, 305, 342, 353
Clean Edge, Inc (2005) 217
Climate Group (2004) 398
combined heat and power (CHP) 264, 320
Community Development Carbon Fund (CDCF) 136, 361
Corporate Average Fuel Economy (CAFE) 232
Cowe (2004) 223

D

"dark spread" 167
David Pearce (2003) 387
de Jong and Walet (2004) 152
Defra (2004d) 253
designated national authority (DNA) 69, 309, 355
Designated Operational Entities (DOEs) 309, 334
Dlugolecki (2004) 283
DTI (2003) 17

E

"Eco-Industrial Revolution" 214

Electricity Supply Board (ESB) 138

Emission Reduction
  Purchase Agreements (ERPAs) 70, 131
  Unit Procurement Tenders (ERUPTs) 89
  Units (ERUs) 52, 91, 130, 317, 359

Emissions Trading Directive (ETD) 253

energy efficiency 39

Energy Sector Management Assistance Programme (ESMAP) 35

energy service company (ESCO) 45

Energy White Paper 204–6, 249

Energy Working Group (EWG) 45

energy-efficiency audit 34

EU Emissions Trading Scheme (EU ETS) 6, 16, 26, 138, 145, 155, 165, 177, 196, 206, 245, 346

European Bank for Reconstruction and Development (EBRD) 9, 34

European Commission (2005) 110, 112

European Federation of Financial Analysts (1996) 223

European Investment Bank (EIB) 134

European Union Allowance (EUA) 156, 166, 260, 296

European Wind Energy Association (2005) 29

export credit agencies 325

expression of interest 92

F

"fair premium" 171

"Finance – Policy" Gap 27

G

"geological sequestration" 194, 393

Global Environment

Centre Foundation (GEC) 313
  Facility (GEF) 326

Global Village Energy Partnership (GVEP) 40

Gluck and Becker (2005) 223

Greenhouse Gas
  Credit Aggregation Pool (GG CAP) 129
  emissions 53, 118, 165, 197, 211
  (GHG) 6, 89, 179, 259, 382
  Risk Solutions 299

Grossman (2003) 373, 382

Group of Eight (G8) Task Force 44, 124

Gurenko (2004) 287

H

Hadley Centre (2005) 5, 14

Haites (2004) 71

Hamilton (2004) 28, 42

Hawley and Williams (2000) 210, 223

heating degree days (HDDs) 172

Henderson Global Investors (2002) 210

Henderson's approach 208

Hohne and Harnisch (2002) 390

I

ICF Consulting (2003) 260

IEA
  (2003a) 25
  (2003b) 26
  (2004) 31

IEA R&D Wind Executive Committee (2001) 31

IIED (2004) 360

Insight Investment (2005) 207

Instantly Available PC (IAPC) technology 195

Institutional Investors Group on Climate Change (IIGCC) 7, 198

integrated planning model (IPM) 265

Integrated Pollution Prevention and Control (IPPC) 245

Intergovernmental Panel on
    Climate Change (IPCC) 5, 271,
    283, 311
International Emissions Trading
    (IET) 77
International Energy Agency
    (IEA) 6, 25, 124
Investment Property Forum (IPF)
    200–1
Investor Network on Climate Risk
    (INCR) 202
IPCC (1999) 272, 279

J
Johannesburg Renewable Energy
    Coalition (JREC) 40
Joint Implementation (JI)
    projects 52, 156, 297, 362
    scheme 112
Jolly and Fukuda-Parr (2000) 365

K
Kiernan (2004) 218
Kommunalkredit Public
    Consulting (KPC) 125

L
Leggett (1999) 15
Li *et al* (2003) 344
Lomborg (2001) 367, 388
Lorenz (1993) 374
Luterbacher *et al* (2004) 373

M
Mansley and Dlugolecki (2001)
    209
Marrakech Accords 78
Mediterranean Renewable Energy
    Programme (MEDREP) 40
Meehl and Tebaldi (2004) 373
memoranda of understanding
    98
Mills, Lacompte and Peara (2001)
    283
Ministry of Economy, Trade and
    Industry 313
Ministry of Environment 313
Mote (2003) 376

N
National Academy of Sciences
    (2001) 294
National Allocation Plan (NAP)
    141, 254, 265
National Development and
    Reform Commission (NDRC)
    326, 335
National Economic Research
    Associates (NERA) 254
National Insurance contribution
    payments (NICs) 251
Natsource's Delivery Risk Model
    137
NERA (2004) 252
New Energy and Industrial
    Technology Development
    Organisation (NEDO) 313
Niederberger *et al* (2005) 359
nongovernmental organisations
    (NGOs) 353

O
O'Brien and Usher (2004) 31
OEMs (original equipment
    manufacturers) 227
official development assistance
    (ODA) 306
Operating and Financial Review
    206, 261
Operations and maintenance
    111
Oppenheimer and Petsonk (2003)
    368
OTC (over-the-counter)
    brokers 162
    swap 170
Oxera (2004) 150

P
Palmer (1999) 374
Panmure (2002) 223
Pearce (2003) 369
Photovoltaic Projects 103–4
Pocklington
    (2000) 253
    (2001) 249
    (2002) 245

Poppe (2004) 344
power-purchase agreement (PPA)
    21, 335, 348
project design document (PDD)
    67, 70, 124, 308
Prototype Carbon Fund (PCF) 129
"prudent fiduciary" equation 212

R
Reinaud (2004) 150
Reinhardt (2000) 152
renewable energy 39
Renewable Energy and Energy
    Efficiency Partnership (REEEP)
    39, 47
Renewable Energy International
    Law (REIL) 41
Renewable Obligation Certificate
    (ROC) 29
Revkin (2004) 398
Rifkin (2002) 17

S
Schär *et al* (2004) 373
Shellenberger and Nordhaus
    (2004) 164
small and medium-sized
    enterprises (SMEs) 43
social cost of carbon 386
Soon *et al* (2003) 375
"spin-off" funds 7
standard test conditions 107
State Environmental Fund 96, 97
State Street Global Advisors 218
Stott *et al* (2000) 375
Stott, Stone and Allen (2004) 373,
    377, 382
Sustainable Energy Regulation
    Network (SERN) 41
Synergy (2003) 358

T
"the big emitters' club" 178
Tol and Downing (2000) 369, 387

U
UBS Warburg (2001) 223
UK Emissions Trading Scheme
    (UK ETS) 177, 252
UK Government (2004) 255
UNCTAD (2004) 359
UNEP Finance Initiative (2002)
    9
UNEPFI
    (2002) 14
    (2005) 364
United Nations Environment
    Programme Finance Initiative
    (UNEPFI) 13, 283
United Nations Framework
    Convention on Climate
    Change (UNFCCC) 66, 78, 89,
    289, 368
Universities Superannuation
    Scheme (USS) 198

V
Venture Capital Trust (VCT)
    vehicle 21
"verified emissions reductions"
    (VERs) 54, 133

W
Walker (2003) 286
Wordsworth, Kwartin and
    Karmali (2004) 261
World Bank (2005) 360
World Bank's Carbon Finance
    Group (WB CFG) 133
World Business Council for
    Sustainable Development
    (WBCSD) 248
World Meteorological
    Organisation (WMO) 373
World Resources Institute (2002,
    2003) 223
World Summit for Sustainable
    Development (WSSD) 40